NEPHI IN THE PROMISED LAND

MORE EVIDENCES THAT
the BOOK OF MORMON IS
A TRUE HISTORY

GEORGE POTTER

CFI
SPRINGVILLE, UTAH

ISBN 13: 978-1-59955-129-6

Published by CFI, an imprint of Cedar Fort, Inc., 2373 W. 700 S., Springville, UT 84663
Distributed by Cedar Fort, Inc. www.cedarfort.com

LIBRARY OF CONGRESS CATALOGING-IN-PUBLICATION DATA
Potter, George, 1949-
  Nephi in the promised land / George Potter.
    p. cm.
  Summary: Study of the location of Book of Mormon events, hypothesizing that they took place in Chile, Peru, and Bolivia rather than Mesoamerica as is usually supposed.
  ISBN 978-1-59955-129-6
  1. Book of Mormon--Geography. 2. Book of Mormon--Evidences, authority, etc. I. Title.

  BX8627.P685 2009
  289.3'22--dc22

2008047475

Cover design by Angela D. Olsen
Cover design © 2008 by Lyle Mortimer
Typeset by Angela D. Olsen
Edited by Melissa J. Caldwell

Printed in China

10 9 8 7 6 5 4 3 2 1

Printed on acid-free paper

DEDICATION AND ACKNOWLEDGMENTS

DEDICATED TO

My Andean Missionary Companions:
Glenn Kimball, Timothy Evans, David Richardson, Dennis Hislop,
Franklin Lewis, Richard Smith, and Stephen MacDonald

My Mission Presidents:
Keith Roberts and Allen Litster

ACKNOWLEDGMENTS

I am indebted to Arthur Kocherhans and David Calderwood for openly sharing their pioneering research; to my editor, A Dennis Mead, for his effort on my behalf and his valuable suggestions; to Diane D. Bersdorff for her review of this work; and to Lyle Mortimer and Lee Nelson of Cedar Fort Inc. for their constant support.

Photographs for this book have been contributed by Mylene d'Auriol Stoessel, David Richardson, Timothy Evans, Arthur Kocherhans, and Liam Quinn. Drawings in the book are by Guaman Poma; the originals are now in the possession of Det Kongelige Bibliotek, in Denmark. The satellite images used in this book are the property of NASA and the Johnson Space Center.

TABLE OF CONTENTS

INTRODUCTION

Blessed art thou, Nephi, because of thy faith, for thou hast sought me diligently,
with lowliness of heart. And inasmuch as ye shall keep my commandments,
ye shall prosper, and shall be led to a land of promise.

1 NEPHI 2:19–20

IN MAY 2008, SCOTT R. WOODWARD, executive director of the Sorenson Molecular Genealogy Foundation, announced that a DNA marker called "Colen modal haplotype," sometimes associated with Hebrew people, had been found in the genes of South American native populations. Although Woodward cautioned against using DNA studies as evidence for or against the Book of Mormon, it was the first time that a Hebrew-specific DNA marker has been found among native people in the New World.[1] The discovery, combined with many recent archaeological discoveries, suggests that we have entered an exciting new period in Book of Mormon research, one that points to South America.

Ever since the coming forth of the Book of Mormon, many scholars and researchers have sought either to disprove the truthfulness of the book or to substantiate its validity and authenticity. In doing so, they have applied a variety of disciplines in an effort to bring their opinions and findings to the general public—depending on their viewpoints or purposes—be they honest attempts to enlighten the minds of those who are seeking additional truths beyond the pages of the book itself or nefarious objectives centered on destroying or discrediting the work for their own gain.

Numerous arguments have ensued relating to the Book of Mormon, and much contention continues to exist today. The purpose of this book is not to perpetuate any argumentation or differing of opinions; enough has been written based on "winning" such arguments. Rather, the intent of the author is: 1) to give credit and appreciation to those honest and sincere scholars, researchers, and scientists who have spent many hours, and even years, pursuing additional findings to confirm the convictions that they already have of the authenticity of the Book of Mormon and the integrity of its translator, Joseph Smith, Jr.; 2) to thank those who have gone ahead with their contributions, and even more so, for the impetus that their research has brought about in the minds of their readers (including the author of this work) to reach out on their own and discover, if possible, additional truths; and 3) to share with his readers the results of his own research along with the conviction that some of the "findings" currently being put forth about Book of Mormon geographical research are, unfortunately, founded on assumptions and not based on fact.

The readers of this book can expect to find many new ideas—concepts that may not only *seem* to contradict previous ideas about the location of the events that we read about in the Book of Mormon, but which *do indeed* represent a series of fascinating facts and archaeological evidences that place those events in a physical environment far to the south of where many people currently consider them to have taken place. The author is keenly aware of the seriousness of his thesis but is convinced that if the readers of this work (be they seasoned researchers and scholars or those who are merely interested in expanding their knowledge of Book of Mormon geography) will read with open minds—searching not for something that either agrees with or opposes what they have heard or believed before, but simply for additional truth, based on numerous incontrovertible findings—they will discover insights that will expand their understanding and conviction of that which is written within the pages of that marvelous work, the Book of Mormon.

The major premise of this book is that the events of the Book of Mormon took place in what today are the countries of Chile, Peru, and Bolivia rather than in Mesoamerica.

One common thesis used by some authors to support a Mesoamerican theory is their conjecture that Joseph Smith identified Central America as the land of Zarahemla. If that were true, there would certainly be ample reason to pursue one's research in the area of Central America. However, after a diligent search for any direct evidence of such a statement by Joseph Smith, I have never found anything to support that assertion. My claim is that Joseph Smith never put his name on a document to that effect, nor to my knowledge did any General Authority who knew the prophet ever claim he made such a statement. The assumption that Zarahemla was located in Central America stems from a series of articles that appeared in the Church's newspaper *Times and Seasons* between September 15, 1842 and October 1, 1842. Although Joseph Smith had earlier expressed his desire to edit the *Times and Seasons*, John Taylor was the editor of the newspaper when these articles were written.[2] Whoever wrote the articles *claimed* that Zarahemla was in Central America. However, this was not the prevailing belief of early Church members, and there is no record that Joseph Smith ever taught such an idea. Whoever did write the articles used the term "we" throughout their arguments. Obviously, "we" means the text was not a prophetic declaration nor even the personal viewpoint of the prophet.

The Church of Jesus Christ of Latter-day Saints takes no position on where the Book of Mormon history took place in the Americas; however, what we do know is the prevailing view of early Church members who knew Joseph Smith: they believed it had been revealed to the Prophet that Nephi's ship landed in Chile. Two highly influential apostles of the Church, Elder Orson Pratt and Elder Franklin D. Richards,

openly taught that the Prophet received a revelation that Nephi's ship landed at 30 degrees south latitude in South America. Both apostles knew Joseph Smith, and it goes without saying that apostles are themselves prophets, seers, and revelators—special witnesses of Christ—and certainly are men who would not have taught a falsehood or a doctrine that conflicted with one taught by Joseph Smith. Evidence supporting this revelation to Joseph Smith is that the words thereof were written in the "handwriting of Frederick G. Williams, Counselor to the Prophet, and on the same page with the body of an undoubted revelation" which is now part of the Doctrine and Covenants.[3]

The Church included the revelation that Nephi landed in Chile as a footnote to the 1879 edition of the Book of Mormon.[4] Indeed, contrary to the revisionist thinking of some later Book of Mormon scholars, B. H. Roberts reminds us that the dominant belief among the early Church members was that Joseph Smith revealed that Nephi landed in South America.[5] The Church appears to have been so certain of this fact, that in 1851 it sent Apostle Parley P. Pratt to South America. After sailing for 64 days from San Francisco, Elders Parley P. Pratt and Rufus Allen arrived as missionaries in Valparaiso, Chile,[6] the very place where it was believed that Nephi's ship landed.[7]

Another argument for the Book of Mormon having taken place in Mesoamerica is that it *uniquely* matches the book's geographic context.[8]

Actually, the Book of Mormon contains very little geographical information from which to draw a definitive conclusion as to where the events within it took place. John E. Clark of

Brigham Young University states: "For the New World, dealing with [Book of Mormon] geography is a two-step exercise. An internal geography must first be deduced from clues in the book, and this deduction must then be matched with a real-world setting."[9] However, the absence of definitive geographical clues makes any deduced "internal geography" to be by definition a hypothetical construct. As such, one can manipulate the self-interpreted parameters of their hypothetical construct to make it fit into any number of possible New World geographical settings.

Since the golden plates were eventually deposited in New York, another popular view is that the Cahokia Mound Builders of North America were the people of the Book of Mormon. However, this notion should not be taken seriously. The Cahokia civilization reached its height between AD 1000 to AD 1100,[10] centuries after the Nephite civilization had vanished. Known sometimes as the Mississippian culture, the Mound Builder's created hundreds of mounds of heaped-up earth, yet not one such structure is mentioned in the Book of Mormon.[11] Indeed, no credible evidence exists that the Book of Mormon–era tribes of North America advanced beyond the Stone Age. They skillfully knapped flint into sharp-edged arrowheads and crude hand tools. However, in comparison, the Nephites civilization mined several metals in abundance, including gold, which does not tarnish or waste away. Of the thousands of archaeological digs throughout North America, none have uncovered worked gold or any other metal artifacts that date to the time of the Book of Mormon. The Nephites were an advanced Iron Age civilization with great cities, highways, a written language, and large herds of domesticated animals. None of these attributes has been found to have existed among the ancient people of North America.

Interest in a North American setting grew when it was announced that European DNA had been found in some Native American tribes in North and South America. However, this has no relevance to the Book of Mormon. Lehi's descendents were certainly not of European origin. As the book states, they were Hebrews from the Middle East. According to the Smithsonian Institute lithic evidence suggests that the European DNA link to Native Americas appears to have happened through the Clovis people (9500 BC) who descended from the Solutrean culture that existed in Europe between 24,000 and 16,500 years ago.[12] In other words, European DNA was widely spread throughout the Americas some 7,500 years before the arrival of the Jaredites.

In our book, *Lehi in the Wilderness*, Richard Wellington and I dedicated a chapter to Nephi, son of Lehi. We acknowledged the young man's legendary accomplishments in the Old World, including his leadership—which saved his family in the wilderness—his struggle to acquire the brass plates of Laban, and the mighty effort the Lord required of him to build a large and solid sailing ship and captain her safely across two oceans. However, these achievements were far surpassed by what Nephi accomplished once he reached the promised land. This book will describe when, where, and how he became the architect of a new civilization, with its crowning jewel being the construction in his lifetime of a temple after the manner of Solomon's. Such a man's accomplishments would not be quickly forgotten. Indeed, one of the premises of this book is that to this day the people of the Andes still remember him by another name—that of the first Inca king, Manco Capac.

And what of the holy library that Nephi started? Today some people doubt the historicity of the Book of Mormon. In this regard, some years ago Hugh Nibley offered a challenge to his students at Brigham Young University.

Since Joseph Smith was younger than most of you and not nearly so experienced or well educated at the time he copyrighted the Book of Mormon, it should not be too much to ask you to hand in by the end of the semester (which will give you more time than he had) a paper of, say, five to six hundred pages in length. Call it a sacred book if you will, and give it the form of a history. Tell of a community of wandering Jews in ancient times; have all sorts of characters in your story, and involve them in all sorts of public and private vicissitudes [daily challenges]; give them names—hundreds of them—pretending that they are real Hebrew and Egyptian names of circa 600 BC; be lavish with cultural and technical details—manners and customs, arts and industries, political and religious institutions, rites, and traditions; include long and complicated military and economic histories; have your narrative cover a thousand years.

Keep a number of interrelated local histories going at once; feel free to introduce religious controversy and philosophical discussion, but always in a plausible setting; observe the appropriate literary conventions and explain the derivation and transmission of your varied historical materials. Above all, do not ever contradict yourself! For now we come to the really hard part of this little assignment. You and I know that you are making this all up—we have our little joke—but just the same you are going to be required to have your paper published when you finish it, not as fiction or romance, but as a true history! After you have handed it in you may make no changes in it. . . . What is more, you are to invite any and all scholars to read and criticize your work freely, explaining to them that it is a sacred book on a par with the Bible. If they seem over-skeptical, you might tell them that you translated the book from original records by the aid of the Urim and Thummim—they will love that! Further to allay their misgivings, you might tell them that the original manuscript was on golden plates, and that you got the plates from an angel. Now go to work and good luck![13]

Why not expand Dr. Nibley's challenge? It is now the twenty-first century, and a growing body of archaeological knowledge can be compared to the account in the Book of Mormon. After passing all the tests required in the professor's original challenge, let us now require that the students prove that their fictitious books are in complete harmony with the current body of archaeological evidence of ancient civilizations that existed in the Western Hemisphere during the same archaeological period as their own made-up story line. Again, good luck!

What makes Book of Mormon research so exciting is that the more you study its contents and origins, the more you appreciate that fact that this remarkable book could not have been concocted by the most knowledgeable historian in 1830, let alone an unschooled farm boy from the backwoods of upstate New York. Indeed, a growing body of archaeological and anthropological evidence from South America overwhelmingly favors the book. The book you are currently reading will use this evidence to present an entirely new paradigm for the Book of Mormon lands. Is the model perfect? No. Does it provide answers to all the questions people ask about the Book of Mormon? No. However, this book will illustrate how a land in the ancient Americas matches Book of Mormon geography, biology, history, and theology, and does so in a compelling fashion, so much so, that one has to wonder how Joseph Smith could have made such an accurate translation in 1830. The new paradigm is centered high in the Andes of Peru, and the more information that is being discovered about this area's past, the more remarkable the Book of Mormon parallels appear to be.

Scientists are just now opening our understanding of the New World's pre-Columbian past. They are opening a new window of discovery. In his landmark book, *1491*, Charles Mann writes:

> One way to sum up the new scholarship is to say that it has begun, at last, to fill in one of the biggest blanks in history: the Western Hemisphere before 1492. It was, in the current view, a thriving, stunningly diverse place, a tumult of languages, trade and culture, a region where tens of millions of people loved and hated and worshipped as people do everywhere. Much of this world vanished after Columbus, swept away by disease and subjection. So thorough was the erasure that within a few generations neither conqueror nor conquered knew that this world had existed. Now, though, it is returning to view. It seems incumbent on us to take a look.[14]

Mann's statement is perhaps truest when it comes to our knowledge of Peru. Brian S. Bauer, archaeologist, formerly of the University of California at Berkeley, explains:

> By the time of European contact in 1532, the Inca [empire of Peru] ruled a population of at least eight million from their capital city in the Cuzco★ Valley.
>
> The Cuzco Valley was the sacred center of the empire and the royal seat of the dynastic order that ruled the realm. Despite the importance of the Cuzco Valley in the prehistory of the Americas, it has been one of the last great centers of civilization in the Americas to be systematically studied. As the heartland of the Inca, the Cuzco Valley has frequently been discussed in the literature, and anthropologists, historians, and archaeologists have long speculated on the locations and importance of its numerous archaeological sites. Yet there has been a surprising lack of archaeological field research in the Cuzco Valley itself.
>
> Until recently, there had been no attempt to systematically survey the Cuzco Valley or to document all of its archaeological sites. As a result, critical issues concerning the cultural history of

---

★ Some authors quoted in this work use the spelling "Cusco."

the valley and the development of the Inca Empire have remained unexplored. Furthermore, we know little about the social complexity of groups that occupied the region before the Inca Empire developed and how the achievements of these earlier people helped to form the foundations upon which the Inca built their great state.[15]

THE CHALLENGES FACED IN WRITING THIS BOOK

The early Book of Mormon prophet Jacob prophesied that the entire literary record of the Nephites would vanish except for the history contained on the plates of the Book of Mormon (Jacob 4:1–2). Having a second written witness to the Nephite history would be extremely helpful. Mann notes, "The biggest difficulty in reconstructing the pre-Colombian past is the absence of voices from that past."[16]

The loss of all other Nephite written records is a tragedy that goes far beyond an understanding of the historical context of our faith. A thousand years of literature is gone. Mann continues:

> "Cultures are like books," the anthropologist Claude Lévi-Strauss once remarked, "each a volume in the great library of humankind." In the sixteenth century, more books were burned than ever before or since. How many Homers vanished? How many Hesiods? What great works of painting, sculpture, architecture, and music vanished or were never created? Languages, prayers, dreams, habits, and hopes—all gone. And not just once, but over and over again. In our antibiotic era,

how can we imagine what it means to have entire ways of life hiss away like steam."[17]

Of course, the destruction of the Inca written records by the Spanish is not the primary reason the world would have lost its knowledge of a possible Nephite civilization in South America. The Lamanites systematically destroyed the religious beliefs of the Nephites circa AD 400 (Moroni 1:2). Furthermore, in the centuries preceding the Spanish conquest, the people living along the Pacific shoreline in Central and South America were visited by, and perhaps influenced to some degree by, the Chinese.[18]

Fortunately, a few sixteenth century Europeans and some native Peruvians recorded the

oral traditions of the Incas that had been passed down to them for thousands of years. However, before comparing the Inca traditions to the events recorded in the Book of Mormon, we should ask the question, "Just how accurate are the Spanish accounts?" For example, without a library, how accurately could an Englishman today recall the events during the reign of William the Conqueror? Even more distant, was King Arthur fact or fiction?

We must also remember the motives of the Spanish chroniclers who recorded the oral traditions of the Incas. Their aims were highly suspect. Each chronicler recorded the Inca traditions and beliefs vis-à-vis their own points of view—and under the influence of their religious sponsorships. For this reason, the Spanish have been accused of systematically erasing the actual Peruvian beliefs, and then forcefully substituting them with their own religious propaganda. In some cases this was the very intent of the Catholic historians who wrote the official account of the Spanish conquest of the Incas.

The often-quoted recorder of Inca folklore, Pedro Sarmiento de Gamboa (fl. 1532–1572), titled one of his accounts "The Fable of the Origin of these Barbaric Indians According to Their Blind Opinions."[19] The bias of the Peruvian chroniclers was likewise apparent in the chronicles of Mesoamerican recorders. Even the K'iche-Maya book the *Popol Vuh*, which is regularly cited by Book of Mormon scholars, was written in the mid-1500's,[20] well after the Spanish conquest, and thus, subject to Judeo-Christian influences.

Sarmiento's book is just one example of how the Spanish accounts were primarily written to camouflage the Spanish atrocities against the natives in Peru, and not an honest attempt to record what the Andean people actually believed at the time of the conquest. In this light, it would then seem even more remarkable if the oral traditions of the Incas, as recorded by the Spanish, actually support the historical events and theology found in the Book of Mormon.

Even with his grossly negative bias against the Incas, Sarmiento is one of the more useful chroniclers. His record will be heavily cited in this book. Gary Urton from Harvard University notes:

> Sarmiento's account is one of the earliest and most detailed versions that we have. As the official historian to Francisco de Toledo, the fourth Viceroy of Peru (1569–81), Sarmiento was charged with compiling a true history of the Inca empire. In undertaking this enterprise, Sarmiento had access to an unusually large number of informants. He tells us, for instance, that he interviewed more than a hundred quipucamayoqs [quipu cordreaders] on historical matters, and he provides us with the names of forty-two of these informants. Furthermore, Sarmiento says that upon completing his account, he had his chronicle read in full, in the Quechua language, to these forty-two descendants of the Inca nobility. All of the men, says Sarmiento, agreed that "the said history was good and true and conformed to what they knew and to what they had heard their [parents and ancestors] say."[21]

Besides Sarmiento, this book draws heavily upon the accounts written by the Spanish

chroniclers Juan de Betanzos, Pedro de Cieza de León, Polo de Ondegardo, and Father Bernadé Cobo.★ These chroniclers claim to have taken care in recording the Inca oral traditions. Cieza de León noted that "the things that I deal with in this history I have observed with great care and diligence."[22] David Calderwood writes of the integrity of Cieza de León:

> The scarcity of paper and ink in the New World only added to his problems. He mentioned that a sheet of paper cost him 30 pesos in Cali, Colombia. The eight books written by Cieza de León required nearly 8,000 sheets of foolscap. He bought paper when he could have been buying a horse! He carried books and manuscripts when he could have been carrying gold![23]

However, even with these historical accounts, the first-hand records of the pre-Columbian Incas will probably never be recovered. The Dominican priest who followed the conquistadors ordered the destruction of every recording device known to the Incas. The desecration of the Inca records was so thorough that even with the help of the Book of Mormon, it is nearly impossible to decipher from the Inca oral traditions what is historical fact from what is mere fable.

Mann points out that "preserved Indian lore throws a brilliantly colored but indirect light on the past. To understand long-ago Indian lives, one cannot avoid the accounts of the first literate people who saw them: European swashbucklers,

★ He is also known as Bernardo Cobo.

What secrets still lie undiscovered in the
17th century San Francisco Library, Lima, Peru?

fortune hunters, and missionaries."[24] Furthermore, Urton warns us:

> While we can obviously follow the
> storyline within a given myth, noting
> that one event is said to have happened
> after another, we cannot sensibly assign
> an absolute date during the period before
> the onset of recorded history in 1532 to
> any one of these events solely on the
> basis of what the post-conquest accounts
> tell us. . . . It is only through the science
> of archaeology, with its radiocarbon and
> other dating techniques, that we can
> securely assign dates to events in the
> pre-Hispanic era and, thereby, begin to
> build up a chronological framework for
> evaluating the historicity of some ele-
> ments of the Inca myths.[25]

After an extensive study of the oral traditions of Mesoamerica and Peru, Calderwood
concludes:

> Although the chroniclers may not
> have been trained historians and their
> writing may not qualify as a good his-
> toriography of pre-Columbia America
> or even of the colonial period, they
> still merit serious consideration. Their
> writings represent the only eye witness
> accounts of the events during the Con-
> quest period. Perhaps Cieza de León
> said it best when he noted that without
> a written account "time so destroys the
> memory of things that only by clues and
> inference can the future ages know what
> really took place."[26]

Calderwood quotes Rolena Adorna:

> The magnificent works produced
> during the viceregal period in Latin

America have been too long overlooked by exegetes seeking a more conventional history of belles letters in Latin America. The problem was not a failure in intellectual and creative endeavors during those centuries, but rather the much more recent failure to appreciate the learned and original contributions of early New World writers.[27]

To add light to what I believe happened in ancient Peru, each point covered in this book will include, where possible, Book of Mormon references related to the oral traditions of the Incas as recorded by the Spanish Chroniclers and to what is presently known about the archaeology and anthropology of the area during the Book of Mormon era. The author respects the incredible efforts made by dedicated archaeologists and anthropologists who attempt to objectively record our human legacy. The Lord has commanded his people to teach one another "things both in heaven and in the earth, and under the earth, things which have been." (D&C 88:77–79). Through the observations and judgments of scientists, the readers can decide for themselves if Mormon's abridgement of the golden plates provides an important key for deciphering what really took place in the Andes over two thousand years ago.

All the same, we must realize that the study of archaeology is much like the art of medicine. Yesterday's medicine is considered witchcraft by today's standards, and today's medicine will be considered barbaric in the coming century. Today's archaeology might contradict an element of the Book of Mormon history; however, that does not mean that in another twenty years the reverse might not be the case. In other words, the conclusions anthropologists and archaeologists draw today, which are based on their rigorous assumptions and interpretations, might or might not hold as new discoveries are made.

In a final note to the reader, due to the complexity and length of the Book of Mormon history and the uses in this manuscript of Quechau and Aymara proper names, Book of Mormon characters' names, and place names, relevant notes have been inserted into citations. Wherever [brackets of this type] are found, they signify that the words therein are an insertion by the author and are not part of the original quotation. I apologize to scholars for these indiscretions; however, I believe these insertions will help the reader to more fully understand the parallels I am presenting.

In our book *Lehi in the Wilderness*, Richard Wellington and I listed eighty-one new evidences documenting evidence that the Book of Mormon is a true history. In my opinion this book presents far more evidences for the book's authenticity.

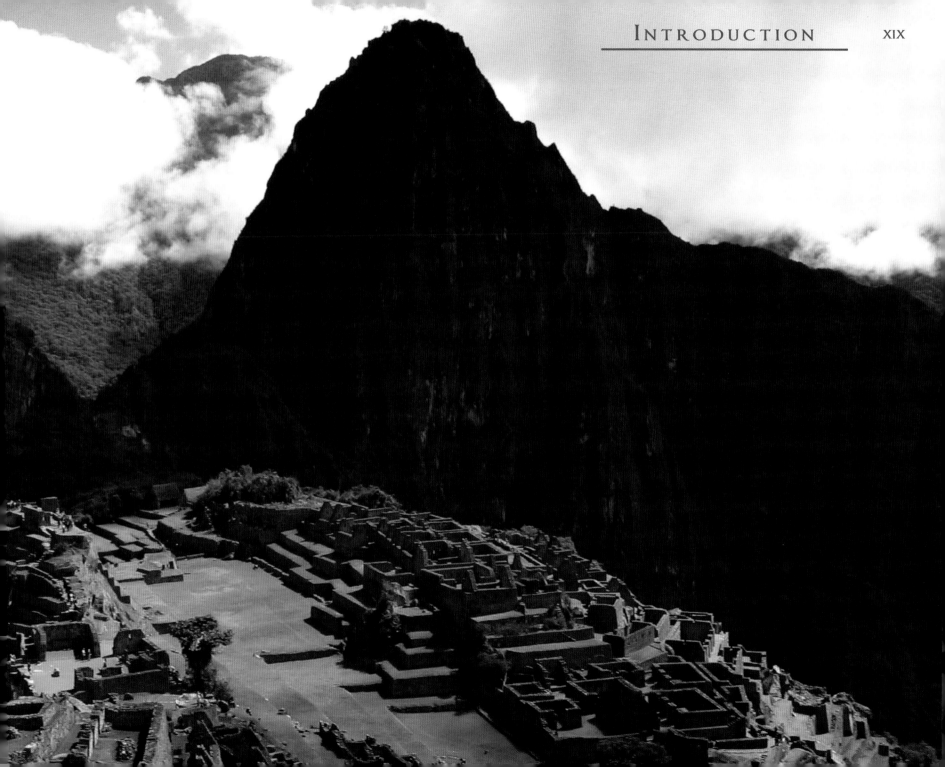

WHY PERU AND NOT MESOAMERICA?

I care nothing for those, even Church doctors, who repeat current prejudices. . . .
As to those who try to impact these doctrines in the wrong order and without preparation,
they are like people who would pour pure water into a muddy cistern.

COPERNICUS

THROUGHOUT CENTRAL AMERICA AND North America one can visit the ruins of mounds and pyramids, and even the remains of accurate celestial observatories. Archaeologists have labeled some these remarkable structures *temples*. As magnificent as these edifices once were, they appear to have had no connection with Nephi's temples or the Book of Mormon. By drawing this conclusion, I will undoubtedly bring upon myself the disapproval of some students of the Book of Mormon who believe otherwise. For this reason, the first two chapters of this book establish a foundation for why the author believes Nephi's temple was built high in the Andes Mountains. Stone upon stone I will present the latest archaeological and anthropological information available that supports the history of the Book of Mormon having transpired in Peru. In so doing, I trust that the readers can weigh the quality of the evidence against all the proposed models for the Book of Mormon and judge for themselves whether we should look to Peru as being

the best candidate for the location of Nephi's temple.

One common argument for the Book of Mormon having taken place in Mesoamerica is that it *uniquely* matches the book's geographic context.[1] Actually, the Book of Mormon contains very little geographical information from which to draw any definitive conclusion as to where the events within it took place. As a result, many other equally logical geographic models for the Book of Mormon lands have been formulated. For example, Joseph Fielding Smith argued against the Isthmus of Tehuantepec and Mesoamerica as being the Book of Mormon lands. He wrote, "Early brethren locate Cumorah in Western New York. It must be conceded that this description fits perfectly the land of Cumorah in New York."[2]

For scholars or anyone else to claim that they have found a region that uniquely matches the geographical clues in the Book of Mormon, they can only do so based on very strong assumptions; that is, they complete their maps by

1

filling in their own ideas "between the lines" in the sacred record. Furthermore, such non-contingent thinking has no place in academia and only hampers our efforts to understand where the Book of Mormon took place. As Ernest Hemingway penned, "truth at first light," meaning that every dawning of new light requires that we redefine what we believe is truth. As time passes, new empirical evidence is discovered, shedding added light on a subject. Twenty years ago, the prevailing body of evidence suggested that Mesoamerica might be a possible contender for lands of the Book of Mormon. However, the new discoveries of the last two decades point to a stronger candidate—Peru.

One commonly held myth is that Peru could not have been the home of the Nephites because the Incas never had a written language. However, scientific researchers now believe that the Incas and their predecessors in Peru did indeed have written languages. The issue of a written language raises an interesting question. "Just what was required for a civilization to have written their religious history on golden plates?" Four technical elements would have been required for a group of people to have compiled the sacred library we now call the Book of Mormon: 1) golden plates, 2) a Semitic language, 3) a vanished written language, and 4) an historical visit in the land by Jesus Christ.

1. GOLDEN PLATES

The New World prophets etched the Book of Mormon on metal plates. The first Nephites (sixth century BC, 1 Nephi 19:1; 2 Nephi 5:15) and the earlier Jaredites (Ether 4:1; 7:9) both would had to have possessed sophisticated metallurgical skills. However, no archaeological

evidence has been discovered of metalworking in Mesoamerica until the first century BC, long after the fall of the Olmec civilization (400–200 BCE), and only scant evidence exists of any metalwork in Mesoamerica before AD 900.[3] That is at least 500 years after Mormon compiled the Book of Mormon, and 1,500 years after Nephi first wrote on golden plates. On the other hand, archaeologists have uncovered extensive Peruvian metalwork dating back to the dawn of the Jaredite Age. Sorenson summarizes it in these words:

Peru's goldsmiths rivaled those of the Kings of Egypt.

Archaeologists only recently learned that metal was being worked in Peru as early as 1900 BC, and it was being traded in Ecuador before 1000 BC [J. W. Grossman, "An Ancient Gold Worker's Tool Kit: The Earliest Metal Technology in

Peru," *Archaeology* 25 (1972): 270–75; A. C. Paulsen, "Prehistoric Trade between South Coastal Ecuador and other Parts of the Andes" (Paper read at 1972 Annual Meeting, Society for American Archaeology). Dates given in these papers need to be corrected backward to accord with bristle-cone pine corrections.] At the same time, all Mesoamerican scholars agree that intercommunication with Peru and Ecuador occurred over a period of thousands of years. Some definitely believe that it was via these voyages that metalworking reached Mexico and Guatemala.[4]

A Neal A. Maxwell Institute (F.A.R.M.S.) online paper states: "Complex and sophisticated metallurgical technologies in the pre-Columbian New World, however, are presently recognized only in the Andes Mountains of Peru and Chile, where copper was smelted from rare copper arsenides, sulfates, and chlorides."[5] Metal, in particular gold, silver, and copper are mentioned throughout the Book of Mormon. Jacob wrote that the land of promise abounds in precious metals (Jacob 2:12). One of the earliest Spanish chronicles of the Incas was written in the 1550s by Juan de Betanzos. According to his interviews with the surviving Inca nobles, the Incas needed to keep records because "some said they had livestock, others, great fields of maize, others, gold mines, others, silver mines, others, much wood."[6] The Inca inventories bring to mind Nephi's account of the resources he found in the promised land—seeds growing exceedingly well, forests, livestock, ore, both of gold, silver, and copper (1 Nephi 18:24–25).

The rich ore deposits of the Andes are legendary. They include the great silver mines of

Potosi, Bolivia, the vast copper deposits of northern Chile and southern Peru, and the gold mines of the Incas. After conquering Peru, Pizarro's brother Hernando, returned to Spain to deliver the crown's share of the initial loot (1/5 only), "carrying so much silver and gold that the ships were ballasted with these metals. . . . He entered Seville with all the treasures. This news excited all Spain because it rang throughout that the House of Trade was filled with golden vessels and jars and other praiseworthy pieces, and of great weight. There was talk of nothing but Peru, and many were stirring to go there."[7] Despite the great quantities of gold and silver stolen by the Spanish, large collections of Inca and pre-Inca metal works still exist. For example, the private collection of Miguel Mujica Gallo in Lima holds 10,000 pre-Columbian gold, silver, or copper artifacts.

The Lord promised Nephi that he would rule a choice land. In terms of precious metals, this definition of choice certainly applied to the Andes. Cobo wrote of the Peruvians' mines:

One of over 10,000 artifacts in Lima's Gold Museum— a tiny remnant of what the Spanish destroyed.

> Some of these *mitas* (labor services performed by taxpayers) provided the labor for the mines of gold, silver, and other metals; the mines that the *mitayos* (laborers in service of the *mitas*) worked for the Inca were numerous and very rich, such as those of Porco [south of Potosi], from which they extracted such rich metals that they contained 50 percent silver, but the most famous were the ones at Tarapacá, in the Diocese of Arequipa. These mines were located in some dry sandbanks where no water is found within twelve leagues of the area and were so rich that the majority of the metal that was extracted from them

was white, refined silver without a mixture of scoria. Lodes were not found in these mines, but rather pockets or isolated nuggets of pure silver that the Indians call *papas* (potatoes); some of them weighed from one-half to one and two *arrobas*, and a nugget has been found that weighed four *arrobas* (an arroba weighs approximately twenty-five pounds).

> There is information about a lode that the Indians have covered up, and they say that it belonged to the Sun, that it was two feet wide and all of pure silver.[8]

A particular skill the Book of Mormon people mastered was the process of hammering gold into very thin plates on which they could write. Archaeologists have discovered that the Peruvians possessed metal-hammering technology during the ages when the words of the Book of Mormon were being etched.[9] Mann writes: "Andean societies vastly preferred to hammer metal into thin sheets, form the sheets around molds, and solder the results. The results were remarkable by any standard—one delicate bust that [Heather] Lechtman [MIT] analyzed was less than an inch tall but made of twenty-two separate gold plates painstakingly joined."[10]

My research leads me to believe that both the Jaredites[11] and the Nephites sailed from the Bronze Age port of Khor Rori (Ophir) in southern Arabia. Building a ship at Khor Rori could explain how metallurgical skills were transferred from the Old World to Peru. William R. Phillips of BYU has suggested that Nephi's skills in metallurgy may have been "learned from the local smiths of the Dhofar [Ophir] or from the Indian traders that passed through nearby trading ports."[12] Recently excavated artifacts at Khor Rori (Ophir) include iron axes, iron nails, an iron knife, an iron razor, and iron melting slag; as well as bronze nails, coins, a bronze bell, and a small bronze plaque.[13] Scholars at BYU believe that the brass plates of the Book of Mormon were actually a copper and tin alloy, that is, bronze.[14] During the first excavation of Khor Rori (Ophir), the American archaeologist Wendall Phillips discovered seven bronze plates with written text engraved on them.[15] As recent as 2007, another bronze plate was discovered at Khor Rori with written text on it.[16] It would appear that when Nephi arrived in the land of promise, he found in abundance an even softer metal on which to write. Gold is found in rich deposits in Peru. According to Inca mythology the founder of the original Inca people, the fair-skinned man named Manco Capac, fashioned two plates of gold.[17] As will be discussed later, Manco Capac possessed many of the characteristics that the Book of Mormon attributes to Nephi who created two sets of gold plates.

The iron artifacts found at Khor Rori remind us that Nephi taught the earliest Nephites to work in iron and steel (2 Nephi 5:15). The ancient Peruvians mined iron ore.[18] On the other hand, iron ore is found in almost every other part of the world except in Central America.[19]

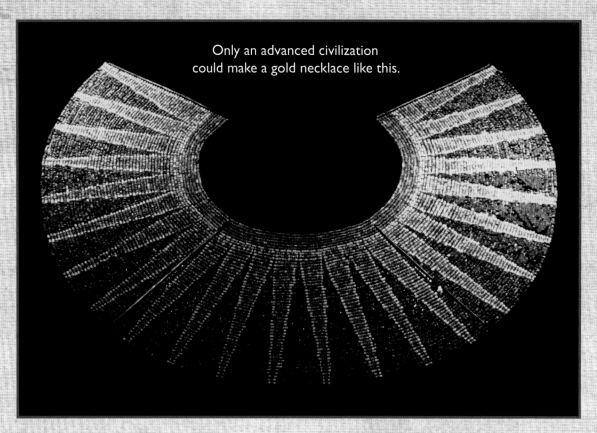

Only an advanced civilization could make a gold necklace like this.

2. A LANGUAGE WITH SEMITIC ROOTS

While there have been attempts by Book of Mormon scholars to trace Mesoamerican languages back to Hebrew or Arabic origins, the evidence for any linguistic linkage is diminutive. A few word sound-a-likes have been suggested, but such matches can be found between any two-language groups. Pre-Columbian Mesoamericans wrote books on bark cloth, a Chinese invention that was undoubtedly brought to Central America by Asian immigrants.[20] The characters used in Mesoamerican scripts were inherited from the Olmec, the mother-culture of the region. Mike Xu of Texas Christian University has convincingly shown that Olmec motifs were inscribed using characters of Chinese origin.[21] As far back as the pioneering work of Alexander von Humboldt (1798), it has been recognized that the amazing Aztec calendar, which they inherited from the Mayans, included months that closely parallel the East Asian zodiac.[22] In comparison, Near Eastern and Native American languages specialist Brian Stubbs cites

Arnold Leesburg's work on lexical similarities between Hebrew and Quechua, the language of the Incas of Peru. Leesburg's lack of linguistic methodology means that linguists ignore it. Nevertheless, a number of his "word comparisons" could feed a competent linguistic treatment, while others may have to be discarded. Observations on Semitic in Quechua have long interested me, and becoming aware of Leesburg's work added to that interest and to previous observations I had made.[23]

The Peruvian language of Quechua belongs to the three-vowel system of languages as does classic Arabic, Aleut, Greenlandic, Sanskrit, Old Norse, and Icelandic.[24] Furthermore, Quechua is similar to Arabic in finite connectivity of its linguistic structure.[25] University of California linguist Mary LeCron Foster concluded that Quechua shows "extensive borrowing from a Semitic language, seemingly Arabic."[26] An example of this is the Arabic word for water, *moya*. The Quechua word for "pasture land," where water would naturally collect is *moya*.[27]

How did the Arabic features find their way into the language of the ancient Peruvians? The Book of Mormon is the history of the Nephite people, who spoke a reformed Egyptian language, which included Arabic characters (JS—H 1:64). This book will use the scriptures to suggest that the Nephites were an elite ruling class that governed a larger constituency of Paleo-Indians, and that not all of the Nephites were destroyed circa AD 400. Father Bernade Cobo wrote: "Apart from the language of Cuzco, which is the general language [Quechua] that the Incas introduced throughout their empire and was the one they used in speaking to their subjects, they knew a different one, which they used only among themselves when they dealt and conversed with those of their own lineage. . . . Now the descendants of the Incas have forgotten this language, although they still remember some words from it."[28]

The secret language of the Inca nobility was called *Callawaya*.[29] The Book of Mormon implies that the Nephite ruling class had such a private language, and it was Egyptian. Jacob recorded that a man came among the Nephites who "had a perfect knowledge of the language of the people" (Jacob 7:4). This could be interpreted to mean that while the Nephite royals and prophets spoke and wrote reformed Egyptian, there was another "language of the people."

The Book of Mosiah (a section of the Book of Mormon) also refers to a private language. When Mosiah's people arrived in Zarahemla, at least three languages were spoken in the city state. First, the Mulekites spoke a corrupted language that could not be understood by the Nephites (Omni 1:17). Second, there was the language of the Nephite general populace. Finally, Egyptian appears to have been the private language of the Nephite elite and the priestly class. In the first chapter of the Book of Mosiah we learn that king Benjamin required that his three sons "should be taught in all the language of his fathers, that they might become men of understanding; and that they might know concerning the prophecies which had been spoken by the mouths of their fathers" (Mosiah 1:2). Obviously, the king's children must have grown up speaking the common language of the Nephites, but here we are told that the king is making a special effort to teach his sons another language, the tongue of his father, Egyptian. Only by understanding Egyptian, could the king "read these engravings, and teach them to his children that thereby they could teach them to their children" (Mosiah 1:2).

The implications seem straightforward. The linguistic context in the Book of Mormon is similar to what is known about the language history of the Incas. Unfortunately, the private language of the Inca nobility was lost and cannot be directly compared to the characters used to write the Book of Mormon. However, this theory would explain why fragments of the Arabic languages can still be found in Quechua, while at the same time, Quechua or any other native American language is not reformed Egyptian.

3. A VANISHED WRITTEN LANGUAGE

The latest research by Gary Urton, the Dumbarton Oaks Professor of Pre-Columbian Studies in the archeology department at Harvard University,[30] supports the oral traditions that the early Incas had a written language that eventually became lost.[31] Indeed, the fact that all traces of Peru's ancient written languages have vanished is a direct fulfillment of Jacob's prophecy. The prophet wrote:

> I, Jacob, having ministered much unto my people in word, (and I cannot write but a little of my words, because of the difficulty of engraving our words upon plates) and we know that the things which we write upon plates must remain; *but whatsoever things we write upon anything save it be upon plates must perish and vanish away.* (Jacob 4:1–2; emphasis added)

Jacob's use of the word "must" implies an unconditional prophecy that all Nephite written records, with the exception of the plates, would

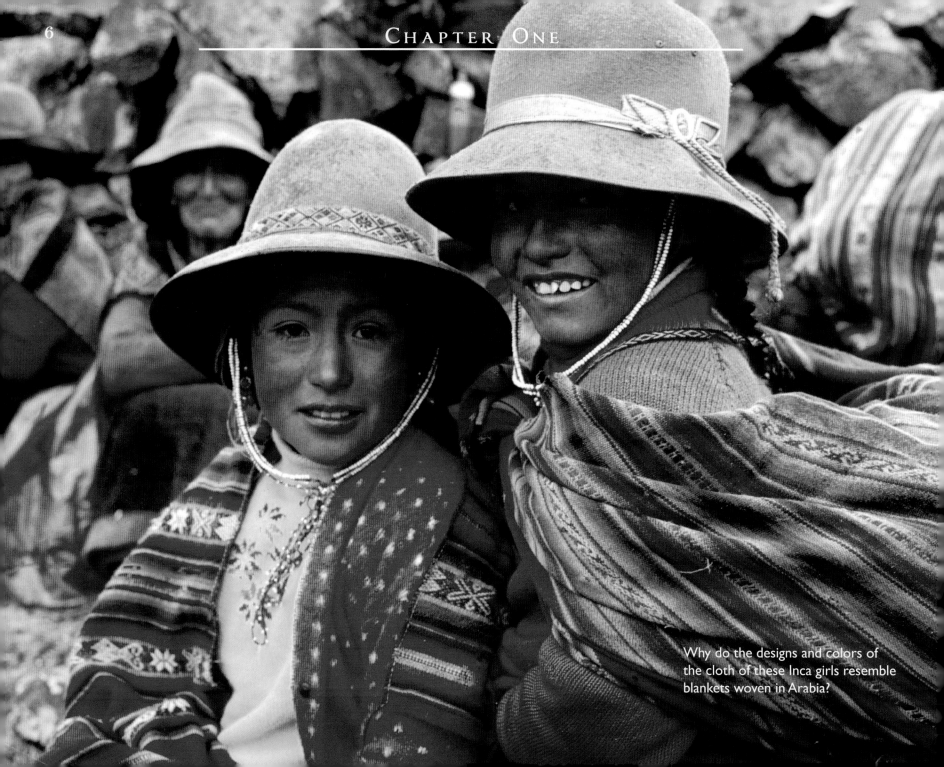

Why do the designs and colors of the cloth of these Inca girls resemble blankets woven in Arabia?

vanish. This appears to be exactly what happened in Peru. In contrast, it is estimated that about fifteen thousand known examples of pre-Columbian writing on monuments, murals, and pottery still exist in Mesoamerica.[32]

Once vanished, is it possible for a written language to return from the dust? The Book of Mormon contains the prophecy of Isaiah that is often used in reference to the book itself. However, the verse might also apply to the recovery of the actual "speech" and "language" of those who were destroyed:

> For those who shall be destroyed [Nephites], shall speak unto them out of the ground, and their speech shall be low out of the dust, and their voice shall be as one that hath a familiar spirit; for the Lord God will give unto him power, that he may whisper concerning them, even as it were out of the ground; and their speech shall whisper out of the dust. (2 Nephi 26:16)

In a dusty unprotected grave in Peru, Urton recently discovered twenty-one bundles of knotted strings. The multicolored tangle of several dozen arm-length knotted strings are called *quipus*. Because the Incas held some of the quipus to be sacred, the Spanish ordered their destruction, and at one point in history, it was believed that all the quipus had been burned. Each knot-type on a quipu and the color of each string had its own meaning, which could only be read by one trained in the code. Thus, while a quipu might appear to be a decorative wall hanging to the untrained eye, in reality it is an amazing seven-bit binary code capable of conveying large amounts of information.[33] Galen Brokaw, an expert in ancient Andean texts at the State University of New York in Buffalo states, "Most

serious scholars of khipu (*quipu*) today believe that they were more than mnemonic devices, and probably much more."[34] Though the only existing *quipus* are from the Inca period, as Mann writes, "It is widely assumed that the Inca built on other, earlier forms of writing that had been developed in the region."[35]

Anthropologist Urton notes,

> It is important to appreciate the role played by one indigenous recording device in particular, the *quipu*, in the collection and recording of Inca myths and histories in early colonial times. *Quipus*, from the Quechua word for "knot," were linked bundles of dyed and knotted strings, which were used by the Incas to record both statistical information that could be interpreted—in some manner that we do not yet fully understand—by experts called *quipucamayoqs* ("knot-makers or keepers") in narrating stories about the Inca past.[36]

One of the early chroniclers, Cobo, wrote of the quipus: "By these recording devices and registers they conserved the memory of their acts, and the Inca's overseers and accountants. . . . On explaining their meaning, the Indians that know them related many things about ancient times that are contained in them. There were people designated for this job of accounting. These officers were called *quipo camayos*, and they were like our historians, scribes, and accountants, and the Inca had great confidence in them."[37] Father Cobo offered an account he was familiar with that demonstrated that the quipus recorded historical information:

> Two Spaniards left together from the town of Ica to go to the city of Castro

Virreina, and arriving at the *tambo* (royal inns along the Inca highways) of Cordoba, which is a day's travel from Ica, one of them stayed there and the other continued his trip; at this *tambo* this latter traveler was given an Indian guide to accompany him to Castro Virreina. This Indian killed the Spaniard on the road and returned to the *tambo*. After some time passed, since the Spaniard was very well known, he was missed. The governor of Castro Virreina, who at that time was Pedro de Cordoba Mejia, a native of Jaen, made a special investigation to find out what had happened. And in case the man had been killed, he sent a large number of Indians to look for the body in the puna and desert. But no sign of him could be found, nor could anyone find out what had become of him until more than six years after he had been killed. By chance the body of another Spaniard was found in a cave of the same desert. The governor ordered that this body be brought to the plaza so that it could be seen, and once it was brought, it looked like the one the Indian had killed, and, believing that it was he, the governor continued with the investigation to discover the killer. Not finding any trace or evidence against anybody, he was advised to make an effort to find out the identity of the Indian who was given to the deceased as a guide at the *tambo* of Cordoba. The Indians would know this in spite of the fact that more than six years had passed because by means of the record of the *quipos* they would have kept memory of it. With this the governor sent for the *caciques* (chief of town) and *quipo camayos.* After they were brought to him and he continued with the investigation, the *quipo camayos* found out by their *quipos* the identity of the Indian who had been given as a guide to the aforementioned Spaniard. The Indian guide was brought prisoner immediately from his town, called Guaytara. . . .

Having given his declaration in which he denied the crime, he was questioned under torture, and at once he confessed for having killed the man and then showed the police where the body was. Police officers went with him to the puna (Andes highlands), and they found the body where the Indian guide had hidden it.[38]

Referred to at times as the Pliny of the New World, José de Costa, a Jesuit missionary, wrote in the sixteenth century that quipus were "witnesses and authentic writing." He wrote "I saw a bundle of these strings on which a woman had brought a written testimony of her whole life and used it to confess just as I would have done with words written on paper."[39]

Today, archaeologists have discovered some 700 quipus, almost all having been retrieved from dusty graves. Their string-and-knot technology for storing information might seem primitive, but actually it was quite advanced. Five hundred years after the fall of the Inca Empire, computers were invented. These twentieth-century digital machines use an eight-bite binary code to store data. The knots provide 128 possible permutations multiplied by 24 different colors. Thus the code used by the cord keepers provided them 1,536 separate units of meaning. This compares to the estimated 1,000 to 1,500 Sumerian cuneiform signs, and double the number of signs in the hieroglyphs of the ancient Egyptians and the Maya of Central America.[40] Indeed, Costa might have been right when he wrote nearly five centuries ago, "Whoever wants may judge whether this [the use of quipus] is clever or if these people are brutish, but I judge it is certain that, in that which they here apply themselves, they get the better of us."[41]

What makes the twenty-one quipus in Urton's study so special is that they might contain an Inca deciphering device similar to the famous *Rosetta stone* that was used to decipher the Egyptian hieroglyphics. The stone now stands in the British National Museum and was the key that unlocked our knowledge of ancient Egypt. The twenty-one quipus in the Harvard group were uncovered from the ruins of the Inca city called Peruchuco. Seven of these quipus start out with the same binary sequence of knots. It is believed that these identical sequences indicated the name *Peruchuco,* the place the quipus came from. Scientists are hopeful that they can use this information and with the help of computers and advance mathematical algorithms, unlock the rest of the code.[42]

Urton and Harvard mathematics graduate student Carrie J. Brezine have been joined by Jean-Jacques Quisquater and Vincent Castus from the Catholic University of Lou-vain in Belgium, and the father/son MIT computer science team of Martin and Erik Demaine. As of January 2007, the team has already found 3,000 different groups of repeated five-knot sequences.[43] If the team continues its astonishing rate of success, they might soon recover the lost language of the quipus, and the world might hear, as Isaiah proclaimed, the voices of "those who shall be destroyed, [which] shall speak unto them out

Examples of Inca quipus. Since the Nephites had great herds of sheep,
what was easier to produce, knotted string or paper?

of the ground." Catherine Julien, a historian of Andean cultures at Western Michigan University, said in reference to the Harvard attempt to decipher the quipus, "We may be able to hear the Inkas for the first time in their own voice."[44]

Even if the quipus are ciphers, they would not have been the only written language of the Nephites. We know that the Nephites engraved reformed Egyptian, and it is also clear that they that had a hand-written language (Alma 30:51–52; Mosiah 2:8). Again, it is important to remember that the Incas told the Spanish that their ancestors once had a written language that was eventually lost.

Why would a nation lose its written language? The Spanish conquest of Peru provides a possible explanation. Conquering nations reduced the probability of a revolt from those they conquered by abolishing their culture, including their religious identity. The easiest way to do that was to destroy their written records. When the Romans finally prevailed over Carthage, they burned their maritime charts so they lost their ability to sail against Rome. When the illiterate Lamanites finally overran the Nephite civilization, it would have been natural for them to have destroyed all of the Nephites written records and in so doing ended forever the Nephite nation.

4. A VISITATION BY JESUS CHRIST

More important than gold or words is the fact that for any nation to have written the Book of Mormon, it must have been visited by the Lord. Indeed the Book of Mormon's main objective is to stand as a second witness of Jesus Christ.

As will be seen in Chapter Eight of this book, there are amazing parallels between the account of Christ's visit to the New World in the Book of Mormon and the oral histories of the Incas of Peru. Despite what many Mormon authors have purported over the years, at the present time there is little mythological evidence that Jesus Christ visited Mesoamerica in AD 34. Furthermore, to assert that the pre-Columbian religious practices in Mesoamerica are even remotely related to the teaching of Jesus Christ is, in my opinion, hard to believe. Adrian Gilbert writes:

> One stumbling block that researchers of Mesoamerican civilization have to overcome is a natural feeling of revulsion towards the cruelty that seems to have been an essential part of the indigenous religions. This cruelty is reflected in the grotesque nature of so much Mesoamerican art and even more so in the preserved literature. There is no doubting that, as witnessed by the conquistadores, the pre-Christian religion of Central America was frightening. The Aztecs in particular practiced human sacrifices on a massive scale. Superstitious to an amazing degree, they would tear out the still-beating hearts of sacrificial victims and offer these as food to the Sun. As if this were not bad enough, they would on other occasions flay their victims while still alive and then wear their skins for rituals that could last for weeks.[45]

The reason they practiced human sacrifice was that they believed their gods needed to be fed. Their favorite food was evidently human life force, most visibly seen in the twitching hearts presented to them on the banqueting table of the temples.[46]

The Aztecs sacrificed some 50,000 human victims each year, and initially believed that Hernán Cortéz was their bloodthirsty bearded white god, Quetzalcoatl.[47] Fortunately, Quetzalcoatl appears to have nothing to do with the Book of Mormon.

Quetzalcoatl did not become the dominant god of Central America until AD 900, well after the conclusion of the Book of Mormon record. It was not until the Xochicaoco's political class started claiming the divine right to rule in the name of Quetzalcoatl that the deity took the main stage in Mesoamerican belief. That is, after the Toltecs began using the name Quetzalcoatl in reference to their rulers.[48] Prior to the Toltecs, Quetzalcoatl was the Olmec and Mayan pagan snake god.

On the one hand, the symbolism associated with Peru's Viracocha white-god traditions appear to be consistent with the Bible and Book of Mormon's description of Jesus Christ. For example, consider the ruins of the city of Tiwanaku (Tiahuanacu) at Lake Titicaca in Bolivia. The city was built around AD 200, the approximate time the Nephite and Lamanite cities were being rebuilt after the appearance of Christ in the New World (4 Nephi 1:7). I visited the ruins of Tiahuanacu during my Peru-Bolivia mission. I was dwarfed by stone statues over four times my height (the tallest is nearly twenty-four feet tall). Some of the giant monoliths portray Viracocha, the bearded white god of the Andes. Every Viracocha image at Tiahuanacu is clearly of a god in the form of a man. Perhaps the most famous icon of Viracocha is the carving of him that adorns the Sun Gate at Tiahuanacu. The carving is of a man holding staffs. The man has an aurora around his head (common artistic convention for signifying deity), a beard, and teardrops falling upon his cheeks (possible symbolism for the love and passion the Lord displayed in the Americas; see 3 Nephi 17:20–21). Clearly, Peruvians' artistic depictions of their white god were in the form of a man.[49]

On the other hand, the white god of Central America was depicted as a beast-fable god. Quetzalcoatl's icons are of humans that have taken on animal characteristics or are entirely the image of a beast—a plumed serpent. Quetzalcoatl images clearly contradict Isaiah's warning against making pagan comparisons to the Lord (Isaiah 40:18). Alonzo Gaskill notes, "Symbolically speaking, they [serpents] remind us of Satan and his teachings, buffetings, temptations, and pitfalls."[50] In the contrary, Peruvian myth scholar William Sullivan notes that the Peruvians believed the serpent was the symbol of "natural and social catastrophes . . . sudden and violent, is a sign of change . . . which first seduced a maiden . . . 'house of the false god.'"[51] Furthermore, in Peruvian lore the serpent was a metaphor for bringing down houses and caused upheavals on the "celestial earth."[52]

How did the snake Quetzalcoatl absorb the characteristics of a bearded white man around the tenth century AD? One plausible explanation is that a Viking or Russian, with his family, sailed off course and found himself as a fair-skinned novelty in the land of the Toltecs. Calderwood suggests that Quetzalcoatl was actually two characters—the ancient feathered-snake idol and a later personage.[53] He cites Doris Heyden in her introduction to *Book of the Gods and Rites*:

> In Durán's time there was utter confusion about Topiltzin-Quetzalcoatl, the

great Toltec priest-king and holy man. The mystery of this man has not been completely clarified in our own times; there are controversial theories about his identity, history, and birth and death dates. . . . Archaeological discoveries have confirmed that the Toltecs formed a great civilization which reached its peak in central Mexico around the year AD 1000. They spoke the Nahuatl language and also introduced metallurgy in the central highlands of Mexico. They left the impressive ruins of Tula.

When the youth became a man, he was made high priest of this cult and adopted the name Quetzalcoatl, their god. He spent most of his life in the city of Tula, or Tollan, where he acquired fame as a holy man. Despite the reverence in which he was held, a conflict between two rival religious sects—one of which urged him to offer human sacrifice—led to a plot against him. Certain sorcerers offered him strong wine, made him drunk, and led him to commit incest with his sister. Disgraced, the priest abandoned Tula and went eastward toward present-day Veracruz. Before his final departure, however, he left various signs of his passing throughout the countryside and promised to return one day.[54]

MESOAMERICA DOES NOT FIT THE BOOK OF MORMON

Besides lacking the above core elements needed just to write the Book of Mormon, it would take a far stretch of the imagination to place the Book of Mormon in a Mesoamerican setting. Brigham Young University Anthropologist John

E. Clark provides this simplified guideline: "Culturally, the Book of Mormon describes an urbanized agrarian people having metallurgy (Helaman 6:11), writing (1 Nephi 1:1–3), lunar and solar calendars (2 Nephi 5:28; Omni 1:21), domestic animals (2 Nephi 5:11), various grains (1 Nephi 8:1), gold, silver, pearls, and 'costly apparel' (Alma 1:29; 4 Nephi 1:24)."[55]

Even an elementary knowledge of Latin American anthropology during ancient times discloses Mesoamerica as presently a poor candidate for the lands of the Book of Mormon.

Mesoamerica

Urbanized in early Jaredite times	No
Gold and Silver	No
Iron Ore	No
Writing	Yes
Metal Plates	No
Lunar and Solar Calendars	Yes
Domestic animals	No
Various grains	Yes
Costly apparel (general populus)	No

In the first century BC, Alma described the Nephites as "having abundance of all things whatsoever they stood in need—an abundance of flocks and herds, and fatlings of every kind, and also abundance of grain, and of gold, and of silver, and of precious things, and abundance of silk and fine-twined linen, and all manner of good homely cloth" (Alma 1:29). Using odd concepts such as "internal logic" or "geographic templates," Book of Mormon scholars have concocted self-defined theory after theory of where the Nephites once lived; however, they have done so while completely ignoring the obvious body of evidence that would actually identify where the Nephites once lived with their metals, ships, herds, flocks,

grains, all manner of cloth, and, most important, the tradition of a visitation of a white god in the form of a man.

A MODEL THAT WORKS

Archaeologists and anthropologists are just beginning to scratch the surface of Peru's history, yet within this limited context compelling evidence abounds that the Book of Mormon is a true history, and that the model found in this book provides a rational basis for proposing possible candidates for Book of Mormon sites. Are these sites the actual places written of by the ancient prophets? Of course, we cannot be certain at this time. Indeed, if one understands the nature and limited scope of the present body of archaeological findings in South America, one would realize how naïve it is to draw definitive conclusions about specific historical features and place-names. For example, this book proposes that the major portion of the Nephite and Lamanite lands of the Book of Mormon are to be found in the southern Andean highlands. The Incas called this area Collasuyu. University of California at Los Angeles archaeologist Charles Stanish writes, "In the last fifteen years, members of the Programa Collasuyu have discovered literally hundreds of new sites. We have begun the slow but immensely satisfying work of documenting, excavating, and theorizing about the entire Titicaca region, not just Pukara and Tiwanaku."[56]

THE TIME FRAME OF THE EVIDENCE PRESENTED IN THIS BOOK

On the one hand, the archaeological record that is unfolding in Peru is clearly showing that the Book of Mormon is in harmony with science.

On the other hand, after decades of research, no credible scientific evidence exists of a single Book of Mormon site in Mesoamerica. Conjecture sure—evidence no. The distinguished Mayanist, Michael Coe, a retired Yale archaeologist, stated: "As far as I know there is not [in 1973] one professionally trained archaeologist who is not a Mormon, who sees any scientific justification for believing [the history of the Book of Mormon], and I would like to state that there are quite a few Mormon archaeologists who join this group."[57]

However, Coe himself was from the old school that thought the cradle of New World civilization was Mesoamerica. Charles Mann writes:

A few decades ago, many researchers would have included jump-starting Andean civilization on the honor roll of Mesoamerican accomplishments. The Olmec, it was proposed, visited Peru, and the locals, dutiful students, copied their example. Today we know that technologically sophisticated societies arose in Peru first—the starting date, to archaeologists' surprise, keeps getting pushed back. Between 3200 and 2500 BC, large-scale public buildings, the temple at Huaricanga among them, rose up in at least seven settlements on the Peruvian coast—an extraordinary efflorescence for that time and place. When the people of Norte Chico were building these cities, there was only one other urban complex on earth: Sumer.[58]

Thus, during the time of the early Book of Mormon Jaredites, a major civilization rose in Peru, with massive public buildings and temples. In 2500 BC the Olmecs were not even on the scene, and it would be another thousand years before the first Olmec cities were built. The Mayans are unlikely candidates for the Nephites since the earliest dating of Pre-Classic Mayan sites is 300 BC, nearly 300 years after the Nephites built their first temple. Even the famed pyramid construction that was once thought to have originated in Mesoamerica is now known to have emerged from Peru centuries earlier.[59]

In contrast, the Peruvian archaeological record provides a timetable that is in harmony with the periods associated with Jaredite, Nephite, and Lamanite civilizations. A candidate for the city of Nephi is the Central Andes during the time that archaeologists define as the Early Intermediate Period (600 BC–AD 200). For the city of Zarahemla, the evidence points to the Northern Titicaca Basin during its Late/Upper Formative Periods (500 BC–AD 400). The early and late Lamanite periods in the land southward, match

Archeological Periods (Civilizations) for Proposed Book of Mormon Lands

CENTRAL ANDES
EARLY INTERMEDIATE
600 BC–AD 200
(LAND OF NEPHI)

NORTHERN TITICACA BASIN
LATE/UPPER FORMATIVE
500 BC–AD 400
(ZARAHEMLA)

EARLY TIWANKU IV
LATE CHIRIPA II
MIDDLE FORMATIVE
600 BC–AD 400
(LAMANITE LANDS)

NORTE CHICO
3500–300 BC
(JAREDITES)

CHAPTER ONE

No, it's not Arabia, but Ica, Peru!

well with the southern Titicaca Basin capital at Tiwanaku and with the Tiwanaku empire that extend from Lake Titicaca into northern Chile and southeast Bolivia during the Early Tiwanaku IV to Late Chiripa 2/Middle Formative Periods (600 BC–AD 400), also called Tiwanaku I, II, III.

THE GEOGRAPHIC SETTING OF THE EVIDENCE PRESENTED IN THIS BOOK

Clark concludes: "Book of Mormon lands encompassed mountains, wildernesses, coastal plains, valleys, a large river, a highland lake, and lowland wetlands."[60] Alan Kolata of the University of Chicago provides a concise description of the almost magical geography of the Inca domain, the primary area of our study:

> Structurally, the Andean natural environment can be divided into five principal physiographic regions: the desert plains of the Pacific coast; the mountainous highlands, or *sierra* basins; the high plateau, or Altiplano of southern Peru and Bolivia; the humid, eastern slopes of the Andes, or *montaña*; and the true tropical rainforest of the Amazon basin. Proceeding east to west from the Amazon basin across the mountainous highlands down to the Pacific coast, climate, precipitation, and vegetation patterns change dramatically, with a general trend toward increasing aridity until one reaches the strip of coastal desert that forms the western edge of the continent from northern Peru to central Chile. The Pacific coastal deserts of Peru and Chile are among the most forbidding tracts of land on earth. The only relief from the monotonous

gray-brown desert landscape is offered by a series of coastal rivers cascading down the western slopes of the Andes. These rivers, naturally enough, have become oases for coastal peoples over the millennia, yielding a series of fertile bands in an otherwise sterile and hostile environment. . . .[61]

In the central Andes, this more heavily watered transitional steppe gives way to multiple intermontane basins hemmed in by the two great mountain chains that form the Andes. The Cordillera Occidental (western) and the Cordillera Oriental (eastern). These high mountain valleys were heavily populated in the prehispanic past and became the core territory for the Inca empire. The indigenous populations of the intermontane basins farmed the rich alluvial soils of the valley floors and extended the spatial reach of food cultivation by constructing contour terraces, frequently connected with irrigation canals which drew water from mountain springs at higher elevations.

Immediately south of Cuzco, the two imposing mountain chains diverge significantly. Interposed between them in an anciently uplifted high plateau is the great Andean Altiplano, which lies between 3,000 and 4,000 masl (10,000 to 13,000 feet above sea level).

The Altiplano proper, defined by the relatively flat depression between the two towering *cordilleras*, runs for over 800 kilometers (500 miles) from north to south, from southernmost Peru to northwestern Argentina, and ranges between 120 and 160 kilometers (75 to 100 miles) from west to east. This enormous plateau, incorporating thousands of square kilometers, comprises the largest area of interior drainage in highland South America. The geologic processes of tectonic uplifting and orogenesis that created this vast, enclosed drainage basin also generated extensive fresh water lakes. The Altiplano and the lakes were formed in the Miocene with the rise of the Andes, and attained their present form in the Pleistocene. Since their formation, the lakes of the Altiplano have been disappearing through evaporative loss. Today only Lake Titicaca on the northern end of the high plateau and Lake Poopó to the southeast remain significant bodies of water. . . .[62]

Immediately to the east of the Andean Altiplano, crossing the great eastern mountain range, which in Bolivia carries the name Cordillera Real, we move quickly into a world entirely different from the bleak, forbidding plateaus of tenuous subsistence agriculture and llama herding. Wild rivers originating in the ancient glaciers of the cordillera cut and gouge the hard rock of the mountains in spectacular displays of headward erosion. Waterfalls cascade violently for hundreds of meters down the vertiginous eastern slopes of the Andes, which become increasingly humid and forested as one descends through roiling banks of damp fog from the high mountain passes. Gnarled evergreens, shrubs, dripping with parasitic wild orchids, cling tenaciously to the fractured black shale and basalt-clad mountainsides. Enclaves of nearly flat land with deep, rich soils are encrusted in the tortuous, almost chaotic jumble of rock formations that form the eastern edge of the Andean chain. These are the opulent hot lands of the montaña, or *yungas* as the Aymara call them.[63]

Beyond the yungas is the vast tropical rainforest of the great Amazon basin. Peru's landscape, especially that of the high Andes and its Altiplano, is spectacular. It borders on the surreal. As a missionary, I stood on the level floor of the Altiplano trying to comprehend that I was actually breathing air at 12,500 feet above sea level. The crystal blue lake waters of Lake Titicaca stretched out before me for some 138 miles. On all sides, the basin was surrounded by snow-capped mountains, some reaching to over 21,000 feet. The Altiplano is the American Tibet, but perhaps it is even more amazing than its Asian counterpart. A hundred miles west of where I was standing is the earth's driest desert, and only a hundred miles in the opposite direction is the greatest watershed on earth, the Amazon jungle. For those fortunate enough to have served missions in Ecuador, Peru, Bolivia, Chile, and Argentina, the images they remember of the Andes will never leave them.

As stunning as the Andean scenery might be, even more impressive are the people who have tamed these great mountains and made this land their home. Charles Mann writes:

Highland Peru is as extraordinary as the Inka themselves. It is the only place on earth, the Cornell anthropologist John Murra wrote. 'where millions [of people] insist, against all apparent logic, on living at 10,000 or even 14,000 feet above sea level. Nowhere else have people lived so many thousands of years in such visibly vulnerable circumstances.'

The author at Lake Titicaca, the "great sea" of the promised land.

And nowhere else have people living at such heights—in places where most crops won't grow, earthquakes and landslides are frequent, and extremes of weather are the norm—repeatedly created technically advanced, long-lasting civilizations. The Inka homeland, uniquely high, was also uniquely steep, with slopes of more than sixty-five degrees from the horizontal. (The steepest street in San Francisco, famed for its nearly undrivable hills, is thirty-one-and-a-half degrees.) And it was uniquely narrow; the distance from the Pacific shore to the mountaintops is in most places less than seventy-five miles and in many less than fifty. . . . In the short traverse from mountain to ocean, travelers pass through twenty of the world's thirty-four principal environments.

To survive in the steep, narrow hodgepodge of ecosystems, Andean communities usually sent out representatives and colonies to live up- or downslope in places with resources unavailable to home. Fish and shellfish from the ocean; beans, squash, and cotton from the coastal river valleys; maize, potatoes, and the Andean grain quinoa from the foothills; llamas and alpaca for wool and meat in the heights—each area had something to contribute.[64]

Why would the Nephites have selected the difficult Peruvian highlands as a place to settle? It must be remembered that to their south they were outnumbered by the Lamanites who were a constant threat to their survival. In Nephi's time, the shoreline of Peru was already ruled over by the powerful Chavín Empire. The steep highland valleys represented an easy-to-defend homeland that seemingly no one else wanted. It is somewhat like the Latter-day Mormon pioneers, who fled their enemies to a high-mountain desert that no one else wanted; and like the Mormon pioneers, it would have taken an industrious people like the Nephites to have created Peru's incredible landscape of mountains partitioned by man-made terraces and crisscrossed with vast irrigation networks.

THE JAREDITES ARRIVE
IN PERU

It was here, then, in confronting the peculiar syntax of the technical
language of myth—where scientific fact and spiritual value lie in
synergic equipoise, the one energizing the other—

WILLIAM SULLIVAN, *The Secret of the Incas*

Driving north along the shoreline from Peru's modern capital of Lima, one sees a barren wasteland. On the left is the Pacific Ocean, and in the distance to the right, the towering Andes Mountains. Between the beach and the great peaks is a dusty desert. This narrow coastal plain has one of the driest climates on earth and presents itself as life-less. One hundred twenty miles north from Lima is a slice of the coastline called Norte Chico. Separated by miles of desert on the north and south, Norte Chico has four river valleys that break up its sterile landscape with strips of lush vegeta-tion. Despite its four snowmelt rivers, Norte Chico appears to be the last place on earth one would look for the birth of a sophisticated civilization.

In 1941, Harvard archaeologists Gordon R. Willey and John M. Corbett worked at the mouth of one of Norte Chi-co's rivers, the Supe. They observed a half-dozen mounds or knolls and reported that they were "natural eminences of sand."[1] They had been fooled by the deceiving desert landscape. Fifty-three years later, Ruth Shady Solies from the National University of San Marcos in Lima discovered in the same area the remains of a 150-acre city that included six large platform mounds, sunken ceremonial plazas, six other complexes of mounds with platforms, and large stone build-ings with residential apartments. The city has been named Caral.

It was quickly apparent that Caral was a very ancient city. Jonathan Hass, an archaeologist for the Field Museum of Natural History in Chicago, and his wife Winifred Creamer, an archaeologist at Northern Illinois University, established in 2000 by radiocarbon-dating that Caral was founded about 2600 BC.[2] That was just the beginning of the discoveries in the area. In the sixty-mile long area that constitutes Norte Chico, the ruins of twenty-four other ancient cities have been dis-covered. From what we presently know, Norte Chico is the site of the New World's first urban complex. Charles Mann writes: "Taken individually, none of the twenty-five Norte

Chico cities rivaled Sumer's cities in size, but the totality was bigger than Sumer. Egypt's pyramids were larger, but they were built centuries later."[3]

The recent discovery of a third millennium BC civilization in the New World that was larger than Sumer surprised archaeologists; however, it is exactly what the Book of Mormon stated was the case when it was printed in 1830. In its account of the Jaredites, the Lord promised the brother of Jared that "there shall be none greater than the nation which I shall raise up unto me of thy seed" (Ether 1:43)

An urban center larger than Sumer in Peru! And with a pyramid mound sixty feet tall and five hundred feet on all sides. Of special interest to students of the Book of Mormon is the fact that only one other city-state civilization existing at that time was Sumer of the tower of Babel and Jaredite fame. How exciting!—a sister civilization that matched that of Mesopotamia in antiquity and achievements. It should be remembered that Sumer in Mesopotamia was the original home of the Jaredites, and that the discovery of Caral is of paramount importance in the study of Book of Mormon historicity. Indeed, for the first time archaeologists have discovered a civilization in the Americas that dates to the era of the early Jaredites. Furthermore, the pyramids of Caral present a striking resemblance to the ziggurat pyramids of Mesopotamia, being composed of sunbaked bricks, terraced with successive receding levels and a ramp on one side.

TWIN CIVILIZATIONS

For Caral to be considered as a viable candidate for the Jaredites' first home, it would need to have met a very specific attribute—one that would seem to have been extremely unlikely in the third millennium BC—i.e., it could not have existed alone; it needed to have had a sister civilization with which it competed, as will be evidenced from the following.

The first Jaredite cities in the promised land were built in the land of Moron (Ether 7:5–6). However, soon after the arrival of the Jaredites in the promised land, it appears that some of them must have broken away from the original colonies and settled *in another region* called the land of Nehor (Ether 7:4). Corihor, the great grandson of Jared, rebelled against his father, king Kib, and fled the land of Moron to the land of Nehor, where he organized a full rebellion and came with an army against the land of Moron. The land of Nehor must have been far enough away from the land of Moron to provide Corihor a refuge where he could organize his rebellion and prepare an army to march against his father. Thus the Book of Mormon not only declares that a sophisticated civilization existed in the Americas in the late third millennium BC or early second millennium BC, but that there were *two rival civilizations*. The official organization that is overseeing the excavation of Caral estimates that the civilization started circa 2660 BC.[4] Archaeological evidence has confirmed that two hundred twenty-five miles north of Caral, *a separate civilization*, the Huaca Prieta, rose up in the Chicama river valley between 2600 and 2500 BC.[5]

WHAT THE BOOK OF MORMON SAYS

Moroni condensed two thousand years of Jaredite history into fifteen short chapters, representing today only thirty printed pages that include numerous footnotes and cross-references. Of course, Moroni had only twenty-four metal plates to begin with (Mosiah 8:9). Remove from this brief narrative the doctrinal passages, and the Jaredite story is short indeed. Still, from this faint glimpse into a long past, we can outline some of the significant events of early Jaredite history:

- A man named Jared ruled over a group of people. His descendants became the Jaredite royal lineage (Ether 1:6–33).

- When the language of the people living in Mesopotamia was confounded, Jared asked his brother, who was favored of the Lord, to pray and ask that their language would not be confounded. His prayers were answered in his favor (Ether 1:34–37), and the language of the extended Jaredite family and their friends was not confounded.

- Jared next asked his prophet brother to "inquire of the Lord" to see if God might lead them into a land "choice above all the earth." Again, the Lord answered the brother of Jared by commanding him to take his family and his friends and "gather together thy flocks, both male and female, of every kind; and also of seed of the earth of every kind; and thy families." Subsequently the Lord met Jared's party in Nimrod (Ether 1:38–41, 2:1).

- From Nimrod the Book of Mormon does not state which direction they traveled, only that the Lord led the Jaredites into a wilderness. Even that "wilderness, yea, into that *quarter where there never had man been*" (Ether 2:4–5; italics added).

Pyramids of Caral. A likely candidate for the first Jaredite city in the promised land.

- After crossing the wilderness, the Jaredites settled for a period in a land they called Moriancumer (Ether 2:13).

- The place Moriancumer must have included a protected harbor, for the Lord commanded the Jaredites to build eight ocean-going barges (Ether 3:1).

- Since the Lord commanded the Jaredites to build barges to cross open oceans "after the manner of barges which ye have hitherto built" (Ether 2:16), the Jaredites must have been a shipbuilding and seafaring family with significant maritime experience (Ether 2:16).

- The Jaredite barges were "driven forth before the wind" (Ether 6:8), thus implying sails. The Sumerians were the first to invent the sail, which they made from canvas that came from cotton they cultivated.

- The design of the Jaredite barges necessitated a source of internal light. The brother of Jared prepared sixteen stones and took them up a mountain to ask the Lord to touch them so they would radiate light. Because of his great faith, the Lord appeared through the veil to the brother of Jared (Ether 3:6).

- When the Lord appeared to the brother of Jared, it appears that the prophet received a "new" or "sacred" name endowment. This conclusion follows from the fact that Moroni never tells us the brother of Jared's actual name. Furthermore, the things that the brother of Jared saw and heard on the mountain had to be sealed up and kept secret by commandment of the Lord (Ether 4:5). Moreover, we know that the brother of Jared passed through the veil (Ether 3:20, 12:21). We learn only later, from the Prophet Joseph Smith, that the name of the brother of Jared was Moriancumer.[6] Thus, the place where the Jaredites built their ships was named after the brother of Jared (Ether 2:13).

- The Jaredites sailed three hundred and forty and four days until they reached the promised land that is known today as the Americas (Ether 6:11).

- The Jaredites went forth upon the face of the land and began to "till the earth" (Ether 6:13).

- When Jared neared death, the people demanded a king. They first selected the oldest son of the brother of Jared, Pagag. He refused, so they selected Orihah, a son of Jared (Ether 6:27).

- Under Orihah the people began to prosper and became exceedingly rich (Ether 6:28). The Book of Mormon does not say in which materials they became rich, but we can assume they must have had an abundance of at least good housing, nourishing food, and fine clothing.

- Orihah reigned in righteousness and begat twenty-three sons, plus one in his old age—King Kib (Ether 7:1–3).

- King Kib's son Corihor rebelled against his father and dwelt in a land called Nehor (Ether 7:4).

- Nehor gathered an army and attacked the land of Moron where Kib lived and took his father captive (Ether 7:5).

- Moron is near the land the Nephites, later called "Desolation" (Ether 7:6).

- Kib bore a son in captivity who later made swords of steel and was able to restore his father to the throne (Ether 7:9). Thus, from the time of the earliest Jaredites, they were advanced metallurgists. They also refined gold and made gold plates (Ether 10:5–7 and Mosiah 8:9).

In summary, within three generations of landing in the promised land, the Jaredites had a king who "did prosper exceedingly and wax great" (Ether 7:19), had a land divided into two kingdoms with their own cities (Ether 7:9, 20), raised armies (Ether 7:5, 9), had bloody battles (Ether 7:16), and had prophets and religious instruction (Ether 7:23).

PROBLEMS WITH A MESOAMERICA MODEL FOR THE JAREDITE LANDS

Although nearly all the popular LDS literature on the Jaredites places them in Mesoamerica, usually associating them with the Olmec civilization, such Mesoamerican models are problematic for several reasons. First, the record of the Jaredites was inscribed on golden plates (Mosiah 8:9), and early Jaredite warriors fashioned swords out of some form of steel (Ether 7:9). However,

Temple at Caral, similar architecture to ziggurats in ancient Mesopotamia.

no archaeological evidence of significant metal-working has been shown to exist in Mesoamerica until the AD ninth century,[7] long after the fall of the Olmec civilization (400–200 BC).[8] On the other hand, the Jaredites were working metal since their earliest years in the New World.

Second, the Bible records seem to indicate that the flood occurred somewhere around 2400 BC.[9] However, Egyptian and Chinese histories predate that time, so the flood could have occurred nearly a thousand years earlier (circa 3500 BC).[10] The Book of Mormon tells us that the Jaredites built barges and sailed them to the New World shortly after the great flood. Within a few generations of their arrival, the Jaredites had already constructed cities, divided into separate lands, and had fought wars (Ether 7:9–12). However, signs of a mother-culture in Mesoamerica started appearing about 1800 BC with the first Olmec cities not having been built before 1200 BC.[11] Even Book of Mormon scholar, John E. Clark stated that the "Jaredites were probably tilling American soil in the Land Northward at least by 2200 BC," but continues, "the earliest known Olmec city was up and running by 1300 BC."[12] Even this late date for the Jaredite arrival leaves a gap of *900 years* without any evidence of the cities the Jaredites were known to have built. To put 900 years with no evidence of cities into perspective, compare the wilderness the Pilgrims of Plymouth found when they landed on Cape Cod 388 years ago to the great cities that exist in New England today. The problem with this deficit cannot be just wishfully ignored. The Jaredite cities mentioned in the seventh chapter of the Book of Ether were constructed nearly a thousand years *before* the earliest Mesoamerican cities appeared on the scene. Where then are those early Jaredite cities that were probably built far earlier than 2200 BC? The only known remains of large city-states in the New World dating back to the era of the Jaredites are the coastal cities of Peru (3200–2500 BC).[13]

Third, the Jaredites domesticated animals that they used in their work (Ether 10:25–26). The Nephites also maintained flocks (2 Nephi 5:11, Enos 1:21, and so forth). The Book of Ether uses Old World names to describe the domesticated animals of the Jaredites: "of cattle, of oxen, and cows, and of sheep, and of swine" (Ether 9:18). On the other hand, the only pre-Columbian animals known to have been domesticated in Mesoamerica and North America were the dog and the turkey.[14] The fact that ancient people in these areas had no animals that resembled a domesticate sheep is no minor disqualifier of these areas as the lands of the Book of Mormon. From the earliest Jaredite to the end of the Nephite nation, animal husbandry was a major economic activity for the people of the Book of Mormon. In the promised land, the term "flocks" was used sixty-three times in the Book of Mormon, being found in the books of 2 Nephi, Enos, Mosiah, Alma, Helaman, 3 Nephi, and Ether. Sheep are mentioned twenty-four times in the Book of Mormon, and herds are noted in the book twenty-three times. The Nephite scriptures refer to the profession of shepherding seventeen times.

Furthermore, herds, flocks, and sheep were important icons in the message delivered by the Lord to the people in the New World. When the Lord, master of all teachers, taught, He carefully selected parables and symbols to match the images of the common everyday life of those that sat before him. For example, in Palestine the Lord often taught principles using the symbolism of the fig tree. However, in the New World, where the fig was not native, the Book of Mormon does not mention the word. In contrast, in the Four Gospels, the Master mentioned sheep thirty-three times, and He continued to use the symbol of the sheep when he taught the Nephites. In addressing the righteous in the New World, Jesus used the symbolism of the sheep eight times, even calling the Nephites the "other sheep I have which are not of this fold" (3 Nephi 15:21).

On the one hand, if the Lord had visited any ancient American people other than His children in the Andes, it would seem highly unlikely that the Lord would have taught them principles using the symbol of an animal they had never seen. If He had, they would have sat there wondering "What is a sheep? What is a fold?" On the other hand, for the symbolism in Book of Mormon to have made contextual sense, it must have taken place in a land where the people understood the meaning of the Lamb of God, one fold, the king's flocks, the good shepherd, and so forth.

Undoubtedly, Joseph Smith had no idea of the types of animals or the advanced husbandry skills of the Peruvians. Yet the Book of Mormon's reference to shepherds and sheep is completely in harmony with ancient Peru. The people of western South America maintained great herds of llamas, alpacas, vicuñas, and perhaps other animals that became extinct over a four-thousand-year period. What is clear is that the Incas had an array of domesticated animals which the Spanish chroniclers described in the following account: "the lords of Cuzco made many and very great sacrifices . . . a large amount of livestock in sheep and lambs was sacrificed as well as deer and all the other animals."[15] The Spaniard Pedro de Cieza de León, described llamas and alpacas as rams, sheep, and lambs[16] and wrote, "Eating those good rams that they found there, which are extraordinary and more flavorful than the excellent ones of Spain."[17] It should not be forgotten that the Nephites sacrificed the firstlings of their flocks.

The domesticated animals of Peru that the Spaniards called sheep, goats, and horses, probably account for what the Jaredites referred to as their "cattle." Noah Webster's 1828 American dictionary defines "cattle" as: "In its primary sense, the word includes camels, horses, asses, all the varieties of domesticated horned beasts of the bovine genus, sheep of all kinds, and goats."[18]

William J. Hamblin writes,

> The Book of Mormon text may have used familiar Egyptian or Hebrew terms for new unknown types of animals which the Nephites discovered in the New World. This opinion has been frequently mocked by anti-Mormons who are apparently unaware of the nature of Pre-Modern naming ambiguities. When Pre-Modern peoples encountered new species for which they didn't have a name, they followed one of two possible courses of action: they either adopted a foreign name for that animal, or they transferred to the new animal the name of an animal with which they were familiar. For example, when the Greeks first encountered a new type of animal in the Nile Valley, they called it the "horse of the river," the hippo-potamos, or hippopotamus. Are we to assume that Greek civilization did not exist at all because they chose to call the Nile

hippopotamus a "horse," rather than adopting the Egyptian name *hebu*? When the Romans first encountered the elephant in the army of Pyrrhus of Epirus in 280 BC, they called it the "Lucca bos, Lucanian cow". . . . If such a linguistic phenomenon in the Book of Mormon is seen as evidence for discounting the very existence of Book of Mormon civilization, must we not also do away with the Greeks, Romans, Maya, and Arabs?[19]

The elephant is never mentioned in the Hebrew Bible. However, the Jaredites called some animal an "elephant" (Ether 9:19). So what did the Jaredites mean by the term *elephant*? In Latin, *ele* means "arch" (extreme: most fully embodying the qualities of his or her kind[20]) and *phant* means "huge." In other words, the meaning of the term elephant in antiquity meant "a huge thing, that of its kind." In Peru the Quechua-speakers called the tapir *ahuara*, meaning "big animal."[21]

However, there is a more straightforward explanation for the elephants in the Book of Mormon. The Jaredite plates were translated (and the word *elephant* inscribed on the plates of the Book of Mormon) by a Nephite. Greek culture was the prevailing language at the time Lehi left Jerusalem. Although the soldiers of Alexander the Great fought against elephants in India, elephants were not seen in the Mediterranean region until Hannibal the Carthaginian (247–183 BC). Prior to their arrival, the Greeks knew that the great beasts had tusks, and therefore considered any animal with "tusks" as being a type of elephant, thus the Greeks called boars "elephants."[22] It would seem only natural then that if the Jaredite record referred to the pig-like peccary with their sharp tusks, they would also call them *elephants*.

Peruvian alpacas. The Spanish conquistadors called them "sheep."

One category, called the giant peccary (*Pecari maximus*), was not discovered until 2007. It is the size of a large dog.[23]

PERUVIAN CREATION MYTHOLOGY

The oral traditions of the Peruvians hint that the Jaredites colonized their shoreline. Urton of Harvard University notes that the Peruvian creator-god was actually a "trinity" of gods,[24] and provides this summary of their creation lore:

> Most versions of this origin myth start by asserting that, in the beginning of time, all was in darkness, as the sun, moon and stars had not yet been created. Into this primeval darkness there emerged the creator Viracocha; . . . [Andeans' bearded White God] In various versions the creator is called Con Tici Viracocha, Thunupa Viracocha, and Viracocha Pachayachachic. . . . certain coastal myths that identify the creator as "maker of earth/time."
>
> In this time and space of darkness, Viracocha, who is described by Betanzos as a lord who emerged from Lake Titicaca, came forth and created the first race of humanity. These first beings, whom some chroniclers identify as a race of giants, lived in the darkness for a period of time but then, for some unspecified reason, they angered Viracocha. Because of his anger and his disappointment with them, the creator brought the first age to an end by a flood.[25]

Father Martín de Murúa, who learned to speak Quechua and Aymara, recorded that "the old Indians state that [after the flood] the brothers saw a rainbow in the sky. Manco Capac told his brothers that the rainbow was a good sign and the world would not be destroyed again by water."[26]

The Jaredites are believed to have been a "very large race of men."[27] Father Bernadé Cobo (1582–1657) was convinced that giants had lived along the Peruvian coast a short period before the first Inca, and he provided several testimonials of Spaniards who had seen the skeletons of giants.[28] The Indians, Cobo explains, "say that giants had come there from the south in large rafts."[29] After the first race of humanity was destroyed by a flood, Peruvian mythology holds that the white god created a second race of humanity, and "he also gave each nation the language they were to speak, the songs they were to sing."[30] Urton notes:

> In the version of the origin myth recounted by Cristobal de Molina, we read a slightly different account of the nature of events at the beginning of time. Molina begins when the world was already populated. Then there came a great flood, the waters of which covered even the highest mountains. The only survivors of this deluge were a man and a woman who, as the waters subsided, were thrown up onto the land of Tiahuanaco. Viracocha appeared and commanded the couple to remain there as *mitimaes* [migrants], the name given to groups of people who were moved by the Inca from their home territory to some other place in the empire.

Molina then says that after the flood subsided, the creator set about repopulating the land, fashioning the ancestors of the different nations of Tahuantinsuyu out of clay, and painting them in the manner of the dress they were to wear.[31] Quoting Molina directly:

> . . . they [Inkas] had an ample account of the deluge. They say that in it perished all races of men and created things insomuch that the waters rose above the highest mountain peaks in the world. No living thing survived except a man and a woman who remained in a box and, when the waters subsided, the wind carried them . . . to Tiahuanaco [where] the creator began to raise up the people and the nations that are in that region."[32]

Though the Andean creator mythology attempts to recall events that occurred at the dawn of human history, it was obvious to the Spanish that the early Peruvians had a basic knowledge of the Creation and the great flood. The Peruvians also appear to have had a communal memory that a large-sized people arrived on their shoreline and that they brought with them the blessings of their first civilization. Yet the most remarkable Peruvian account of the flood was recorded by Sarmiento:

> It is related that everything was destroyed in the flood called *una pachacuti*. It must now be known that Viracocha Pachayachachi [bearded white god], when he destroyed the land as has been already recounted, preserved three men, one of them named Taguapaca, that they might serve and help him in the creation of new people who had to be made in the second age [dispensation], which was done in this manner. The flood being passed and the land dry, Viracocha determined to people it a second time, and, to make it more perfect, he decided upon creating luminaries to give it light [sixteen stones of the Jaredites?]. With this object he went, with his servants, to a great lake in the Collao [Jaredites built

Did her ancestors watch over the flocks of the Book of Mormon people?

barges], in which there is an island called Titicaca [South America?].[33]

The Incas believed that the first people who arrived in their land called it *Pirua* (corrupted by the Spanish into *Peru*). Earlier Spanish chroniclers were told by the Indians that the name *Pirua* was derived from the name "Ophir," the same name as the famous Biblical sailor (Genesis 10:29; 1 Kings 10:11, 22). The seamanship skills of Ophir might even explain how in antiquity commerce took place between the Old and New Worlds. This is evidenced by the New World plants of coca and tobacco having been found in the graves of Egyptian mummies starting in 1070 BC.[34]

Like the later European colonizers in the Americas, the Book of Mormon people followed the custom of naming the lands they migrated to after the places they had left behind, such as Bountiful (Alma 22:29), Midian (Alma 24:5), Ishmael (Alma 17:19), and Jerusalem (Alma 21:1–2). Because the Peruvian natives believed they were descendants of Ophir,[35] it would follow that the Biblical character Ophir left the Old World harbor named after him, and sailed to Peru. Book of Mormon scholar Janne M. Sjodahl cites, "Fernando Montesinos. . . records the theory that Ophir, a 'grandson of Noah' settled 'Hamerica,' as he spells the name, 340 years after the deluge, and that 'Peru,' the name, is derived from 'Ophir.' "[36] Montesinos believed that God led Ophir to Peru, gave them commandments, but that they became greedy and a war broke out over land and material possession."[37] James Adair wrote: "But Vatablus reckons it was Hispaniola, discovered, and named so by Columbus: yet Postellus, Phil. Mornay, Arias Montanus, and Goropius, are of the opinion that Peru is the ancient Ophir."[38]

Cobo conjectured that there were four reasons why many Spaniards believed that in discovering Peru (Piru) they had located Biblical Ophir:

First, the authority of Admiral Christopher Columbus. . .[who believed] he had discovered the land of Ophir; second, the similarity and relationship between these two names Ophir and Peru. . . .

The third conjecture that moves them to adopt this opinion is the abundance of gold, precious and exquisite woods, and many apes, peacocks, and other unusual and very valuable things that Solomon's ships brought from Ophir. . . .

The fourth and last reason is the long period of time that those ships [Solomon's] took on the trip, which was three years.[39]

In 1989 US explorer Gene Savoy, who is credited with discovering forty-three "lost cities" in the Andes, declared that he found a King-Solomon-era icon for the land Ophir on three stone tablets in Peru. According to an article posted on the website of the Neil A. Maxwell Institute (FARMS) at BYU: "At the Grand Vilaya he [Gene Savoy] discovered carved stone stela inscribed with what may prove to be the only known example of pre-Columbian linear writing found *in situ* in South America."[40] It should also be remembered that Nephi knew the name Ophir, for it was engraved on the small plates (2 Nephi 23:12).

Why is Ophir a clue for understanding where the Jaredites landed in the New World? The answer lies in the fact that Ophir was the brother of Jerah. Jerah fled Mesopotamia with Ophir and his other brothers at the time of the confounding of the languages. The family initially migrated to southern Arabia[41] (Genesis 10:26–30). The leader of the family was Jerah,[42] who appears to be the family leader named Jared in the book of Ether. Reverend Charles Forster, a former preacher in the Cathedral of Christ, Canterbury, provides these variant spellings for Jerah, *Jarah* (Arabia Felicis), *Jarach, Jare* (St. Jerome), *Jerhä* by modern Arabs.[43] Smith's Bible Dictionary (London, 1863, 1:964) states that "Jared" is the Jered of I Chronicles 1:2. According to the Smith and Sjodahl's commentary on the book of Ether, some early Bible translations spelled Jerah, "Jared."[44] Their parallel stories in the books of Genesis and Ether make it probable that Jerah of the Bible and Jared of the Book of Mormon are the same person (Genesis 10:25–30; 11:1–9).[45] One element of those stories is that the brother of Jerah (Ophir) and the brother of Jared (Moriancumer[46]) each had a harbor named after them (I Kings 10:11, 22; Ether 2:13). It would follow then that Ophir and Moriancumer were also the same person. That said, we are left with the distinct possibility that Peru is actually named after the great Book of Mormon colonizer known to us as the "brother of Jared."

At first it might seem confusing that the brother of Jared was named Ophir in the Bible but did not go by that name in the Book of Mormon. Moroni's abbreviated version of the book of Ether was included in the sacred Nephite record referred to as the Golden Plates. The original Jaredite plates were probably written entirely in the New World, and probably did not name the brother of Jared as Ophir or Moriancumer. To understand why, we must remember that something special happened to the brother of Jared (Ophir) just before he left the Old World for the promised land. It appears that the brother of Jared was given a "new" or "sacred" name endowment when the Lord appeared to him (Ether 3:13). Under similar circumstances, new names were given to Abraham, Israel, Paul, and other prophets. In other words, it appears that the man Ophir, who went up the mountain with his sixteen stones, came down the mountain as Moriancumer.

HARBOR OF OPHIR, WHERE THE JAREDITES BUILT THEIR BARGE

Richard Wellington and I have presented compelling evidence that Nephi's ship embarked for the promised land from the frankincense harbor of Khor Rori on the Indian Ocean in southern Arabia.[47] Local Khor Rori historian Ali Shahri, who has been invited to make presentations at Brigham Young University, is a member of the Shahri tribe. He has published a book that traces his genealogy to the man Ophir.[48] His family still owns the land surrounding the harbor of Khor Rori, and Shahri claims that Khor Rori is the Biblical port of Ophir and the property of his tribe. If true, then the port Khor Rori is not only the place where Nephi built his ship, it is also the port where Solomon's ships of Tarshish were sent to bring back gold, peacocks, and other riches from Ophir (I Kings 10:11, 22). It is generally accepted by Biblical scholars that King Solomon's Tarshish was probably a port on the Indian Ocean (see LDS Bible Dictionary). It has also been put forward by noted historians that Ophir is the original name for Khor Rori.[49] Indeed, it appears that growing evidence indicates that the Jaredites and the Nephites built their ships at the same harbor in southern Arabia.

THE RELIGION OF THE WHITE GOD COMES TO THE PROMISED LAND

The Jaredites brought their religion with them to the promised land. If the civilized Jaredites of Mesopotamia settled Norte Chico in Peru, then perhaps it is possible to find evidence that a new monotheistic religion appeared along the Peruvian coast around the time the Jaredites arrived in their promised land. The Mesopotamians were descendents of Noah and originally believed in the One True God. Norte Chico is the site where the first artifact with the icon of the staff god, or the bearded white god *Viracocha*, was found in the Americas. The gourd on which the icon was carved dates back to 2180 BC. Mann writes:

> Norte Chico chiefdoms were almost certainly theocratic, though not brutally so; leaders induced followers to obey by a combination of ideology, charisma, and skillfully timed positive reinforcement. . . .

> The only known trace of the Norte Chico deities may be a drawing etched into the face of a gourd. . . . When Creamer found the gourd in 2002, the image shocked the Andeanists. It looked like an early version of the Staff God, a fanged, staff-wielding deity who is one of the main characters in the Andean pantheon. Previously the earliest manifestation of the Staff God had been thought to be around 500 BC [approximate time of Nephites]. According to radiocarbon testing, the Norte Chico gourd was harvested between 2280 and 2180 BC. The early date implies, Haas and Creamer argued, that the principal Andean spiritual tradition originated

Several clues support the idea that when the Jaredites left Mesopotamia they crossed Arabia to Khor Rori. First, like Nephi, the Jaredites needed a protected harbor in which to build their ships and a port that had available all resources required to build large ocean-going vessels. These tangible and intangible resources appear to have been available at Khor Rori at the time of the Jaredites.[50]

Second, after traveling north to Nimrod to gather provisions, the Lord met the Jaredite party, then led them into the wilderness (Ether 2:1). According to Hugh Nibley, in the Bible the word "wilderness" usually meant "desert." The great desert nearest Mesopotamia is Arabia.

However, it was not just any wilderness that the Jaredites crossed, the Lord led them "forth into the wilderness, yea, into that *quarter where there never had man been*" (Ether 2:5; italics added). If the Jaredites traveled in a direct course from Babel to Khor Rori (Ophir), they would have needed to cross the largest sand desert in the world, the famed *Empty Quarter*, the *Rub al-Khali*, so named because no man has ever lived there. To this day, the only trail through the Empty Quarter, the *Dakakah* trail, ends at the ancient frankincense harbor of Khor Rori. Thus, it is possible that the Jaredites left from the harbor of Ophir (Moriancumer) and arrived in a promised land they called "New Ophir," or "Peru."

in the Norte Chico, and that this tradition endured for at least four thousand years, millennia longer than had been previously suspected. . . . Over the millennia, this god or gods transmuted into Wiraqocha [Viracocha], the Inka creator deity, whose worship was brutally suppressed by Spain.[51]

During Book of Mormon times, the Peruvian white god was always depicted as a man holding staffs and was the dominate god of Peru until the Incas (AD 1400–AD 1532) started worshipping the Sun.

Cabello Valboa wrote that God had instructed Ophir to construct temples once they arrived in Peru. Both the people of Caral and those of the later Chavin civilization to the north of Norte Chico constructed temples. John H. Rowe cites the great Chavín temple near Trujillo as one of the most remarkable remaining Pre-Columbian structures.[52]

THE FIRST CIVILIZATION OF THE AMERICAS

Traditional archaeology claims that primitive man stumbled upon stone tools some 1.5 million years ago. If so, then during the next 1.5 million years very little changed in the lifestyles of our ancestors. According to scholars, around 3000 BC, as if by some miracle, the first civilization suddenly bloomed at Sumer in Mesopotamia. After 1.5 million years of glacier-speed progress, as if within the twinkling of an historian's eye, mankind suddenly invented agriculture, metalwork, government, irrigation, textiles, sailing, fishing, and a complex theocracy. Science has no explanation as to why mankind, after sleeping so long, could become so intelligent so fast and in

Virocha on the Sun Gate at Tiahuanacu

one place only. If scientists cannot explain what happened in Mesopotamia around 3000 BC, what chance do they have of explaining how this same miracle could have occurred in Peru only a few hundred years later? Indeed, the discovery of the ancient urban center in Peru's Norte Chico has left archaeologists with a puzzling paradox. How could man have invented what we now call civilization at approximately the same time but on opposite sides of the world?

PERU BEFORE THE JAREDITES

As noted before, the barren coastal plain of Norte Chico is an unlikely candidate for giving birth to a sophisticated civilization. Archaeologists

believe that before the third millennium BC the coastline of Peru was inhabited by native people whom they refer to as Paleo-Indians. These native people had a technology that seems to have been just above that of the first humans back in 1.5 million BC. Mann describes their society in this manner:

Peru's first known inhabitants appear in the archaeological record sometime before 10,000 BC. According to two studies in *Science* in 1998, these people apparently lived part of the year in the foothills, gathering and hunting. When winter came, they hiked to the warmer coast. At Quebrada Jaguay, a dry streambed on the nation's southern coast that was one of the two sites described in *Science*, they dug up wedge clams and chased schools of six-inch drum fish with nets. They carried their catch to their base, which was about five miles from the shore. Quebrada Tacahuay, the other *Science* site, was closer to the shore but even drier: its average annual rainfall is less than a quarter inch. The site, exposed by the construction of a road, is an avian graveyard. On their annual travels between the foothills and the shore, Paleo-Indians seem to have visited the area periodically to feast on the cormorants and boobies that nested on the rocks by the beach.

By 8000 BC, Paleo-Indians had radiated through western South America. Their lives were similar enough to contemporary hunter-gatherers that perhaps they should now be simply called Indians. . . . Some groups had settled into mountain caves, skewering deer-size vicuña on spears; others plucked fish from the mangroves swamps; still others stayed on the beach as their forebears had, weaving nets, and setting them into the water.[53]

What is the probability that the Paleo-Indians of Peru could have created an autonomous and sophisticated civilization along the barren shoreline of Peru? Mann continues:

> Sometime before 3200 BC, and possibly before 3500 BC, something happened in the Norte Chico. On a world level, the eruption at the Norte Chico was improbable, even aberrant. The Tigris-Euphrates, Nile, Indus, and Huang He Valleys were fertile, sunny, well-watered breadbaskets with long stretches of bottomland that practically invited farmers to stick seeds in the soil. Because intensive agriculture has been regarded a prerequisite for complex societies, it has long been claimed that civilizations can arise only in such farm-friendly places. The Peruvian littoral is an agronomical no-go zone: barren, cloudy, almost devoid of rain, seismically and climatically unstable. Except along the rivers, nothing grows but lichen.
>
> "It looks like the last place you'd want to start up something major," Creamer said to me. "There doesn't seem to be anything there to build it on."[54]

The Neolithic Revolution is the invention of farming, an event whose significance can hardly be overstated. "The human career," wrote the historian Ronald Wright, "divides in two: everything before the Neolithic Revolution and everything after it." It began in the Middle East about eleven thousand years ago. In the next few millennia the wheel and the metal tool sprang up in the same area. The Sumerians put these inventions together, adding writing, and in the third millennium BC created the first great civilization. Every European and Asian culture since, no matter how disparate in appearance, stands in Sumer's shadow. Native Americans, who left Asia long before agriculture, missed out on the bounty. "They had to do everything on their own," [Alfred] Crosby [University of Texas] said to me. Remarkably, they succeeded.[55]

THE INVENTION OF GOVERNMENT

The early Jaredites formed a centralized government, with kings who ruled over cities and lands. At latest, this appears to have occurred in the late third millennium BC, a time when complex civic organizations were still rare. Mann notes of Peru:

> Because human beings rarely volunteer to spend their days loading baskets with heavy rocks to build public monuments, Hass, Creamer, and Ruiz argued that these cities must have had a centralized government that instigated and directed the works. In the Norte Chico, in other words, *Homo sapiens* experienced a phenomenon that at that time had [happened] only once before, in Mesopotamia, the emergence, for better or worse, of leaders with enough prestige, influence, and hierarchical position to induce their subjects to perform heavy labor. It was humankind's second experience with *government*.[56]
>
> It's one of only two places on earth . . . where government was an invention. Everywhere else it was inherited or borrowed. People were born into societies with governments or saw their neighbors' government and copied the idea. Here [Peru], people came up with it themselves.[57]

It seems far more likely that a group of people, that is the Jaredites, migrated from Mesopotamia to Peru around 2200 BC, and patterned their new government after the one they knew in Mesopotamia, than to believe that after eons of time two separate groups of people simultaneously invented a new form for ordering human society. Indeed, it is easy to answer the question, "Where did government come from?" In the Old World, it was established by Noah as the patriarchal order. In the New World, a similar order was implemented by the Jaredites.

If the Jaredites introduced the Paleo-Indians of Peru to religion and government, then it would seem probable that they would have transferred the technologies of Mesopotamian to the New World. Following are some other examples of new technologies that came into existence in Peru during the early Jaredite period. That any one of these technologies could have been discovered without some form of external stimulus is highly improbable.

THE INVENTION OF METALLURGY

In 1998, Yale University anthropologist Richard L. Burger and Yale geologist Robert B. Gordon discovered thin gold and copper foils in Peru. The foils date to 1410–1090 BC. These ancient dates were confirmed by testing the carbon atoms that had collected on the sheets. The gold foils were worked cold, that is, pounded with stone hammers into foils between 0.1 and .05 millimeters thick (.004 to .002 inch).[58] The hammering technique for making golden foils or metal plates is an example of a rarely known technology. However, in antiquity such hammered plates were fabricated in the Near East, including bronze plates that were discovered at the harbor of Khor Rori, where it seems likely the Jaredites built their barges.[59]

The Book of Mormon informs us that well before Nephi fabricated his plates, the Jaredites had created their own book of gold plates (Mosiah 8:9). Nephi started creating golden plates once he was in the promised land (1 Nephi 19:1). Therefore, it is conceivable that Nephi learned how to hammer plates of gold in the Americas from a people who had been taught the technique from the Jaredites. The chronicler Fernando de Montesinos claimed that giants had come to Peru and that they had steel instruments. It is also believed that the Araucano Indians of Chile used lead weapons against the conquistadors.[60]

Although there has been no archaeological evidence of steel having been used in Peru, the metal mentioned in the Book of Mormon could have been a copper-alloy or a form of iron that would have rusted away long before our era.

THE INVENTION OF FARMING

If it were not for a transfer of technology from the Old World, how did the Paleo-Indians of Peru suddenly discover how to cultivate food on irrigated fields? Mann writes:

Researchers have long known that a second, independent Neolithic Revolution occurred in Mesoamerica. The exact timing is uncertain—archaeologists keep pushing back the date—but it is now thought to have occurred about ten thousand years ago, not long after the Middle East's Neolithic Revolution. In 2003, though, archaeologists discovered ancient seeds from cultivated squashes in coastal Ecuador, at the foot of the Andes, which may be older than any agricultural remains in Mesoamerica—a third Neolithic Revolution.[61]

To feed Norte Chico's burgeoning population, Shady [Ruth Shady Solies] discovered the valley folk learned how to irrigate the soil. Not given an environment that favored the development of intensive agriculture, that is, they shaped the landscape into something more suitable to their purposes.[62]

A hammered Gold plate, Fereñafe, Museo Sicán, north coast of Peru

How the Peruvians "learned" to farm is the real question. The Jaredites were no strangers to the advanced agricultural techniques of the Mesopotamian valley. They brought their seeds with them (Ether 2:3), and upon reaching the promised land they immediately began tilling the earth (Ether 6:13). Of special interest in Book of Mormon research is that the main crop cultivated by the farmers in Norte Chico was cotton, a traditional crop of Mesopotamia. The Jaredites would also have been familiar with the irrigation systems in Mesopotamia. Archaeologist Alan Kolata notes of the Peruvian coastal plain:

The levees and natural flood plains of these rivers [flowing from the Andes to the Pacific] originating in the highland collecting basins are the fragile life line of the coast, permitting year-round cultivation of food and tree crops. With the advent of wide-spread artificial irrigation in the Andes at some point in the second millennium BC, these naturally watered floodplains were extended laterally to incorporate entire valleys and, eventually, multiple valley networks into large-scale agricultural production systems.[63]

THE INVENTION OF CLOTH AND THE PERUVIAN TEXTILE REVOLUTION

Growing and breeding cotton and learning how to produce textiles from it are complicated processes. Only four species of cotton have ever been domesticated—two in the Americas and two in the Middle East and South Asia. Cotton was unknown in Europe until the thirteenth century AD. The men aboard Columbus's ship wore flax and wool cloth. Mann points out that "South American cotton (*Gossypium barbadense*) once grew wild along the continent's Pacific and Atlantic coasts. . . . In the Andean past, the long, puffy bolls of South American cotton, some varieties naturally tinted pink, blue, or yellow, were the soft underpinning of Andean culture."[64]

The Jaredites produced silks and fine linen (Ether 9:17). Certainly, the Book of Mormon usage of the word silk did not refer to thread made from the thread of an Asian worm. The sacred record was written in Reformed Egyptian and contained Arabic words (JSH 1:64). The English word "silk" comes from the Arabic word *salaka*, which means "any thread."[65] In some Arabic dialects *salaka* means soft and *selk* means thread or wire. Thus in the original terminology of the Book of Mormon silk simply meant soft

thread, and its usage by Joseph Smith in translating the Book of Mormon attest the exactness of his translation. The cotton textiles produced in ancient Norte Chico were of such quality that they were the main element for regional trade. It was the medium in which the Peruvians created visual arts and was used as a medium for exchange and savings.[66] Calderwood cites of the Peruvians: "Cieza de León stated that the Indians could weave as good a tapestry as any woven in Flanders from the wool of their flocks, and so fine a weave that it seemed of silk rather than of wool."[67]

THE INVENTION OF FISHING AND MARITIME TECHNOLOGY

Before leaving Mesopotamia, the Jaredites had built boats (Ether 2:16). Subsequently, they made eight barges that successfully completed a transoceanic crossing to the Americas. To have achieved such a feat, the Jaredites must have been skilled and experienced seafarers before they commenced building the barges that took them to the New World. Although it was a surprise to archaeologists, the latest discoveries support the theory that the rise of civilization in Peru was based on a maritime economy. In 1995, University of Florida anthropologist Michael Moseley proposed the MFAC hypothesis: the Maritime Foundation of Andean civilization.

The MFAC hypothesis—that societies fed by fishing could have founded a civilization—was "radical, unwelcome, and critiqued as an economic impossibility," Moseley later recalled. Little wonder! The MFAC was like a brick through the window of archaeological theory. Archaeologists had always believed that

in fundamental respects all human societies everywhere were alike, no matter how different they might appear on the surface. If one runs the tape backward to the beginning, so to speak, the stories are all the same: foraging societies develop agriculture; the increased food supply leads to a population boom; the society grows and stratifies, with powerful clerics at the top and peasant cultivators at the bottom; massive public works ensue, along with intermittent social strife and war. If the MFAC hypothesis was true,

early civilizations in Peru [were] in one major respect strikingly unlike early civilizations in Mesopotamia, Egypt, India, and China. Farming, the cornerstone of the complex societies in the rest of the world, was in Peru an afterthought. . . .

The MFAC hypothesis was radical, its supporters conceded, but the supporting evidence could not be dismissed. Bone analysis shows that late-Pleistocene coastal foragers "got 90 percent of their protein from the sea—anchovies, sardines, shellfish, and so on."[68]

Ancient Peruvians fished in reed ships using cotton fishing nets made at Caral.[69] The reed sailing ship was invented in Mesopotamia. Besides fabricating cotton sails, the Sumerians used cotton nets to catch fish. If the Jaredites arrived in Peru, they undoubtedly would have discovered the great fishery of the Humboldt Current, one of the richest fisheries in the world. It would only seem natural that the shipbuilding and ocean-going Jaredites from Mesopotamia would continue building ships in the promised land and exploit the Peruvian fishery.

THE INVENTION OF OCEAN-GOING REED SHIPS WITH SAILS

If the Jaredites' barges landed in Peru, they were probably not the first foreign ships to land in South America. The Bering Strait theory for the early habitation of the Western Hemisphere is now under serious revision. The problem is that South America was inhabited 32,000 years ago.[70] That would place humans in South America prior to the ice-free corridor through the glaciers that permitted migrants from Asia to reach the southern ice-free lands before they died from starvation.

Ancient Peruvians fished in reed boats using cotton fishing nets.

Recent discoveries in Chile suggest that humans have lived there for more than thirty thousand years. The new discoveries prompted Mann to state, "Perhaps the first Indians traveled [to Chile] by boat, and didn't need the land bridge."[71]

The Spanish chronicler Cabello Valboa (a great-nephew of Vasco Nuñez Balboa [with a "B"], who discovered the Pacific for the Europeans) wrote that according to the legend of the Incas, in primordial times, the Peruvian coastal valleys were invaded by people from the sea in a fleet of balsas or rafts.[72] Again, the Jaredites came to the New World in eight barges. They were shipbuilders whose home of origin invented the sail and had a long legacy of building large ocean-going balsa vessels.

The Peruvians were still building ocean-going balsa ships when Columbus reached the New World. The first encounter the Spaniards had with the Incas was "in the form of an Inka ship sailing near the equator, three hundred miles

from its home port, under a load of fine cotton sail. The Inca balsa had a crew of twenty and was easily the size of a Spanish caravelle."[73] The Spaniards encounter with the Inca ship was the first sign that an advanced and wealthy empire was to be found farther south, and even more important, it was the first time Westerners were seeing evidence that a Jaredite-style empire existed in Peru. Aboard these Inca balsas, the Spanish found "many pieces of silver and gold as personal ornaments . . . including breastplates; tweezers and rattles and strings of clusters of beads and rubies; mirrors decorated with silver, and cups and other drinking vessels. They were carrying many wool and cotton mantles and Moorish tunics . . . and other pieces of clothing coloured with cochineal, crimson, blue, yellow and all other colors, and worked with different types of ornate embroidery, in figures of birds, animal, fish and trees. They had some tiny weights and weigh gold . . .

Drawing of Mesopotamian reed ship. Where did the Peruvians learn to build reed boats and ships?

There were small stones in bead bags: emeralds and chalcedonies and other jewels and pieces of crystal and resin."[74]

Smaller versions of Peruvian reed boats are still utilized by the *Uros* Indians on Lake Titicaca, the highest navigable sea in the world. The Lake Titicaca basin was settled around 1200 BC, perhaps by the last remnant of the Jaredites. Thor Heyerdahl compared the reed boats of Peru to the reed boats of Mesopotamia. When he built a replica of a Mesopotamian ship, he called it the *Tigris*; however, he used Bolivians from Lake Titicaca, not Iraqis, to construct the *Tigris*.[75] The *totora* reed shipbuilding technology could have reached Peru much earlier than Lehi. The Jaredites migrated from Mesopotamia where the sailing ship was invented. The similarities between the reed boats of Mesopotamia and Peru are amazing, including the reed animal head placed on the bow of their boats.

Are we to believe that all of these inventions spontaneously occurred in the New World just after they were discovered in Mesopotamia? As difficult as a voyage of eight barges from the Near East to the New World would have been, it is far more rational to believe the Jaredite account in the Book of Ether than it is to assume all these technologies were invented by the Paleo-Indians of Peru without contact from Mesopotamia.

THE INVENTION OF OVERLAND CARAVAN COMMERCE

Another astonishing parallel between the Near East and Peru was the domestication of the camel or camelid and their utilization for long-distance overland trade. The earliest record of camel caravans is reported in the Bible when Joseph's brothers sold him to a caravan bound

Reed boat with animal-head bow on Lake Titicaca, Peru

for Egypt. Eventually the famous Frankincense and Silk routes transported large sums of goods between China and the Middle East. Archaeologist Alan L. Kolata describes the caravan routes of Peru:

> On the contrary, after about 2000 BC, large pack trains of llamas traveling along these vertical axes between the established villages and towns of the highlands and coast were a common scene throughout the southern Andes. Over time and space, these llama caravans were organized in different ways. Most often, the Andean caravans were operated by politically independent pastoral societies. These pastoral nomads followed predetermined trade routes, visiting communities on the coast and in the high Andean basin in a fixed season round. . . . reciprocal kinship bonds were essential to a system that demanded high-risk ventures over the trackless, desertic wastes of the southern Andean *Altiplano*. Caravan traders would not hazard a perilous journey without the assurance of a guaranteed consumer for their products and, just as importantly, family-style hospitality at the end of the trail.[76]

The pre-Hispanic llama caravans were made up of as many as 2,000 animals,[77] each llama being able to transport an 80-pound load over Inca highways through the great Andes.[78] The Old World caravan routes operated in a very similar fashion. A quote from Kolata seems like a reference to the famous Arabian incense trail; however, it was made about the Aymara Indians living around Lake Titicaca: "Caravans bearing aromatic and hard woods, resinous shrubs, and blocks of pure salt still come down to the shores of the lake as they have for at least 100 generations."[79]

WHAT HAPPENED TO THE WHEEL?

If the Jaredites transferred to Peru the Mesopotamian technologies of metallurgy, writing, irrigated farming, textile fabrication, the sail, reed ships, and government, why didn't the Inca civilization incorporate the wheel? Since the wheel was invented in Mesopotamia around 4000 BC, the Jaredites must have known about it. Charles Mann provides a possible explanation, "Because of the Pleistocene extinction, the Americas lacked animals suitable for domestication into beasts of burden; without animals to haul carts, individuals on rough terrain can use skids almost as effectively."[80] Carts and chariots would have been difficult to use on the pre-Columbian Peruvian stone highways that summit passes as high as 15,000 feet, and often included long stretches of steps.

It is also interesting that the Jaredites wrote that they had horses and asses (Ether 9:19), and the Nephites recorded that they used chariots (Alma 18:9, 20:6). Until the remains of a horse are found in the Americas that carbon-14 dates to the time of the Nephites, we must ask ourselves which animal in the New World would have reminded the Jaredites and Nephites of a horse; at least to the point that they gave the animal the name horse, after a similar animal they knew in the Old World. In my opinion, the best candidate for *Jaredite horses or asses* is the llama (*Lama*) of the Andes. Although the llama is a member of the camel family, it does not have a hump and has the general appearance of a small

Llama Chariot

If the Inca called Spanish horses *llamas*, wouldn't Nephi call these *horses?*

horse. A smaller animal that had the appearance of a horse would make sense since the Book of Mormon refers to horses, but never mentions a man riding one or a cavalry. When the Spaniards first saw the Peruvian peccaries (*Tayassu pecari*) they called them *puercos* (or hogs)[81] ("swine," Ether 9:18).

Actually, the peccary *is* related to the pig. In his chronicle *The Discovery and Conquest of Peru*, Pedro de Cieza de León referred to peccary or tapir flesh as "hog meat."[82] Likewise the Spanish had no names for the South American puma, jaguar, and rhea, so they called them lions,[83] tigers,[84] and ostriches.[85] If the Europeans called peccaries *pigs*, is it any less likely that the Jaredites would have called llamas *horses?*

But do we have any direct evidence that the Peruvians considered llamas to be horses? The answer is yes. When Betanzos translated the Inca legends from Quechua into Spanish, he used the Spanish word *oveja*, sheep, for the llama.[86] Thus, as the Spaniard quoted the Inca account of the arrival of the conquistadors (substituting *sheep* for *llama*), we see that the Incas thought the conquistadors' horses were llamas, or by logic, to them their llama was a kind of horse. Betanzos recorded: "They [the Spaniards] bring a kind of sheep [meaning llama] on which they ride and travel. These sheep [llamas] are very big, much larger than ours;"[87] and "Wherever they wish to go, these sheep [llamas] carry them there. And if they wish, these sheep [llamas] run with them

on their backs."[88] If the Incas called the horse a llama, doesn't it make sense that when the Nephites saw the llama for the first time they called it in reformed Egyptian a "horse" and its smaller cousin the alpaca an "ass"?

As the Old World used the horse and the ass, the Indians use the llama and the alpaca—as beasts of burden. It is even feasible that as a weapon of war the Nephites could have harnessed several llamas to chariots with wheels or skids. The Romans used camels to pull chariots, so why couldn't the Nephites use llamas for the same purpose?[89] And today several websites offer instruction on how to train llamas to pull carts.[90] I have lived in Arabia for fifteen years, so at first the notion of harnessing a member of the camel family to a chariot seemed odd. I thought it was impossible to have a camel trained to pull a cart. Having seen camels used in Arabia only as pack animals, I assumed they could not pull a cart. However, on visiting India, I saw hundreds of Arabian camels pulling heavily laden carts. So why do not the Arabs use camels to pull carts? The answer is simple, the wheel is not suitable for the mountains and sand dunes of Arabia. Likewise, the wheeled cart is not suitable for the mountainous terrain of the Andes, and it is reasonable to see why the technology was abandoned by the Peruvians by the time of the Incas.

Economics could also have played a role. Richard W. Bulliet of Harvard University's Center for Middle Eastern Studies wrote:

Once, in ancient times, the Middle East teemed with carts and wagons and chariots, but they were totally driven out by the coming of the camel.

For all the discussion there has been among archeologists about why advanced societies such as those in pre-Colombian Central and South America never invented wheeled transport, there has been little notice taken of the amazing fact that Middle Eastern society willfully abandoned the use of the wheel, one of mankind's greatest inventions.

It was the long, slow pace of the camel, two and a half miles an hour, 20 miles a day, for weeks on end, that spelled the demise of the wheel. Because of the primate state of harnessing technology in the ancient East, where even a horse could not be harnessed effectively to pull a heavy load, the camel could not be hitched to a wagon.

The ox cart was equally slow, and in the competition the camel had certain positive advantages.

These advantages meant that camel transport was about 20 percent cheaper than wagon transport, according to the prices issued by the Roman emperor Diocletian in the third century AD."[91]

Since a packed camel is a faster and more economical form of transportation than the ox or camel cart, it only makes sense that eventually the Nephites would abandon llamas pulling carts and wagons and use them exclusively as pack animals. A similar fate could have befallen chariots pulled by llamas. In the long run they were ineffective in the Andes Mountains.

Although it appears that the horses of the Book of Mormon were probably llamas, it is noteworthy to mention that horses lived on islands just off of Peru not long before the coming of the Spaniards. Tupac Inca, who reigned as Inca

The Inca Highway, a stairway that ran the length of South America.

from AD 1397–1464, built a *balsas* ship navy that carried 20,000 warriors, and sailed to the island of Avachumbi and Ninachumbi, returning back "with him black people, gold, a chair of brass, and a skin and jaw bone of a horse. These trophies were preserved in the fortress of Cuzco until the Spaniards came. An Inca now living has charge of this skin and jaw bone of a horse. He gave this account, and the rest who were present corroborated it."[92] The skin of the horse was still recognizable, suggesting that the horse skin probably belonged to Moorish sailor who had come to the New World prior to Columbus, rather than to a horse that dated to Book of Mormon times. Still, horses seem to have been living in proximity to the Americas prior to Columbus.

DISBURSEMENT AND DEMISE OF THE JAREDITES

Andeanist Gary Urton states, "Archaeologists divide Peruvian prehistory into five major periods, primarily on the basis of continuities and changes in ceramic shapes and styles over time and across space. Three of these periods are known as 'horizons,' a term that is meant to indicate that these were periods of relative unity in art, architecture, ritualism and economy over broad regions in the central Andes."[93] The first of these periods or civilizations ended in 200 BC,[94] the time period when the last Jaredite king was discovered by the people of Zarahemla (Omni 1:21). From the evidence presented above, it is likely that the Jaredites brought the first real civilization to the

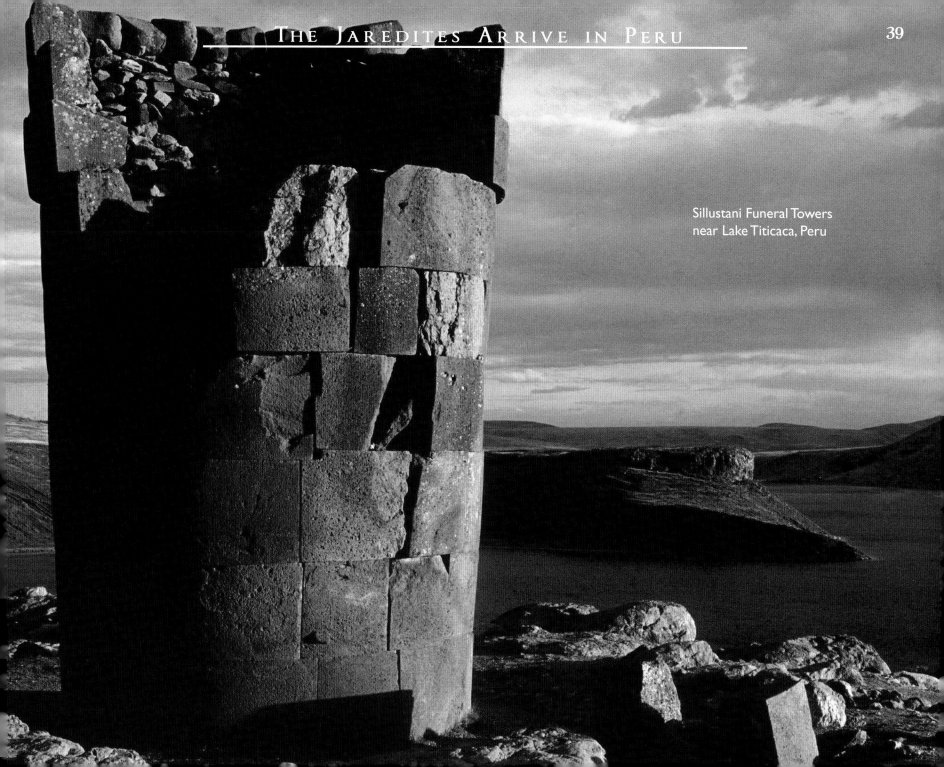

Sillustani Funeral Towers
near Lake Titicaca, Peru

Americas, and their demise marked the end to the Western Hemisphere's first great culture. Furthermore, it seems reasonable that as millions of Jaredites were being slaughtered in a civil war that would end with the complete destruction of their civilization, at least some of the Jaredites would have launched balsa ships and sailed northward to Mesoamerica. Such a migration by refugees would provide one possible explanation of how the worship of a bearded white god and the working of metal eventually reached Mexico and other parts of Central America.

Although the last battle between the armies of Shiz and Coriantumr took place at the hill Cumorah, the preceding great battles where millions were slain took place in the "land of Desolation," which was to the north (Ether 15:2, 10, 11; Helaman 3:5–6). In chapter four, I will explain how the Book of Mormon's description of the Jaredite battle sites, the land of Desolation, matches the landscape of the Peruvian shoreline. Just south of Norte Chico are the valleys that surround present-day Lima, Peru. Incredible as it might seem, the Incas called this area "the land of the people of desolation." Sullivan writes: "Peoples native to the Huarochirí area, the origin of the 'strong and rich . . . *people of desolation*' is not known (emphasis added)."[95] Clearly, the Book of Mormon indicates the origin of the "people of desolation"; they were the Jaredites from Mesopotamia.

The Spanish priest Avila recorded the myths of the men of Peru's central Pacific area near Lima. One myth describes a people whose history seems to parallel the Jaredites' sad fate and identifies them as the people of desolation. Avila recorded:

> In the four preceding chapters we have already recounted the lives lived in ancient times.

Nevertheless, we don't know the origins of the people of those days, nor where it was they emerged from.

These people, the ones who lived in that area, used to spend their lives warring on each other and conquering each other. For their leaders, they recognized only the strong and rich.

We speak of them as the Purum Runa, "people of desolation."[96]

Joseph Fielding Smith offered this summary of the history of the civilization known as the Jaredites:

> On this land the Jaredites multiplied and prospered, sinned and were punished, repented and were forgiven— during a long period of years. They had among them men holding the priesthood and a Church organization. The Lord established his covenants with them as he did with Abraham and Israel. They built cities and became skilful and cunning workmen in gold and silver and had a thorough knowledge of the coming of Jesus Christ. Eventually through sin their civilization crumbled. They killed their prophets. Plague and constant warfare decimated them until eventually they were entirely destroyed. Their last king, Coriantumr, lived to see another people come to possess the land which he and his people had lost through transgression, in fulfillment of the prediction of their first prophet, Mahonri Moriancumer.[97]

While serving an LDS Mission on the Altiplano of Peru/Bolivia, my companion Glenn Kimball and I spent a preparation day visiting the ruins known as the towers of Sillustani. We hitched a ride on an Indian flatbed truck to the ruins that were located in remote hills about 35 miles from Lake Titicaca. Today the towers are a popular tourist site, but in 1970 few people knew of the towers, and that day we found ourselves alone at the ruins. Both Glenn and I were born with an extra portion of curiosity. Near the stone towers were smaller *chullpas*, white stone burial towers. The chullpas had small holes in one side into which a person can snake his way into the interior of the tower.

We squeezed our way in and found the interior was only a well-like shaft that fell straight down into the darkness below. As foolish as it might seem today, without a rope, we both worked our way into the shaft and precariously climbed down the seemingly bottomless pit. As we descended, I wondered more than once if we could make our way back up the shaft. We reached the floor about fifteen feet below the small entrance.

When we reached what we thought was the floor of the shaft, we found that whatever was below our feet cracked as we applied our full weight. As our eyes adjusted to the very dim light, we discovered that we were standing upon a deep pile of bones. We picked up skulls and found that they were far larger than the heads of the Aymara Indians who now live around the lake and were even larger than the typical head of a modern-era six-foot-tall man. We were reminded of a statement about the Jaredites that was published in the early Mormon newsletter, *The Evening and Morning Star*: "They were a very large race of men; whenever we hear that uncommonly large bones have been dug up from the earth, we may conclude that was the skeleton of a Jaredite."[98]

Overview of Nephites and Lamanites in the Andes

In this world we are exiled from our home
in the land in the world above.

QUECHUA SAYING

When the Spaniards arrived in Peru, the Incas ruled the greatest empire on earth. It was larger than the Ming Dynasty of China or the Great Zimbabwe.[1] Yet, the Incas at that time were only trying to emulate an even greater period in their history. It was a vain effort to restore the "glories of their cultures" at the time of the legendary Manco Capac and the earliest Incas. Were these earlier and perhaps even greater empires of the Andes the Nephites and Lamanites of the Book of Mormon? To answer that question we must go back into the oral traditions of the Incas, to the time when the Viracochas or white people first arrived among the native population.

Some myths state that the white men arrived by sea,[2] while most accounts say the Viracochas originated on an island of Lake Titicaca. Both accounts hold that the white people were sent by the creator god. The giant Lake Titicaca lies in a mystical land, like a scene from Tolkien's Middle Earth. During my mission, I served in the Lake Titicaca basin, a high plain,

the Spanish call the Altiplano. The Andes mountains consist of two ranges that run parallel for 2,500 miles. Between the two chains of mountains, is the high valley of the Altiplano. Starting in southern Peru, the Altiplano runs south for 600 miles, reaching far into western Bolivia, northern Chile, and Argentina. The maximum width of the Altiplano is 120 miles.

During the four months I lived on the Altiplano, I had the opportunity to meet several groups of professional mountain climbers. As they passed through the town of Juliaca on route to challenge another Andean peak, they would stop to greet us, the only two Americans in the town. Those that had climbed the Himalayan mountains told me that the Altiplano reminded them physically and spiritually of Tibet. According to Inca lore, the Altiplano's Lake Titicaca is their version of the Garden of Eden, the place from which all humanity emerged.

While on the Altiplano, I wondered if long ago other missionaries had walked the same paths as I. Did Nephi and later Jacob and Joseph teach the gospel here? Could it have been possible that the Creator himself, Jesus Christ, visited his sheep that surrounded the dark blue waters of Lake Titicaca? According to Sarmiento, four brothers came to Peru claiming to be the "sons of Viracocha Pachayachachi, the Creator, and that they had come forth out of certain windows to rule the rest of the people. . . . Thus they introduced the religion that suited them."[3]

What is interesting to students of the Book of Mormon is that archaeologists estimate that a new religion was introduced to the people in the Altiplano circa 500 BC—roughly the time of Nephi's arrival in the promised land. Because this new religion used in its temples stone stelae of a man and woman and a two-headed serpent, archaeologists have called it the *Yaya-Mama*, sometimes written *Yaya-Uma*, (Father—Mother) religion.[4] The Metropolitan Museum of Art states: "ca. 500 BC. The *Yaya-Mama* (meaning "Father-Mother" in the Quechua language) religious tradition is believed to have flourished in the southern Altiplano. Male-female imagery of paired deities is carved on stone stelae at ceremonial sites in the Lake Titicaca region."[5] Also worth noting about Yaya-Uma is that *um* means "mother" in classical Arabic, while in some dialects of Arabic the word for "mother" is pronounced *Yuma* or *uma*.[6] Yaya has a similar pronunciation to *YHWH*, the Hebrew name for Jehovah. *YHWH* was written in the French *Revised Second Version of the Bible, Yahve*.[7] The Arabic name for god is *Allah*, with the "ll" in Spanish having the "y" sound, forming *ayah*. Since Egyptian was the original first language of the Nephites (Mosiah 1:4,

Could these beautiful girls be descendants of the Lamanites?

Mormon 9:32), it is most interesting that one of the names the Peruvians called their bearded white god was *Illa*.[8] Change the first *I* to an *A*, and you have *Alla*, the Arabic name for God. Furthermore, the Arabic name *Yahya* is derived from the Hebrew name *Yochanan* (John), meaning "YHWH (Jehovah) is gracious."

It is not hard to understand why some of the earlier Spaniards in Peru believed that the Inca had a previous knowledge of Adam and Eve. Alan Kolata of the University of Chicago writes:

> In Cristóbal de Molina's version of the same myth, these two culture heroes

are the Andean Adam and Eve: the primeval male-female pair and the children of Viracocha [Christ]. Like the other variants of the theme of genesis, the events of the myth begin after a universal flood: "all the created things perished through him [Viracocha] except for a man and a woman, who remained in a box, and when the waters receded, the wind carried them to tierra Guanaco [city of Tiahuanaco on shores of Lake Titicaca]" Viracocha orders the pair to remain in Tiahuanaco, and gives them, as surrogates of the Creator, dominion over the people they are charged with calling forth from the sacred landscape.[9]

The Yaya-Mama (Adam and Eve) religion, was part of the early Peruvians' overall faith in Viracocha, the Andean white god who created the earth's first parents, Yaya-Mama. If the Nephites colonized the Altiplano, we should not be surprised to find the story of Adam and Eve forming a central element in the Peruvian religion. The story of Adam and Eve was recorded on the brass plates that were used to teach the Nephites (1 Nephi 5:11), and the principles associated with our first parents were major doctrines of the Nephite religion. If Adam had not transgressed, he would not have fallen, and Adam fell that men might be (2 Nephi 2:19–25). The Holy One of Israel suffered the pains of all who belong to the family of Adam (2 Nephi 9:21).

On the one hand, the Incas believed that the person who brought the new religion to them was Manco Capac, their first king. The first Inca king had fair skin and was called a son of Viracocha (the Inca's name for the bearded white God). Viracocha [Christ] was the Creator god of all things, including our first parents, Adam and Eve. On the other hand, Nephi the first king of the Book of Mormon, considered himself a son of Christ and took upon himself the Lord's name. Furthermore we know that the early Nephites (circa 500 BC) taught that Christ was the "Creator" God (2 Nephi 9:5).

Before we go into the general body of evidence for specific Book of Mormon place names, such as the city of Nephi, this chapter will provide a general overview of the Book of Mormon account and will discuss evidence indicating that the history of the Book of Mormon is in harmony with what is known about the people who lived in the southern Andes during the same period.

WHAT THE BOOK OF MORMON SAYS

The ancient authors of the Book of Mormon provided a chronological tracking in their record. Their timeline began when Lehi and Sariah, their four sons, and the rest of their family left Jerusalem and embarked on a journey into the wilderness. It is probable that their journey into the wilderness started in the year 597 BC.[10] A brief summation of the Nephite history would include these major milestones:

- Lehi and his four sons leave Jerusalem for Arabia.
- Nephi takes over the leadership of the family in the wilderness (Mosiah 10:13).
- After eight years in the Arabian wilderness, Nephi builds a ship and sails with his extended family to the promised land (later called the Americas).
- Shortly thereafter, the Mulekites leave Jerusalem and arrive in the promised land in the same region of the Americas where the Nephites were living.
- Under Nephi's command, the family arrives in the promised land.
- Once ashore, the Lehites' first order of business is to pitch tents and plant the seeds they brought from Jerusalem.
- The family takes several journeys into the wilderness where they discover forests, animals, and ore deposits.
- Obeying the Lord's commandment, Nephi makes golden plates and starts engraving on them two records of his people.
- Jacob writes that they had lived on an Isle of the Sea (2 Nephi 10:20).
- Lehi dies and Nephi is forced to separate from his older brothers, thus bringing about two competing nations, the Nephites and the Lamanites.
- When the Nephites and Lamanites first arrived in the promised land, they were both considered to have been a fair-skinned people.
- Nephi becomes the founder of the first Nephite city and builds therein a temple like unto Solomon's.
- Within one generation of landing in the Americas, the Lamanites locate the Nephite settlement and feudal wars begin.
- Jacob warns the Nephites that if they don't repent they will lose the land of their first inheritance (city of Nephi).
- Nephites become wicked, and the Lord warns Mosiah to flee the city of Nephi.
- Mosiah discovers the city of Zarahemla and the Mulekites.
- King Benjamin drives the Lamanites from the land of Zarahemla.
- A period of great wars ensues between the Nephites and Lamanites.
- As the Lamanite threat grew, the Nephites colonize the land of Bountiful and the land northward.
- Samuel predicts the birth of Christ.
- The Nephite capital and the chief temple is relocated to the city of Bountiful.

- At the death of Christ, three days of darkness engulf the land, during which cities are destroyed and the geography of the land is changed.
- Christ appears to the house of Israel in the New World, his first appearance occurring at the temple at Bountiful.
- Christ sends forth his apostles to convert the people in all the land.
- A two-hundred-year period of peace allows the Nephites and Lamanites to prosper and rebuild their cities.
- The Nephites and Lamanites become wicked people.
- Circa AD 400 sees the complete destruction of the Nephite civilization.

To find candidates for the people of the Book of Mormon, we must first isolate the archaeological periods of central and southern Peru that coincide with the Book of Mormon record. According to the archaeological classifications, only the first two Inca horizon periods would apply to the Nephites—the Early Horizon 900–200 BC, and the Early Intermediate 200 BC–AD 500.[11] So what evidence do we have that the Peruvians of these periods were the Nephites?

ARRIVAL OF THE NEW ETHNIC GROUP: THE FAIR-SKINNED VIRACOCHAS

Betanzos recorded that the Inca name *Viracocha* "means 'god.' . . . When the Spaniards came to this land, they [the Incas] used this name for them and thought they were gods."[12] As the first three Spanish conquistadors entered the Inca capital at Cuzco, it is reported that when "the old men and women of these towns saw them,

they immediately offered their eyelashes and eyebrows and blew them in the air right in front of them. They called them *Ticci viracocha pachay-achachic runa yachachic*, which means 'gods from the ends of the earth, creators of the world and of the people.'"[13]

We now know why the Peruvians thought the Spaniards were gods. Like their god Viracocha, the Spaniards had the form of a man, wore beards, and had white skin. Cobo noted that the Incas called all native men, *runa*, and all white men *viracochas*.[14] Thus, Viracocha is the white god, and Viracochas was the name given to any white men. Keeping this in mind, Thor Heyerdahl reminds us that according to Peruvian legend, white people called Viracochas came from across the sea in boats.[15] The Incas also believed that their ruling nobles were "white-skinned."[16] Calderwood documented several reports that the Inca nobility were fair-skinned,[17] including the following:

> Pedro Pizarro, who participated in the conquest of Peru, claimed that the people of the Incas Indians, at the time of the arrival of the Spanish, were white or light-skinned. Pizarro described the Indians: "The people of this kingdom of Peru were white, a light brown color, and among the lords and ladies, they were even more white, like the Spaniards." It would appear that he was referring only to the Inca nobility and not to all of the Indians in Peru.[18]

Calderwood further cites the Indians in Brazil telling "about a white king wearing long robes and living in the mountains far to the west."[19] The reports of fair-skinned people in the Andes at the time of the Spanish conquest

appear to have been recently substantiated through genetic studies. Research on Human Lymphocyte Antigens (HLAs) indicates that the Quechua-speaking Indians of Peru [possible descendents of the Nephites] have DNA markers linking them to ancestors who lived in the Near East, Arabia, and Europe. The studies include HLA samples from pre-Columbian Peruvian mummies.[20] (See Appendix 3 for further details about DNA studies.)

Another Spanish chronicler wrote that the Indians reported: "They had heard from their forefathers that all [ruins] that are there appeared overnight. Because of this and because they also say that bearded men were seen on the islands of Titicaca . . . I say that it might have been that before the Incas ruled, there were people in parts of these kingdoms, who came from no one knows where, who did these things, and who, being few and the natives many, perished in the wars."[21]

In other words, the original settlers, or better said the first civilizers of the Lake Titicaca region, were fair-skinned people who first arrived by sea and then migrated to the great lake and were eventually killed off through warfare with the non-white-skinned people. The fact that the Incas took upon themselves the name of their bearded white god is certainly consistent with the Book of Mormon people, who called the righteous people the "children of Christ" (Mosiah 5:7).

It is important to concentrate our study on only those tribes that were likely to have been Nephites, and having had some probability of practicing the gospel of Christ during the Book of Mormon period. Although the Nephi elite (Viracochas or Incas) might have ruled over a vast area, that does not necessarily imply that the gospel was lived by the tribes they ruled.

The Peruvians' long noses are a characteristic of the Middle East.

The limited accounts in the Book of Mormon of missionary work before the visitation of Christ seems to suggest that the gospel's scope was limited in the same way it was restrained in the Old World. That is, the full gospel was preached to only the descendents of the Hebrews and not to their neighbors. If this was the case in Peru, then finding the Nephites among all the Peruvian ancient civilization is not an easy task. Archaeologist Gary Urton notes:

> One of the most salient facts of life in the pre-Columbian Andes was the great ethnic diversity characterizing the subjects of the Incas. Such diversity seems to have had at least two important consequences for the shape and substance of myths in the empire. One was that this diversity itself needed an explanation. Why were people so different in terms of their languages, dress and other customs and habits? Did near, or even distant, neighbors who seemed so fundamentally different from one another have different origins? Or did all the people in the empire have a single origin?[22]

In a Peruvian context, it would appear that the pre-Meridian Nephites would not have taught the gospel in its fullness to natives tribes they ruled over. That would not necessarily have meant that the Nephites would not have tried to teach the natives to worship the One True God, while at the same time allowing them the agency to retain their own beliefs and idols. Urton writes:

> Answers to questions such as these, which are represented in the contents of the myths themselves, lead us to distinguish two quite distinct bodies of origin myths. On one level, peoples in different

parts of the empire appear to have insisted on the distinctiveness of their individual origins, and the myths resulting from these locally based myths and ideologies or origin display a multiplicity of creator deities and places and times of origin. We have a few dozen such origin myths from various parts of the empire, including the Lake Titicaca region, the north coast of Peru, and the central and northern highlands of Peru. What is important to recognize is that such myths exist in sufficient number to assure us that peoples in different parts of the empire promoted their individual origin myth, and their unique place of origin in the landscape, as components of ayllu or ethnic group identity and unity.[23]

A CLIMATE COMPARABLE TO PALESTINE

Author and filmmaker Arthur J. Kocherhans has researched the lands of the Book of Mormon people for forty years. As a young man, Arthur served an LDS mission in Mexico and Central America. However, his research brought him to the conclusion that Mesoamerica could not have been the place where Lehi and his family disembarked in the promised land. The more he extended his research, the more he believed that, as Joseph Smith, Jr. reportedly taught, Nephi's ship ended its voyage in Chile. Citing 1 Nephi 18:24–25, Kocherhans writes:

"The Book of Mormon is specific about FOUR identifiable characteristics of the Lehi colony landing place:

1)   They traveled by sea driving before the WINDS and they have a compass for guidance.

2)   They land and plant their SEEDS from the land of Jerusalem, which GROW EXCEEDINGLY.

3)   They go into the FOREST and find animals.

4)   They also locate ORE of 'both' gold, silver, and copper."

Kocherhans concluded: "Because of these scriptural requirements, Central America becomes self-eliminating as a landing place for the Lehi colony since two factors are missing. The climate and the ores."[24]

The Nephites brought seeds with them to the land of promise (1 Nephi 18:24). Some of these seeds were from Jerusalem, while others might have been collected in Arabia (1 Nephi 16:11). The lack of Eastern Hemisphere crop varieties in the Americas suggests that the Nephites either

These children are learning to till the earth from their fathers, just as their fathers learned from many previous generations.

quickly phased out the use of plants from the Old World (that is, they must have favored native varieties), or they eventually moved to another ecological zone where their seeds no longer thrived. Still, for at least one growing season, the Nephites successfully harvested Old World varieties of vegetables and grain (1 Nephi 18:24). In his book, *Lehi's Isle of Promise*, Kocherhans raises the question of where seeds from Jerusalem could have grown in the Americas.

The earth is made up of many climates and so agriculture varies all over the world. But here Nephi is telling the reader that "seeds" from the land of Jerusalem grew "exceedingly" where the colony had disembarked from their long voyage. Is this information given in the scripture without purpose? Probably not, so let us look for understanding and search the world climates. . .

From the climate maps it will be observed that the west side of Central America falls in a Monsoon region, and the east coast is recognized as a rainy tropical region. Therefore, seeds from the land of Jerusalem, which is a Mediterranean subtropical region, would NOT grow "exceedingly" on either coast of Central America. It appears that we would do well not to ignore these basic facts of agriculture.

Observe now South America. There is a small area with a Mediterranean subtropical climate on the west coast of today's Chile. Lehi could have successfully planted all his seeds, which he had brought from the land of Jerusalem, at this location and they would have grown "exceedingly."[25]

Having traveled extensively in South America and Arabia, I have concluded that one of the reasons the Lord had Lehi spend eight years in the harsh Arabian environment (1 Nephi 17:4), is that it mirrors the climate and growing conditions along the Peruvian-Chilean shoreline—the driest desert on earth. One of the plants that appears to have been transported to the New World were wine grapes. Wine seems to have been a common beverage among the Nephites and Lamanites. Jacob, who was born in the Arabian wilderness, speaks of its use during his lifetime (2 Nephi 5:9). King Noah "planted vineyards round about in the land; built wine-presses, and made wine in abundance" (Mosiah 11:15). Perhaps with time the grape vines died off from lack of care or the result of disease or from one of the severe droughts and floods that periodically occur in Peru due to the climatic oscillations called El Niño.

On the one hand, we know that today the slopes of the Andes, in particular Chile, produce some of the world's best wines. The ancient vineyards might have died off, but the process of making wine was not lost. When the Spaniards arrived, they found that the Peruvians were making wine from palms.[26] On the other hand, Mesoamerica has no comparable wine growing region. Writing shortly after the Spanish conquest of Peru, the chronicler Pedro de Cieza de León stated that the Nazca Valleys in the foothills along the southern Peruvian coast produced the best wine in the realm.[27] Another explanation for wine being mentioned in the Book of Mormon is that the Spanish referred to the Inca chicha, an alcoholic drink made from corn, as "wine,"[28] which in turn would make King Noah's vineyards fields of maize and not grapes. Father Bernadé

The Book of Mormon described a land where grains grew in abundance, not the tropics.

Cobo reported that the young Inca women called acllas (chosen women or sometimes called the virgins of the sun) spent part of their time making "wines" or chichas (corn beer).[29]

Lehi's family brought multiple seeds with them from Jerusalem, and successfully planted them while they lived in their tents next to the sea. However, there is very little evidence that Middle East plants were introduced to the New World from the Old World around 500 BC. So what happened to the seeds they brought with them that were initially so successful?

Nephi provides a possible clue. After harvesting crops, they left the shoreline and journeyed in the wilderness (1 Nephi 18:25). We know that when Nephi used the word "journey" it meant a migration, as in their journeys in the wilderness in Arabia. Furthermore, it seems that only during

their journey, and not while they are camped by the shoreline, they discovered a forest with animals in it (2 Nephi 18:25). In northern Chile and Peru, the shoreline is a barren landscape that has the appearance of the surface of the moon. However, within forty miles one climbs into the Andes Mountains where both forest and large game are found, such as horses (llamas), asses (alpacas), and wild goats (Andean huemul)[30] (1 Nephi 18:25). Note that the animals Nephi saw and described on their journey are associated with mountains, not tropical jungles. A mountainous terrain also seems indicative of Nephi's reporting that they discovered deposits of gold, silver, and copper.

Thus, it appears that the Nephites left the shoreline where their seeds from Jerusalem thrived and entered a mountainous climatic zone. This would necessitate the abandonment of their

Fields of barley and quinoa
in the high Andes.

Mediterranean subtropical crops for more durable varieties that could grow in frigid conditions. Perhaps it is for this reason that after the Nephites journeyed from their first seashore camp "seeds from Jerusalem" are never mentioned again (for example, 2 Nephi 5:11).

We learn something about the new crops the Nephites adapted from Mosiah who describes them as corn, wheat, barley, *neas* (a plant grown by the people of Zeniff, perhaps papas Quechua word for potatoes), and *sheum*. The grains wheat and barley could have been the Altiplano native grains varieties, like *quinoa*.

We also know that Nephite grains would not grow without rain (Helaman 11:13:17), and that periodically the people of the Book of Mormon were subject to drought and famine (2 Nephi 1:18, 6:15; Mosiah 9:3; Alma 10:22; 53:7; Helaman 10:6, 11:4, 13:9; Ether 9:28, 9:30). Thus, quite a climatic change existed between their first camp along the shoreline where seeds from Jerusalem grew and the semi-arid mountainous region where grains only grew when it rained. The Book of Mormon descriptions of changing crops, forest, ores, and mountain-dwelling animals appear to match well two climatic zones of Peru and Chile. The first is the shoreline where today the farming of vegetables exists in the diluvial valleys, and the second, the high Andes where Peru's staples of grains and potatoes grow in a climate dramatically affected by the El Niño drought cycles.

NEPHITES DISCOVERED ORE

The Nephites did not report finding fibers in the promised land from which paper could be made; however, they did find gold in abundance, and the metal was Nephi's chosen

medium for recording the sacred record of his people. Referring to the Lehites landing site, Kocherhans provides the following insight:

> He [Nephi] explains: "we did find all manner of ore, both of gold, and of silver, and of copper." Here there are "three" minerals following the word "both." Now our test of understanding comes.
>
> Is the Book of Mormon consistent? Can we go by word definitions? Can we take the Book of Mormon literally with this apparent conflict? Can we give it unqualified acceptance?
>
> The answer is YES, we can, even though we are required to look for understanding. I find a genius in this sentence. It says "both" of gold, and of silver: two precious metals. Gold and silver are two, and therefore "both," but as a unit of precious metals are one. Add copper to the unit of precious metals and then "both" again applies identifying two units: the precious metals unit and the copper unit. . . .
>
> I have searched up and down the American west coast for references to mineral deposits and only in Chile have I been able to find gold and silver as a unit. Close observation will reveal that this unit of two or "both" is within the Mediterranean Subtropical climate of that country; and then that unit is surrounded by the unit of copper. Thus the unit of gold and silver, as precious metals, and the unit of copper are available to match scripture requirements."[31]

To support his position, Kocherhans provides a Rand McNally map of the mineral deposits in Chile.[32]

A NEW RELIGION COMES TO THE ANDES INDIANS

As noted earlier, archaeologists believe that a new religion based on a bearded white deity, and including a lore that parallels that of Adam and Eve, was introduced in southern Peru around 500 BC. We know that this was roughly the same time that Nephi appointed Jacob and Joseph to be teachers of the gospel to his people [circa 544–421 BC]. However, we can glean much more from the Inca oral traditions about their ancient religion.

Like the Pilgrims of Plymouth, Lehi's family came to the New World as religious refugees. First and foremost they were looking for a place where they could establish a homeland, wherein they could worship God according to their own desires. Faith in God was the paramount driving force in the lives of Lehi, Nephi, Jacob, and undoubtedly many other members of the family. Thus, if they were successful in colonizing an area in the Americas and instituting a Christian faith, we should be able to find distant traces of that faith still among the Amerindians of Peru at the time of the Spanish conquest. That is to say, even though the faith of the Nephites and Lamanites was deeply corrupted by the fourth century AD, we should still be able to find within the oral tradition of the beliefs of their ancestors vague hints that their ancient faith was Christianity. Here are a few of the possible clues:

INCA FOREFATHERS BELIEVED IN THE BEARDED WHITE GOD, VIRACOCHA

When the Spaniards arrived, they erroneously reported that the Incas primarily worshipped the sun and that they believed their king (supi Inca)

to be the son of the sun. However, this was only a very late development in the Inca religious history. In earlier eras the chief god of the central and southern Andes was Viracocha. Urton writes: "A more troublesome and difficult issue concerns the chronological relationship between the worship of Viracocha [White God] and the worship of the sun. Some chroniclers suggest that the Inca worship of the sun was a late development, coming only after the expansion of the empire [AD 1400] beyond the boundaries of the valley of Cuzco and with maturity of the imperial bureaucratic organization. Others argue that the worship of Viracocha [always] superseded the worship of the sun."[33] Either way, Abinadi reminds us that apostate Nephites, like the later Incas, had the practice of worshiping graven images of heavenly bodies (Mosiah 12:35–37, 13:12, 25–26).

William Sullivan confirms the dominant position of Viracocha in the Peruvian belief system: "Throughout all these centuries, the teaching of Wiraqocha [Viracocha/Jesus Christ] remained the essential cultural tool for mastering the complexity of the physical environment of the Andes. Down to the present day and impermeable to time, there endures among the Andean peasantry the fundamental religious principle of Andean agricultural society, taught by Wiraqocha."[34]

Even up to the fifteenth century AD, when the Inca were supposedly worshipping the sun, their concept of God is surprisingly similar to the Book of Mormon concept of deity. At that time, the Emperor Inca Yapanque prayed to the creator god Viracocha Pacha-yachachic. Betanzos reported that "Viracocha came to him in the form of a man and spoke to him: 'My son, do not be distressed. The day that you go into battle

with your enemies, I will send soldiers to you with whom you will defeat enemies, and you will enjoy victory.' "[35] From this account, it appears that the Incas believed in a God in the form of a man, who cared for his creations and came to their aid when needed.

So intimidated were the Spanish priests with the Peruvians' belief in their bearded white god that the training manual for Jesuit missionaries called *The Extirpation of Idolatry* instructed the missionaries that "their very first duty, upon entering a village, was to get their hands on the lineage *waka* shrine [to Viracocha] and destroy it."[36]

VIRACOCHA, THE WHITE GOD, VISITS PERU

According to Inca oral traditions, in ancient times their land had been plunged into darkness, then "there suddenly appeared, coming from the south, a white man of large stature and authoritative demeanor. This man had such great power that he changed the hills into valleys and from the valleys made great hills, causing streams to flow from the living stone" (compare 3 Nephi 8).[37]

Early Spanish chroniclers were told by the Peruvian Indians that:

. . . they heard it from their fathers, who in their turn had it from the old songs which were handed down from very ancient times. . . . They say that this man traveled along the highland route to the north, working marvels as he went and that they never saw him again. They say that in many places he gave men instructions how they should live, speaking to them with great love and kindness and admonishing them to be good and to do no damage or injury one to another, but to love one another and show charity to all. In most places they name him Ticci Viracocha.[38]

"Wherever he [Viracocha] passed, he healed all that were sick and restored sight to the blind."[39] Viracocha was not only the Creator and healing God, he was also the Savior. The Spanish discovered that the Incas "prayed to Viracocha for pardon of their sins."[40]

Could Viracocha have been anyone save the Lord Jesus Christ? Thus, for the purpose of this book, we will refer to this great being as Viracocha [Christ].

SIMILARITIES TO THE LAW OF MOSES

The Books of Moses were recorded on the brass plates that the Nephites possessed in the promised land (1 Nephi 5:11), and the Ten Commandments were taught among them (Mosiah 13). Pedro de Cieza de León, Miguel Cabello Valboa, Felipe Guaman Poma de Ayala, and other chroniclers reported evidences that the South American natives performed practices and observed laws similar to those of Israelites and Christians. Calderwood notes:

> The Law of Moses and especially the observance of the Ten Commandments appeared to be similar to religious tenets that were kept in many areas of the New World. The punishment for breaking one of these New World "Ten Commandments" was frequently carried out in a manner similar to the ancient Israelite customs of meting out punishment.[41]

Like the Israelites, the Peruvians kept an eternal flame in their temple reminiscent of the eternal flame of Leviticus; they stoned to death those who committed adultery, executed murderers, severely punished thieves, prohibited homosexual practices, and taught their youth to remain morally pure.[42]

DISPENSATIONS OF TIME: THE FIVE AGES

William Sullivan believes that "To understand how the astronomical level of Andean myth worked, it is necessary to know something about its great overarching schema, the tradition of five Ages of the World, culminating with a Fifth Age, unilaterally declared, as it were, by the Incas."[43] Spanish chronicler father Martín de Murúa penned that "since the creation of the world until this time, there have passed four suns without [counting] the one which presently illumines us. The first was lost by water, the second by the falling of the sky on the earth. . . the third sun they say failed by fire. The fourth by air: they take this fifth sun greatly into account and have it painted and symbolized in the temple Curicancha [Coricancha, the Inca temple in Cuzco] and placed in their *quipus* [knotted cords used for counting and record-keeping] until the year 1554."[44]

The end of the fifth Sun represented to the Incas the depopulation of the land by the Spanish conquest, and also marked the Last Age or latter-days, when the land would be destroyed. Sullivan writes of Peruvian mythology:

> The use of the term "Sun" as the chronometric equivalent of "world-age" was a practice common to the Incas and the Aztecs, and at this point it is not necessary to elaborate on the specific reasons for this usage. The indigenous term for "world-age" that had pan-Andean usage was the word *pacha* . . . .
>
> The precise meaning of the word *pacha* is critical for understanding Andean mythical thought.[45]
>
> The Quechua word *pacha* means, one, and only one, thing: place and time simultaneously.[46]
>
> The Quechua term *pacha*, recognizable to us in its mythical sense of "world-age," is the irreducible matrix of Andean myth and culture. . . . This terminology places the concept of *pachakuti* squarely within the framework of the various world-ages described above by Murúa, involving successive "destructions" of the "space-time world". . . very much from other traditions where "worlds" are destroyed and new ones created.[47]

Chronicler Guaman Poma de Ayala described a "sun-age" as enduring for a thousand years, and drew an illustration descriptive of each first four ages.[48]

Is there a correlation between the doctrine of gospel dispensations found in the Bible and the Book of Mormon, and the Inca ages of the Western Hemisphere? The first gospel dispensation ended with Enoch, the second with the destruction by flood, the third dispensation closed with the destruction of the Jaredites, the fourth the era came to an end with the demise of the Nephites, and finally the fifth dispensation, closed with the destruction of the Inca Empire at the hands of the Spanish in preparation for the commencing of the Last Days. Poma provided this general outline of the Inca's World Ages:

INCA FIRST AGE
FIRST ONE THOUSAND YEARS, [ADAM TO ENOCH]

Began during a time of primordial darkness [compare Genesis 1:2].

People lived with only rudimentary technology.

First people wore clothing made of leaves [compare Genesis 3:7].

People first worshiped God, but then they lost faith and began worshiping other creator deities [compare Genesis 4:4, Moses 3:7].

First age of the Inca ended in an unspecified manner.

INCA SECOND AGE
[ENOCH TO NOAH]

People were more advanced than previous thousand years.

Had clothing of animal skins [compare Genesis 3:21].

Lived simply and peacefully, without warfare [no wars recorded in Genesis 6].

They recognized Viracocha [the white god, compare Genesis 5:24].

Ended in a flood [Genesis 6:17, Alma 10:22].

INCA THIRD AGE
[JAREDITE PERIOD IN PERU]

Age of *Purun Runa* ("wild men") [compare Ether 15:16–22].

More complex society [compare Ether 7:11].

People made clothing of spun and dyed wool [Ether 9:18; 10:24].

Practiced agriculture, mining, and making jewelry [compare Ether 4:11, Ether 6:18].

Population grew beyond previous levels [compare Ether 7:11].

People [Jaredites] migrated into the previously uninhabited lowlands [compare Ether 6:12–13].

There was a marked increase in conflict and warfare [compare Ether 7–15].

Each town had its own king [compare to Ether 7:20].

The people as a whole worshipped the creator [is another Peruvian name for Viracocha-Christ; compare Ether 6:17]

INCA FOURTH AGE
[ROUGHLY 600 BC–AD 400 NEPHITES/LAMANITES]

Age of Auca Runa "warlike people" [compare 2 Nephi 26:2].

Earlier part of the Inca empire occurred within age [legendary time of first Inca, Manco Capac—likely Nephi, son of Lehi, first king of Nephites; 2 Nephi 5:18].

World divided into four quarters [Alma 43:26, 52:10, 56:1, 58:30, 35; Ether 14:15 during Nephite era].

Warfare increases [Mormon 1–8].

People lived on mountain tops in stone houses and fortifications, called pucaras [compare Alma 51:27 and 48:8–9].

Ayllus Quechua word meaning "family," "lineage" or "part" [means "tribe";

compare Jacob 1:13]—of which there were perhaps tens of thousands of members spread throughout that part of the Andes with the Inca Empire.

Technology and material conditions greatly improved [compare 2 Nephi 5:11–17].

Not specified how it ended.

INCA FIFTH AGE
[LAMANITE EMPIRE TO SPANISH CONQUEST, AD 400–1531]

Age of kingships.

Decimal bureaucracy.

Empire organized by its religion [compare 4 Nephi 1:41–42].

Incas start worshiping the "demons of Cuzco" [compare Mormon 4:14–21].

The Fifth Thousand years ended with the coming of the Spanish.[49]

THEY TOOK UPON THEM HIS NAME

According to the Native American Felipe Guaman Poma de Ayala, his Inca ancestors believed that the first Incas were called *Vari Viracocha Runa* (men of god Viracocha). The Incas believed that the men of god Viracocha were brought to Peru by God, and "they had a light and a knowledge of the Creator of heaven and earth."[50] However, the *Vari Viracocha Runa* eventually lost their writings and forgot the commandments of God.

When the fair-skinned Spanish arrived in Peru, they called themselves the "Christians," the same name by which they were known in Iberia for having defeated the Muslims. However,

the Incas did not call the Spaniards Christians. Instead, they used the term "Viracochas," after their great creator god Viracocha [Christ]. The Spanish Chronicler Cieza de León wrote that the Inca warriors used the Quechau phrase, "*Viracochas, udcaxamo!*" which means, "Christians, come quickly!"[51] and "*Viracochas, ancha misque nina*," which means, "Oh, Christians, how very sweet is the fire to me."[52] It is somewhat ironic that the Incas gave the same name to the murdering, plundering, and raping conquistadors that they gave their ancestors, who were named after the Creator of the World. One must wonder if the Incas might have realized at some level that their ancestors, the people who took upon themselves the name of the god Viracocha, had also been Christians. The Book of Mormon tells us that the true believers in Christ called themselves "Christians" (Alma 46:14–15). Was it possible that the inscription Joseph Smith translated as "Christian" read on the Gold Plates "Viracocha"?

THE BELIEF IN A PREMORTAL EXISTENCE

The Spanish who conquered the Incas never quite understood what the Incas meant by their traditional phrase: "In this world we are exiled from our homeland in the world above."[53] We know from the Book of Mormon that the Nephite prophets taught the doctrine of the premortal existence (Alma 13:3).

MOTHER EARTH

The Nephites referred to the "mother earth" to which all flesh shall return (2 Nephi 9:7). The Andean people still celebrate "mother earth."

PERUVIANS PRACTICED ANIMAL SACRIFICES

Blood sacrifices did not start with the Law of Moses; rather it was the *sacrament* of the Old Testament:

> And [God] gave unto them commandments, that they should worship the Lord their God; and should offer the firstlings of their flocks for an offering unto the Lord. And Adam was obedient unto the commandments of the Lord. And after many days, an angel of the Lord appeared unto Adam, saying, Why dost thou offer sacrifices unto the Lord? And Adam said unto him, I know not, save the Lord commanded me. And then the angel spake, saying, This thing is a similitude of the sacrifice of the Only Begotten of the Father, which is full of grace and truth; Wherefore, thou shalt do all that thou doest, in the name of the Son. And thou shalt repent, and call upon God, in the name of the Son for evermore. (Moses 5:5–8)

If ancient Peru periodically had righteous Christian observers, then we would expect to find that in some form the practice of animal sacrifice would have existed in ancient Peru. When the Spanish arrived they observed the Incas still sacrificing sheep (Mosiah 2:3, probably alpacas or llamas), lambs, and birds (John 2:14).[54] Betanzos, recorded that the throats of the sheep and lambs were slit in the presence of the Inca,[55] apparently to collect the blood or to prepare the meat in a manner consistent with the Law of Moses (Leviticus 3:17). Sarmiento also mentioned that the Incas sacrificed lambs (young llamas or alpacas).[56] Apparently, the Incas sacrificed animals in a

manner similar to what the Nephites did two thousand years before. "And they [the Nephites] also took of the firstlings of their flocks, that they might offer sacrifice and burnt offerings according to the Law of Moses" (Mosiah 2:3). Cieza de León noted that the traditional sacrifice required a "lamb of one color without spots"[57] and that "they made great sacrifices according to their custom. They killed many animals, whose blood they sprinkled on the altars where there were channels to make the offering."[58]

The Incas observed three main ritual events. One held during the December solstice, the longest day of the year in the Southern Hemisphere. In one of the most authoritative texts, Avila refers to it as the *capac hucha*. During the ritual tens of thousands of llamas were sacrificed with the blood being collected in small clay vessels and distributed throughout the empire. There is debate over why the animals were sacrificed, but one meaning of the word *hucha* is "sin."[59] Perhaps the *hucha* ritual was reminiscent of the "sacrifice for sin" or "sin offering" that was practiced in ancient Israel (Numbers 15:30–31, Leviticus 4:2, 22, 27; 5:15, 17) and by the early Nephites who understood the sin offering and made offerings in accordance with the law of Moses (2 Nephi 2:7; Mosiah 2:3).

From at least the time of Moses, incense was an important offering in the Hebrew temples (Exodus 30:34–36), where high priests had to make a duty offering twice at day (Exodus 30: 7–8, 30–34). To enter the Holy of Holies the high priest was required to carry an incense burner as he entered the sanctuary (Numbers 6:24–26). We should not be surprised then that within the remains of Yaya-Uma (Adam-Eve) temples in Peru ceramic incensories have been found.[60] Indeed, archaeologists have discovered a widespread distribution of incensories at sacred sites between Cuzco and Lake Titicaca.[61]

PERUVIANS' CONCEPT OF THE RESURRECTION

The Peruvian Indians had a saying, "*Cay pacha tu coptin atarixunxi llapan chic caocarispa aichantin ymanamcuna canchic*," which means "When this world comes to an end, we will all rise up with life and with this flesh as we are now."[62] Hearing this Peruvian saying, the Spanish chronicler Betanzos wondered, "Someone made them understand this; they know it very well."[63] Of course, students of the Book of Mormon know who taught the principle of the resurrection in the promised land:

Yea, this bringeth about the restoration of those things which have been spoken by the mouths of the prophets. The soul shall be restored to the body, and the body to the soul; yea, and every limb and joint shall be restored to its body; yea, even a hair of the head shall not be lost; but all things shall be restored to their proper and perfect frame. (Alma 40:22–23)

A Progression of Three Afterlife Kingdoms

When the Spanish arrived in the New World, they found that the natives had a strong belief in the immortality of the human soul and that they believed they would be with their earthly spouses in the next life.[64] They mummified their nobles and, according to Garcilaso de la Vega, buried them "with everything that belonged to their bodies" including fingernail and hair clippings so they could "rise up more quickly"[65] (compare Alma 40:35). However, the Spanish priests had trouble understanding the Inca mythology of three heavens. With their belief in only a heaven and a hell, the Spanish could not reconcile what the Incas were teaching their children about the hereafter. Sullivan explains:

According to the indigenous view at the time of the Conquest, the cosmos was composed of three domains: *hanaq pacha*, literally "the world above" [heaven]; *kay pacha*, "this world"; and *ukhu pacha*, "the world below"[LDS concept of paradise and spirit prison].

The Spanish blithely assimilated their "worlds" to the Christian concepts of "heaven," "earth," and "hell."

An exception to this practice is found in the writing of Spanish chronicler Santillán, who apparently listened a bit more carefully, noting that the dead returned whence they had come "which was beneath the earth [paradise]; and that someone who died as a result of just punishment for theft or other sins went to hell [inferno]. . . [spirit prison].

In this world we are exiled from our homeland in the world above [in heaven with the Father] ("*Caypachapim hanacpacha llactanchic-manta hahuanchananchic.*") If ordinary people went to ukhu pacha, the "world below" [equivalent to LDS paradise or spirit prison] when they [first] died, what did they [the Incas] mean by claiming that their ultimate abode lay "up there," in the sky [equivalent of LDS concept returning to Father in Heaven after paradise]? Who was confused?[66]

The fact that the vast bulk of perfectly innocent Andean humanity journeyed at death to ukhu pacha, "the world below" [spirit world], apparently didn't stop them from referring to the sky when asked about the ultimate abode of the dead [celestial kingdom].[67]

Obvious parallels exist between the Inca lore of life after death and the gospel plan of salvation with a preliminary paradise for all people, and a later hell or heaven above after the final judgment. Calderwood believes that the pottery paintings of the Moche people suggest that the Peruvians might have understood the existence of the "spirit world" as early as the Jaredite era.[68]

Law of Chastity Similar to the Law of Moses

During the final Inca period, well after Book of Mormon times, the Peruvian Indians still practiced some laws reminiscent of those in the Bible. Betanzos recorded: "The Inca ordained that the married woman or *mamacona* who commits adultery, when proven guilty would be stoned to death by everyone outside the city. . . . And if the testimony could not be proven, the one who had given it would die in the same place and in the same way as the adulteress would have died."[69] If an Inca woman's husband died, and she wanted to remarry, "she would be married to the closest relative of her husband."[70]

A New Civilization Appears in the Andes

Although it is impossible to restore that which time has eroded away and what man has turned into ashes, the Book of Mormon provides a timeline on which we can hang archaeological and mythological information as a way of understanding the history of ancient Peru. Thus, if the Nephites ruled a region of Peru roughly between 575 BC and AD 400, we should be able to detect their distant signals on the radar screen of Andean archaeology. The latest science shows the unique markings of an ancient Book of Mormon culture having existed in Peru. For example: The Metropolitan Museum of Art notes of the Central and South Andes between 1000 BC and AD 1, "In the final centuries of the period, more stratified and warlike cultures emerged, particularly on the north and south coasts of Peru. They introduced new technologies and imagery in art and architecture."[71] Sullivan writes:

dry-stone walls" [compare 2 Nephi 5:15] and taught the people how to construct irrigation canals [compare 2 Nephi 5:11]. These emissaries from Titcaca were credited with creating the order of Andean society [see 2 Nephi 5:10]. Those who absorbed this teaching took the name Huari [Nephite; see 2 Nephi 5:9].[74]

Significantly, the record of this tradition accords with the archaeological record, which indicates some sort of interchange, on the level of ideas rather than trade, between the Titicaca basin and the Andean sierra as far north as Ecuador dating back perhaps five centuries before Christ.[75]

AN INDUSTRIOUS PEOPLE

Nephi had no respect for slothful people. An energetic lifestyle was valued by the Nephite society since the time of its founder. Nephi declared: "I, Nephi, did cause my people to be industrious, and to labor with their hands" (2 Nephi 5:17). The prophet-king taught that "because of their cursing which was upon them (the Lamanites) they did become an idle people" (2 Nephi 5:24). It appears then that the actual curse on the Lamanites had nothing to do with their skin color, which was only a distinguishing factor. In Nephi's opinion his elder brother's descendents had become cursed because they were lazy people. Since Jacob taught his people not to belittle the Lamanites because of the color of their skin (Jacob 3:9), he seems to confirm that the Lamanites' darker skin was not a curse, rather the cursing was the Lamanites' idle lifestyle, which in turn distanced them from the Lord. The Nephites' emphasis on work was

We are now looking at the historic moment of the formation of the "vertical archipelagos" that transformed Andean civilization. According to the archaeological record, evidence of terracing and irrigation first began to appear in the Titicaca basin about 500 BC [arrival of Nephi and his brothers] and then began rapidly to spread throughout the Andean highlands in general at the onset of the Early Intermediate Period that is about 200 BC [the move to Zarahemla]."[72]

Llama [members of the camel family] caravans were the bloodstream of the vertical-archipelago system.[73]

The Aymara, Paleo-Indians who lived at Titicaca before the Nephites, called the people who came and changed their food preparation and diet, the huari. Sullivan adds:

According to these traditions the "Huari" were a race of white, bearded giants who had been created at Lake Titicaca, whence they had set forth to civilize the Andes. . . . [they] "laid up probably rooted in the belief that idleness leads to sinfulness. The people of Alma were industrious (Mosiah 23:5); the people of the church prospered because they were industrious (Alma 4:6); the Anti-Nephi-Lehies became very industrious (Alma 23:18); and the converted Lamanites covenanted that they would labor rather than be idle (Alma 38:12).

To what degree the Inca culture at the time of the Spanish conquest could still have reflected elements of an ancient society is debatable. However, the Peruvians, up to the time that the Spanish crushed their society underfoot appear to have been the New World's foremost "workaholics." Their leaders abhorred idleness. Inca Yapanque, the founder of the later Inca Empire taught that "idle people tore the nation apart, they should tolerate no idleness in their nation or in the other nations and provinces but, rather, all should work and practice all kinds of activities."[76] Betanzos notes the rules of the Incas:

Taking into consideration the laziness and great pretentiousness in which the young men of Cuzco were reared, the Inca ordained the following: When a boy reached five years of age, his parents and relatives should impose on him part of their work and servitude. They should send the boys out to bring firewood and straw, to collect snails and mushrooms, and to catch birds. They should also be sent to the fields to irrigate, cultivate, and do other farmwork. . . . With regard to girls, at five years of age their mothers should require that they go to the fountains for water, not alone but, rather, accompanied by their servant girls. These little girls should also go to the fields to pick vegetables that they eat. They should

also be taught to cook, spin, and weave garments for both men and women.[77]

. . . the children of each one of the towns and provinces from a young age [should] be taught by their parents the farming and jobs done by their parents. From a young age these children should be accustomed to serve Cuzco and to avoid idleness.[78]

Even when the Inca soldiers were guarding bridges, they were ordered to "make cords of cabuya and ropes and cables of those twigs so that when the bridges needed to be repaired they would have the materials ready and these guards would not be idle."[79]

The Inca youth would have made good poster-children for the Mormon pioneers' icon of the *deseret*, the hard working honey bee. They were also a perfect match for another Mormon animal analogy—the packrat.

PERU THE GREAT GRANARY, A CURIOUS STORAGE CULTURE

Peruvians had the ancient world's foremost preparedness program. Not only did they carefully preserve huge grain stashes, they also stored supplies of clothing and other essential items. They even named their land after their storage program. Sullivan writes:

Pirua [Peru], and its Aymara variant *pirua*, refers to a kind of building, a round storehouse for grain. These structures relied for their stability, as did the Ages of the World, on four sturdy pillars, around which were worked wattle and daub into a round shape. . . . The *pirua* was the ancient granary of the peasantry.

Arriaga and Acosta both noted the ceremonies of the peasantry concerned with guarding their crops in the *pirua*.[80]

The Incas believed that their god Viracocha [Christ] had "given them food and the way to preserve it."[81] Can you think of any other religion where food preservation is a part of the official curriculum? Besides being prepared for the hereafter, the Peruvians had a long history of being prepared for the here and now, and for uncertainties such as famines. Mann writes: "The Spanish invaders were stunned to find warehouses overflowing with untouched cloth and supplies. But to the Inka the brimming coffers signified prestige and plenty; it was all part of the plan. Most important, Tawantinsuys [Four Quarters—the Inca name for their empire] "managed to eradicate hunger," the Peruvian novelist Mario Vargas

Llosa, though no fan of the Inka, noted: "Only a very small number of empires throughout the whole world have succeeded in achieving this feat."[82]

Betanzos recorded: "These storehouses were so well supplied with all of the things necessary for their lives and needs that in them there was even footwear for rams made of *cabuya*, which is used like hemp in Spain. There were not only storehouses for garments and wool and the other necessities, but there were also large corrals of livestock along with this. The corrals, just like the storehouses, were well supplied for these provisions and benefactions."[83]

Perhaps the Peruvians learned to keep large stores of provision because of the long sieges put on the Nephites by the Gadianton robbers. "But behold, this was an advantage to the Nephites; for it was impossible for the robbers to lay siege sufficiently long to have any effect upon the Nephites, because of their much provisions which they had laid up in store" (3 Nephi 4:18). The First Presidency of The Church of Jesus Christ of Latter-day Saints has advised: "We encourage Church members worldwide to prepare for adversity in life by having a basic supply of food and water and some money in savings. . . . We encourage you to store as much as circumstances allow. May the Lord bless you in your home storage efforts."[84] The LDS Church strongly advises its members to maintain where possible a one-year supply of food, medical supplies, and other basic needs such as clothing and hygiene materials. While Mormons today stuff storage items into every feasible cranny of their homes, the Latter-day Saints are still no match for the Incas who at times accumulated sufficient supplies for ten years.[85] The Inca capital had dozens of storages houses, but these were

Ancient grain silos at Rachi, Peru. Their god taught the Incas to store food.

insignificant when compared to the thousands of units that were located in the largest provincial centers.[86]

The manner in which the Incas stored their reserves was ingenious, and it should be remembered that the Incas believed that Viracocha [Christ] had taught them how to preserve their food. Cobo wrote:

> Ordinarily these storehouses or warehouses were built outside of town on a high, cool, and windy place near the royal road. . . . The Indians put these storehouses in high places so that what was stored in them would be kept from getting wet and humid and from spoiling in any way; and by dividing the *buhios* [huts with thatched roofs] in the aforementioned way, the Indians tried to prevent damage from fires so that if one of them caught on fire, since the fire could not be put out, no more would be lost than the contents of the house that was burning, and the fire would not spread to the rest.[87]

To keep insects away from their stores of grains and vegetables, the Incas lined the bottom of their granaries with a variety of mint called Muña (*minthustachys mollis*). Remembering that Lehi's family spent eight years in the Arabian wilderness and had to preserve their food during their journey, it is interesting to note that the Arabs still use a variety of mint to keep insects from their food. The Arabs even place mint leaves in their hair as an insect repellent.

The Inca storage system acted somewhat along the lines of a welfare distribution system. The stores were assigned to three different groups of people: the community, the religious functionaries, and the royals. The last share, that of the Incas was also used as an empire-wide storehouse. Cobo expounded:

> These same storehouses he [the Inca] ordered alms to be given to the poor and needy, and after the province was supplied, with the necessary provisions, he had them supply the needs of other surrounding provinces; and thus foods were carried from one province to another, and not infrequently, foods were transported from the storehouse of the coastal plains to the sierra and vice versa. All this was done with so much care, order, and speed that nowhere was anything lacking nor was anyone in dire straits, even though there were lean years; for the provision went from person to person where they were needed, and what was left over or not necessary was kept in the storehouse for times of need. These storehouses were always very well supplied because ordinarily there was food gathered from ten or twelve years back.[88]

Cieza de León gave this account of the amazing storage program of the Incas:

> As this kingdom was so vast, as I have repeatedly mentioned, in each of the many provinces there were many storehouses filled with supplies and other needful things; thus, in times of war, wherever the armies went they drew upon the contents of these storehouses, without ever touching the supplies of their confederates or laying a finger on what they had in their settlements. And when there was no war, all this stock of supplies and food was divided up among the poor and the widows. These poor were the aged, or the lame, crippled, or paralyzed, or those afflicted with some other diseases; if they were in good health, they received nothing. Then the storehouses were filled up once more with the tributes paid the Inca. If there came a lean year, the storehouses were opened and the provinces were lent what they needed in the way of supplies; then, in a year of abundance, they paid back all they had received.[89]

No Frills Society

The Peruvian storage houses give us a sense of the nature of Inca culture. While many ancient cultures were aesthetically abstract and immoderate, the Peruvian civilization was a frugal, no-nonsense, practical society centered on religion and preparedness. Sullivan cites:

> The Maya, it seems, lived in imagination because we have at hand vivid pictures for contemplation in the mind's eye: Tikal, Palenque, the Carcól, and so on. With the exception of Machu Picchu, no such images of the Inca exist. It is not that the Spanish destroyed the great architectural treasures of the Andes, although they destroyed many buildings. The true monuments of Inca civilization exist in a context too humble for ready transmission to modern sensibilities. The Incas were arguably the world's finest stonemasons, but they did not lavish their skill on ornate temple complexes. Instead they built soil.

In the Andes, where the basis of wealth is land and the currency labor, a substantial portion of the labor of the people—their taxes—was converted into soil through the construction of agricultural terrace walls. To this day, at such places as Pisca and Chincheru, tier upon tier of massive stone terraces wrought of exquisite Inca masonry graced the hillsides. These walls were built to create land for the Sun, land that the Incas chose to create rather than to requisition from the people, land that produced the surpluses used to thwart famine. Behind these walls the soils were carefully laid in layers to ensure drainage and promote friability and aeration. The masonry itself, a mosaic of interlocking irregular polygons, represents tens of thousands of man hours of labor.[90]

PRIESTLY CULTURE

Sullivan explains that during the Peruvian Age of Viracocha (Christ), the political order was "not based on force or deception, but belonged to the priest-astronomer, who by merit of superior insight alone was able to command respect."[91] During the first two hundred years after Christ's visit to the Nephites and Lamanites, there appears to have been no other political organization than the Church. It was only after the people divided themselves into classes and started false churches that conflicts arose and we read of militaries being formed (4 Nephi 1:1–30).

Even during Inca times, the high priest played an important role in Peru. Calderwood states:

Concerning the organization of the

priesthood among the Incas, Cieza de León noted that the high priest, called a Villacumu, meaning sorcerer who speaks, held his position for life. The high priest was married and so revered that he competed in authority with the Lord Inca. He had power over all the shrines and temples, and appointed and removed priests. The priests were of noble lineage

and powerful families, and this dignity was never conferred on men of low station, however great their merits. Cieza de León also mentioned that the priests were greatly venerated, and even the Inca nobility obeyed them in whatsoever things they ordered.[92]

INCA MANNER OF DRESS

The Nasca people of Peru lived near the Pacific shoreline during Book of Mormon times. Helaine Silverman from Columbia University and Donald A. Proulx from the University of California, Berkeley studied Nasca mummies. They found that the Nasca people wore "mantles, tunics, turbans and turban bands, head cloths, headbands, loincloths, slings, pads, and fringes. Although most people probably went barefoot, leather sandals have been found in some Nasca cemeteries."[93] The clothes found in the Peruvian tombs appear to be like the apparel one would have found in an ancient Middle Eastern boutique—complete with head cloths and headbands. Alan Sawyer discovered that the Nasca used textile work to distinguish status differences in Nasca society.[94] Silverman and Proulx note that Nasca Peruvian textiles included: "needle-knitting or the cross-knit loop stitch used to produce extraordinary three-dimensional textiles, plainweave, double cloth, gauze, tapestry and plaiting. Plainweave textiles could be superstructurally decorated by magnificent embroidery."[95]

It is important to remember that Nephi and his family did not dress like Bedouin shepherds. They were from the upper economic level of society and undoubtedly wore the prevailing Greek fashions of their day. Although the Incas lived a full millennium after the Nephite Empire disappeared, the Spanish found the Inca elite class dressed in a Hellenistic style.

Historian John Hemming described Inca clothing:

> Their clothes—one suit for everyday wear, one for festivals—were constantly darned but rarely washed. Men wore a breechclout: a piece of cloth passed between the legs and fastened to a belt in front and behind. Above they wore a white sleeveless tunic, a straight-sided sack with openings for the head and bare arms, hanging down almost to the knees: this gave them the appearance of *Romans* or medieval pages. Over the tunic they wore a large rectangular cloak of brown wool, knotted across the chest or on one shoulder. The women wore a long belted tunic, rather *Grecian*, hanging to the ground but slit to expose the legs when walking. . . . Both sexes went barefoot or wore simple leather sandals bound to their ankles (emphasis added).[96]

Loren McIntyre found that "in the University of San Antonio Abad, in Cuzco [the Inca's capital city] there is a ceramic head of an Inca warrior wearing a sling [see Mosiah 9:16] on top of his head in a wrap-around fashion.[97] The figurine brings to mind how the Arabs wrap cords around their heads to hold their headdresses in place.

USE OF SIGNET RINGS

Not only did the Inca dress like people in ancient Jerusalem, but they sealed their documents in the same manner. Authorized Incas wore on their hand a very interesting item. Similar to an event in the motion picture, *Ben Hur*, in which Charles Heston pressed his adopted Roman father's signet ring into the pallet sealing

9 *Festival of the Sun*

an agreement, this same ancient authorization tool was used in pre-Columbian Peru. Kolata writes,

> A striking find of a terra cotta ring from one of these houses strengthens the inference that the residents of this sector of the city [Tiwanaku], although perhaps not of the highest social stratum, were nevertheless considerably wealthier and of higher status than the urban commoners and rural folk who constituted the bulk of Tiwanaku's population. This piece carries an embossed, stylized representation of a masked human wearing an elaborate crown. The intaglio design makes it clear that the ring functioned as a signet device for marking, or sealing objects as the property of the owner.

Such signet rings are rare in Tiwanaku, suggesting that they were the property of a restricted class of people. They may have belonged to elite of a rank immediately below that of the royal lineages who were charged with conducting some of the day-to-day affairs of the state.[98]

CUSTOMS ASSOCIATED WITH HAIR

Like the early Christians in the Old World, Inca men wore their hair cut short (1 Corinthians 11:14). Betanzos observed that "the custom in Cuzco was for everyone to wear their hair very short and cut off."[99]

In another Peruvian hair-cutting custom, we can see yet another possible connection to the Hebrews of Palestine. The Hasidic Jewish do not have their hair cut until their third birthday. The hair-cutting ceremony is called *upsherin*. Betanzos recorded a similar ritual among the Incas.

> When Atahualpa reached his first birthday, his father ordered that his hair be cut so that the lords of Cuzco could perform this ceremony and offering because cutting the hair of such a recently born child was their custom. So they cut his hair and performed a solemn ceremony. All the lords and ladies of Cuzco offered their gifts. In this hair cutting ceremony [*Rutuchico*] his father named him Atahualpa. You should know that they had a custom to celebrate a fiesta four days after the birth of a son. One year after the birth they celebrated another in which they cut his hair.[100]

The Hebrew-like ritual of cutting a babies' hair was not native to Peru, but was started by the foreigner, the very first Inca king, even Manco Capac [Nephi].[101]

UNCLEAN AFTER BIRTH

Hebrew women who gave birth to a male child were considered unclean and were required to be separate for seven days (Leviticus 12:2). Inca women who bore male children were separated for four days in a room where the sun could not be seen.[102]

SHIELDS MADE FROM WOVEN CLOTH

Domesticated animals played an important role in both the Inca and Nephite societies. The Nephites were counseled to pray for their flocks (Alma 34:20, 25); the Nephite women worked cloth for clothes (Mosiah 10:5, Helaman 6:13). The Nephites were known for their "fine clothing"

and also protected their soldiers with armor of thick cloth (Alma 43:19). Peruvian alpaca and vicuña wool is prized as some of the finest on earth. Mann notes: "Andean textiles were woven with great precision—elite garments could have a thread count of five hundred per inch—and structured in elaborate layers. *Soldiers wore armor made from sculpted, quilted cloth that was almost as effective at shielding the body* as European armor and much lighter. After trying it, the conquistadors ditched their steel breastplates and helmets wholesale and dressed like Inka infantry when they fought" (emphasis added).[103]

CONCERN FOR ANCESTORS

The Lord's true religion teaches the need to tie together the generations of man. Of course, many other cultures revere their dead. Still, one

would think that a Nephite culture would have taken special care to remember their dead. Sullivan writes:

> The ideal of reciprocity has deep roots in Andean civilization, which sought from its inception to build bridges between the world of the living and the unseen worlds, the worlds of the gods and of the ancestors. It was to the ancestors that the gods had revealed their plan for humanity. It was from the ancestors that the living had received the body of traditions and skills that made agricultural civilization in the Andes possible. To forget the ancestors was to sever the ties of reciprocal obligation that ensured the welfare of both the living and the dead in their separate modes of existence.[104]

ADVANCED TECHNOLOGIES:

The first solar observatories in the Western Hemisphere were created by the Peruvians. The oldest of these are the towers of *Chankillo*, a series of thirteen stubby towers built along a ridge. The towers mark the sun's progress across the sky. It is by far the oldest astronomical observatory in the Americas, dating back to the fourth century BC.[105] Lehi held the keys to temple work, and must have had some officiating capacity within the temple of Jerusalem, which itself was aligned to mark the movements of the sun. Furthermore, Lehi, whose native tongue was Egyptian, must have had considerable roots in Egypt, a civilization that based much of its mythology on tracing the sun.

Besides metallurgy, astronomy, sophisticated irrigation systems, and the ancient world's finest stone masonry, the Peruvians exhibited some other surprising technologies. McIntyre notes:

> Toothaches and headaches afflicted the Incas, as they do people today. Silver crowns for capping teeth, made by an Inca prosthetist half a millennium ago, display an astonishing similarity to crowns used in 20th century dentistry.

> Holes in an Inca skull were incised with bronze trepanning instruments like . . . knife, tweezers, chisels, hammer, scalpel, and needle. Trepanning was a surprisingly successful operation for mace wounds, skull fractures, tumors, headaches, and—very likely—exorcism of evil spirits.

> In 1953, Peruvian surgeons preparing a treatise on Inca trepanning sharpened this very set of tools to prove their utility. They operated on a man suffering speech impairment from a brain lesion, using a tourniquet around his head Inca-style to stop bleeding. The man recovered. Ceramic jugs from the coast shows a doctor straddling his patient while performing a trepanation.[106]

A WORLD DIVIDED BY HATE

It is hard to read the Book of Mormon without feeling a deep sadness for the disharmony and hatred that existed among the descendents of Lehi's sons. How different it would have been if Laman and Lemuel would have accepted the will of the Lord and allowed their righteous younger brother to lead the family. The feud they fostered was never resolved, and as a result, the thousand-year history of the Nephites is one of nearly constant warfare between the Lamanite and Nephite nations.

The Book of Mormon states that the Lamanites and Nephites were separated by a border that ran from the sea on the east to the sea on the west (Alma 22:27), and that the Lamanites were primarily in the land to the south (Alma 22:33). In the next chapter, we will see why Lake Titicaca is an excellent candidate for the Book of Mormon's "east sea." If this is the case, then the Lamanites would be represented by the Aymara-speaking people who lived on the southeast end of Lake Titicaca, their capital being at the city of Chiripa and later at Tiwanaku. The Nephite people would have been the Quechua-speaking people to the north and west of the lake, with their capital city of Zarahemla having been the ruins of the city the archaeologists have labeled Pukara (meaning *the fortress city*). The Aymara tribes or nations ruled a vast expanse of land, which included Bolivia and parts of Chile and Argentina. The Quechua people controlled the central Andes and probably included the tribes that eventually controlled Cuzco and the Inca Empire at the time of the Spanish conquest. Historically the two linguistic groups have always been bitter enemies. Alan Kolata writes: "In symbolic terms, Tiwanaku represented the recognized boundary marker that delineated the fault line, or point of cleavage between two archetypal social groups [Nephi/Lamanites]."[107]

A religious, ethnographic, linguistic, and cultural fault-line ran straight through the heart and soul of the ancient Andean peoples. That heart was Lake Titicaca, and the history of the lake is that of a broken heart. At 12,500 feet above sea level, the lake's basin provides only limited natural resources that had to be shared by these two competing nations. Sullivan describes the relations: "Pucara [Pukara/Zarahemla], which flourished from about 200 BC until about AD 200, constituted a rival polity of Tiahuanaco (Tiwanaku) [Lamanites]. The relationship between these two cities appears to have ranged from intense competition to open hostility. . . . Until its complete disappearance in the fourth century [time of the comprehensive destruction of the Nephites], Pucara appears to have been the main rival—perhaps the only serious rival—of Tiahuanaco in the Titicaca basin.[108]

Placing the Nephites at Pukara, on the northwest side of the lake between 200 BC and AD 400 provides some interesting possible insights into the Nephite society. First, it appears to have been a "dry" state. Within the ruins of Pukara archaeologists have found no containers for the brewing or consumption of beer, a traditional beverage throughout Andean history. On the Aymara [Lamanite] side of the lake, fancy decorated ceramic *chicha* cups have been excavated indicating that drinking beer was a social activity.[109] The evidence seems to suggest that the Quechua-speaking people during the time of Zarahemla were a sober people while the Aymara were heavy drinkers.

Second, Nephi discouraged his people from mixing with the Lamanites, and throughout the Book of Mormon we see very little interaction, except for wars, between the civilizations. Likewise the Quechua-speaking people of Pukara and the Aymara people of early Tiwanaku did not mingle. For over four hundred years the two nations lived in proximity within the Titicaca Lake Basin. Yet with their capital cities being only ninety miles apart, not a single piece of Aymara (Tiwanaku) pottery shards have ever been discovered at the Pukara excavations.[110] Clearly, it was not proper for the Quechua (Nephites) and the Aymara (Lamanites) to mix.

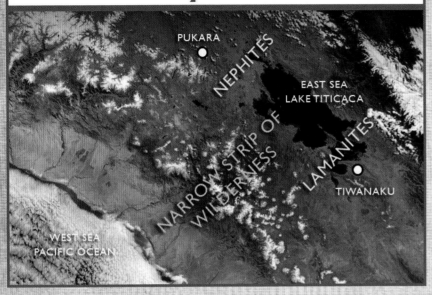

Narrow Strip of Wilderness

PUKARA

NEPHITES

EAST SEA
LAKE TITICACA

NARROW STRIP OF WILDERNESS

LAMANITES

TIWANAKU

WEST SEA
PACIFIC OCEAN

EL QVARTOCAPITAN
APOMAITACIVGA

Third, the Quechua had a centralized government located at its capital, Pukara. The Aymara seem to have had a more Lamanitish tribal organization, which Mann describes as "Less a centralized state than a clutch of municipalities under the common religio-cultural sway of the center."[111] As the two civilizations matured, we see that the Nephites maintained a centralized government ruled by kings or chief judges. The Lamanites, on the other hand, appear to have conducted their affairs as a loose confederation of tribes, with multiple kings or chiefdoms (e.g., King Lamoni being a king at the same time other Lamanite kings were also reigning, and Lamoni's father concurrently reigning as the chief king of the Lamanites).

Fourth, the Lamanites appear to have had

little respect for the Nephite religion. Sullivan points out that the famous Thunderbolt Stela found at Tiahuanaco has been shown, thanks to the research of Sergio Chavéz, to have been broken from its base in Arapa (then under the control of Pukara) and transported ninety miles by raft across Lake Titicaca to Tiwanaku.[112] In other words, during a time of victory over the Quechua (Nephites), the Aymara (Lamanites), as a sign of supremacy, broke off a huge stone religious icon of the Pukara temple and hauled the massive block all the way back to their own capital city.

Fifth, the Quechua people on the west of the lake specialized in the maintenance of large herds of domesticated animals—an economic system consistent with that of the Nephites in the Book of Mormon. The Aymara, occupying the more fertile southeastern shores, like the Lamanites, raised crops and hunted.[113]

Bouyee-Cassagne reminds us that Lake Titicaca, the highest navigable lake in the world, is unique in many ways: "as an element of Aymara [Lamanite] thought, Lake Titicaca is not merely a specific geographical location: it is at once a centrifugal force that permits the differentiation of the two terms in opposition and a

centripetal force that ensures their mediation. In the symbolic architecture, the *taypi* . . . is crucial to the equilibrium of the system."[114] In other words, the blue waters of Lake Titicaca appear to have been the mediating element that periodically allowed the two enemy nations, the Nephites and the Lamanites, to live next to each other in an uncomfortable peace.

The hatred between the Quechua and Aymara people was not language based. Indeed there were at least four principal languages spoken in the Lake Titicaca basin. Aymara or proto-Aymara might not even have been the original language of the people along the southern shores of Lake Titicaca.[115] If Nephi's ship actually landed in South America, then we can probably trace the hatred between the Quechua and Aymara people back to a power struggle between two brothers in the sands of the Arabian wilderness.

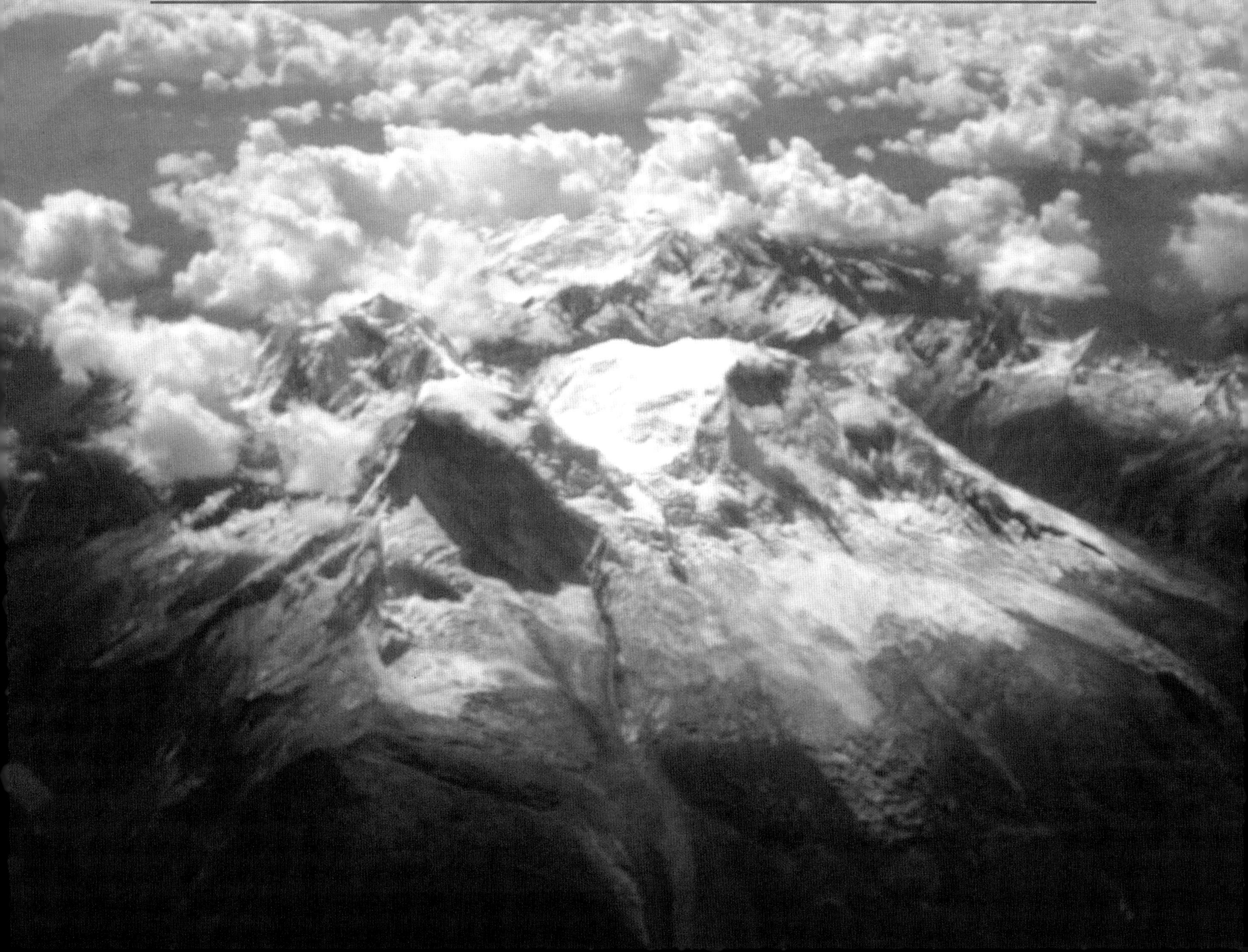

Geopolitical Model for the Book of Mormon in Peru

And so you start again like children,
knowing nothing of what existed in ancient times,
here in your own country.

Plato, *Timaeus*

If the Book of Mormon's history transpired in Peru, then there should have been Peruvian hegemonies that reasonably resembled our limited knowledge of the Nephite and Lamanite kingdoms. If not, then it is unlikely that Peru was the land of the ancient American prophets.

Ancient Quechua's (Nephite) Economic Pattern

An admired practice of the Mormon pioneers was the principle of reciprocity. The first settlers to arrive in the Salt Lake Valley grew crops for the saints who would arrive after them. The Perpetual Emigration Fund Company brought Saints to Utah from Europe, with the understanding that once they arrived, they would earn the funds to finance the next wave of immigrants to Zion. Working side by side, the Utah pioneers built massive irrigation projects, temples, and other public works that are still blessing the people of several western U.S. states, as well as parts of Canada and Mexico.

Sullivan notes that reciprocity was a characteristic of the pre-Columbian Peruvians:

> The core value of Andean civilization was reciprocity. It remains to the present day the operative principle of indigenous life in the Andean village. Groups of men work together, now preparing one another's fields for planting, now working together to make adobes for a newly married couple's first house. Young children tend the flocks. While the women spin and weave, the men collect llama dung on the high slopes for use in the agricultural fields. When it is time to plant, men open the earth with a foot plow, the chaclla, while women place seed in the earth. Everyone in the village participates in the annual cleaning of the irrigation ditches. One hand washes the other.[1]

71

Like their fathers before them, native Peruvians prepare to work the fields together.

The Inca Empire that the Spaniards discovered has been praised by many and condemned by others. What is known about the economic system of the Incas is that it was unique, and oral traditions indicate that elements of it date back to the earliest Incas. As such, we can compare elements of the Inca system with the order Christ taught when he visited the Nephites and Lamanites. The Book of Mormon tells us that after the Lord's visit to them, "there were no contentions and disputations among them, and every man did deal justly one with another. And they had all things common among them; therefore there were no rich and poor, bond and free, but they were all made free, and partakers of the heavenly gift" (4 Nephi 1:2–3). The Inca lands were divided one-third to the Inca or state, one-third for religious functions, and one-third as common community property divided among the private citizens. The lands were allocated according to their family needs. No taxation was exacted in terms of money or goods, just a heavy tribute paid by providing the labor for the national and religious lands, and for other public works when needed. The labor for taxes was called mitimaes. Polo de Ondegardo provides this description of the Inca order:

> The lands set apart for the tribute of the Inca and of religion were sown and reaped in the same order; but it must be understood that when the people worked upon them, they ate and drank at the cost of the Ynca and the Sun. This work was not performed by gangs, nor were the men told off for it, but all the inhabitants went forth except the aged and infirm, dressed in their best clothes, and singing songs appropriate for the occasion.[2]

From this private property no tribute

of any kind was exacted, even when it was considerable in amount. But all were obliged to do their part in producing the tribute demanded from the community. It is not right, therefore, that they should now be taxed by the head, but rather according to their estates. If there are a thousand Indians in a Repartimiento, among whom there are five hundred mitimaes who never possess any sheep, and if the tribute amounts to five hundred head, it is impossible to raise it. Consequently, when, by reason of the flocks, the tribute is to be paid in sheep, it is necessary to ascertain to whom the sheep belong, and to assess the mitimaes and the natives separately. Thus the difficulty will be overcome, and the injustice will be avoided. The community is composed of rich and poor, and the tribute of sheep should be distributed among those who breed them, without including any poor man who happens to have acquired a single sheep. For this immunity should be granted, and the matter is of sufficient importance to justify this digression.[3]

Although the Incas took great care in dividing the empire, its provinces, towns, and villages into quarters, there seems to have been no effort to divide the actual land into private properties. In other words, the villagers held their communal lands in common and distributed only the right to work the fields. Cobo explains how the Peruvians held land ownership over a thousand years after the last Nephites: "It is understood how the land used by the Indians belonged to the community of an entire town; . . . and the work of cultivating them was done on a communal basis, and the individual who did not work in sowing got no share of the harvest.[4] In the cases of war or other emergency, when a man was called away from his village, "the community themselves worked the fields of the absent men without requesting or receiving any compensation beyond their food, and, this done, each one worked on his own fields."[5]

ANCIENT AYMARA (LAMANITE) ECONOMIC PATTERN

As noted in the previous chapter, the Aymara people had a less centralized government than their Quechua neighbors. Their society was structured around tribal chiefdoms, a pattern that seems to match the very little we know about Lamanite government. When we read about the Lamanites in the Book of Mormon, we must remember that it is from their enemy's point of view. The Lamanites were pictured by the Nephites as being a slothful and unclean people. If the Lamanites were the Aymara, then the Nephite bias appears to have had an element of truth in it. Kolata notes that the Aymara [Lamanites] never developed a written language.[6]

The lands of the traditional Aymara-speaking people ranged from the southern shores of lake Titicaca, which extend down into the entire Bolivian highlands, to northern Chile and Argentina and into the vast area of the Amazon basin called the Beni. Despite their lack of a written language or a strong centralized government, the Aymara were able to rule over a vast area of land, recruit large armies, control many resources, and organize long overland trade routes. The same seems to have been true of the Lamanite Empire —it was impressive and eventually overpowered the Nephites.

Four Seas of Nephite Lands

NORTH SEA
ATLANTIC OCEAN

EAST SEA
LAKE TITICACA

WEST SEA
PACIFIC OCEAN

SOUTH SEA
LAKE POOPO
AND SALT FLATS

To this day, very little is known of the lands that fell under the influence of the Aymara. Mann described his visit to the Beni, (which means "of the tribe" in Arabic) lands which were part of the Aymara confederation:

> Below us lay the Beni, a Bolivian province about the size of Illinois and Indiana put together, and nearly as flat. For almost half the year rain and snowmelt from the mountains to the south and west cover the land with an irregular, slow moving skin of water that eventually ends up in the province's northern rivers, which are upper tributaries of the Amazon. The rest of the year the water dries up and the bright green vastness turns into something that resembles a desert. This peculiar, remote, often watery plain was what had drawn the researchers' attention, and not just because it was one of the few places on earth inhabited by some people who might never have seen Westerners with cameras.[7]

Scattered across the landscape below were countless islands of forest, many of them almost-perfect circles—heaps of green in a sea of yellow grass. Each island rose as much as sixty feet above the floodplain, allowing trees to grow that otherwise could not endure the water. The forests were bridged by raised berms, as straight as a rifle shot and up to three miles long. It is [Clark] Erickson's [University of Pennsylvania] belief that this entire landscape—thirty thousand square miles or more of forest islands and mounds linked by causeways—was constructed by a technologically advanced populous society more than a thousand years ago.[8]

The Beni is a case in point. In addition to building roads, causeways, canals, dikes, reservoirs, mounds, raised agricultural fields, and possibly ball courts, Erickson has argued, that the Indians who lived there before Columbus trapped fish in the seasonally flooded grasslands. The trapping was not a matter of a few isolated natives with nets, but a society-wide effort in which hundreds or thousands of people fashioned dense, zigzagging networks of earthen fish weirs (fish-corralling fences) among the causeways. Much of the savanna is natural, the result of seasonal flooding. But the Indians maintained and expanded the grasslands by regularly setting huge areas on fire.[9]

Beginning as much as three thousand years ago, this long-ago society—Erickson believes it was probably founded by the ancestors of an Arawak-speaking people now called the Mojo and the Bauré—created one of the largest, strangest, and most ecologically rich artificial environments on the planet.

Lake Titicaca was known to the Incas as "the great east sea."

These people built up the mounds for homes and farms, constructed the causeways and canals for transportation and communications. . . . In Erickson's hypothetical reconstruction, as many as a million people may have walked the causeways of eastern Bolivia in their long cotton tunics, heavy ornaments dangling from their waists and necks.[10]

NEPHITE "WHOLE EARTH" SURROUNDED BY FOUR SEAS

By the first century BC, the Nephites spread across the "whole earth from the sea south to the sea north, from the sea west to the sea east" (Helaman 3:8). The Quechua word *cocha* means both "sea" and "large lake."[11] Thus, the Incas called both the Pacific Ocean and Lake Titicaca *cocha*. The Peruvians were an amazing seafaring people. They certainly knew that South America was surrounded by oceans on all four sides. But they didn't need to venture that far to find the four seas of ancient Peru. The Pacific Ocean to their west is obviously the west sea. Polo de Ondegardo tells us about two other seas. At the summit of mount Vilcanota and the La Raya pass: "This road to the lake of Vilcanota, the point where the Collao begins. Two powerful rivers flow out of this lake, one going to the *north sea*, and the other to the *south*" (emphasis added).[12] The Incas believed that the rivers that flowed north into the Amazon basin emptied into the "north sea" or Atlantic Ocean.[13] The waters that flowed south from the La Raya pass, ended up, with an intermediary stop in Lake Titicaca, in the large saline Sea of Poopó at the south end of the Altiplano.

Maps today show these large bodies of water as lakes, but once again, the Inca word for lake and sea were the same. The sea of the east was the aforementioned sacred sea of the Incas, the 138-mile-long fresh water lake, Lake (Sea) Titicaca.

A Land of Mountains and Deserts

Hugh Nibley taught that the word *wilderness* "has in the Book of Mormon the same connotation as in the Bible, and usually refers to desert country."[14] He also taught that the word *border* (or *borders*) usually referred to "mountains." In the Semitic language the words for *mountain* and *borders* share a common derivation. That is, the Hebrew word *gebul* means "borders." *Gebul* is a cognate of the Arabic *jabal* (jebel, djebel), which means "mountain."[15] Dr. Nibley also confirmed that in the ancient Mesopotamian and Egyptian languages the word for *borders* meant "mountains."[16] Arthur Kocherhans believes that placing the descendents of Lehi in the Andes mountains is a direct fulfillment of the blessing that Joseph of Egypt received from Israel.[17] Lehi was a descendent of Joseph who was promised that his seed would be "progenitors unto the utmost bound of the everlasting hills" (Genesis 49:26). Not only do the great South American Andes fit the description of "everlasting hills," placing the Nephites and Lamanites in the range's highest inhabitable valleys (up to 13,000 feet above sea level), it is also indicative of the mountains' "utmost bounds."

Without knowing the probable meaning of the words *wilderness* and *borders* in the Book of Mormon, it would appear that there are few descriptions of the terrain in the land of the Nephites. However, the opposite is likely the case.

The word *wilderness* (desert) is used 214 times in the Book of Mormon (often used in proximity to the seashore), and the word *borders* (mountains) is used 65 times, suggesting that much of the Book of Mormon lands were deserts by the sea or mountains, a perfect description of Peru.

Sjodahl provided a more direct reasoning for the Book of Mormon lands having been mountainous. He writes:

ANTI

There are several words in the Book of Mormon in which "anti" is one of the component parts, as for instance, ani-Anti, the name of the Amalekite village in which Aaron, Muloki, and Amnah preached the gospel (Alma 21:11). Anti-Nephi-Lehi, the name of a king and also of a people (Alma 24:1–5); antion,

a piece of gold used as money (Alma 11:19); Antipas, the name of a mountain (Alma 47:7); Antum, the name of the country in which hill Shim was situated (Mormon 1–3), and onti, the name of a piece of silver used as money (Alma 11:6), are instances of the use of the word *anti* in the Book of Mormon.

The Indian (Quechua) word corresponding to *anti* is, I believe, *anta*, which Garcilasso de la Vega tells us means "copper." From *anta*, the magnificent mountain chain that forms the backbone of South America was called the Andes, possibly because of the metal, especially copper, found in these mountains.

In the Book of Mormon, *anti* means a mountain, or a hill. When it is used to denote a country it probably means

The Nephites called such places "Wilderness."

a hilly or mountain country, and when the name is applied to a city it may indicate location in a mountain region. In the same way the Anti-Nephi-Lehi may have been located in a hill country.[18]

Anti appears in Antisuyu, the name given by the Peruvians to the eastern part of their vast domain; that is, to the part that was traversed by the loftiest ridges of the Andes mountains. That proves, beyond questions, that the Peruvians used the word exactly as we find it used in the Book of Mormon.

ANTIPAS was the name of a mount or hill on the summit of which Lamanite armies on one occasion had gathered themselves for battle (Alma 47:7). This is a genuine Indian word. On the mountain slope of the Cordillera, in the upper Amazon basin, there is, according to Dr. Brinton, a tribe of Indians, of the Jivaro linguistic stock, known as the Antipas. They are described as "rather tall, of light color, with thin lips, aquiline noses, straight eyes, prognatic jaws, hair black or with reddish tinge."[19]

The Book of Mormon place name "Manti" provides a very interesting line of thinking that seems to support Sjodahl's argument. We can start by breaking down the word into "M-anti," remembering that *anti* means "mountains," and there was actually a hill of Manti (Alma 1:15). Since Manti meant hills or mountains, this would confirm the fact that *borders* meant "mountains" in the Book of Mormon, for we read of the Nephites defeating the Lamanites near the "borders of Manti" (Alma 27–54).

Other verses use *borders* [mountains] to describe "Manti" (Alma 16:6–7, 43:32). Furthermore, the headwaters of the Sidon river was near Manti (Alma 43:24–25); headwaters of rivers are normally found high in the mountains. There was also a valley in Manti (Alma 43:27), implying either mountains or hills that formed the valley. There was a hill Riplah in the land of Manti that was so large it could conceal a Nephite army (Alma 43:31–35).

Finally, an interesting application of Sjodahl linguistic key is that over time Book of Mormon words evolved into Quechua words as the ending *i* changed to an *a*. Manti was in the vicinity of Antiparah (Alma 56:14), and according to Sjodahl's reasoning *anti* can be translated into the

Quechua word *anta,* which means copper. Using the same linguistic rule, the Book of Mormon city, land, or hill of Manti would be translated into Quechua as Manta. The Quechua name for the place from which Viracocha [Christ] left Peru after his mission was called "Manta."[20]

The name of the Nephite King Limhi transposes to Lima, the Quechua place name that is still used for the name of the Peruvian capital, which was originally called Ciudad de los Reyes, or City of the Kings.

Limhi could also relate to Limatambo (meaning the "Inn of Lima") an Inca site west of Cuzco.[21]

The city of Lehi could become the city of Laha (Inca town near Lake Titicaca).

Anti from the Book of Mormon becomes Anta, name of a town northwest of Cuzco.[22]

Onti was the Nephite word for a silver coin (Alma 11:6). Transpose the "i" for an "a" and you have Onta while Anta is the Quechua word for copper.

Finally, there is the story found in the Book of Second Nephi, which in Arabic would be the book of "Dhu Nephi." It is the story of Nephi leading his people into the wilderness and finding himself on an island (2 Nephi 10:20). Chapter 5 will present evidence that Nephi lived for a short period on an island in Lake Titicaca. For now, we will exchange an *a* for the *i* to form Dhu Nepha for Second Nephi. The Inca oral tradition of Thu-nupa has several parallels to the story of Nephi. Osborne writes: "Thunupa appeared on the Altiplano [where Lake Titicaca is located] in ancient times, coming from the north with five disciples [Laman, Lemuel, Sam, Jacob, and Joseph]. A white man of august presence, blue-eyed, and bearded, he was sober, puritanical, and

The Inca's true highway through the clouds.

preached against drunkenness, polygamy, and war."[23]

HIGHWAYS IN THE MOUNTAINS

The Incas built an incredible highway network that was longer than the Roman highway system and was comparable in quality to the roads that led to Rome.[24] The Inca highway system had some 25,000 miles of surface tracks and was in its time the biggest road system in the world.[25]

One Spaniard described the Inca roads: "He proceeded on his journey through that land— which, although it is a level country, it is very rough, with high mountains that seem to reach the clouds and descend again infinitely into profound valleys. Although this is true, the royal highway of the Incas, who were so powerful, is also so well made and built through slopes and sections that one almost does not feel the height of the mountains."[26] The Inca road system ran straight through the Andean mountains forming parallel north-south tracks running nearly the entire length of the great mountain range. At times the Inca highways were paved with gypsum cement.[27]

Inca Highway at Nevado Pariacaca with an elevation of over 15,000 ft.

The Nephites were great "highway" builders (Helaman 14:24). The Book of Mormon records that during one short expansion period "many highways were cast up, and many roads made, which led from city to city, from land to land, and from place to place" (3 Nephi 8:13). In other words, the Nephites had a vast highway system that interconnected their empire. We also know that the Nephites were experts in cement.

It is interesting that the Nephites distinguished between "roads" and "highways."

Kocherhans draws our attention to the great height of the Andes and cites the words of the Book of Mormon: "Many places which are now called valleys which shall become mountains, whose height is great. And many highways shall be broken up" (Helaman 12:23–24).

He lists the following heights of some of the tallest peaks in the Andes:

Santa Marta	19,309 ft.
Chita	17,589 ft.
Tolima	18,436 ft.
Huila	18,700 ft.
Cotopaxi	19,498 ft.
Chimborazo	20,702 ft.
Huascaran	22,180 ft.
Vilcanota	20,644 ft.
Misti	19,200 ft.
Sajama	21,320 ft.
Llullaillaco	22,145 ft.
Ojos del Salado	22,405 ft.
Mercedario	21,810 ft.
Aconcagua	23,080 ft.
Tupungato	21,810 ft.
Malpu	17,388 ft. [28]

There are many other towering peaks in the Andes, such as Mount Illimani in Bolivia that towers 21,184 feet above sea level. Cobo writes of the Inca highways:

The Incas had two royal roads constructed that ran the length of their kingdom from the province of Quito [Ecuador] to the Kingdom of Chile, which is nine hundred leagues (2,500 miles), one along the plains and seacoast and the other inland through the provinces of the sierra. In some places, it was thirty leagues from the coast, in others fifty or sixty, more or less, according to the lay of the land. Apart from these roads, which ran together from one end of the kingdom to the other like parallel lines, there were in different places four to six other transverse roads going from one side to the other; these cut across the

Starting construction on a traditional Inca bridge.

two main roads already mentioned. The length of these transverse roads was equal to the width of the Peruvian Empire. The most important of these ran through the city of Cuzco, crossing the long road of the sierra [the one running through the high Andes][29]

Hammond Innes explains that the Inca roads included "pack animal stairways [that] climbed as high as 15,600 feet," and suspension bridges that utilized "rope cables, some as thick as a man's body slung the roads across deep river gorges."[30] McIntyre writes that he discovered an Inca bridge still being maintained in our day:

That marvelous "Bridge of San Luis Rey" collapsed about 1890 after five centuries of heavy usage.

Within a week (we) were jumping with joy on the brink of the upper Apurimac gorge, our shouts echoing from the opposite cliff. We had found the chaca still hanging! Three hundred feet below us, swaying over a deep green pool, it gleamed like Inca gold. Downstream the voices of the Great Speaker, the Apurimac [river], warned of rapids beyond a dark defile.

We clawed down the precipice to approach the span, which hung 60 feet above the river.

Suddenly a voice cautioned. "Don't cross! The bridge is dying!" It was our first meeting with Luis Choqueneira.

He told us: "I am one of the chaca camayocs [keepers of the bridge]. My people feel sad about abandoning the keshwa chaca for a new steel bridge upstream. So we're going to rebuild it when the New Year comes, just as we have done every year since Tupa Inca ordered our ancestors to do so."[31]

In all, some 22,000 feet of hand-spun rope go into reconstruction of the span, which sways 60 feet above the river.[32]

Cieza de León reported that the Inca bridge at Vilcas had a span of 166 pasos (approximately 400 feet).[33]

Maintained along the entire highway system were royal lodgings and storehouses to facilitate the travel of the nobles. There were also the huts of the famous chasques, (meaning receivers of messages) every quarter of a league (.65 miles). Until I was a missionary in Peru and learned of the tradition of the message runners, I wondered how the Nephites were able to communicate so speedily. For example, King Benjamin asked to have all the people in the land, both the people of Zarahemla and the people of Mosiah, be brought together. The very next morning the people had already gathered to the temple (Mosiah 1:10,

2:1–2). The chasque network explains such phenomena. Pulitzer Prize winning science reporter Gareth Cook notes, "They [Incas] even put together a kind of Bronze Age Internet, a system of messenger posts along the major roads. In one day, Incan runners amped on coca leaves could relay news some 150 miles down the network."[34] Cobo describes the incredible casque network of roads and runners:

> In each one of these huts two Indians always resided, and therefore, in every pair located together at intervals stated above (.65 mile), four men were stationed. They performed the job of runners and messengers, who with incomparable speed carried the orders and commandments of the Inca to the governors and caciques of the whole kingdom, and the runners brought the news that was sent to the Inca at his court or wherever he was located. Therefore, in a very brief time the Inca knew what was happening in all of his states and word was spread there of all that he ordered.[35]

These chasques ran with such speed that in ten or twelve days the Inca had an answer in Cuzco from the orders that he sent to Quito, even though these two cities are four hundred leagues (approximately 1,040 miles) apart, and in one day, twenty-four hours, it was normal for a message to travel fifty leagues (approximately 130 miles).

The Incas also used the runners and messengers when they felt like having something especially delicious that needed to be brought from far away; if, while he was in Cuzco, the Inca felt a desire to some fresh fish from the sea, his order was acted upon with such speed that, although that city was over seventy leagues (180 miles) from the sea [and at an altitude of over 10,500 feet], the fish was brought to him very fresh in less than two days. . . . [in comparison] letters were carried from this city of Lima to the city of Cuzco in three days over one hundred and forty leagues (460 miles) of very bad road over very broken sierras. Now it takes the Spanish mail by horse twelve to thirteen days to do the same.[36]

The chronicler Montesinos wrote that the chasquis originally carried written messages, not the quipos.[37]

THE FOUR QUARTERS OF THE ANDES WORLD

Actually, no civilization ever called itself "The Inca Empire." When the Spaniards arrived in Peru, they found a people who called themselves "Incas" and who lived in a kingdom called Tahuantinsuyu, meaning "the four united quarters."

At the heart of the land of Tahuantinsuyu was its central temple in the capital of Cuzco. The division of the land into quarters was not made by the "later" Incas, but by their earliest ancestors. From its mythical beginnings their kingdom had been divided into four quarters: Chinchaysuyu, Antisuyu, Collasuyu and Contisuyu.

Brian Bauer describes the geography of Tahauntinsuyu:

> Both of the Cuzco moieties were, in turn, further divided in half. These four quarters, or suyus (divisions), radiated

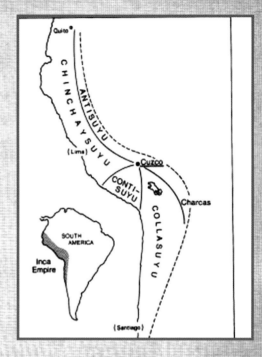

from the Coricancha [Cuzco main temple] as the center of Inca world. . . . The indigenous name for the Inca Empire, Tawantinsuyu (the four parts together), was derived from the four great spatial divisions that together made up the realm. The Hanansaya quarters [upper or the land northward], consisting of the regions of the northwest, and northeast of Cuzco, were called Chinchaysuyu and Antisuyu respectively. The Hurinsaya division included the two southern quarters [lower or land southward]: Collasuyu to the southeast and Contisuyu to the southwest. The Inca Empire was seen as the sum of these four parts, and for the Inca, the Coricancha [main temple] marked its centers.[38]

Likewise, the Nephites divided their land along an east-to-west axis. The Book of Alma provides a description of the land ruled over by the chief Lamanite king. His lands were bordered by a narrow strip of wilderness, "which ran from the sea east even to the sea west" (Alma 22:27). We learn later that there was another line that separated Bountiful (land southward) and the land Desolation (the land northward) (Alma 22:31–32). The Book of Mormon people did not stop there, they divided the land again into quarters (Alma 43:26, 51:10, 56:1, 58:30, 58:35; Ether 14:15) during Nephite period. If the Nephites divided their land at its founding, then Nephi undoubtedly oversaw the subdivision. Urton notes of the Peruvian legends:

> One myth that does account for the division of the Inca world into four quarters at the beginning of time is provided by Garcilaso de la Vega in his work, Commentarios Reales de los Incas. Garcilaso says that after the waters of the deluge receded, a man (unnamed in this myth [Nephi]) appeared at Tiahuanaco [city at Lake Titicaca]. This man was so powerful that he divided the land into four parts, giving each quarter to one of four kings. Manco Capac [candidate for Nephi] received the northern quarter, Colla the southern [Laman?], Tocay the eastern [Jacob?], and Pinahua the western [Joseph?].[39]

The reasons why Lemuel and Sam were not provided lands will be discussed later.

THE CITY OF NEPHI (CUZCO, THE NAVEL OF THE WORLD)

Historically, the Hebrews believed the center point of their world was the temple in Jerusalem. The temple was the holy shrine that they knelt toward when they prayed. The Inca universe evolved around their temple at Coricancha in Cuzco, which their legendary first king Manco Capac first constructed. The Inca temple was the center point of an elaborate network of lines that turned the Andes into a massive solar calendar. The Book of Mormon records that the first Nephite king, Nephi son of Lehi, constructed a temple, which undoubtedly served as the central point of reference for his kingdom. In chapter 6 a full discussion of why Cuzco is the best candidate for the city of Nephi will be provided. For now, we will assume that the original name for the Inca capital of Cuzco was the city of Nephi.

THE LAND OF NEPHI (THE INCA ANTISUYU QUARTER)

The northeast flank of the Inca Empire was the quarter they called Antisuyu, or as Sjodahl explains, the quarter of the mountains. In fact, Antisuyu was almost entirely composed of the great Cordillera Oriental, the tallest mountains of the Andes. The land of Nephi was also a mountainous land. Alma camped at the waters of Mormon, which was in the land of Nephi. We read in the Book of Mosiah that there was "a place which was called Mormon, having received its name from the king, being in the borders [mountains] of the land having been infested, at times or seasons, by wild beasts. Now, there was in Mormon a fountain of pure water, there being near the water a thicket of small trees" (Mosiah 18:4). This micro description of a place in the land of Nephi reminds me of the mountains, panthers, and tropical forest that surround Machu Picchu. We are later told in the sacred account that idle Lamanites inhabited the borders (mountains) of Nephi (Alma 22:28).

The central city of Cuzco was part of the Antisuyu quarter. As noted, this quarter was originally given to the first Inca king Manco Capac, the man who founded Cuzco and built the Inca's first temple in the city. The natural comparison here would have the Inca northeast quarter, Antisuyu, being a candidate for the land of Nephi.

THE LAND SOUTHWARD (SOUTHEAST INCA QUARTER OF COLLASUYU)

Collasuyu's northern boundary was believed to have passed through the La Raya pass between Cuzco and Lake Titicaca and continue as far south as Argentina and Chile. It was by far the largest of the four quarters of Tahuantinsuyu, but the least understood. The Inca myths have very little to say about the southern quarter. From a Book of Mormon viewpoint, this would be expected since the book was written by the Nephites in the land Northward. If we assume that the ancestors of the Quechua-speaking Indians were associated with the extinct Nephites then we know that they would have had very little interaction with their Lamanite (Aymara) enemies in the southern quarter (Alma 22:29, 33). The lack of knowledge about the southern quarter, suggests that the ancient Incas could somehow have been associated with the Nephites and had little interaction with the Lamanites who lived in the southern part of the land (Alma 16:6, 22:23, 31:3). Urton explains:

Lake Titicaca, with 22,000 foot-tall mountains on its east side.

Proposed Southeast Quarter,
Northeast Area Zarahemla
Adapted from Chávez 1992 and
Majica and Klarich.

The origin myths we have discussed thus far pay curiously little attention to what would become the major geographic, demographic and political division defining the Inca world, that of Tahuantinsuys, "the four united quarters." An especially puzzling omission in the origin myths concerns the quadrant of Collasuyu. This quarter of the empire, which included the territory south-east of Cusco, extended not only from the capital to Lake Titicaca but also much farther to the south-east, into central and southern Bolivia and on the north-west Argentina. Now, if the work of creating proceeded from Lake Titicaca to the north-west [from Titicaca to the city of Nephi], what were the origins of the peoples of Collasuyu, to the south-east of Lake Titicaca [the Lamanites]? Were the powerful nations and confederation of nations of Bolivia (the Qara Qara and Charka, for example) not created at the same time and in the same manner as those of the other three quarters of Tahuantinsuyu? There is no body of myths that would settle our unease about the Inca disregard of this portion of the empire.[40]

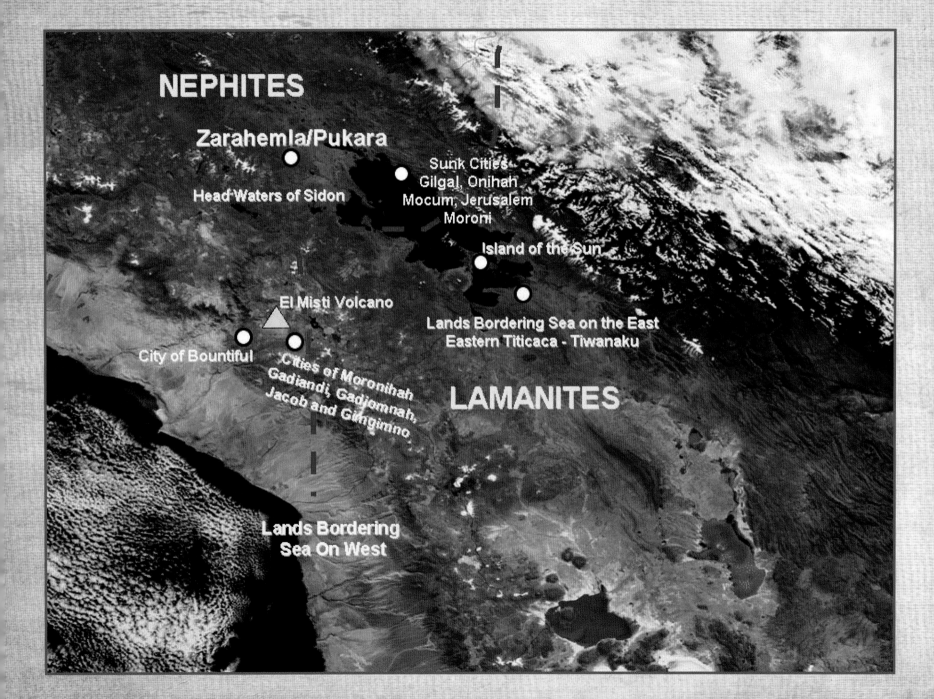

NEPHITES

Zarahemla/Pukara

Head Waters of Sidon

Sunk Cities
Gilgal, Onihah
Mocum, Jerusalem
Moroni

Island of the Sun

El Misti Volcano

Lands Bordering Sea on the East
Eastern Titicaca - Tiwanaku

City of Bountiful

Cities of Moronihah
Gadiandi, Gadiomnah,
Jacob and Gimgimno

LAMANITES

Lands Bordering
Sea On West

There was one exception to the lack of knowledge about the southern quarter. The Incas knew a great deal about the very northern part of the southern quarter or the Lake Titicaca basin. Lake Titicaca was the sacred area where they believe their god, Viracocha, created the world. The Book of Mormon also contains a great deal of information about the northern part of the land southward. It was the land called Zarahemla. Perhaps more information is provided about this small area than any other land mentioned in the Book of Mormon. Chapter 7 will cover the archaeological evidences for the land and city of Zarahemla having been located in the northwest side of Titicaca Basin of the Altiplano. For now, we will assume that the city of Zarahemla was located at the ruins of the city of Pukara along the winding banks of the Pukara River, our candidate for the River Sidon.

Briefly stated, the ruins at Pukara are a likely candidate for Zarahemla for these four reasons: First, it was populated by the Quechua-speaking people who were disliked by the Aymara whose capital was on the southeast side of the lake. This fits the Book of Mormon description of the Nephites and Lamanites being divided by a strip of wilderness that stretches between two seas. On the northwest side of the sea were the people of Pukara, and the southeast side were their enemies, the tribes of the early Tiwanaku civilization (Chiripa).

Second, the city of Pukara came in prominence at roughly 200 BC, the same time as the arrival of Mosiah at Zarahemla.

Third, Pukara is south of Cuzco, which is how Zarahemla was situated in reference to the City of Nephi. Mosiah and his party were led "through the wilderness until they came *down*

into the land which is called the land of Zarahemla" (emphasis added, Omni 1:13). The word for *down* in Semitic languages refers to "south." Quechua follows the same convention, with *up* meaning "north" and *down* meaning "south."[41] Zarahemla being located south of the City of Nephi is confirmed in the Book of Helaman when Nephi, son of Helaman, goes to the land of Nephi to preach the gospel to the Lamanites (Helaman 5:20), and later returns to Zarahemla "from the land northward" (Helaman 7:1).

Fourth, the original land of Zarahemla (Pukara) was bordered by the sea on the west (Pacific) and by the sea on the east (Titicaca). The map on the opposite page is based on a map by University of California at Santa Barbara archaeologist Elizabeth Klarich, which shows the lands of the Pukara Empire starting at Titicaca and running to the Pacific.

Just as the ancient Inca quarter of Collasuyu was divided into separate areas of two feuding enemies—the Quechua versus the Aymara people—the Book of Mormon's southern quarter was divided between two enemies. The Lamanite king we know as the father of Lamoni lived at the same time as the Pukara Empire. The Book of Mormon states that the Lamanites during his reign inhabited the lands southward and describes how Zarahemla was separated from the lands he controlled:

> The king sent a proclamation throughout all the land, amongst his people who were in all this land, who were in all the regions round about, which was *bordering even to the sea, on the east and on the west*, and which was divided from the land of Zarahemla by a *narrow strip* of wilderness, which ran from the

> *sea east even to the sea west, and round about on the borders* [mountains] *of the seashore, and the borders of the wilderness* which was on the north by the land of Zarahemla, through the *borders* [mountains] *of Manti, by the head of the Sidon,* running the *east towards the west*—and thus were the Lamanites and Nephites divided. (Alma 22:27; emphasis added)

The strip of wilderness that separated the enemies ran from east to west, which was true of the border that separated the Quechua Pukara and Aymara people. The boundary went from the sea on the East (Lake Titicaca) to the sea on the west (Pacific), which means that both the Lamanites and Nephites controlled lands on the east sea (Lake Titicaca) and the west sea (Pacific Ocean).

The Nephite-controlled lands and the Lamanite lands were separated by a "narrow strip of wilderness" (desert land). There is a track of arid land that lies between Lake Titicaca and Pacific Ocean that fits the label of a narrow strip of wilderness. The distance between the two bodies of water at today's Peru-Chile boarder is a mere 145 miles. This would be roughly the same width as the Isthmus of Tehuantepec in Mesoamerica, that some suppose is the Book of Mormon's "narrow neck of land." However, the Isthmus of Tehuantepec bridges north and south seas, not east and west bodies of water.

From Lake Titicaca a narrow canyon runs west through the arid mountains down to the Moquequa Valley just north of today's Chilean border. This valley passes through a mountain range that runs as far north as Pukara and the head waters of the Pukara river. Here we have likely candidates for the mountains of Manti and

Huallamarca temple, near downtown Lima: Is this what remains of the land of Desolation?.

the river Sidon. Between the mountains and the seashore is the wide coastal plain that is part of a desert (wilderness). Thus, not only does the Book of Mormon's land southward match the general topography of the Inca's Collasuyu quarter, the southernmost quarter of ancient Peru also matches an important Book of Mormon prerequisite, "a narrow strip of wilderness" between a sea on the east and a sea on the west.

THE LAND NORTHWARD (INCA NORTHWEST QUARTER OF CHINCHASUYU)

As described in chapter 1, the only area in all the Western Hemisphere that had large cities, metal working, and the religion of a white god in the time period of the early Jaredites was the civilization located along the shoreline one hundred and twenty miles north of present-day Lima. The ruins of its ancient cities are found in the region called Norte Chico. In the Book of Omni, we learn that the land of the Jaredites was in the area the Nephites knew as the "land northward" (Omni 1:22). It seems somewhat coincidental that the name of this area today still incorporates the term *norte* (north). Being on the shoreline, and in the northern half of the Inca world, it is safe to match the Book of Mormon "Land Northward" to the Inca quarter called Chinchasuyu that started at Pachamaca, some twenty-five miles south of Lima and continued north along the coast to Ecuador.

LAND OF DESOLATION

The southern end of the Book of Mormon "land northward" was called "the land of Desolation," not because of a lack of vegetation, but because when the Mulekites landed there they found it was full of the bones of dead Jaredites. "It being so far northward that it came into the land which had been peopled and been destroyed" (Alma 22:30). The Land of Desolation was on the western seashore, being the place where the Mulekites landed and near the place from which Hagoth set sail for Polynesia (Alma 63:5). Furthermore, Desolation bordered with the land Bountiful to its south (Alma 22:30). As noted in chapter 2, the Incas called the shoreline just north of Lima (Rimac Valley) to Pachamaca on the south of Lima the land of the people of Desolation.[42] The Inca land of Desolation has the exact same features as those described in the Book of Mormon: a seashore (Ether 14:12), plains by the seashore (Ether 14:13–15), a wilderness (probably meant desert) (Ether 14:4), and inhabited valleys leading east into mountains that were near the sea (borders; see Ether 13:29, 14:26).

The Inca Land of Desolation included a very important feature—a narrow passage that lead from the northeast quarter to Cuzco and the two southern quarters. The main Inca highway ran through the passage. Sullivan writes:

> This area lies on the western, seaward slopes of the Andean cordillera. Access to this entire region—draining the Cañete, Mala, Lurin, and Rimac rivers, each flowing west to the Pacific—came through a *single high pass*. In both Inca and Spanish colonial times, the *main route from the southern and south central Andes to the central Pacific coast lay through the pass,* where the Inca carved steps into living rock on the flanks of a towering volcanic mountain called Pariacaca.[43] (emphasis added)

It is important to remember that the route between the Nephite main cities to the lands northward and Desolation had to go through a narrow (mountain) pass (Alma 50:30) which we know led to the sea (the Pacific through an east-to-west passage).

The Incas had one more quarter. It started on the Pacific Ocean and ran south from Pachamaca roughly to today's Peru-Chile border. The quarter's eastern and southern borders were the Inca's southeast quarter, Collasuyu. In Book of Mormon geographic terms, the lands south of the Chilean border were the wilderness areas of the land southward, a region occupied by Lamanites. So what was the land south of Desolation, but north of the Chilean border? The description of the domain of the Lamanite king makes it quite clear—it was the land of Bountiful.

THE LAND OF BOUNTIFUL (THE INCA QUARTER OF CONTISUYU)

The Land Bountiful is south of the Land of Desolation (Alma 22:31) and ran from the "east" (eastern quarter of Zarahemla or southwestern Inca quarter of Collasuyu) to the "west sea" (Pacific Ocean) (Alma 22:33). Thus, the final piece of the puzzle, the land Bountiful, fits perfectly into its place as the Inca's quarter of Contisuyu.

SMALL NECK OF LAND

Along the border that separated the land northward from the land southward and the land of Bountiful was a feature referred to as a "small neck of land." This feature is one of the most misunderstood features of Book of Mormon geography.

As a result, there have developed over time many popular misconceptions about its nature and location. As with all the Book of Mormon sites, we have very limited information available to identify it. Readers of the Book of Mormon usually assume that the "narrow neck of land" defines a geographical feature, but a closer examination of its context in the Book of Mormon shows that it describes an important military fortification that must be defended to stop a Lamanite invasion. John Sorenson notes of the narrow neck of land: "Mormon was speaking of a fortified line of defense."[44] The most commonly cited clues to its nature are found in the Book of Alma.

> And now, it was only the distance of *a day and a half's journey*—for a Nephite, on the *line* Bountiful and the land Desolation, from the *east to the west sea*; and thus the land of Nephi and the land of Zarahemla were nearly surrounded by water, there being a *small neck of land between the land northward and the land southward*. And it came to pass that the Nephites had inhabited the land of Bountiful, even from the east [Andes mountains] to the west sea, and thus the Nephites in their wisdom, with their *guards and their armies, had hemmed in the Lamanites on the south,* that thereby they should have no more possession on the north, that they might not overrun the land northward. (Alma 22:32–33, emphasis added)

As important as what is written in this verse is what is not written. The verse does NOT say the "small neck . . . ran from the *east sea* even to the *west sea*," nor does it state that it ran between the east to the west seas (plural). Rather the small neck of land ran from *the east*

to the *west sea*. Clearly, the phrase is only referring to one sea, the Pacific and a place called
the east. A similar phrase would be "the Union
Pacific railroad ran from the East to the Pacific
Ocean."

This is probably a new notion to readers of
the Book of Mormon, but there are two reasons
for believing that there was no sea on the east
side of the small neck of land. First, a Nephite
could cross the "*line*" on the small neck of land
in one and one half days. There is nowhere in the
Western Hemisphere where one can start at the
Pacific Ocean and walk to another separate large
body of water (sea) in one and a half days. For
example, the first westerners to cross the Isthmus of Panama were Vasco Nuñez de Balboa and
his men in 1513. Even with the help of Indian
guides, it took them twenty-three days to cross
the torturous jungle of Panama. The tropical
jungle of the Isthmus of Tehuantepec is 137 miles
across at its narrowest point, a distance of over
four times the width of Panama. Neither of these
Mesoamerican geographic features could have
been the narrow neck of land. (See end notes for
explanation.)[45]

Second, what was being traversed in a day
and a half was not a crossing between two bodies
of water, but a "line" between two lands: "Yea,
to the line which was between the land Bountiful and the land Desolation" (3 Nephi 3:23) and
"it was only the distance of a day and a half's
journey for a Nephite, on the line Bountiful and
the land Desolation" (Alma 22:32). Furthermore,
the Book of Mormon tells us that the Nephites
fortified this line (3 Nephi 3:23, 25). It would
appear then that the "line" was a fortified border
line, a road or a defensive line which must have
had a length of no more than forty to fifty miles.

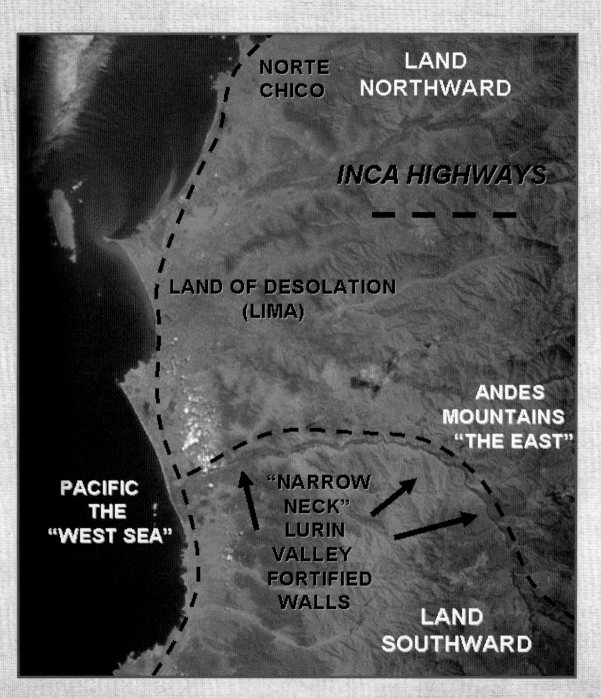

One definition Webster's provides for a "line" is "disposition made to cover extended military positions and presenting a front to the enemy."[46] The Noah Webster's original 1828 American Dictionary of English Language defines a line as "a trench or rampart; an extended work in fortification."[47] Again, it is important to remember that whenever the small neck of land is mentioned in the Book of Mormon, it is specifically in reference to military defenses needed to protect the land northward from the Lamanites in the south.

Two decades prior to my analysis, F. Richard Hauck (MA in anthropology from Brigham Young University and a PhD in anthropology from the University of Utah), formulated the same conclusion in his book, *Deciphering the Geography of the Book of Mormon*. Hauck writes:

> One of the traditional assumptions of Book of Mormon scholars and casual readers alike has been to equate the "narrow neck of land" with an isthmus. Because this assumption has been widely accepted without careful examination, it has complicated and confused the numerous attempts made to identify the setting of the book, for the identification of the proper isthmus is frequently the primary focus of attempts to identify the Book of Mormon geography. Careful analyses of all the references in the text to this topographic feature fails to identify the presences of two seas flanking the transportation corridor. The west sea is clearly evident in the descriptions given in the text, but the east sea is never specifically mentioned as being associated with the narrow corridor. Since two bodies of water flanking a

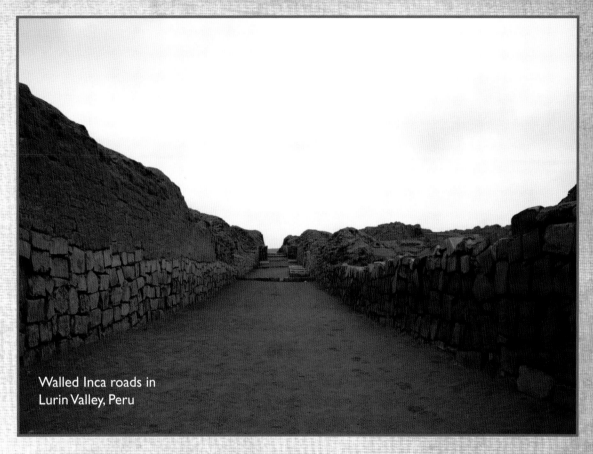

Walled Inca roads in Lurin Valley, Peru

narrow strip of land create an isthmus, the "narrow neck of land" as described in the Book of Mormon does not qualify as an isthmus. The description of a transportation corridor narrowly constricted on the west flank by the sea and on the east flank by a possible mountain barrier does, however, qualify as a land bridge.[48]

The question remains. "What was on the east of the line?" It appears to have been a highly secured mountain pass that was a strategic gateway between the northward and southward lands. We learn in Alma 52 that the narrow entry or neck leading from the land of Bountiful into the land northward was a "pass," presumably a narrow mountain pass through the Andes. Noah Webster's 1828 dictionary defines a pass as "a narrow passage, entrance or avenue; a narrow or difficult place of entrance and exit; as a pass between mountains."[49]

The prophet Mormon described the narrow neck of land as a "passage" that led to the land southward from the land northward

Remains of ancient wall that protected the access northward from the Lurin Valley

(Mormon 2:29). Mormon also described this important military feature as a "pass":

> I did cause my people that they should gather themselves together at the land of Desolation, to a city which was in the borders, by the narrow pass which led into the land southward.
>
> And there we did place our armies, that we might stop the armies of the Lamanites, that they might not get possession of any of our lands; therefore we did fortify against them with all our force. (Mormon 3:5–6)

The narrow pass or neck is described in the Book of Mormon as a "point" (Alma 52:9). Webster's defines a *point* as "a geometric element determined by an ordered set of coordinates; . . . a narrowly localized place having a precisely indicated position; . . . [or] a particular place."[50] A strategic road through a narrow mountain pass between two geopolitical lands would form a strategic military point, which was so vital that this single point would allow the Lamanites to attack in the Nephites from every side. (Alma 52:9). Webster's 1828 American Dictionary includes these definitions of a "point.": "a small

space; as a small point of land," "the place in which anything is directed."[51] Both these definitions could apply to a narrow passage through the mountains.

Hauck notes of the "narrow neck of land:"

> Throughout Nephite history, this strategic west sea land bridge was critical to their defense of the land northward. Nephite protection of the entrance into this corridor began as early as the first century BC based on the information given in Alma 22:32–34. The Nephi defensives strategy repeatedly included the defense of the entrance into this corridor. It was defended from fortifications at Judea and in the land of Bountiful between 67 and 65 BC, and again from 35 to 31 BC. This corridor became the Nephite place of refuge during a war with the Gadianton robbers between AD 17 and 22. Last of all, it was a pertinent defensive asset to the Nephites in their final war, for it helped them block Lamanite access to their resources and population in the land northward during 48 years of bloody warfare.[52]

So what information do we have that can help us find a candidate for the small and narrow pass in Peru?

- It was a track of land that separated the land of Desolation on the north and the land of Bountiful on the south.

- The small neck was a "passage" or "pass" which suggest a mountain passage (Alma 52:9, Mormon 2:21, 3:5–6).

- It started in the "east" and ended at the "west sea."

- From the "east" to the "west sea" took a Nephite one and a half days to cross.

- It included a "line," which in antiquity probably meant a defensive wall. We know that the narrow pass had great military significance, for if the "pass" fell, the Lamanites could possess the land northward. Moroni ordered Teancum to "secure the narrow pass" (Alma 51:30–32, 52:9; Mormon 3:5–6). In a later attack by the Lamanites the same strategic place is simply called "the line which was between the land Bountiful and the land Desolation" (3 Nephi 3:23) with no mention of a narrow neck of land.

- It was a narrow track of land that included a "point" of military significance.

- The Jaredites built a "great city by the narrow neck of land" (Ether 10:20).

Is there in Peru a narrow, yet strategic, transportation corridor that starts at the Pacific and ends in the mountains that possessed these seven characteristics at the time of the Jaredites and Nephites? The answer is yes, and it is not hard to

Strategic Line of Defense— The Narrow Neck of Land

LAND OF DESOLATION

ANDES MOUNTAINS THE "EAST"

INCA HIGHWAY ALONG COAST FROM LAND SOUTHWARD TO LAND NORTHWARD

GREAT WALL DEFENDING WAY TO NORTH

LURIN VALLEY NARROW NECK OF LAND

FORTIFIED MAIN INCA HIGHWAY FROM CUZCO

identify. It is right where we would expect it— the Lurin Valley where it is located exactly between the Incas' land of the people of Desolation and their southeast quarter of Contisuyu [Bountiful]. Here are the reasons why the Lurin Valley qualifies as a candidate for the Book of Mormon's narrow neck or passage of land:

1. The border between the Incas' northwest and southwest quarters was located roughly at the Lurin Valley.

2. As noted above, Sullivan informs us that the area the Incas called the land of the people of desolation had a "single high pass. In both Inca and Spanish colonial times, the main road from the southern [land Bountiful] and south central Andes [City of Nephi and Zarahemla] to the central Pacific coast [Desolation and the land Northward] lay through the pass, where the Incas carved steps into living rock."[53] The pass is found in the Andes at the eastern end of the narrow Lurin Valley that runs from the mountains down to the shoreline. The Lurin valley was extremely important for military reasons. Not only did the passage to Cuzco run through it,

but it was also the junction with the Inca's shoreline highway from the south. The Inca coastal road was along a sixty-mile narrow passage that led from what appears to be the land Bountiful north along the sea. This shoreline passage does not widen until it reaches the Lurin Valley. Losing control of the Lurin valley would have meant that the Lamanites could attack the land northward from both the southeast (the land southward) and the south (land of Bountiful).

3. The narrow neck ran from the "east" to the ocean. The term *east* might seem vague to the reader, but to an Inca it had a very specific meaning. As noted earlier, the entire Inca Empire was divided along a north–south axis, dividing the land into the west and the east. Once the Inca road reached the Andes it would have been in the eastern quarter or Antisuyu (the mountain quarter). In Inca terminology, the narrow neck of land would have run from the mountains of Antisuyu (the east) to the Pacific Ocean.

4. The distance from the Pacific Ocean up the Lurin Valley to the Andes Mountains is approximately forty-five miles—a distance a Nephite could have walked in a day and a half.

5. The Inca highway that ran from the shoreline mouth of the Lurin Valley to the Andes appears to have been fortified. The Spanish chronicler Cieza "describes this section of the highway as being some fifteen feet wide, protected by a strong wall roughly the height of a man."[54] A wall

the height of a man! The wall that ran the entire length of the Lurin Valley from the shoreline to the Andes was, undoubtedly, a line of defense to halt invading armies from the south. What words would a writer in antiquity use to describe a narrow highway with tall walls on both sides, that ran for several miles? Would the words, "neck of land" have been indicative of this manmade feature? Even more descriptive of a "line" is a great wall that was built on the north side of the mouth of the Lurin Valley. Today, the remains of the wall, approximately fifteen feet wide at the base and of equal height, can still be seen. Although only remnants of the wall still exist, it appears to have run from where the protective mountains ended to the seashore, thus, forming one last line of defense. For invading armies from the southeast and south to be able to enter the lands northward, they first had to overrun the wall.

6. The Lurin Valley is a narrow valley; however, on its east end is a very narrow passage or gorge through the mountains that would constitute a military "point" of defense. Cobo described just how narrow the pass was on the road up the Lurin Valley: "The part of this road of the plains that reaches the sierra and broken land was made by hand with much work and skill. If it passed through hillsides with cliffs and slabs of rock, a narrow path, only wide enough for one person leading a llama or sheep, was dug in the boulders itself; and this type of construction did not run very far, but as soon as the boulder or slab

was passed, the road widened again. . . . Along the parts of these hills and slopes where there was some ravine or narrow gorge that cut off the road, even though it was three or four estados deep, rock walls were also made from below and built up to the level of the road."[55] The narrow pass at the Andes end of the Lurin Valley appears to be the place where the Spanish conquistadors feared for their lives as they returned from to Cajamarca. Hernando wrote: "The road was so bad that they [the Inca warriors] could have easily taken us there or at another pass which we found between here and Cajamarca. For we could not use the horses on the roads, not even with skill, and off the roads we could take neither horses nor foot-soldiers."[56] Indeed the junction on the Inca roads in the Lurin valley was a major military position with a key "point" that was easy to defend. The point was the place where the Inca highway passed through a narrow river gorge near the summit of the valley.

7. The final criterion for any candidate for the narrow neck or pass was that it was near a great city that was built by the Jaredites. The city was constructed near the end of their era. Located at the mouth of the Lurin Valley are the ruins of the city Pachamaca. With its massive pyramids, it would appear to meet this criterion. Unfortunately, the earliest dating for Pachamaca is AD 200.[57] Also, Pachamaca was on the fortified highway, not "near" the pass, as described by the Jaredites. However, just 2.5 miles north of Pachamaca, at Huaca Villa Salvador, is the excavation of a more

ancient city. The ruins date to the end of the Early Horizon Period 1000 BC to 250 BC, placing it firmly within the context of the late Jaredites. The ceramics at the site have an influence from the northern Peru coastline, which would be consistent with the Jaredites at Norte Chico having had a satellite city in the important Lurin Valley.[58]

Using the Book of Mormon's criteria for the narrow neck of land, we see that there was an excellent match in ancient Peru. Perhaps some of the confusion surrounding the location of the narrow neck of land is because many people believed it was an isthmus. At first glance this appears to be the case since we are told that the land of Nephi and the land of Zarahemla were nearly surrounded by water (Alma 22:32). A more careful reading indicates that it is the lands of Nephi and Zarahemla that are nearly surrounded by water, not the narrow neck of land. The land of Nephi and the land Zarahemla were large land masses, the borders of which had water along them. It is easy to see how a Peruvian model would fit this description for these two lands. Zarahemla, the Pukara Empire, ruled from the shores of Lake Titicaca to the Pacific Ocean, including the southwest quarter (Bountiful).

The land of Nephi we have matched to the Inca Quarter Antisuyu. The eastern border of Antisuyu was the Amazon basin which the Incas called the north sea. The northward quarter included only the people who lived in the cities that existed along the coastal plain while the quarter of Nephi (Antisuyu—the mountain quarter) took in "all" the mountain people, thus extending the border to within twenty miles of the Pacific.

PROPOSED GEO-POLITICAL MAP OF BOOK OF MORMON LANDS

We can now compare my proposed Peruvian geographic model of the Book of Mormon lands to the so-called "internal geography" of the Book of Mormon developed by scholars at Brigham Young University to try justify a Mesoamerica template. My comments are placed in brackets to explain where I either differ or agree with this interpretation. Quoting John E. Clark's views entitled "Geography" posted on the Maxwell Institute BYU online website:

An Internal Book of Mormon Geography. Numerous attempts have been made to diagram physical and political geographies depicting features mentioned in the text, but this requires many additions and is difficult to accomplish without making approximate relationships appear precise (Sorenson, 1991). The description presented below of the size and configuration of Book of Mormon lands and the locations of settlements within it summarizes the least ambiguous evidence.

Book of Mormon lands were longer from north to south than from east to west [correct]. They consisted of two land masses connected by an isthmus ("a narrow neck of land") flanked by a "sea east" and a "sea west" (Alma 22:27, 32). [incorrect.; the Book of Mormon states that the "narrow strip of wilderness" not the "narrow neck of land" separated two seas. The narrow neck of land ran from the "east" (mountains) to the "sea west"]. The Jaredite narrative took place entirely in the land northward (Omni 1:22; Ether 10:21), but details are insufficient to place their cities relative to one another [incorrect; the Book of Ether reports at least one early migration of the Jaredites to the land southward, even as far south as Zarahemla (Ether 9:31). We also know that Coriantumr was found in association with Zarahemla. It would also seem likely that over a two-thousand-year history the Jaredites would have extended their settlements far from their original coastal cities in the land northward]. Most of the Nephite narrative, on the other hand, took place in the land southward. [correct]. Travel accounts for the land southward indicate that the Nephites and Lamanites occupied an area that could be traversed north to south by normal travel in perhaps thirty days [this is a strong assumption, but it appears reasonable].

The land southward was divided by a "narrow strip of wilderness" that ran from the "sea east" to the "sea west" (Alma 22:32) [correct]. Nephites occupied the land to the north of this wilderness, and the Lamanites, that to the south [correct; the Nephites were the Quechua-speaking Indians on the north side of Lake Titicaca, and the Lamanites were their Aymara counterparts on the south side of the lake]. Sidon, the only river mentioned by name, ran northward between eastern and western wildernesses from headwaters in the narrow strip of wilderness (Alma 22:29) [incorrect; the headwaters of the river Sidon were to the north of Zarahemla (Alma 22:29), thus the river flowed southward. Also the verse does not state that the river flowed in the "narrow strip of wilderness."] The Sidon probably emptied into the east sea—based on the description of the east wilderness as a rather wide, coastal zone-—but its mouth is nowhere specified [correct; the river Sidon probably emptied into the east sea (The headwaters of the Pukara River are north of the ruins of Pukara, my candidate for Zarahemla). The river runs southward, past Pukara, and finally empties into the east sea, Lake Titicaca].

The relative locations of some important Nephite cities can be inferred from the text. Zarahemla was the Nephite capital in the first century BC. That portion of the land southward occupied by the Nephites was known as the "land of Zarahemla" (Hel. 1:18) [correct]. The city of Nephi, the original Nephite colony, by this time had been occupied by the Lamanites and served at times as one of their capitals for the land south of the narrow wilderness divide (Alma 47:20) [incorrect; verse 20 does not state that the city of Nephi was in the land southward. The city of Nephi was probably north of the land of Zarahemla, for when Mosiah fled the city of Nephi, he went "down" to Zarahemla (Omni 1:14), and when some of the Nephites wanted to return to the city of Nephi from Zarahemla, they traveled "up." In Hebrew and Quechua, *down* implies south and *up* signifies north].

Based upon the migration account of Alma, the distance between the cities of Zarahemla and Nephi can be estimated to be about twenty-two days' travel by a company that includes children and flocks,

mostly through mountainous terrain (cf. Mosiah 23:3, 24:20–25) [roughly the distance between Cuzco (city of Nephi) and Pukara (city of Zarahemla)].

The distance from Zarahemla to the narrow neck was probably less than that between Zarahemla and Nephi [There is no basis in the scriptures for this speculation]. The principal settlement near the narrow neck was the city of Bountiful, located near the east sea (Alma 52:17–23) [Incorrect. Bountiful was located near the narrow neck of land by the west sea; there is no mention of an east sea. Furthermore, Hagoth sailed from near Bountiful and Desolation on the west sea (Alma 63:5)]. This lowland city was of key military importance in controlling access to the land northward from the east-sea side [incorrect, the west sea; Nasca (city of Bountiful) is on a lowland plain about ten miles from the Pacific Ocean].[59]

The few geographic clues we have of the Book of Mormon lands, all clearly fit comfortably into a geopolitical setting that archaeologists have established for a New World region. A Peru model for the Book of Mormon not only fits within a recognized scholastic context for Peru, it also matches the archaeological periods established by scientists. Furthermore, an early-Inca model for the sacred book provides an economic and cultural structure with characteristics similar to what one would expect of the Nephites and Lamanites. It also contains the mineral and animal resources mentioned in the Book of Mormon, and as we shall see in the next chapter, Peru's oral traditions correlate remarkably well with specific accounts recorded on the golden plates.

Matthew Potter stands where the conquistadors feared an attack—the dangerous passage on the Inca highway, through the narrow Lurin Valley.

THE JOURNEYINGS OF NEPHI

V

Ah Viracocha, ticci capac
The sun, the moon,
The day, the night,
The seasons of ripening and rain

They are not free,
From Thee they take their order,
Thee they obey.

PRAYER OF
MANCO CAPAC TO
THE WHITE GOD

I traveled nearly 75,000 miles through the Arabian outback retracing Lehi's trail. The wilderness terrain was so harsh that, at times, I wondered how Lehi's family could have survived such a saga. The Arabian Desert is one of the most hellish environments on earth. As I retraced the prophet's footsteps, I often wondered, "Why would the Lord have made Lehi's family suffer eight years in such a land?" There were shorter routes to the Americas, so why Arabia? Hot and dry, without rainfall for months. The only farms to be found near the trail were at the small oases and mountain washes.

Surprisingly, the Arabian scenery was familiar to me. I had once lived in a similar land. It was during my mission when I served along the coastal plain of Peru, the driest of all deserts. In places along the Chilean and Peruvian coast it has not rained for over one hundred years. The cold Humboldt Current runs near the shoreline while the sun bakes the land near the Pacific. Because of the temperature differential, the moisture is sucked away from the thirsty shoreline.

Knowing that the Prophet Joseph Smith taught that Nephi's ship landed in Chile[1] in the sixth century BC, I am amazed at how similar the landscape of Arabia, the place where the ship embarked, compares to the shoreline of Chile and neighboring Peru. Comparing the two deserts, we can now start to understand why the Lord sent Lehi through Arabia. Before setting foot in the promised land, Nephi had to know how to survive among foreign people in an arid and hostile landscape. After leading his family through Arabia (Mosiah 10:13), Nephi had all the desert savvy and leadership skills he would need to survive along the barren shoreline of South America. He knew how to dig for water in dry streambeds, grow food in very arid conditions, how to elicit the friendship and aid of nomadic people, lead caravans of camels, and most important—to rely on the Lord. By the time Nephi crossed Arabia, built a large sailing ship, and crossed the Pacific, he was well prepared to rule a promised land. Not only was the young leader able to successfully establish a beachhead in the

Chilean desert, it appears that a short time later he led his people "into the wilderness" to southern Peru (1 Nephi 19:1). So who was waiting to greet Lehi's family when they arrived in South America?

A LOCALIZED AND ELITIST PARADIGM FOR THE NEPHITES IN PERU

An often debated Book of Mormon question is whether or not Nephi encountered native tribes when he arrived in the New World. The archaeological and geographic storyline of the Americas provides ample evidence that it was next to impossible for the Nephites to have occupied the entire Western Hemisphere or any localized part of it without having shared the land and bloodlines with prior settlers.[2] The most recent genetic and archaeological evidence indicates that Native American peoples descended from the approximately 1,000 to 5,000 Asians who entered the Americas from the Bering Strait between 10,000 and 11,000 years ago.[3]

The assumption that the Nephites and Lamanites interacted with native tribes is referred to as the "Local Colonization Hypothesis" or sometimes called the "Limited Geographic Hypothesis," with the word "local" proposing that the land of the Book of Mormon people was limited to a particular region of the Americas and not the land mass of both continents. The LDS Church authorities appear to have endorsed the Limited Colonization Hypothesis when they announced in November 2007 that the introduction to the Book of Mormon would be changed from "they (the Lamanites) are the principal ancestors of the American Indians" to the Lamanites are "among the ancestors of the American Indians."[4]

Limiting the Nephites and Lamanites to a specific region carries with it some important implications. Michael Whiting of Harvard University writes:

The local colonization hypothesis is more limited in scope, includes many more complicating factors from a genetic perspective, is much more difficult to investigate by way of DNA evidence and, in my view and that of Book of Mormon scholars, is a more accurate interpretation of the Lamanite lineage history. This hypothesis suggests that when the three colonizing parties came to the New World, the land was already occupied in whole or in part by people of an unknown genetic heritage. Thus the colonizers were not entirely isolated from genetic input from other individuals who were living there or who would arrive during or after the colonization period. The hypothesis presumes that there was gene flow between the colonizers and the prior inhabitants of the land, mixing the genetic signal that may have been originally present in the colonizers. It recognizes that by the time the Book of Mormon account ends, there had been such a mixing of genetic information that there was likely no clear genetic distinction between Nephites, Lamanites, and other inhabitants of the continent. This distinction was further blurred by the time period from when the Book of Mormon ends until now, during which there was an influx of genes from multiple genetic sources. Moreover, the hypothesis suggests that the Nephite-Lamanite lineage occupied a limited geographic range. This would make the unique Middle Eastern genetic signature, if it existed in the colonizers at all, more susceptible to being swamped out with genetic information from other sources.[5]

Decades earlier Hugh Nibley wrote that "The ethnological picture becomes very complicated as we learn that the real foundations of the New World civilization were not laid by Lehi's people at all, . . . numerous survivors of archaic hunting cultures of Asiatic origin that had thousands of years before crossed the North Pacific."[6] Since I served a mission in Bolivia and Peru in 1969–1971, well before DNA analysis was possible, I have held to a version of the local colonization hypothesis My missionary assignments included La Paz, Bolivia; Juliaca on the Peruvian Altiplano; Cuzco, in Peru, the capital of the Inca Empire; and Lima and Trujillo on Peru's arid coastal plain. I also had an assignment that required me to visit Northern Chile. Early on, I became convinced that the Lamanites integrated quickly into the pre-existing tribes of inhabitants of Peru, and that the Nephites did so to a somewhat lesser degree. The words of Jacob seem to support this hypothesis:

"I shall call *them* Lamanites that seek to destroy the people of Nephi, and *those who are friendly to Nephi*, I shall call Nephites." (emphasis added, Jacob 1:14). Who are "them"? A rather vague reference if Jacob is describing his brothers, sisters, nieces, and nephews. And who are "those friendly to Nephi"? It seems only logical that these would have been native people who had allied themselves to the impressive young leader named Nephi. However, Nephi didn't just integrate with a native populace—he became their beloved king (Jacob 1:10).

A small group of Inca nobility ruled over
subjects numbering in the millions.

The question begs to be answered, "How
could Nephi with his small family group have
become king over a multitude of native people?
There are several historical parallel events, including one that took place in Peru. Two thousand
years after Nephi, only one hundred and seventy
Spaniards subjugated the Inca kingdom of Peru, a
nation estimated to have had eight million inhab-
its. The results may have been the same, but the
means used by Nephi and the Spaniards would
have been substantially different.

By the time Lehi reached the promised land,
he was "stricken in years" (1 Nephi 18:17). Nephi
had long since taken over the leadership of the
family while they were in Arabia. Besides Nephi,

Lehi had five other sons, six princes in all when
they landed in the promised land. However, the
two youngest sons, Jacob and Joseph were born
while Lehi was in Arabia and would have been
less than ten years of age when they arrived in the
Western Hemisphere. The four elder sons were
married men, with their own children as old as
Jacob and Joseph. During the first years the family
was in the promised land, the four older brothers would have been the principle elders of the
family of Lehi. These four brothers would have
been the men who represented the Lehites when
they confronted native tribes. However, one son,
the youngest was clearly the ruler. His oldest
brother, the jealous and violent Laman, had tried
to kill Nephi on several occasions.

Understanding the Lehites' leadership structure presents a fascinating question, "Were
Laman, Lemuel, Sam, and
Nephi the legendary first
Incas?" The Peruvians believe,
the first Incas were white men
who arrived by sea.[7] In Betanzos' recounting of the Inca
oral traditions, instead of the
Viracochas coming from the
sea, he has them coming forth
from a cave. Coming out of the
hold of a ship, could be likened
unto coming from a cave. He
records, "four men came out
with their wives in the following order. The first one, Ayar
Cache [Laman the oldest] came
out with his wife, who was
named Mama Guaco. After
him another, called Ayar Oche
[Uchu, Lemuel], came out and

after him his wife, named Cura. After this one,
another came out, called Ayra Auca [Sam], with
his wife, named Ragua Ocollo (Mama Ocollo).
After these, came another called Ayar Manco,
whom they later called Manco Capac [Nephi]
which means King Manco. After him came his
wife, whom they called Mama Ocollo."[8]

As we follow the story of the four founding
brothers, it will become highly plausible that they
were Laman (Cache), Lemuel (Oche or Uchu),
Sam (Auca) and Nephi (Manco). For now, it is
interesting to note that both Manco Capac and
Nephi were the fourth sons of their father, and
each became the king over their elder brothers.
Furthermore we note that they are reported to
have come out of the cave with their family in the
order of their age, which is the same manner in
which Lehi's sons entered Nephi's ship (1 Nephi

18:6). A quick overview of Peruvian lore shows that the eldest Cache (Laman) was violent and strong, so his brothers eventually found a way to separate themselves from him,[9] and Oche (Lemuel) died approximately the same time as the separation from Cache (Laman). That leaves only Manco (Nephi) and Auca (Sam) having reached Cuzco Valley (land of Nephi). The Inca Auca (Sam) was married but never had children,[10] which would explain why there were no "Samites" mentioned in the Book of Mormon (Jacob 1:13).

According to Peruvian mythology, the four brothers were called Viracochas, because they had a white skin. Just as one would expect if four taller Hebrews (1 Nephi 4:31) landed among a shorter native people of Asian origin, the four brothers seemed to have made a big impression on the local population. The dress of the Lehites would also have made an impression. We know that Lehi had been a wealthy man in Jerusalem, and even though they suffered hardships in the wilderness, they still brought into the desert the trappings of their upper-class lifestyle. The story of the appearance of the four original Viracochas and their wives to a primitive people is consistent with what one would anticipate: Betanzos recorded:

> From inside the cave [hold of the ship] they brought out their handsome golden halberds. The men came out dressed in garments of fine wool woven with gold. On their necks they brought out some bags, also of elaborately woven wool; in these bags they carried sinewed slings. The women also came out dressed very richly in cloaks and sashes that they call chumbis, well woven with gold and

with fine gold fasteners, large pins about two palms long, which they call topos. These women also brought the ware with which they would serve and cook for their husbands; this included pots and small jars and plates and bowls and drinking tumblers all of fine gold.[11]

Lehi had "left gold and silver, and all manner of riches" (1 Nephi 4:16) and had these in an "exceeding great" quantity (1 Nephi 4:25). However, the family would still have to have taken their clothes and fancy cooking pots, plates, bowls and drinking tumblers. So impressed were the Indians with the gold utensils of the first Viracochas, that the Inca nobles wore large gold spoons to distinguish themselves from the commoners.

Undoubtedly, Nephi and his brothers towered over the Paleo-Indians of Peru. The Spanish conquistadors reported that the Inca nobility were tall people like themselves. Unlike the architecture of the Mayans, whose doorways and ceilings were of nearly pigmy-scale proportions, the Inca buildings were constructed for tall people. While exploring Lake Titicaca, our five-foot-tall Aymara Indian guide told my son and me that his people had been "conquered by the Incas who were tall like you." I am five feet ten inches tall, while my son, Matthew is six foot two inches tall.

The Spanish chroniclers wrote that the four white brothers and their wives announced to the native Paleo-Indians in Peru: "We are born strong and wise, and with the people who will here join us, we shall be powerful. We will go forth from this place to seek fertile lands and when we find them we will subjugate the people and take the lands, making war on all those who do not receive us as their lords."[12]

HOW THE NEPHITES BECAME THE RULERS

The Bible recounts the hardships and wars that Moses and the children of Israel faced in acquiring their promised land of Palestine. The Nephites must have experienced similar difficulties, yet the Book of Mormon does not describe the Nephites having faced conflicts outside their own internal feuds. However, it must be remembered that 1) the literary convention of the day was to not mention the lesser nobles and commoners; thus as expected the Book of Mormon only just slightly discusses women, children, or Ishmael's descendents, let alone any interaction with native people.[13] Second, the small plates were exclusively dedicated to religious matters and would not have included an account of the wars and civil affairs the Nephites had with native tribes (Jacob 1:3–4).

The long history of the Americas is that of docile populations that were swept over by the next wave of aggressive invaders from the north. The Peruvian invasion that we know the most about was by Francisco Pizarro and his small band of conquistadors. The bold Spaniards conquered the highly organized and well-armed soldiers of the late Inca Empire.

In his popular book *Guns, Germs,*

and Steel, Jared Diamond describes how more technically advanced civilizations are able to dominate significantly larger societies who lack a comparable level of technology. The accounts of the conquistadors provide ample evidence that germs and steel were the key factors that helped the Spaniards defeat the Incas.

However Diamond forgot three other strategic advantages Pizarro utilized to secure his initial victory over the Incas: 1) Pizarro instituted a new religion to replace the native faith. The new faith helped control the Indians by teaching them that they could only acquire salvation through the Spanish priests, 2) he formed alliances with the Peruvian tribes who hated the Incas, and 3) Pizarro manipulated the native royal class, vis-à-vis intermarriages between the Spaniards and the daughters of the Inca nobility.

GERMS

We have no record in the Book of Mormon of plagues that may have been brought to the New World by Lehi's family. All the same, it is a high probability that the silent killers of the Eastern Hemisphere diseases could have killed off many native people, including their ruling elite. This would have opened a power vacuum for Nephi and Laman to fill.

STEEL

Diamond conjectures that steel technology was the key factor in who ruled whom. For example, the hardened copper-plated weapons of the Incas were no match for the steel swords of the Spanish. There is much speculation as to what the exact metal composition was of the steel mentioned in the Book of Mormon. What we do know is that Nephi felt it was imperative that he make swords after the manner of the sword of Laban (5 Nephi 5:14), and that he wield Laban's sword in defense of his people (Jacob 1:10). Indeed wars seem to have played an important role in the rise of Nephi's kingdom (1 Nephi 19:4), as well as in its destruction, since the Lamanites were a numerous and fierce band who used swords, bows, axes, and all manner of weapons (Mormon 6:7).

During the rebellion between two Inca lords just before the arrival of the Spanish, they fought with "helmets, battle-axes, clubs, halberds, macanas, lances, and shields."[14] A macanas was "a sword-shaped double-edge war club made of hardwood."[15] When the Spaniards arrived, an envoy tried to describe the Spanish sword to the Inca king: "The Inca was amazed to hear this and remarked that those long things that cut would

be what was called 'macana' (the Inca wooden sword)."[16] It is interesting that the descendants of the Lamanites and Nephites still used a weapon with the shape and function of a sword, however, it appears that with the demise of the Nephite society and their technology (circa AD 400), the Peruvian's ability to smelt hard metal alloys for weapons was lost. The fact that iron smelting went to the grave with the Nephites, is evidenced by the reaction the first orejón (Inca elite) had when Pizarro gave him an iron axe. Cieza de León wrote that this gift, "strangely pleased him [the Inca deputy], esteeming it more than if they had given him one hundred times more gold than it weighed."[17]

Nephi's sword of Laban must have had a huge impact as a weapon in defending his people and the native tribes that aligned with him. To any

natives confronting Nephi's mighty sword, it must have been a frightening experience. In the hands of a strong man like Nephi, a sword the quality of Laban's would have been unstoppable against primitive clubs and spears. For example, the robbers who tried to steal King Lamoni's sheep made the mistake of raising the clubs against a highly skilled swordsman. Ammon was no superman, but he was the son of the king, and was undoubtedly trained in the military arts. As a prince he would have had a sword of the highest quality. When the band of robbers attacked, Ammon was confident. He possessed a metal sword and the knowledge of how to use it (Alma 17:37–39).

The Spanish had the same advantage against the Incas nearly two thousand years later. The Spanish possessed even stronger metals. As a result, Francisco Pizarro's army of 168 Spaniards butchered an Inca army of 40,000 men. It is estimated that during the first battle six to seven thousand Indians were killed and many more had their arms cut off and suffered other wounds. In contrast, not one Spaniard was killed that day.[18] Diamond studied the battle, and discounted the advantage the Spanish guns and horses gave the conquistadors. He writes. "Far more important [than guns] were the Spaniards' steel swords, lances, and daggers, strong sharp weapons that slaughtered thinly armored Indians. In contrast, Indian blunt clubs, while capable of battering and wounding Spaniards and their horses, rarely succeeded in killing them."[19]

One thing we learn from Nephi's account is that he never backed down. Whether it was to acquire the brass plates from Laban and his private army, or when his rebellious brothers and the sons of Ishmael out numbered him, Nephi always stood tall. He was a large man and was afraid of no one. Nephi had a steel sword and used it in the defense of his people (Jacob 1:10).

Put yourself in the sandals of a native Indian chief in ancient Peru. Nephi enters your village to seek an alliance with your people. It is a primitive lawless age when villages would prey upon each other. The young man is strong and a full foot taller than the largest man in your village. You cannot believe your eyes when you see Nephi's sword, wondering how such a weapon could be made. You have heard stories of how this giant has killed or wounded scores of men who attacked his camp. Nephi tells you that the creator god has made him ruler of the land, promises you peace and prosperity if you will submit to his rule, and even promises to make similar swords for your warriors if they would fight beside him. If I were such a chief, I think I would sign up and do so immediately.

The Lamanites hated the Nephites, who they believed had deceived and robbed their forefathers. Sarmiento gives what appears to be a Lamaniteish view of the four white-skinned brothers who arrived in Peru. His account gives us an insight into the general lack of technology of the native people. From his report, it appears that the Paleo-Indians were unorganized and laid back. They saw the white brothers, especially Manco Capac [Nephi], as an aggressive invader seeking the domination of the easy going natives. Sarmiento writes:

> Thus all eight brethren, four men and four women, consulted together how they could tyrannize other tribes beyond the place where they lived, and they proposed to do this by violence. Considering that most of the natives were ignorant and could easily be made

to believe that which was said to them, particularly if they were addressed with some roughness, rigour, and authority against which they could make neither reply nor resistance, because they are timid by nature, they sent abroad certain fables respecting their origin, that they might be respected and feared.[20]

Although Latter-day Saints hail Nephi's right to rule the Promise Land as a reward for his faithfulness (1 Nephi 2:22), his older brothers passionately and violently resented their younger brother's rule over them and his acting as their "teacher." The archaeological timeline of the Americas suggests that there were many native tribes in Peru in the sixth century BC, and we can assume that many of them would not have shared the same proactive vision as Nephi. These less

industrious people would have preferred aligning themselves with Laman. Those tribes who placed themselves under the umbrella of the Lamanites must have labeled Nephi as an aggressive colonizer bound on eliminating their passive lifestyle. To them, Nephi was a white Viracocha outsider who used his religion to claim he was their rightful ruler.

Furthermore, it would seem likely that the Lamanites became extremely jealous of the Nephites who prospered under Nephi's leadership. Sarmiento continues: "They [Nephites] took the name of Inca, which is the same as lord. They took 'Ccapac' as an additional name because they came out of the window 'Ccapac-tocco,' which means 'rich,' although afterwards they used this term to denote the chief lord over many.[21]

RELIGION

Above all, Nephi was a devoted servant of the Lord and his people. Certainly, he must have been appalled by the blood that was spilled between his people and the Lamanites. I wonder if he ever enjoyed a time of peace during his lifetime? If military means were needed to obtain the right to rule in the promised land, such aggressive measures probably played a minor role. Nephi had a tool much more effective than the sword. It was the word of God. Nephi made great efforts to teach his people true principles for living their lives (2 Nephi 5:19). He "consecrated Jacob and Joseph, that they should be priests and teachers over the *land of my people*" (2 Nephi 5:26; italics added). Here we see that Nephi is using the phrase "land of my people" only thirty years since they left Jerusalem (2 Nephi 5:27), and probably less then twenty years from having arrived in the promised land. He writes of being a king over a land of people, not a small family group. Clearly, Nephi had formed a growing alliance of native tribes.

Sarmiento wrote that the native Peruvians were both afraid of the newcomers and ready to accept their god. "They [Nephi & his brothers] said that they might be respected and feared. They said that they were the sons of Viracocha Pachay-achachi [Christ], the Creator, and that they had come forth out of certain windows to rule the rest of the people. As they [Nephites] were fierce, they made the people believe and fear them, and hold them to be more than men [children of God], even worshipping them as gods. Thus they introduced the religion that suited them."[22]

TRIBAL ALLIANCES

Just as there were people who were "those who are friendly to Nephi" (Jacob 1:14), the statement implies that there were those who were not friendly to Nephi. The young first king of the Nephites was what we would call today a "mover and a shaker." On the one hand, the Inca legends tell us that the Peruvian Indians before the arrival of the four brothers were lazy and primitive. On the other hand, Nephi had his people observe the commandments, keep the judgments and statutes of the law of Moses, sow seeds, raise flocks, make weapons, build building, work wood and metals, and build a large temple (2 Nephi 5:10–16).

In parallel to Nephi, the first Inca king Manco Capac dedicated his life to the service of his people and won their submission through his service to them. Cobo recorded about Manco Capac, "With such good works as the Inca performed for his subjects, they came to like him better each day; and in order to enjoy the same benefits, strangers willingly submitted to his rule. Thus he came

to rule over the whole Valley of Cuzco and the sierras that surround it, and in this district he found many towns. Although they were small at first, they grew steadily as time passed. The Inca [first king] made useful laws to teach his vassals praiseworthy customs and to increase the size and ensure the success of his state."[23]

It is understandable that the majority of the laid-back natives would not have been attracted to Nephi's or Manco Capac's regimen—"I, Nephi, did cause my people to be industrious, and to labor with their hands" (2 Nephi 5:17). Although Laman can best be described as a vile person, willing to kill his own father, he presented an alternative lifestyle to that of the Nephites. He demanded nothing of the Indians that followed him; they could remain in their primitive state while he would provide them swords. Like his younger brother, Laman was probably of large stature and in possession of the same military skills that Nephi displayed to the natives. Under Nephi's leadership, those not willing to improve their lives had a real choice—they could remain pretty much as they were under the passive leadership of Laman, who permitted his people to "become idle people, full of mischief and subtlety" (2 Nephi 5:24).

MANIPULATION OF THE EXISTING NOBILITY VIS-À-VIS INTERMARRIAGE

In accordance with their Hebrew tradition, the first generation of "Nephites" desired to keep their bloodlines pure. Following Nephi's warning to his people not to mix with the Lamanites, Jacob wrote that the Lord declared "that I (the Lord) might raise up unto me a righteous branch from the fruit the loins of Joseph" (Jacob 2:25). However, it is probable that by this time the

Lamanites had already begun intermarriage with native Peruvians of Asian origins. As a result, the descendants of Laman had a darker skin. Nephi was no geneticist, but could see the results and warned his people, for "cursed shall be the seed of him that mixeth with their seed, for they shall be cursed even with the same cursing" (2 Nephi 5:23); that is, a primitive and debased way of living. It appears that as king, Nephi did not permit his own family members to intermarry with the native Peruvians.

By not approving intermarrying with the Lamanite people, the Nephite prophets were not racists (Jacob 3:9), rather they were obeying the law of Moses, to which they were subject at that time. It is interesting that the later Inca nobility, who might have been in part blood descendents of Nephi, appeared to have observed the same law. J. M. Sjodahl wrote of the Incas, "and no one was allowed to go outside his own community or kindred for a wife. In this respect they observed the law of Abraham, Isaac, and Jacob (Genesis 24:4, 28:2)."[24] Betanzos wrote of the Inca emperor that "the Inca who is lord has a principle wife, and she has to be from his family and lineage, one of his sisters or first cousins."[25] Brigham Young noted that Abraham married his half-sister according to the Bible: "They were commanded never to go out of their own family—the family of Abraham—to seek a partner for life. . . . but there is a discrepancy in the record, for it is stated in his own writing that she was the daughter of his older brother."[26] Thus Abraham did not marry his sister, but his niece who was considered a family or tribal sister. Without the option of intermarrying with native people, the first Nephites would have had to practice the same inter-family marriage traditions of their ancestors. Hugh Nibley

this people, which I have led out of the land of Jerusalem" (Jacob 2:32; emphasis added). Were the "fair" skinned Nephite daughters suffering because their husbands were taking on darker-skinned native women?

At the time Jacob condemns the Nephites for polygamy, the Lamanites apparently had ceased the practice (Jacob 3:6), and would by then already have become predominately a native blooded people. Thus, Jacob warns his brethren, "I fear unless ye shall repent of your sins [polygamy] that their skins will be whiter than yours" (Jacob 3:8), Not that Jacob is prejudice to skin color, clearly he is not (Jacob 3:9, nor was Nephi, see 2 Nephi 26:33); he is just stating a genetic and cultural reality of having children born and reared by Paleo-Indian mothers: "Because of your filthiness, bring your children unto destruction, and their sins be heaped upon your heads in the last day" (Jacob 3:10). Despite the warnings, we see that five hundred years later some of the Nephites were freely intermarrying with the Lamanites (Alma 3:19; Helaman 3:16).

The biological, not moral, nature of the Lamanites darker skin appears to be confirmed over five centuries after Nephi's death when the Lamanites, who "united" with the Nephites, became "white like unto the Nephites and their young men and their daughters [the next generation after intermarrying] became exceeding fair, and they were numbered among the Nephites" (3 Nephi 2:14–16). Webster's 1828 Dictionary defines *unite* as "to join; to connect in a near relation or alliance; as, to unite families in marriage."[28]

There was probably a practical reason why the Nephites and Lamanites sought wives and

wrote: "Since it has ever been the custom among the desert people for a man to marry the daughter of his paternal uncle (bint al-ammi) it is hard to avoid the impression that Lehi and Ishmael were related."[27]

After Nephi's death, the Nephites seemed to have openly practiced the intermarrying of native women. The Book of Mormon tells us that "the people of Nephi, under the reign of the second king, began to grow hard in their hearts, and indulged themselves somewhat in wicked practices, such as like unto David of old desiring many wives and concubines, and also Solomon,

his son" (Jacob 1:15). The obvious question is, "If this were only the second generation of Nephites, where did all these extra wives and concubines come from, if not from the indigenous women of Peru?"

Obviously, if the Nephites intermarried with the native tribes, they would also have become a darker-skinned people and would have over time lost the Hebrew genetic markers. Jacob makes one more possible reference to the interracial aspects of this unauthorized practice of polygamy. He quotes the Lord saying, "I will not suffer, saith the Lord of Host, that the cries of the *fair* daughters of

Pre-Inca cloth: provides evidence of
fair-and dark-skinned subjects.

spread across the Andes, with the Inca ruler and his kin taking only secondary wives (no longer principle wives) from the noble houses of vanquished ethnic groups. This strategy continued well into the Colonial Period, with high-ranking Cuzco elites offering their women to the Spaniards in hopes of building alliances with the newly established power in the Andes.[31]

Without alliances with native tribes, it is hard to understand how, within Jacob's own lifetime, (a man who was born in the Arabian wilderness), both the Nephites and Lamanites had become "numerous" in the promised land (Jacob 3:13). Alliances also provided a probable meaning to what Nephi meant when he wrote "my children and those who were called my people" (2 Nephi 5:14).

WHY WOULD NEPHI HAVE WANTED TO RULE OVER OTHER TRIBES

It is fair to ask, "Why would Nephi have wanted to drastically increase the number of people in his kingdom?" There are at least three reasons that stand out. First, he probably believed he was following the instruction of the Lord, to rule over a promised land.

Second, having just arrived and being surrounded by native populations, Nephi faced what anthropologists call the "Big Man" environment of primitive chiefdoms. It was eat or be eaten by the next "Big Man," and as we know, Nephi's stature, leadership skills and faith made him a powerful "Big Man." It is also important to understand that he was on a mission to inherit the land the Lord had promised him, and he needed

concubines from the native tribes. Strategic marriages have long been practiced as a means of building strong political and military alliances. Such bonds could have been a stable means to insure defensive alliances, since the mixed children of these marriages represented the royalty and welfare of both households. For example, Solomon formed political alliances by marrying foreign women. The same practice was used by the Incas some two thousand years later to expand their empire into the largest empire in the Americas. Bauer writes: "The previously independent groups that inhabited the Cuzco region were brought to the emergent Inca state through a variety of mechanisms, including alliance formations, wife exchange amongst chiefs, and outright conquest."[29] Cobo reported of the Incas "these Indians do not value anything as

highly as having many wives."[30] Bauer explains how alliances by marriage played an important part in the building of the later Inca Empire.

Tracing the intermarriage of the elite Inca with women from rival ethnic groups reveals the gradual expansion of Cuzco-based regional alliances over time. Although the earlier Inca rulers [early Nephites] are said to have married the daughters of community leaders from within the Cuzco Basin, and the last Inca emperors considered their full sisters as principal wives, several generations of interethnic regional marriage alliances occurred between Cuzco and other powerful groups of the heartland during the period of state formation. The Inca modified this practice as their empire

to control the local tribes so that they did not turn upon him under the leadership of a rival chief.

Third, Nephi had a dangerous rival, not from the native tribes, but from his own elder brothers, who wanted him dead so they could assume the leadership of the family (2 Nephi 5:1–3). While Nephi was preaching against intermarrying, it appears that Laman, Lemuel, and the sons of Ishmael were busy taking on native wives and having darker-skinned children. By taking wives and concubines of the princesses of native tribes,

Laman and his cohorts were quickly building a large confederacy against the Nephites.

As unorthodox as the local colonization hypothesis might seem, it helps explain the multitudes of people, the wars, and a few other seemingly unexplainable events that took place during the first generation of the Nephites in the promised land. For example, there is the story of a "Nephite" man, yet seemingly a stranger, who comes among the Nephites preaching a false version of the gospel. Jacob wrote that "there

came a man among the people of Nephi, whose name was Sherem" (Jacob 7:1) He led "away many hearts" (Jacob 7:3) and was "learned, that he had a perfect knowledge of the language of the people" (Jacob 7:4).

If Sherem was a member of the Jacob's extended family, why did he have to "come among the people," and why would Jacob simply not have identified to us what Sherem's blood relationship was in the traditional Middle Eastern matter, that is, *Sherem, son of Nephi, son of Lehi*? Furthermore, if this Nephite was a descendent of Lehi, why would Jacob have had to mention that he had learned the language of the people? One possible explanation is that Sherem was a "gentile-Nephite" of native Peruvian stock that had been taught the gospel, but never really understood its basic truths. Sherem was educated, having a perfect knowledge "of the people" (Quechua), but not the private language used within the ethnic Nephite circles, which was reformed Egyptian.

Sherem was a grown man in Jacob's lifetime; he knew the Law of Moses but did not accept the need for a Christ. Sherem's ignorance of the role of the Savior suggests that a member of his own tribe, who likewise had not fully grasped its most fundamental concepts, possibly taught him the gospel. Otherwise, if Sherem had been taught the gospel at the feet of Lehi, Nephi, or Jacob—all great men who knew the Lord personally—such a cleft of understanding would seem unlikely. Try as one may, the story of Sherem makes no sense in the context of the Nephites living in isolation as a small family group and without interaction with other people.

PRIVATE LANGUAGE USED ONLY BY THE ELITE

A well documented fact is that the Nephite elite and the Inca elite spoke a private language not shared by their general populace. Linguistically, this suggests that a small group of people integrated into a larger population, and that a core group retained their original language. This would be consistent with the theory that a small group of Nephites landed in Peru, and subsequently became a small ruling elite who spoke reformed Egyptian, while the masses spoke Quechua. In similar fashion, when the Jews were exiled to Babylonia, they quickly adopted Aramaic, the language of the larger population already living in Babylonia. Only the educated and priestly elite of the Jews retained the ability to speak Hebrew. This is the reason why, at the time of Christ's birth, the Jewish populace no longer spoke Hebrew.[32]

THE NEPHITES—AN ELITIST SOCIETY

As the Nephites became numerous, perhaps to some degree by intermarrying with affiliate tribes, it appears that an elitist core developed. This group avoided marrying outside the family. Nephi was specifically given the right to rule in the promised land (1 Nephi 2:20–22), and his descendents undoubtedly felt they constituted the royal bloodline. This possibly explains why a descendant of Nephi was selected to be the king (Mosiah 25:13) even though the Nephites were outnumbered by the Mulekites in Zarahemla (and certainly the native Indians). It would also explain why six hundred years later, at the Nephites darkest hour, a ten-year-old boy is given the Nephites' sacred record (Mormon 1:2).

At sixteen years of age, the same lad is placed in charge of the army during his nations' last stand. The boy was Mormon, who tells us that he was sober (Mormon 1:2) and large in stature (Mormon 2:1). Being serious and tall does not explain why an inexperienced sixteen-year-old boy would have been entrusted with the physical and spiritual fate of his nation.

However, many historical precedents can be cited of a people rallying to war under the leadership of a youthful crown prince, who had been mentored since birth to command battles and lead a kingdom. Mormon gives us a clue that this might have been what happened in his case. Mormon knew that his abridgement of the plates should only contain vital information, yet twice he goes to the effort of recording his own lineage on the golden plates. Mormon must have felt it important that future readers of the record know that he is both a "pure" (3 Nephi 5:20) descendent of Lehi and that he was specifically "a descendent of Nephi" (Mormon 1:5). His son Moroni followed the same protocol (Mormon 8:13). Of course, the only way Mormon would have known he was a pure-blooded descendent of Nephi, a man who had lived a thousand years before him, is that his family laboriously kept detailed records of who married whom for over a millennium. If this long family record was proof of his right to rule, we can understand why such a record was necessary—both for the family and the stability of the Nephite state.

Having to inform us that he was a "pure" Lehite, Mormon implies that most of the people he ruled were non-pure Lehites. If this scenario holds true, the Nephite society was probably composed of three classes of people, 1) a small royal family of fair-skinned elite, 2) a blended nobility of natives whose ancestors had intermarried with the Nephites to form close alliances, and 3) a darker-skinned populace of the common people. By contrast, the Lamanites were a larger alliance of native tribes who were led, at least for a short period, by the descendents of Laman, but had over the centuries, lost any sense of the Hebrew blood lineage.

Of course, the above description of the Nephite society is conjecture; however, it does compare well with what is known about the pre-Columbian Peruvians. The Incas were divided into three main groups: 1) the Inca Royal Blood elite who had a white-skin[33] and a private language, 2) the non-royal tribes that were loyal to the Incas and who were allowed to live in the Cuzco Valley (these were called the Inca of Privilege, *Inca de Privilegio*);[34] and 3) the common class.[35] The conquistador Pedro Pizarro reported, "The people of this kingdom of Peru were white, a light-brown color, and among the lords and the ladies, they were even more white, like the Spaniards."[36] Juan de Betanzos reports that when Francisco Pizarro captured the Inca Atahualpa, he was accompanied by an Indian woman who was "very white and beautiful." Poma de Ayala described the Inca nobility as white, and in particular, noted that their women were white and very beautiful.[37] Furthermore, he described other Peruvian Indians as being dark-skinned.[38] Indeed, while the Inca nobility was light skinned, the Incas themselves referred to their vassals or servants as *yanakuna,* which literally translates to "blacks."[39]

WHERE DID NEPHI'S SHIP LAND?

As noted previously, Arthur Kocherhans spent forty years trying to identify key Book of Mormon sites, and concluded that Nephi's ship landed at what today is La Serena, Chile, although as we will show, he soon thereafter migrated to Peru.[40] Kocherhans followed four specific branches of reasoning when trying to locate the probable site where Lehi's family disembarked—wind patterns, a climate that could sustain seeds from Jerusalem, a local forest with animals, and a location where "both" gold and silver and copper were found.[41] If we add a "wilderness" (desert) and "borders" (mountains) we have even stronger evidence that Kocherhans' conclusion is accurate. La Serena is located 30 degrees south in Chile, the exact latitude where Joseph Smith Jr. reportedly taught that Nephi's ship landed.[42]

At 30 degrees south in Chile, we find something that is rare along South America's Pacific coast—a sheltered harbor. Without calm waters, the Lehites' landing would have been a shipwreck with probable losses of their provisions (seeds), their tents, and the lives of family . Furthermore, La Serena is located along the most arid shoreline in the world, yet, like a miracle, a river flows out of the Andes and empties into the Pacific in La Serena bay.

A growing body of archaeological evidence states that there was some kind of migration along the shoreline of Chile in the period when Nephi's ship arrived. Archaeologists have found that a distinct change in human development occurred along the Chilean coast during what is called the "Formative Period" from 1000 BC to AD 500.[43] DNA research shows the existence of a genetic shift during the Formative period along the northern Chilean coast, and during this same period the native maritime societies started incorporating farming technologies.[44]

Arthur Kocherhans stands before the calm waters of La Serena harbor, Chile.

In this regard, we know that the first activities Nephi describes his people performing when they arrived in the land of promise is pitching their tents and farming.

Finally, not on the seashore, but as Lehi's family journeyed into the wilderness away from the sea, they discovered a forest with many wild animals (1 Nephi 18:25). A Spanish chronicler describes leaving Peru's Ica Valley, which is similar to La Serena, and traveling up the valley from the barren shoreline and into the Andes: "In this valley there are great forests of algorrobales and many fruit trees . . . deer, doves . . . and other game."[45]

WAS NEPHI THE FIRST INCA KING?

Nephi and Manco Capac were unique, even among great kings. Both were given the right

Wild Vicuña on the Altiplano in Peru.

to rule their people by Viracocha/Jesus Christ. The Lord promised Nephi that he would rule over his brothers (1 Nephi 2:22). Manco Capac was selected king of his people by Viracocha, the bearded white god [Christ]. Sullivan retells Inca lore: "According to a myth recorded by Pachakuti Yamqui, the god Wiraqocha [Viracocha/Christ], just before leaving the 'earth,' via the river Chac-amarca [on waters and ship], met with the father of the yet-unborn Manco Capac and *left for the child his 'staff.'*"[46] A leader's staff is a universal sign of the right to rule.

Lehi undoubtedly ordained Nephi to be the patriarch over his posterity (2 Nephi 1:24–28). It would appear that when he ordained Nephi to lead the family, he gave him his patriarchal blessing at the same time. Evidence of this conjecture is found later in the Book of Mormon when Lehi neared death. At that time, Lehi gave Laman, Lemuel, Joseph, and Jacob blessings, but not Nephi (2 Nephi 1:28–29). A staff is a "badge of office" or keys to preside, and in the case of Manco Capac, they were given to him by God, but through his father.[47]

The Spanish priest Bernadé Cobo wrongfully associates Manco Capac [Nephi] with the sun. Actually, the original Peru icon of the sun represented a god who had the body of a man.[48] However, it is well documented that Viracocha [Christ] was the god who gave the right of leadership to Manco Capac. Cobo wrote that the Inca god "himself spoke like an older brother to Manco Capac in the following way: 'You and your descendants will subjugate many lands and peoples, and you will be great rulers. Always regard me as your father, and pride yourselves on being my sons, without ever forgetting to venerate me as such.'"[49]

We can learn more about Manco Capac from the priest Cobo, who had only disdain for anything Inca including their religion. It seems that the only exception was his admiration for their first king. Although the priest tries to portray Manco Capac as a worshipper of many gods, which Manco Capac was not, Father Cobo describes the noble Inca in these words:

Once the Inca Manco Capac was in command of that small community and republic of barbarians, he treated them in a humane and familiar manner, more like brothers than with the authority of a superior [compare 2 Nephi 1:25–26, 33:1]. He employed all of his ingenuity in striving for the welfare and increase of his subjects [compare 2 Nephi 1:25]. The first thing he did was to divide the population of Cuzco into two groups of Hanan Cuzco and Hurin Cuzco. . . . He puts matters pertaining to religion in order, [compare 2 Nephi 5:10] designating the gods [Manco Capac only worshipped Viracocha] that they had to worship and teaching them the way that these gods [only Viracocha] were to be venerated and invoked, especially his father. . . . [Viracocha/Christ]. He built temples [compare 2 Nephi 5:16] and appointed ministers and priests [compare Jacob 1:18] for the service and rituals of the temples; he established the ceremonies, rituals, and sacrifices with which the gods [Viracocha/Christ] should be venerated . . . [compare 2 Nephi 5:10].
    The king set himself to teach the men all of the tasks that are theirs, such as the work in the fields, how to make ditches from the rivers in order to irrigate, and the proper times for sowing and harvesting their crops [compare 2 Nephi 5:11]. He instructed them in the use of clothes and footwear of the type they used thereafter and the majority still use today. The Coya, or Queen, took care to teach the women to spin and weave wool and cotton, as well as other tasks and occupations of their profession [compare to Mosiah 10:5].
    With such good works as the Inca performed for his subjects, they came to like him better each day; and in order to enjoy the same benefits, strangers willingly submitted to his rule [compare 2 Nephi 5:18]. Thus he came to rule over the whole Valley of Cuzco and the sierras that surround it, and in this district he found many towns. Although they were small at first, they grew steadily as time passed [compare 2 Nephi 5:13]. The Inca made useful laws to teach [compare 1 Nephi 2:22] his vassals praiseworthy customs and to increase the size and ensure the success of his state [compare 2 Nephi 5:13, 17].[50]
    . . . since the Incas felt sure that they all descended from Manco Capac [called themselves Nephites], his body and idol were adored by all of the families and *ayllos* [family tribes, compare 2 Nephi 5:9].[51]

It is presumptuous to compare anyone to the enlightened, brilliant, bold, and most of all faithful Nephi. However, in the Peruvian oral traditions of their first king Manco Capac, we seem to have a serendipitous match. Cobo continues:

The Inca [Manco Capac] took special care to erect a temple. . . . He selected for this a very spacious and prominent site, and on it he started to build the great temple of Coricancha; it was not such a magnificent edifice as it later became, but of humble and crude workmanship with adobe walls. . . . [compare 2 Nephi 5:16]. Finally, the first Inca established the kingdom by winning the good will of those who approached him [compare 2 Nephi 5:17] and by showing himself to be humane, affable, and very religious and well informed with regard to things pertaining to the divine rituals [compare 2 Nephi 32:9] and understanding the gods [only Viracocha/Christ] especially his father the Sun [Viracocha/Christ] [compare to Nephi 31:20–21], whose worship Manco Capac and his successors established throughout their kingdom [compare 2 Nephi 5:19].

Having reached old age, when he felt the approach of death, the Inca ordered his most important subjects to gather together before him, and he told them that it was time for him to return to the sky; his father the Sun [icon for Viracocha/Christ] was calling for him to come there. The most important thing that he entrusted to them in that hour, for the love that he had shown to them, was to keep peace and harmony among themselves and to be as obedient and faithful to his eldest son, Cinchi Roca, as they had been to him. Having said this, he died [compare Jacob 1:9]. His subjects were visibly stricken with grief, for they loved him as a father [compare Jacob 1:10].[52]

The Incas believed that Manco Capac was the son of a *curaca*[53] (a local official and head of a high-ranking lineage). As we know, Lehi was a man of importance in Jerusalem, otherwise, why would he have been a threat to the elders there. Furthermore, Nephi tells us that he was born of "goodly parents" (1 Nephi 1:1), and indicates that his father had substantial wealth (1 Nephi 3:25). We are told that Lehi, "as he went forth prayed unto the Lord, yea, even with all his heart, *in behalf of his people*" (1 Nephi 1:5; italics added). "His people" suggests that Nephi's father was the head of a lineage or tribe.

Sarmiento provided another interesting aspect of the life of Manco Capac. He fought wars, and the people chose him to lead them[54]—yet two more specific parallels to the life of Nephi (Jacob 1:10, 2 Nephi 5:9).

Manco Capac was said to have been "a man of good stature, thin, rustic."[55] Nephi noted that he was a man of "large stature" (1 Nephi 4:31).

WHEN DID MANCO CAPAC LIVE?

Fabricated genealogies by the fourteenth-century AD Inca Yupanqui claimed that Manco Capac lived only nine generations before him and that he was Manco's direct descendent. This is impossible. Manco Capac was the founder of the ancient, not the later, Inca civilization. His mummy and a large stone image of him were discovered by the Spanish not in the city of Cuzco, but in the ruins of the nearby Wimpillay.[56] This ancient town was the most important city in the valley during the Inca Late Formative Phase (500 BC–AD 200).[57] If the Spanish had not burned the preserved mummies of the Inca kings, we might have had Manco Capac's DNA!

Inca Yupanqui's creation of a false genealogy to show that he was a descendant of the great Manco Capac is no more surprising than the European monarchs having falsified their genealogies to show that they were descendants of the house of David.[58] Manco Capac was given the staff to rule by god himself, and Inca Yupanqui wanted to show the people that he had the same right to rule over them by being Manco Capac's direct descendent. Sullivan explains: "Although, for reasons including political expediency, the Incas projected their own ancestry back into the thick of the events."[59] Archaeologists now believe that the first eight generations of Inca kings, date far back into antiquity when the first Incas appeared in Peru. Recent archaeological findings tentatively point to Manco Capac's reign as having been circa sixth century BC.

The early chronicler Fernando de Montesinos claimed that there were 105 Inca kings, some of which were actually from the Wari people. Until recently, scholars ignored Montesinos' account of the Incas because he claimed that the Incas had a written language. Not only do Harvard University archaeologists now believe that the Incas did have a written language,[60] a closer study of the archaeological evidence is discovering that Montesinos' record of the Inca kings is the only record that can be relied upon with any level of confidence. Juha Hiltunen of the University of Oulu in Finland writes: "The dynastic lists recorded in Montesinos' chronicle can be correlated with the current prehistoric periodization in the Andes with promising results. In this new way of looking into the Andean past, we can consider that the Middle Horizon and Late Intermediate Period Wari kings may have been recorded into this unique written source, the only one available to us from its time."[61]

If the last of the 105 ruling Inca kings, Huayna Capac, died in AD 1527 from the smallpox plague that was brought to the Americas by the Spanish, when would the first king have reigned?

We can estimate an approximate date for Manco Capac's reign by comparing the average length of the reigns of the British monarchs from AD 704 to the present day. Accurate records were maintained during this time span. The Saxon kings who ruled for 362 years reigned for an average of 16.5 years. The English kings and queens who ruled after the Norman invasion reigned for 941 years with an average tenure of 22.5 years.[62] The combined average reign since AD 704 would be 20.8 years. Since the English monarchs included women, who on the average live longer then men, I propose rounding the average length of rule to an even 20 years. By multiplying the 20 years average reign times 105 Inca kings, the total would be 2,100 years from the first to the last Inca ruler. Subtracting 2,100 years from AD 1527 tells us that Manco Capac would have taken power sometime around 570 BC. Thus, if Manco Capac was Nephi, then our best guess as to when he reigned is during early sixth century BC, well within the period the Book of Mormon gives for the reign of Nephi.

WHY WOULD NEPHI HAVE BEEN MUMMIFIED?

If Nephi was Manco Capac, it might seem odd to Latter-day Saints that Nephi's body would have been mummified. Rather than odd, it is another witness that the Book of Mormon account is in perfect historical harmony. Nephi was from the house of Joseph (1 Nephi 5:16) and the tribe of his son Manasseh. Unlike the other tribes of Israel, the tribes of Manasseh and Ephraim had roots in the courts of Egypt. When Israel died, Joseph ordered that the Egyptian physicians embalm his father—a mummification process that took forty days (Genesis 50:1–3). Of Joseph's death, The Torah states, "Joseph died at the age of one

hundred and ten years; and he was embalmed and placed in a coffin in Egypt." Thus, Joseph was mummified and his body was not buried in the ground, but placed in a sarcophagus.

When the children of Israel left Egypt, they took only the bones of Joseph (Exodus 13:19), but not the remains of the other eleven patriarchs. This implies that Joseph, second in command of all Egypt, was the only son of Israel that was mummified. Did this family tradition get passed down to Lehi's family? The Lehites considered their native language to be Egyptian (1 Nephi 1:2), and according to Hugh Nibley:

> He, (Lehi) was of the tribe of Manasseh, which of all the tribes retained the old desert ways and was most active in the caravan trade. He seems to have had particularly close ties with Sidon. . . [for the name appears repeatedly in the Book of Mormon, both in its Hebrew and Egyptian forms, which at that time was one of the two harbors through which the Israelites carried on an extremely active trade with Egypt and the West. He was proud of his knowledge of Egyptian and insisted on his sons learning it] (Mosiah 1:4).[63]

Whether the Lehites mummified their dead or not, the practice existed in Peru well before the sixth century BC[64] and might have Jaredite associations.

NEPHI'S NAME

It would seem natural then that when Nephi died, his own family and the natives over which he ruled would desire to practice the Egyptian and Peruvian tradition of mummifying his body. Like Joseph of Egypt, Nephi was loved by

his people, and when he died they were "desirous to retain in remembrance his name" (Jacob 1:10–11). For this reason the Nephites called their kings "Nephi" (Jacob 1:11). Lynn and Hope Hilton remind us that in Arabic, Nephi is pronounced "NAFI."[65] The Incas called all their kings the INCA or INKA. Rearrange the letters and you have "NACI" or "NAKI". Could "INCA" have been the encoded Quechua name for NAFI [Nephi], the name of the kings in the secret language of the Cuzco elite? This rearranging of the letters might appear to be nothing more than a word game, but it should be remembered that the Nephites intentionally "altered" their usage of the characters of the reformed Egyptian language (Mormon 9:32). It would also explain why, according to Hugh Nibley, the sacred text of the Book of Mormon contains Egyptian (possibly private) names[66] (Laman, Lemuel, and Sam) while the Incas might have referred to the same people, Manco Capac's brothers, by their Quechua names (Cachi, Uchu and Auca).

Finally, in remembrance of the great Nephi, Jacob wrote that "Whoso should reign in his stead were called by the people, second Nephi, third Nephi, and so forth" (Jacob 1:11). Manco Capac means King Manco. Montesinos wrote that *Manco* Capac reigned twenty-one years, his son Cayo *Manco* Capac followed him, and he was followed by his son, Sinchi Ayar *Manco*,[67] thus retaining the appellation *Manco* in their names and titles.

As compelling as the parallels are between Nephi and Manco Capac, it is impossible to know for certain that they were the same person. All the same, to develop the paradigm proposed in this book, we shall consider them one and the same.

NEPHI'S THREE JOURNEYS IN THE PROMISED LAND

Comparing Nephi to Manco Capac can begin with the Nephites disembarking on the shores of the promised land. It seems clear that Nephi realized that the beachhead where his family landed was not the land "choice above all other lands" that he had been promised. However, his first order of business after disembarking in the promised land was to restock the family's food supply (1 Nephi 18:23–25). Thus, Nephi wrote that they pitched their tents, planted seeds, and harvested in abundance. With a plentiful harvest, the family now had the provisions they needed to search for lands that were more fertile.

Nephi wrote that they journeyed in the wilderness, apparently surveying the resources in the lands they passed through. The Book of Mormon states that under Nephi's leadership the entire family made several "journeyings" (1 Nephi 19:1). Thus, the role played by Nephi in the early colonization of the promised land should not be underestimated. In this light, we can compare Nephi to the legendary founder of the Inca people, the great Manco Capac, and see if these two great men were one and the same. If Nephi was the first Inca king, then it follows that Peru was the land where the first Nephites settled.

When Nephi used the word *journey* he referred to a migration of the family from one place to another—for example, when the Lord commands Lehi that they should leave the valley of Lemuel and journey with his family in the wilderness (1 Nephi 16:9). After using the plural term "journeyings" (1 Nephi 19:1), Nephi again used the word "journey" at the time he separated from Laman and Lemuel (2 Nephi 5:7). Thus, it appears that Nephi led at least three journeys or

Isle of the Sun

Lake Titicaca

migrations in the promised land before settling in the city of Nephi. What parallels are there between Nephi's journeys with the oral traditions of the migrations led by the founder of the Inca people, Manco Capac?

1) Manco Capac arrived by sea along the Pacific Coast of South America, but was known to have migrated to the mountains of the Altiplano and Lake Titicaca and later settled in the Cuzco Valley. On a journey from the Pacific Ocean to Lake Titicaca, Manco Capac would have witnessed the same resources Nephi reported on his family's first migration, e.g. forests, wild animals, and ore deposits (1 Nephi 18:25).

2) From Lake Titicaca, Manco Capac did not go directly to Cuzco. The family first lived in a cave at Pacariqtambo in the mountains west of Cuzco. Again, Nephi's record implies that they made at least three migrations. For now, we will

assume that Manco Capac's migration from Lake Titicaca to Pacariqtambo can be matched with Nephi's second journey.

3) From the cave at Pacariqtambo, and before continuing their journey to Cuzco, Manco Capac decided that the family must separate themselves from their violent brother Ayar Cachi [Laman]. Manco Capac's separation from his violent brother Ayar Cachi before settling in Cuzco is reminiscent of Nephi's separation from Laman and Lemuel before settling the city of Nephi (2 Nephi 5:1–8). Manco Capac's migration from Pacariqtambo to Cuzco is indicative of Nephi's third and final migration.

Urton writes of Manco Capac's last migration, "The principal figure was Manco Capac, who was destined to become the founder-king of the empire. The Incas set off with people who lived around Tambo T'ogo [allied tribes of Pacariqtambo] in search of fertile land on which to build their capital. Following a long period of wandering, they finally arrived at a hill overlooking a valley of Cuzco [city of Nephi]. Recognizing by miraculous signs that this was the home they had long sought, the Incas descended from the mountain and took possession of the valley from the local inhabitants."[68]

FIRST JOURNEY—FROM THE PACIFIC BEACHHEAD TO LAKE TITICACA

The Peruvians called the first Incas or four white brothers Viracochas, which some historians believe meant "foam of the Sea."[69] This odd meaning was possibly derived from the fact that the four brothers arrived in the land upon the sea, like the sea foam that is carried on waves to the shore. The four Inca brothers did not stay long at the Pacific shoreline. Instead, they migrated to an island in Lake Titicaca.

The Book of Mormon does not disclose where Nephi led the family when they left the seashore and headed into the wilderness. However, Nephi hints that he had moved into the towering Andes Mountains, for on occasions he was "carried away upon exceedingly high mountains" (2 Nephi 4:25).

Eventually the Nephites settled in the land of Nephi, a large area where many cities existed and over which wars were fought and long missions served. The place where the Nephites finally settled does not appear to have been an island. However, Jacob made an interesting insertion on the golden plates. He wrote that they had lived upon an "Isle of the Sea" (2 Nephi 10:20). Here again, is another possible parallel between the history recorded in the Book of Mormon and the oral traditions of Manco Capac. Loren McIntyre (*National Geographic Magazine*) notes, "According to a legend still learned by Andean school children, the first Inca, Manco Capac, wandered northward from Titicaca. Reaching Cuzco, he founded a dynasty whose armies and disciplined society would spawn one of the world's great empires."[70] In other words, before settling in Cuzco, Manco Capac had lived at Lake Titicaca; and according to the legends of the Incas, Manco Capac and his people lived on an island.

The Incas thought of Lake Titicaca as a concha or "sea." The giant body of water has an area of 3,200 square miles and is nearly 1,000 feet deep. Lake Titicaca has scores of islands, but one, the Island of the Sun, is very special. It was the home of Manco Capac before he migrated to the north. Following only the central temple in Cuzco, the Island of the Sun was the second-most sacred site for the Incas. University of California at Los Angeles archaeologist Charles Stanish writes of the Island of the Sun:

Cobo also describes a large architectural complex that is today called the Chincana, and notes the presence of a small set of buildings now called Mama Ojlia [Manco Capac's wife] and a set of natural marks on the bedrock which were believed to be the footsteps of mythical Inca, Manco Capac [Nephi]. On the other hand, some features that Cobo mentions, like a round altar stone in front of the rock no longer exist. . . .

The far-side of the [Sacred] rock descends much of the distance down to the lake. Cobo calls this broad descending side, "the convex side of the stone," and says it was covered in cumbi, a finely woven cloth. He stated that the plaza side of the rock was covered with sheets of gold and that an altar was located in the prominent concavity near its center.[71]

The author believes that the Chincana on the Isle of the Sun is perhaps one of the most sacred antiquity sites for Latter-day Saints. Its exceptionally beautiful setting is matched by its possible historical significance. First of all, it is believed to be the very place where Viracocha created the universe and all things within it. Second, it was the first temple built by Manco Capac, and includes an altar of unhewn stones (Nephites practiced animal sacrifices, 1 Nephi 5:9). Third, the Chincana is where the Incas believe that Viracocha descended a second time to earth to teach the people how to live together in prosperity and peace, to heal the sick, and to raise the dead.[72]

The design of the Chincana suggests that it was an ancient temple of the truth faith. An Inca trail leads from the shore of Lake Titicaca up to the temple. Originally, before reaching the altar, the patrons had to pass through three doors (or rooms) along the trail. After the third door, they came to the altar. A few feet from the altar was the west face of the sacred rock, which was believed to have contained the face of Viracocha watching over the altar. The natural feature believed to be their Lord's face was covered in pure gold, highlighting Viracocha's crown, eyes, nose, mouth, and beard. The back side of the rock that featured the image of Viracocha, an area covering approximately 150 feet by 60 feet, was entirely covered with fine cloth. Just north of the altar is a structure believed to have been built by Manco Capac. It is known as the temple of Viracocha. The temple contained the "fountain" of the Incas, a small spring that still flows from the temple down to the lake. Since the altar was used for animal sacrifices, the spring is an essential element for a temple because Mosaic sacrifices had to be washed.

IS THERE ARCHAEOLOGICAL EVIDENCE THAT A PERSON LIKE NEPHI LIVED ON THE ISLAND OF THE SUN?"

We know that both Nephi and Manco Capac were great teachers and were leaders who were loved by their people because of the knowledge they shared with them. The Island of the Sun is located on the southeast end of Lake Titicaca. Archaeologists have discovered that there was a marked change in the level of civilization in this area starting approximately 500 BC, and classified the period as Tiwanaku IV.[73]

Nephi's settling his colony on the isle of the Sun would also explain why the chronicler Cieza de León reported the legend that bearded white men lived on an island in Lake Titicaca.[74]

Initially settling on an island probably made a great deal of sense to Nephi. The island is fertile, has springs of sweet water, and most important, it would have been a natural fortification against any tribe trying to eliminate the newcomers. This first migration of the Nephites might have taken place within months, one growing season, from the time Lehi's family reached the promised land. The family would still have been a small group of virtual strangers, not yet knowing the native languages and still trying to bridge friendships and alliance with the indigenous peoples. It would have been a high-risk environment and, being surrounded by water on an island with steep cliffs, would have provided a safe refuge.

If the Nephites lived on an "isle in the sea" (2 Nephi 10:20) in Lake Titicaca before they founded the city of Nephi (2 Nephi 5), then there appears to be a chronological conflict in the Book of Mormon. However, a closer look at The Second Book of Nephi indicates that the book is composed of four parts. The first four chapters are Lehi's prophesies and blessings. Chapter 5 is Nephi's entire history of his kingship, from the time he separated from his brothers until forty years had passed away from the time they left Jerusalem (2 Nephi 5:34). Chapters 6–24 are Jacob's lectures on faith, including his insertion of the words of Isaiah. Finally, Chapters 25–33 are Nephi's parting message to his people.

In other words, the only historical events Nephi recorded on the Small Plates were: 1) a short note that they arrived in the land of promiseplanted crops, and journeyed in the wilderness (1 Nephi 18:22–25); 2) That he was commanded to make plates on which he wrote that they had had "journeyings in the wilderness" (1 Nephi 19:1); and 3) his condensed history which is found in Chapter 5. The details of their journeyings in the promised land before settling in the land of Nephi would have been recorded by Nephi on his Large Plates, which were his secular history of his people. When Nephi gave the small plates to Jacob, he instructs him that he "should not touch, save it were lightly, concerning the history of this people, which are called the people of Nephi. For he said that the history of his people should be engraven upon his other plates (Jacob 2–3). Even so, in the second book of Nephi, Jacob appears to have inserted a small historical reminder to his family that they had once lived on an isle in the sea. Jacob was not giving a history lesson, rather he was emphasizing a spiritual point he was trying to convey. In the sermon, he recounts events that had previously happened to the family including the time they crossed the sea and the time, probably years before they settled in the city of Nephi, when they lived on an isle of the sea (2 Jacob 10:19–20).

SECOND JOURNEY FROM LAKE TITICACA TO PACARIQTAMBO

It seems likely what while living on their isle in the sea, Nephi and his brothers made alliances with the local tribes. Yet for some reason, Nephi continued his "journeyings." There must have been a good reason why Nephi decided to leave the isle of the sea. Using the journeys of Manco Capac as a type, two possible reasons come to mind. First, the legendary first Inca king traveled

One of the three doors
leading to the altar on
the Isle of the Sun.

They first formed an alliance with the Tambo Indians, who lived in the mountains thirty miles west of Cuzco.[77] Urton records:

> After the ancestors [Manco Capac and his brothers], emerged from Tambos Toco, they allied themselves and prepared to go with them in search of fertile land; upon finding good land, they vowed to conquer the people who lived there. Sarmiento describes this turn of events as follows:

> *And agreeing among themselves on this [plan of conquest], the eight ancestors [the four brothers and their wives] began to stir up the people who lived in that part of the mountains, setting as the prize that they [the Inca ancestors] would make the people rich and that they would give them lands and estates which they conquered and subjugated. From an interest in this [proposition], there were formed ten groups or ayllus, which means, among these barbarians, a lineage or faction.*[78]

The ten ayllus [families or tribes] of Tambo Indians founded at Tambo Toco were destined to become the principle groupings of commoners in Inca Cusco. They were complemented in the social organization of the capital by the ten royal ayllus [tribes] kings. Shortly after their creation and emergence from Tambo Toco [caves], the eight ancestors set off with their entourage—the ten ayllus of Tambo Indians—walking northward in the direction of Cusco valley. Along the way, the ancestors [Nephites] tested the earth by plunging a golden bar [Nephi's staff], which they had brought with them from Tambo Toco, into the soil. They were searching for fertile land that would be suitable to call home.[79]

north in search of fertile land.[75] The isle of the Sun is fertile, but is not large enough to provide enough food for a permanent settlement. Second, Sarmiento reports that Manco Capac's violent brother, Cachi [Laman] "committed great cruelties and was oppressive both among the natives of the places they passed, and among his own people. The other brothers were afraid that the conduct of Ayar Cachi would cause their companies to disband and desert, and that they would be left alone."[76] In other words, as fast as Manco Capac

[Nephi] was building alliances with native tribes, his wicked brother was alienating the natives. If Cachi was Laman, then it seems that Laman committed some vile acts against the native people at Lake Titicaca, such as perhaps kidnapping their daughters or killing someone. To keep the peace, Manco Capac needed to move on.

The Inca legends provide a destination for this second migration. According to tradition, the four Inca brothers did not conquer the indigenous people of the Cuzco Valley by themselves.

According to Michael Mosley, Peruvian "yllus [tribes] were often named after their founders [Nephites], who were heroic figures, if not mythical ones, and could turn into stone or some special object. They secured lands for their people [land of Nephi], established codes of behavior, and were models for proper life [teaching of Christ]."[80]

It appears that when Manco Capac left Lake Titicaca in search of fertile lands, he had eyed the fertile Cuzco Valley, but did not yet have the necessary forces to seize the valley. Instead, he and his family camped at Pacariqtambo cave in the homeland of the Tambo Indians. It was there that Manco Capac forged an historic alliance between his family and the ten tribes of the Tambo Indians. The Tambo tribes agreed to become subservient to Manco's leadership, and together they plotted to conquer the people in the Cuzco Valley.

Once in the valley, the Tambo tribes became the Incas' "common ancestors," not the "commoners," as Urton suggests. That is, they became the second tier of Inca nobility, probably intermarried to some degree the lesser members of the Incas (Nephites) and became "the Privilege Incas." The Tambo Indians were so to speak the right-hand men for the Incas, and were their link to the common class of affiliate tribes.

I conjecture that Nephi's second journey was from the Island of the Sun on Lake Titicaca to the cave at Pacariqtambo, and here the stage was set for the final march to the land of Nephi. The only problem still facing Nephi was a rising rebellion within his own family.

THIRD JOURNEY FROM PACARIQTAMBO CAVE TO CUZCO VALLEY

The apostle Orson Pratt taught that, "Shortly after the Nephite colony was brought by the power of God, and landed on the western coast of South America, in the country we call Chili [Chile], there was a great division among them."[81] The Book of Mormon informs us that this division was necessary and divinely directed.

"And it came to pass that the Lord did warn me, that I, Nephi, should depart from them and flee into the wilderness, and all those who would go with me. . . . we did take our tents and whatsoever things were possible for us, and did journey for the space of many days and did pitch our tents" (2 Nephi 5:7).

Three questions need to be answered with respect to Nephi's third journey:

1) From whom was he fleeing?

2) Who were "all those who would go with" him?

3) Where did they go?

The Book of Mormon tells us that Nephi was fleeing from his elder brothers who sought to kill him (2 Nephi 5:1–2). That group would have been headed by Laman and included the sons of Ishmael and any native people who affiliated themselves with Laman.

As for "all those who would go with" Nephi, they could have been the ten tribes of the Tambo, the allies of Manco Capac. Nephi's record suggests that when he separated from his elder brothers he took with him more than just his immediate family. Nephi listed the principal members of his original party and then adds "all those who would go with me were those who

believed in the warnings, and the revelations of God; wherefore, they did hearken unto my words" (2 Nephi 5:6). Of course, those that hearkened to his words could have been the members of his own family whom he had already listed, but such an unnecessary redundancy inscribed on golden plates seems unlikely. The implication is that there were nonfamily members who followed Nephi. These would have been people to whom Nephi taught the revelations of God, and who hearkened to his words. In turn this would imply that Nephi was teaching the revelations of God to the native people, i.e., the Tambo Indians. Since Nephi served a successful mission while in the Arabian desert (D&C 33:8), teaching a limited version of the gospel to natives in the promised land is exactly what one would expect of this faithful man.

One of the revelations Nephi would have shared with the Tambo Indians was the dream of the tree of life. When the Spanish arrived, they found that the Incas had fitted the entrance of the Pacariqtambo cave of the Tambo tribes with golden doors and had placed a golden tree at the cave.[82]

We are now ready to try to answer the final question, "Where did they go?" If our Manco Capac equivalence holds, then Nephi led his people to the Cuzco Valley where Manco Capac founded the city of Cuzco, our candidate for the city of Nephi. According to Sarmiento, the four brothers searched eight years for fertile land before settling in Cuzco.[83] If Nephi's journeyings in the promised land took eight years, then we can add this to the eight years Lehi's family journeyed in Arabia (1 Nephi 17:4). We must also add the two to four years that it would have taken to build a ship and sail it to the New World. In total, Nephi possibly led his family for as many as twenty years without a permanent home!

By this time, the crude Laman must have been completely poisoned to Nephi's leadership, and was preparing to murder his brother (2 Nephi 5:3–5). However, in Manco Capac's case, we see that it was his violent elder brother's own behavior that was hampering the family's effort to secure a peaceful homeland. As a result, during this third leg of Manco Capac's search for fertile land, he decided that it was time to separate from his evil-tempered brother. The Incas considered the separation of the brothers as one of the most significant events in their entire history. This breech finally divided the family into two warring nations. Urton provides a digest of what happened:

> The ancestors [Manco Capac and his three brothers] and their entourage then came to a place called Haysquisrro. It was here that a momentous event occurred that resulted in the separation of one of the ancestors [Laman] from the group.

According to various versions of the Inca origin myth, Ayar Cachi [Laman] was known universally as a boisterous, rowdy and cruel character; he was also very handy with a sling. Cieza (de León) tells us that Ayar Cachi could launch stones from his sling flying up to the clouds. In addition, Ayar Cachi stirred up trouble in all the towns the ancestors passed through, and he disturbed the peace and harmony among the ancestors [Lehi's family] and their allies. According to Sarmiento, "the other siblings feared that because of his bad behavior and tricks, Ayar Cachi would disturb and alienate the people who were traveling with them, and that they would be left alone" [the Tambo Toco Indians would leave them].

These concerns led the ancestors, under the direction of Ayar Manco [Nephi], to concoct a ruse to rid themselves of this troublesome character. Manco told Ayar Cachi [Laman] that they had left several items [brass plates, Mosiah 10:16] in the cave of origin, Tambo Toco. These included a golden cup (topacusi) [Liahona?], some seeds [1 Nephi 8:1, 16:11, 18:6, 18:24], as well as an object called a napa. The latter had the form of a miniature decorative llama, which, in Sarmiento's words, was an "insignia of nobility". . . . At first, Ayar Cachi [Laman] refused to return to the cave. However, Mama Huaco, the most forceful and bellicose of the sisters (and according to Betanzos, the wife of Ayar (Cachi) [Laman], jumped to her feet and began berating Ayar Cachi, calling him a lazy coward. Shamed into action by Mama Huaco's words, Ayar Cachi agreed to return to the cave.

On his trip back to Tambo Toco, Ayar Cachi [Laman] took with him a man from among the Tambos Indians, named Tambochacay ("Tambo entrance-barrier"). Unbeknownst to Ayar Cachi, the other ancestors had persuaded Tambochacay to dispose of the troublesome Ayar Cachi [Laman] when they reached the cave. Arriving at Tambo Toco, Ayar Cachi went inside to retrieve the articles. Tambochacay immediately closed off the entrance to the cave with a huge boulder, trapping Ayar Cachi inside for all time.[84]

Sarmiento's original recording of this event adds this comment about Cachi [Laman]:

Ayar Cachi [Laman] was fierce and strong, and very dexterous with the sling. He committed great cruelties and was oppressed both among the natives of the places they passed, and among his own people.[85]

Pedro Sarmiento De Gamboa recorded this Inca oral tradition in 1572, over two thousand years after Nephi broke away from Laman. However, two sentences in Sarmiento account have convinced the author that the first Inca King, Manco Capac, was none other than Nephi. Sarmiento wrote:

> They called Ayar Cachi [Laman] and said to him, "Brother! Know that in Ccapac-tocco we have forgotten golden vases called tupac-cusi, and certain seeds, and the napa, which is our principle ensign of sovereignty." The napa is a sheep of the country, the colour white, with a red body cloth, on the top earrings of gold, and on the breast a plate with red badges such as was worn by rich Incas when they went abroad.[86]

COULD MANCO CAPAC HAVE BEEN ANYONE OTHER THAN NEPHI?

Beyond the many corollaries already present between Manco Capac and Nephi, there are four additional ones, which make it seemingly impossible that the two men were not one and the same.

1) Laman was notoriously lazy and uncommitted. He thought he would die during the relatively short trip from Jerusalem to the Valley of Lemuel. He gave up trying to obtain the plates from Laban. He wanted to forgo the family's journey to the promised land while they

Did Nephi build this temple? Isle of the Sun.

were still in Arabia, kill his father and brother, and return to Jerusalem. He refused to help Nephi build his ship. Rather than being industrious, he allowed his descendents to become slothful. Put bluntly, Laman was next to impossible to motivate. So let us consider this question, *"If Manco Capac was not Nephi, how could he have known of the one thing that would motivate Laman [Cachi] to return to the cave?"* When the Lord warns Nephi to separate from Laman, He tells Nephi what Laman desires—to kill him so Laman himself could "rule over this people." Laman wanted more than anything to eliminate his younger, but stronger, brother so he could rule over the people. Now consider carefully what it was that Manco Capac told his elder brother Cachi (Laman). He told him that he had left in the cave the "napa, the principle ensign of sovereignty!" In other words, Manco Capac said to Cachi "If you return to the cave you will find the ensign that designates the right to rule."

2) We need to understand exactly what the napa was, this most important icon of the Inca king. It was a white sheep (most likely an alpaca), and it had a red body cloth draping it.[87] Recall how in the Inca account Manco Capac's father received the staff, the symbol of the right to rule

from the Lord Viracocha [the bearded white god]. It was the staff of the Lord, and would have represented God's power and authority. The napa was in the figure of the sheep. Nephi taught that Jesus Christ was the Lamb of God (1 Nephi 13:34–36). The napa sheep was white, as was Viracocha—the bearded white go. Finally, the napa wore a red body cloth, symbolic of "the blood of Christ that was shed (in Gethsemane) because of sin."[88] When the Master was whipped, stripped, and had a crown of thorns placed on his head, the Romans put a scarlet robe upon him (Matthew 27:28). In other words, the napa seems to have been symbolic of Jesus Christ. Furthermore, Manco Capac was the first Inca to wear the maskapaycha, a scarlet-colored fringe that covered the forehead which was the foremost symbol of the ruler.[89]

3) Manco Capac received the staff of Viracocha (Christ) as his ensign indicating to all that he was the rightful king. The napa was only a figurine of a sheep, so why would Cachi (Laman) be so desirous to obtain it? Sarmiento indicated that it was the "principal ensign of sovereignty." He went on to note that the napa was "carried in front of all on a pole with a cross or plume of feathers."[90] Therefore, it appears that the napa's pole was Viracocha's staff of royal authority.

4) Finally, why was Manco Capa's napa the most important symbol of the right to rule in ancient Peru? Perhaps the Book of Mormon provides the answer. In the promised land, Nephi was exclusively given the right to rule. Applying Sjodahl's linguistic rule that Semitic words that ended in "i" evolved into Quechua words through the exchange of the ending "i" with an "a," we can reverse the process by changing the Quechua word napa into the Book of Mormon

word napi. According to Lynn & Hope Hilton, the name Nephi in Arabic is Nafi.[91] In other words, the name of the symbol of sovereignty for the Incas was possibly "Nephi," the very name of the man the Lord ordained to rule in the Americas (1 Nephi 2:20–22).

It is not certain what actually happened to Cachi (Laman). Some legends state that he was trapped and died in the cave, while other accounts say he escaped and settled in a place near Cuzco.[92] As for Lemuel, it appears that Nephi did not have to separate himself from him for Uchu (Lemuel)

was turned into stone (died) before the party reached the Cuzco Valley.[93]

Finally, it is interesting to note that the oral traditions of the ancient Peruvians, which presumably were passed down by surviving Lamanite posterity, claimed that Cachi (Laman) had been tricked by Manco Capac (Nephi) into returning to the cave. This story of the brothers would be consistent with the Book of Mormon's description of how the Lamanites viewed the dealings of Nephi with Laman. King Lamoni's father stated, "These Nephites, who are sons of a liar, Behold, he robbed our fathers; and now his children are also come amongst us that they may, by their cunning and their lyings, deceive us, that they again may rob us of our property" (Alma 20:13). Of course, this bias on history is exactly what a student of the Book of Mormon would expect the Indians to have told the Spanish. According to Sarmiento's notes, descendants of Cachi (Laman) were among those who lived in Cuzco at the time of the Spanish conquest.[94]

In Betanzos' record of the four brothers, he states that after they separated from Cachi (Laman), Manco Capac took care of Cachi's wife.[95] As his sister-in-law she would have been considered in the Middle Eastern sense a sister to Manco Capac. Betanzos continued that "Ayar Manco (Nephi) received Ayar Oche's [Uchu/Lemuel's] wife, Cura, to care for her. . . . Manco Capac and his companion, Ayar Auca (Sam), left their settlement, taking with them the four women already mentioned (their own wives plus the wives of Laman and Lemuel). They walked toward the town of Cuzco."[96] This oral tradition of the founding of Cuzco, certainly brings to mind the account in the Book of Mormon, where

Nephi wrote that he took "also my sisters," when he settled the city of Nephi (1 Nephi 5:6, 15).

THE LAND OF THE NEPHITES' INHERITANCE

Urton continues with his account of the four Inca brothers:

> Having rid themselves of Ayar Cachi, the ancestors moved on and arrived next in the immediate environs of the valley of Cusco at a place called Quirirmanta, which is at the foot of a mountain called Huanacauri. Ascending Huanacauri, the ancestors viewed for the first time the valley of Cusco. Heaving the bar of gold with which they had been testing the soil into the valley, they saw the entire shaft sink into the earth. From this indication, as well as by the sign of a rainbow that stretched over the valley, the ancestors [now the Nephites] recognized that this was their long sought-after home [the land choice above all other lands] and they prepared to descend.[97]

According to Sarmientos' chronicles, when Manco Capac settled in Cuzco, he removed the ten "barbarian" tribes away from the city including the "lineage of Ayar Cachi" [Lamanites].[98] In other words, Manco Capac did not want his people mixing with those he considered barbaric. The first Inca king's attitude parallels Nephi's sentiments regarding the traditional behavior of the Lamanites and his desire that his people not mix with them (2 Nephi 5:21–23).

Ironically, Manco Capac's (Nephi's) effort to keep the Inca royalty's bloodlines pure was in vain. Cobo recorded: "He [Cinchi Roca, the son of Manco Capac/Nephi] sought to have his son marry, for he wanted him to remain with a legitimate wife so that there would be legitimate children according to their laws, but the youth did not accept the marriage that his father arranged; this caused Cinchi Roca much grief, and being old and very honored, he came to the end of his days."[99] It is noteworthy that this would have occurred in a time corresponding to when Jacob was warning his people against taking multiple wives—seemingly from native people.

ORGANIZING THE CHURCH

Having settled in the land of Nephi (Cuzco Valley), Nephi ruled over his own family, his aligned tribes (Tambos), and the native people that subjugated themselves to him in the surrounding valleys. As his domain grew, he called his younger brothers to be "priests and teachers over the land of my people" (2 Nephi 5:26), seemingly a large and dispersed community. It appears that Nephi could no longer personally administer the gospel and carry out the affairs of government. To accommodate the instruction of his people, Nephi needed to organize the Church and send his brothers out into the "land" to teach the "people." His brothers were still young adults, but they had been tutored in the gospel by two of the greatest prophets of all ages, their father Lehi and their brother, the king.

In his calling as a teacher, Jacob says to the people "Behold, if ye were holy I would speak unto you of holiness; but as ye are not holy, and ye look upon me as a teacher." (2 Nephi 9:48). Certainly Jacob was not teaching the sons of Nephi, Sam, Zoram, Joseph, and his own children. Nephi wrote of his brothers and Zoram: "We did observe to keep the judgments, and the statutes, and the commandments of the Lord in all things, according to the law of Moses" (2 Nephi 5:10).

Surely, these righteous fathers had taught their own children to observe the commandments. So who were the "unholy" people of whom Jacob was called to be the teacher and priest? It must have been the people Manco Capac (Nephi) described as the "barbarian" tribes, the poor Incas that the Nephites and the Tambos had subjugated. Later in Nephi's own account he seems to address those in his kingdom that are not of his immediate family with a degree of unfamiliarity: "My people, ye are a stiffnecked people; wherefore, I have spoken plainly unto you, that ye cannot misunderstand. And the words which I have spoken shall stand as a testimony against you; for they are sufficient to teach any man the right way" (2 Nephi 25:28).

In later years, Jacob wrote of his lifelong mission as a teacher to his "people" (Jacob 1:7). The Nephites had already separated from the Lamanites, so Jacob is teaching among the Nephites only, and doing so within the walls of the temple (Jacob 1:17). He reported, "We labored diligently among our people, that we might persuade them to come unto Christ, and partake of the goodness of God" (Jacob 1:7). "Wherefore, we would to God that we could persuade all men not to rebel against God, to provoke him to anger, but that all men would believe in Christ." (Jacob 1:8). If Jacob taught only his blood-kin, his words about "all men" would imply that the children and grandchildren of Lehi had no foundational teaching of Christ. His words would seem much better suited as an effort to teach pagan tribes to worship Jesus Christ.

NEPHI'S PROMISED LAND

The Inca nobility performed an annual pilgrimage to the Island of the Sun in Lake Titicaca.

The Incas have long believed that the lake was the original homeland of Manco Capac and the other Viracochas, the bearded white men, who were the first Incas. For this reason, it is interesting to contemplate whether Nephi had initially decided to settle on the Isle of the Sea, and was only forced to move on because of hostilities that arose because of the cruel actions Laman heaped upon the local natives. The Altiplano with its Lake Titicaca is a special place, perhaps even a promised land.

Perhaps there is a specific type or template for a promised land. Anyone who has studied the geography of the Salt Lake Basin and the Altiplano of Peru-Bolivia cannot help but recognize the similarities. A like type was noted by the early Utah pioneers when they discovered that the geography of Salt Lake Valley paralleled geographic attributes of Palestine. Both areas had a large fresh water lake that was connected by a river to a dead or salten sea. A poster published by the Rio Grande Western Railroad showed maps of "Deseret" and "Canaan." The railroad published the poster in an effort to draw Mormon settlers to Salt Lake City. Between the two maps was the title, "The promised land!" [100]

Nephi was also given a "promised land." Having been born in the land of Jerusalem, it would not have been lost to him that the fresh waters of Lake Titicaca emptied southward via the Desaguardero River into a huge salten lake the Incas called the sea of Poopó. [101] The Altiplano's geography fits the same rare pattern of Palestine and the Salt Lake Valley, but on a much grander scale.

NEPHI'S PROMISED LAND

FRESH WATER LAKE TITICACA

DESAQUARDERO RIVER

SALT WATER LAKE POOPO

SALT FLATS 4250 Sq Miles

City of Cuzco

THE CITY OF NEPHI

VI

"Cam cuzco capaca"
"You are the king of Cuzco."

HYMN TO VIRACOCHA

McIntyre, a writer for the *National Geographic*, states:

From the waters of Titicaca—according to one Inca origin legend—Manco Capac [Nephi], the first Inca, and his sister-wife, Mama Ocllo, emerged after their creation by the sun. The couple wandered with a golden staff until they found a fertile valley where it sank easily into the earth. There they founded Cuzco [City of Nephi], which means "navel" in Quechua and "richest of the rich" in the secret Callaway tongue. Both meanings fit the great religious and political center of the empire, its temples laden with gold, its warehouses bulging with weapons and clothing.[1]

From what is known about pre-Columbian Cuzco, it is not hard to understand why it was known as the "richest of the rich." The Lord promised Nephi, "ye shall prosper, and shall be led to a land of promise; yea, even a land which I have prepared for you; yea, a land which is choice above all other lands" (1 Nephi 2:20). Of course Nephi was faithful, and through hard work and providence, the Nephites did "prosper exceedingly" (2 Nephi 5:13).

Cieza de León recorded:

In the month of October of the year of the Lord fifteen hundred and thirty-four the Spanish entered the City of Cuzco, head of the great empire of the Incas, where their court was as well as the solemn Temple of the Sun and their greatest marvels.

Although treasure for Atahualpa's ransom was taken [from Cuzco] to Cajamarca, and Quizquiz [Inca general] robbed what has already been related, and even though the Indians thought of destroying it and took a great deal, it did not seem to make a dent in how much remained. It was a marvelous thing and worthy of contemplating because no loot equaled this one, nor in all the Indies was there found such wealth. Neither a Christian nor a pagan prince has or possessed such a wealthy region as the one where this famous city was founded. The high priest abandoned the temple, where [the Spanish] plundered the garden of gold and the sheep and shepherds of this metal along with so much silver that it is unbelievable, and precious stones which, if they were collected, would be worth a city.

Indeed, when the Spaniards entered and opened the doors of the houses, in some they found heaps of very heavy and splendid gold pieces, in others large silver vessels. It irritated them to see so much gold. Many left it, scoffing at it, not wanting to take more than some delicate and fine little jewels for their Indian women. Others found beads, feathers, gold ingots, and silver in bullion; indeed, the city was full of treasures. In the fortress, the royal house of the Sun, they found unseen and unheard of grandeur because the kings had deposits there of all the things that can be imagined and thought about.[2]

Archaeologist Bauer writes of Cuzco: "Within the city, spectacular elite and religious buildings expanded to fill the entire area between the two rivers, and a large plaza capable of holding thousands of people was built."[3] Sancho arrived five months after the first three Spaniards entered Cuzco:

The city of Cuzco is the principal one of all those where the lords of this land had their residence; it is so large and so beautiful that it would be worthy of admiration even in Spain; and it is full of the palaces of the lords, because no poor people live there, and each lord builds there his house, and all the caciques do

likewise, although the latter do not dwell there continuously. The greater part of these houses are of stone, and others have half the façade of stone. There are many houses of adobe, and they are all arranged in very good order. The streets are laid out at right angles, they are very straight, and are paved, and down the middle runs a gutter for water lined with stone.[4]

Cuzco was a city primarily built from ashlar stone. The Incas' beautiful stonework, considered the finest in the ancient world, can still be seen today because of its unique earthquake resistant design. Cobo was in Cuzco in 1653 and wrote of the Inca masonry:

. . . an entire section of a wall that still remains in the city of Cuzco, in the Convent of Santa Catalina. These walls were not made vertical, but slightly inclined inward. The stones are perfectly squared, but in such a way that they come to have the same shape and workmanship as a stone for a ring of that sort that jewelers call "faceted." The stones have two sets of faces and corners, so that a groove is formed between the lesser faces of the fitted stones, separating the faces in relief. Another skillfully made feature of this work is that all the stones are not of the same size, but the stones of each course are uniform in size, and the stones are progressively smaller as they get higher. Thus the stones of the second course are smaller than those of the first, and the stones of the third course are also smaller than those of the second, and in this way the size of the stones diminishes proportionately as the wall become higher. Thus the above-mentioned wall

of the structure, which remains standing to this day, has a lower course of ashlar blocks of more than one cubit in diameter, while the stones of the upper course are the size of azulejos [ornamental tile]. This wall is two or three estados high. It is the most skillfully made of all the Inca structures that I have seen. We said that the Indians did not use mortar in these buildings, that all of them were made of dry stone. . . But this does not mean that the stones were not joined together on the inside with some type of mortar; in fact it was used to fill up space and made the stones fit.[5]

Of course, the Spanish did not enter Cuzco to admire it, but to loot it. Cuzco had already been looted once by the Spanish when Sancho recorded the second plundering: "Truly it was a thing worthy to be seen, this house where the melting took place, all full of so much gold in plates of eight and ten pounds each, and in vessels, and vases and pieces of various forms with which the lords of the land were served, and among other very sightly things were four sheep in fine gold and very large, and ten or twelve figures of women of the size of the women of that land, all of fine gold and as beautiful and well made as if they were alive."[6]

One of the most amazing sights the Spanish saw in Cuzco was its huge plaza, a portion of which makes up today's large Plaza de Armes in central Cuzco. Out of reverence to Viracocha (Christ) who left Peru by sea, the Inca covered the entire plaza in two and a half feet of beach sand that they hauled over the Andes Mountains from the Pacific. Polo de Ondegardo stated in 1559, "because the plaza is large and the number

of loads [of sand] brought into it was countless."[7] Within the sand floor of the plaza were buried many gold and silver vases and tiny figures of llamas and men.

Of course, the Cuzco the Spanish entered would have been quite different from the valley Manco Capac (Nephi) would have looked on for the first time. In his day, the Cuzco Valley must have been unblemished, with large forests, wild animals, and villagers who lived a primitive lifestyle. Garcilaso de la Vega witnessed the deforestation of the valley by the Spaniards. In 1604 he wrote: "I remember that the valley of Cuzco used to be adorned with innumerable trees of this valuable variety, but within the space of a very few years it was almost stripped of them, the reason being that they provide excellent charcoal for braziers."[8] Bauer writes: "Perhaps the largest concentration of forest lay to the north-west of Cuzco, in a vast and rolling area between the city and the slope of Huayna-corcor. Based on the large number of projectile points found during our survey work in these hills, it seems that the northwestern end of the valley continued to be a favored hunting region throughout prehistory. This remained true even in Inca times, as we know that the Inca maintained a royal hunting lodge there."[9] Betanzos recorded: "In the place and site which is called today the great city of Cuzco in the province of Peru, in ancient times, before there were any lord orejones, Inca Capacuna, as they called their kings, there was a small town of about thirty small, humble straw houses."[10]

Archaeologists have classified the period ca. 1500–500 BC in the Cuzco Valley (the period just prior to the Nephite Age) as the Middle Formative Period. Bauer states of this prehistoric age: "The Middle Formative Phase in the valley is represented by a series of undifferentiated settlements, which began as hamlets and grew increasingly large through time. We can speculate that these villages would have had leaders (so-called Big Men), whose positions of authority were highly unstable."[11] The architecture during that time was basic—"although some adobe walls were identified, no large architectural features that could be classified as public works were found. . . . While each village. . . was likely relatively self-sufficient, each developed its own local specialties, as the restriction accompanying [sedentariness] limited direct or easy access to resources. . . . No direct evidence was found to indicate social stratification or craft specialization based on principles other than age and sex."[12]

MANCO CAPAC (NEPHI) TAKES THE CUZCO VALLEY

The large gold plates of Nephi contained the secular history of the family. Thus, as we might expect, the small gold plates that are included in the Book of Mormon tell us nothing as to how Nephi acquired the land of Nephi. Turning to Inca oral history, we find an interesting account of how the ingenious Manco Capac took charge over the people of the valley without shedding a single drop of blood. Sarmiento tells us that Manco Capac (Nephi) fashioned two plates of gold, one of which he wore on the front of his body, the other on his back. Manco then positioned himself on the hill of Huanacauri, overlooking Cuzco where, at the moment of sunrise, he appeared as a resplendent, god–like figure. The locals were awed by his appearance, whereupon Manco descended from Huanacauri to Cuzco and became the ruler of the valley.[13]

This curious story leads one to wonder if during the two thousand years since Manco Capac's entry into Cuzco the story became somewhat distorted. Did Manco Capac really create two plates of gold to wear, or did he create two "sets of golden plates"—a large set and a small set? Could he have read the words of God from the gold plates and convinced the natives that he was their rightful leader? A similar event took place when Mosiah entered the domain of the people of Zarahemla. They rejoiced at Mosiah's coming for he had the plates of brass, and thereafter they made him their king. (Omni 1:14–19).

On the one hand, such metal plates from which one could read and the finely crafted sword of Laban would have made profound impressions on the primitive people. On the other hand, if Nephi did wear golden plates into the land of Nephi, the Book of Mormon provides a possible explanation. The Nephites wore breastplates into battle, and the local natives could have witnessed his impressive armor and steel sword and decided to surrender the valley (Alma 43:19–21). We also know that the breastplate of the Urim and Thummin was buried by Moroni along with the golden plates. *Urim* and *Thummim* are Hebrew terms for "lights" and "perfections."[14] The Urim and Thummim was made of "two stones in silver bows—and these stones, fastened to a breastplate" (JSH 1:35). Could Nephi have worn the Urim and Thummim as he entered the land of Nephi, and by doing so, radiated an incredible "light" that testified to the native people that they should subjugate themselves to the young leader? Whatever happened that day, we see that both Manco Capac and Nephi knew how to fabricate gold plates, a very rare technology in the New World in ancient times.

Urton tells us that once in the valley of Cuzco, Manco Capac and his people went to the leader of the natives and "told him they had been sent by their father, the sun [Inca corruption of Viracocha the White God], to take possession of the town. Alcavicca, the native leader, and his followers acceded to this request and made room for the six ancestors. Then Manco Capac [Nephi] took some maize (corn) seeds that he had brought with him from the cave of Tambo Toco, and with the help of Alcavicca and the other ancestors he planted the first corn field in the valley."[15] Scientists have found evidence that show that maize is observed for the first time in the Cuzco Valley at around 600 BC, a dating that tightly coincides with Nephi's entry to the city of Nephi.[16]

THE SETTLING OF THE CUZCO VALLEY

On reaching the site where Manco Capac decided to build the city of Cuzco (Nephi), a tragedy occurred. Bauer writes, "When Manco Capac and his companions finally reached the place that would become the centre of the city of Cuzco, the plaza of Huanaypata, Ayar Auca [Sam] was transformed into a stone pillar."[17] Auca's demise would indicate that Sam must have died shortly after the founding of the city of Nephi. This left only Manco Capac (Nephi), his four sisters, and the boy Cinchi Roca (Nephi's son) to build the city of Cuzco.[18]

In comparing the Inca lore to the Book of Mormon account, we find that from the time Nephi separates from his older brothers, the Book of Mormon never again mentions Laman, Lemuel, or Sam. According to Inca legend, Viracocha (Christ) had specifically granted Cuzco and the northern quarter of the land to Manco

Exquisite earthquake-proof walls
form foundations for Spanish
buildings in Cuzco.

we began to raise flocks, and herds, and animals of every kind . . . we began to prosper exceedingly, and to multiply in the land. . . . I did teach my people to build buildings, and to work in all manner of wood, and of iron, and of copper, and of brass, and of steel, and of gold, and of silver, and of precious ores, which were in great abundance. (2 Nephi 5:10–15)

THE SEEDS THEY SOWED

As previously noted, Manco Capac has been credited with the introduction of maize into the Cuzco Valley. Nephi reported planting seeds in the land of Nephi, but no longer specifies that the seeds are from Jerusalem. A possible scenario is that Nephi brought maize from the Island of the Sun in Lake Titicaca, or the cave

Capac (Nephi).[19] The inference is that Nephi, Jacob and Joseph were the only sons (princes) of Lehi who settled in the land of Nephi. This is the reason why it is proposed that the four quarters of the land would have been distributed to Nephi, Jacob, and Joseph, with the final quarter being the domain of the Lamanites.

After long years of wandering without a permanent home, it seems that Nephi wasted no time in turning his vision of a new righteous society into a reality. Nephi provided this brief synopsis:

We did observe to keep the judgments, and the statutes, and the commandments of the Lord in all things, according to the law of Moses. And the Lord was with us; and we did prosper exceedingly; for we did sow seeds, and we did reap again in abundance. And

at Tambo, to Cuzco. "Daniel Gade . . . working in the nearby [to Cuzco] Vilcanota Valley, notes that in Inca times this zone was characterized by the cultivation of tubers (such as oca, añu, and ullucu) and native seeds crops (such as quinoa and tarwi). Harvests on the valley slopes vary greatly from year to year because of frost and hail damage."[20] Maize was also grown in the Cuzco Valley. The Nephites, would not have used the common Quechua words for quinoa (cheno-podium quinoa from which bread is made) and tarwi (lupinus mutabilis sweet, a grain legume) to describe these New World grains. They would have used Egyptian grain names for these grains on the golden plates. Furthermore, the Nephites had no word for potatoes and other South America tubers, since these did not exist in Egypt.

These native high Andes crops could easily have been the crops harvested in Zarahemla: "even with all manner of seeds, with seeds of corn, and of wheat, and of barley, and with neas, and with sheum" (Mosiah 9:6–9).

NEPHITE FLOCKS AND HERDS

Bauer notes of Cuzco in the Late Formative Period (500 BC–AD 200): "Great quantities of llama bones show that they kept large numbers of domestic animals. Pottery is well made and abundant, and a high percentage of decorated ware is found in the refuse."[21] He explains:

> Agricultural intensification continued during the Late Formative Phase, and we know that quinoa, beans, and presumably potatoes held critical roles in

the local economy. It is clear, however, that maize also played a part in the Late Formative diet. Maize pollen, dating to 500 BC has been recovered. . . . Camelid herds would also have been kept in the upper elevations of the valley during this era. As in earlier times, these herds met a wide variety of needs for the people, including food, wool production, and beasts of burden. Nevertheless, deer hunting still continued throughout this period as well.[22]

BUILDING A CITY OF FINE BUILDINGS

Cobo provides this description of the transformation made by Manco Capac and his wife:

> They divided up in that valley, the

Incredible Inca stonework is witnessed by this large block with twelve corners: Cuzco.

prince [Nephi still not anointed king] on the one hand and the princess [his wife] on the other, in order to call together its inhabitants and win them over with reasoning and benefits. The prince and the princess let it be known that they were children of the Sun [Viracocha/Christ], sent to provide the people with instructions and benefits. The barbarians, who saw how well dressed and adorned they were, with clothing so different from their own, started to respect them, and on the advice and orders of these children of the Sun [Viracocha/Christ], the barbarians called one another together; and with the skills that the Incas [Nephites] gave them, they built houses on the site where the city stands today, and it was divided into two barrios: one with the people who were attracted by the prince, and the other with those who were brought together by the princess; the former was called Hanan Cuzco and the latter Hurin Cuzco, meaning "Upper Cuzco" and "Lower Cuzco"; and this was the feeble beginning of the city of Cuzco and the empire of the Incas.[23]

TRANSFORMING LIFE IN THE LAND OF NEPHI

After so many journeys in the wilderness, the Nephites finally had a homeland where they could build a city and a society where, by living the commandments, the people "prosper[ed] exceedingly" and where precious metals were found in abundance. Years later, Jacob wrote of the Nephites continuing to have an abundance of silver, gold, and all manner of precious ores (Jacob 2:12).

The Nephites were known for the "costliness" of their apparel (Jacob 2:13; Alma 1:6, 4:6, 5:53, 31:28; 4 Nephi 1:24; Mormon 8:36). The clothing worn by the Inca nobility was perhaps the finest in the ancient world. The quality of Inca weaving was amazing. Cobo informs us that the Inca king:

> wore a cloak and a shirt, with *ojotas* [sandals or shoes] on his feet; in this respect he followed the custom of the common

people, but his clothing was different from the usual in that it was made of the finest wool and the best cloth that was woven in his whole kingdom, with more brilliant colors and finer-quality weaving. The *mamaconas* (virgins of the Sun) made this clothing for him, and most of it was made from vicuña, which is almost as fine as silk . . . other clothing was very colorful and showy with very small feathers woven into it, and other clothing was covered with ornaments of gold, emeralds, and other precious stones; this was the finest formal attire and corresponds to our embroidery, cloth of gold or silver, and brocades.

. . . a Spaniard touched his cloak, and, noticed that it was softer than silk, he asked him what his clothes were made of; the Inca responded that they were made from some birds that fly about at night . . . bat wool.[24]

HOSTILITIES AGAINST THE CITY OF NEPHI

While building the city, Nephi reports of having to forge swords to prevent his people from being destroyed by the Lamanites (2 Nephi 5:14). The Lamanites lived within eyesight of the city of Nephi (Mosiah 20:8) and seem to have lived south of the city, for when they attacked the Nephites, they "had come up" or north (Mosiah 20:9) to the city. Clements Markham writes that a tribe of Indians called Ayamarcas—a similar name to Aymara-speaking (Lamanite) enemies of the Quechua speaking Incas—"seem to have occupied the country about 15 miles S.S.W. of Cuzco."[25] If the Ayamarcas were Aymara-speaking, this would tell us where the descendents of

Laman initially settled. Having enemies so close to the city would be consistent with the hostilities Nephi reported. Sarmiento writes of one incident between the two groups: "When the Ayamarcas saw that the Huayllacans [from Cuzco] had broken their word, they were furious and declared war, considering them as enemies. War was carried on, the Huayllacans defending themselves and also attacking the Ayamarcas, both sides committing cruelties, inflicting deaths and losses, and causing great injury to each other. . . . both sides saw that they were destroying each other and agreed to come to terms to avoid further injury."[26]

NEPHI BUILDS A GREAT TEMPLE

The most impressive building in ancient Peru was the temple in Cuzco. We can safely assume that the same was true in the city of Nephi. "I, Nephi, did build a temple; and I did construct it after the manner of the temple of Solomon save it were not built of so many precious things; for they were not to be found upon the land, wherefore, it could not be built like unto Solomon's temple. But the manner of the construction was like unto the temple of Solomon; and the workmanship thereof was exceedingly fine" (2 Nephi 5:16).

According to legend, Manco Capac first settled in the Cuzco Valley at a place called Catitampucancha, a small square in Inca times, which today is found inside the monastery of Santo Domingo in the city of Cuzco.[27] On this site Manco Capac built a great temple, which was remodeled several times until its final rebuilding by the Inca Empire a few decades before the Spaniards arrived.[28] Bauer notes: "At the center of the city stood the Coricancha (Golden

Monastery of Santo Domingo now stands on ruins of the Coricancha.

Enclosure) or what the Spaniards [incorrectly] referred to as the Templo del Sol (Temple of the Sun)."[29] Cobo wrote:

He [Manco Capac] selected for this a very spacious and prominent site, and on it he started to build the great temple of Coricancha; it was not such a magnificent edifice as it later became, but of humble and crude workmanship with adobe walls. This is because in that unrefined period the technique of stonework that their successors achieved later had not been seen or used. Thus, this Inca only began the magnificent temple of the Coricancha (which means "golden

house"), and the other kings who succeeded him raised it up to the magnificence and loftiness it had attained when the Spaniards found it.[30]

THE SACRED CENTER OF THE INCA UNIVERSE

Bauer described the temple of the later Inca Empire: "This great sanctuary [Nephi's temple] was located on a slight rise [temple mount] in the heart of Cuzco, near the confluence of the two small, canalized rivers that flow through the city. It was built out of the exquisitely cut stone blocks for which the Inca are justifiably famous. . . . The Coricancha was actually a series of buildings and courtyards surrounded by a large exterior wall."[31] From a distance similar to that which the Mormon pioneers had to transport the stones quarried for the Salt Lake Temple, the blocks for the "Golden Enclosure" were brought from the quarry of Rumicolca some twenty-one miles away.[32]

Starting at the magnificent temple complex, the Incas addressed the location of every street, village, city, province, and quarter of the kingdom. Bauer explains: "The importance of the Coricancha [Nephi's original temple] cannot be underestimated. The Inca Empire was seen as being composed of four great geopolitical quarters that radiated out from this complex. For the Inca, the Coricancha marked the central and most sacred spot in the universe."[33]

The Inca temple was aligned along the cardinal points and the celestial bodies. Due east of the temple, at the equinox, was mountain Pachatusan with a pillar for measuring space-time.[34] A "ray" or road "ran due east" from the Temple of the Sun to the mountain Pachatusan, the "support pillar of space-time," that was used to observe the fall and spring equinox.[35] "The high altar was at the east end,"[36] and the gold-plated sides of the

Like the temple in Jerusalem, the Cuzco temple (Coricancha) was surrounded by walls.

Inca temple faced the rising sun to the east.

Joseph Fielding McConkie notes of the temple in Jerusalem:

> It should not go unnoticed that the [temple] gate was always to be located on the east side of the tabernacle. The first of the sun's rays would always point themselves to it. This heavenly light would thus reveal the beauty of the multicolored gate as the light of heaven reveals Christ as "the way, the truth, and the life". . . the orientation of the East Gate of the Temple of Jerusalem was such that on the days of the spring and fall equinoxes the first rays of the rising sun, heralding the advent of the glory of God, could penetrate into the Holy of Holies. Joseph Smith said that the coming of the Son of Man will be as the light of the morning coming out of the east.[37]

The Coricancha temple was more than just important—it was sacred and holy, and only people who had properly prepared themselves could enter its single gate. When the Spanish entered the gate they desecrated the temple. "The Christians went to the buildings and, with no aid from the Indians, who did not want to help, saying that it was a building of the Sun and they would die."[38] One of Pizarro's foot soldiers reported: "We entered the Houses of the Sun and the Villac Uma, who was like a priest in their religion, said, 'How did you enter; anyone who enters must fast for a year first and must carry a load and be barefoot.' "[39]

THE TEMPLE TREASURE

The Cuzco temple that the Spanish destroyed was something the world had not seen before or afterwards. Its decorations were perhaps the most costly of any building built up to that time. It was a wonder of the world with its wall sheathed in pure gold on the side where the sun rose and of gold alloy on the other.[40]

The very name of the temple, "Golden Enclosure" or "house of gold," was given because of the incredible wealth of gold that was embedded in the temple's chapels and its walls, from ceilings to floors. It contained an altar of pure gold and, like Solomon's temple, a large fountain in its courtyard.[41] However, unlike the temple in Jerusalem, with its brazen sea font, the fountain of the Cuzco temple was cast in gold. The temple featured a life-size gold statue of the Viracocha (Christ).[42]

Although the Indians are believed to have hidden most of the gold of the temple from the conquistadors, the amount of gold looted by the Spaniards from the Cuzco temple is remarkable. Francisco de Xerez, the secretary of Francisco Pizarro, provides us this accounting of the first of several shipments of treasure from the temple. He wrote in 1534:

> [They saw] a house in Cuzco plated with gold. The house is very well made and square and measures three hundred and fifty paces from corner to corner. [The Spanish used Roman Pace, passus, 4.57 feet.] They removed seven hundred of these gold plates from the house that in all weighed five hundred pesos [roughly 5 pounds each]. And from another house the Indians removed a total of two hundred pesos, but because it was of very low (quality), having (only) seven or eight karats, they did not accept it. They did not see more than these two plated

houses, because the Indians did not allow them to see the whole city. . . .

All this gold arrived in one hundred and seventy-eight loads, with four Indians carrying each load in a litter. They brought very little silver.[43]

According to Bauer, "The Coricancha contained many of the finest gold and silver objects of the empire,"[44] including "a seat of very fine gold,"[45] and perhaps as many as 2,800 sheets of lesser-quality gold that covered parts of the complex.[46] The lesser-quality sheets were a composite of gold and copper. The artistic traditions of Cuzco and the fact that Peru was the only place in the New World that had such metallurgic skills during the second century BC, provides a remarkable comparison to the architects in the city of Nephi who "built many elegant and spacious buildings; and he [king Noah] ornamented them with fine work of wood, and of all manner of precious things, of gold, and of silver, and of iron, and of brass, and of ziff, and of copper. . . . And he also caused that his workmen should work all manner of fine work within the walls of the temple, of fine wood, and of copper, and of brass. And the seats which were set apart from the high priests . . . he did ornament with pure gold (Mosiah 11:8, 10–11).

WHO HELPED MANCO CAPAC (NEPHI) BUILD THE ORIGINAL TEMPLE AT CUZCO?

Once Manco Capac (Nephi) and Ayar Auca (Sam) went into the Cuzco valley, they built a house or temple. Betanzos recorded the legend:

He [Manco Capac or Nephi] liked the place now occupied in this city of

Cuzco by the houses and monastery of Santo Domingo, which used to be the houses of the Sun [the Inca Temple]. . . .

Manco Capac and his companion, with the help of the four women, made a house [temple] there without allowing the people of Alcavicca [primitive natives the people Nephi called stiffnecked] to help, even though these people wanted to. The two of them [Nephi and Sam] and the four women stayed in the house. Having done this, Manco Capac and his companion, with the four women, planted some land with maize.[47]

In other words, it appears that Manco Capac (Nephi) did not allow non-believers to help build the temple, even though they wanted to. Furthermore, and as we might expect of Nephi or of Brigham Young, Manco Capac started building the temple even before he taught the people how to plant corn.

Manco Capac's reverence for the temple does not seem to have been shared by later Incas. When the Spanish arrived, they found the icons of other gods in the temple. It should be remembered that the later Incas tried to consolidate their military conquest by plundering the pagan gods of those they conquered and having them forcefully brought to the temple in Cuzco.[48] Thus, the temple at the time of the conquest housed idols from other religions. In a similar fashion, in times of unrighteousness, the temple in Jerusalem housed pagan gods, for example, the image of the Babylonian goddess Ishtar and at other times the gods of the invading Romans.

When the Spaniards first set their eyes on the temple, it had been over a thousand years since the fall of the Nephites and the last known record

of priesthood authority and temple keys. Without question, the religion the Spanish found the Incas practicing was apostate and far removed from the faith the Nephites once practiced. Over the centuries, many idols and superstitions worked their way into the Inca religion in the same manner and over the same time period as the Christian apostasy. When the priests melted down the golden idols in the temple at Cuzco, they replaced them with less valuable idols of Christian saints and the Virgin Mary.

ROOMS OF THE CUZCO TEMPLE

Cieza de León stated [1553] that "within the [temple] complex were four structures of central importance. The gateways and doors as well as many other parts of these structures were covered with sheets of gold." He also indicates that there were "two benches [altars] along an east-facing wall, upon which the light of the rising sun fell."[49] Leading into the temple's interior patio were twelve doorways.[50]

Michael Mosley explains, "Cuzco's most extraordinary temple, the Coricancha [Golden Enclosure], was located in the puma's tail [Cuzco was laid out in shape of a puma]. It was a grand cancha [building] with a single entry, enclosing six wasi-like chambers arranged around a square courtyard. One chamber, richly bedecked with gold, was dedicated to the sun [compare to "celestial"; see 1 Corinthians 15:40–41; D&C 76:70] and held Inti's image; a second [chamber], clad in silver, belonged to the moon [compare to "terrestrial"; D&C 76:71] and held her image. Other structures contained images or symbols of Viracocha [Christ], Ittapa the lord of thunder, Cuichu the rainbow, and various celestial bodies" [compare to "telestial"; D&C 76:109].[51]

Rooms associated with the sun, moon, and celestial bodies compare well to the rooms found in modern Latter-day Saint temples.

However, the Golden Enclosure was dedicated to the sun god. If it was once a House of the Lord, why would the Incas have dedicated it to an idol? Of course the Incas had long since lost the correct concepts associated with the religion of Jesus Christ. However, we should not then be too surprised that for a century prior to the arrival of the Spanish, the Incas started worshiping the image of the sun. But just what did the image of the sun actually represent to the Incas?

Bauer explains: "Various early colonial writers state that the image [of their Sun god] was in the image of a man."[52] Was the sun icon a distorted image of their bearded white god Viracocha, who promised to return to them like the rising sun? "The Prophet Joseph Smith repeatedly discoursed on the well-established figure of the rising sun as a symbol of the second advent of Christ."[53] The gold sheets that adorned the Cuzco temple faced the rising sun. And he taught that "This is the light of Christ. As also he is in the sun, and the light of the sun, and the power thereof by which it was made" (D&C 88:7); and that Christ's "countenance shone above the brightness of the sun" (D&C 110:3). Still, the AD fifteenth-century Incas were wrong to "re-dedicate" the Golden Enclosure to the sun. Without a prophet in their midst, it is easy to understand the source of their confusion.

In the temple were also symbols of the Lord of thunder and the rainbow. The rainbow was a symbol of gratitude to Viracocha (Christ), who had led Manco Capac to Cuzco and set a rainbow above the valley to indicate that this was the place where the people should settle.[54] As for

The exquisite stonework of the Cuzco temple.

Lord of thunder, we need to remember that an important Nephite name for Jesus Christ was the "voice of thunder" (1 Nephi 17:45; Mosiah 27:11, 27:18; Alma 29:2, 36:7, 38:7), a name that obviously is associated with the times He spoke to the Nephites and the earth shook. Thunder was also associated with both the prophecy announcing the coming of the Lord to the Nephites (Helaman 14:27), and his actual appearance to them (3 Nephi 8:6).

Garcilaso de la Vega described special niches within the interior of the temple that illustrate that the Incas spared no expense in the temple's interior decorations:

> They had molding around the edges and in the hollows of the tabernacles, and as these moldings were worked in the stone they were inlaid with gold plates not only at the top and sides, but also the floors of the tabernacles. . .
>
> In two of these tabernacles in a wall facing east, I remember noticing many holes in the moldings made in the stonework. Those in the edges passed right through while the rest were merely marks on the walls. I heard the Indians and the religious of the temple say that those were the places in which the precious stones were set. [55]

THE TEMPLE'S OUTER COURTYARD

Nephi's temple was built after the manner of Solomon's (2 Nephi 5:16). King Solomon's temple had an outer plaza or courtyard which measured 500 cubits square or roughly 729 feet measured in ancient cubits.[56] The temple in Cuzco had a courtyard surround by twenty-foot-tall walls that measure 625 feet by 500 feet.[57]

Model of the courtyard of Coricancha

As one historian states of Solomon's Temple, "a plaza or courtyard surrounding the sacred residence of the god marked with stones, is a feature common throughout ancient Semitic religions."[58] The famed Salt Lake City Temple has a courtyard in which several beautiful statues are found, including the Christus statue in the Visitors' Center.

The Spanish chronicler Cieza de Leon wrote "Coricancha, the temple of the Sun, contained many precious objects even after its exterior had been stripped for Atahualpa's ransom. Gold and silver life-size models of men, women, llamas, and maize filled the garden. In the center of the temple was a large gold disk of the sun, and replicas of the moon, the stars, and a representation of Illapa, the thunder."[59] One of the statues was of the lord Viracocha (Christ). One observer writes:

> It seemed that in the early sixteenth century, before the Spanish began to demolish Peruvian culture in earnest, an idol of Viracocha [Christ] had stood

in the Holy of Holies of the Coricancha [temple]. According to a contemporary text, the *Relacion anonyma de las costumbres antiques de las naturales del Piru*, this idol took the form of a large marble statue of the god—a statue described as to the hair, complexion, features, raiment and sandals, just as painters represent the apostle Saint Bartholomew. Other accounts of Viracocha likened his appearance to that of the Saint Thomas.[60]

Of course, no one in ancient Peru would have known what Bartholomew or Thomas looked like. However, there is a written record of one Jew who actually visited Peru at the time of the first apostles. He was Jesus Christ, and a description of his visit to the New World is found in the Book of Mormon.[61]

THE GOLDEN GARDEN (GARDEN OF EDEN)

Sullivan provides this description of the Inca temple:

> The first Spanish outriders to reach Cuzco were overwhelmed by the golden garden in the outer courtyard of the Temple of the Sun. It contained life-size effigies of maize and other food plants, of flowers, of golden llamas. By a font of gold stood enormous gold and silver urns overflowing with maize and other sacrificial offerings. The interior walls were clad in gold, and facing the rising sun was an image of the Sun encrusted in emeralds and other precious stones. Countless golden vessels bore the images of every living thing—birds, snakes, crayfish, and caterpillars.[62]

Without understanding why the Incas had a golden garden in their temple, the concept might seem odd as a way to adorn a temple of Jesus Christ. Since the initial Mormon temples usually incorporated a "Garden Room," the symbolism should not be lost on Latter-day Saints. However, the most interesting historical precedent is Solomon's temple, which was also adorned with sheets of gold and had an orchard of gold trees.[63]

Another feature of the Cuzco temple that needs to be understood is why it was lavished with so much gold. The Incas placed no commercial value in the metal. To them it was only a means of reminding them of the glory of god. Alonzo Gaskin writes of the religious symbolism of the metal:

Gold also symbolized the celestial, divine, or godly nature of a thing. Commentators make this connection partly because gold is pure, incorruptible, precious, and glorious. The Apostle Paul established an ancient connection between gold and things celestial when he stated: 'There are also celestial bodies, and bodies terrestrial: but the glory of the celestial is one, and the glory of the terrestrial is another. There is one glory of the sun, and another glory of the moon, and another glory of the stars. . . . (1 Corinthians 15:40–41). Joseph Fielding McConkie wrote, "Gold is the color of the sun, it represents divine power, the splendor of enlightenment, radiance, and glory. Because of its great value, and its radiance, gold is known to us as the possessions of kings and great kingdoms. It is a symbol common to scriptural descriptions of God and the heavenly kingdom."[64]

THE TEMPLE'S GOLDEN FONT AND ALTAR OF PURE GOLD

Hemming notes of the Cuzco temple's golden font: "The font was more substantial. Juan Ruiz de Arce witnessed ceremonies being performed at it during the first year of the Conquest. In the centre of the courtyard is a font, and beside this font is an altar. . . there remains in our convent a large stone font that is octagonal on the outer side. It is over a vara and a half [five feet] in diameter and over a vara and a quarter deep [roughly four feet]."[65] Of course, Solomon's temple also had a great fountain in its courtyard. Likewise the courtyard of the Jerusalem temple had a large brazen altar, while the temple's Altar of Incense had a gold overlay.[66]

The sheer volume of gold found in the temple's garden is staggering. In his *Royal Commentaries of the Inca* (1609) Garcilaso de la Vega writes:

In the time of the Incas, this garden . . . was entirely made of gold and silver; and there were similar gardens about all the royal mansions. Here could be seen all sorts of plants, flowers, trees, animals, both small and large, wild and tame, tiny, crawling creatures such as snakes, lizards, and snails, as well as butterflies and birds of every size; each one of these marvels being placed at the spot that best suited the nature of what it represented.

There were a tall corn stalk and another stalk from the grain they call quinoa, as well as other vegetables and fruit trees, the fruits of which were all very faithfully reproduced in gold and silver. There were also, in the house of the Sun, as well as in that of the king, piles of wool made of gold and silver, and large statues of men, women, and children made of the same materials, in addition to storerooms and recipients for storing the grain they called pirua, all of which, together, tended to lend greater splendor and majesty to the house of their god, the Sun.

All of these valuable works were made by the goldsmiths attached to the Temple, from the tribute of gold and silver that arrived every year from all the provinces of the Empire, and which was so great that the most modest utensils used in the temple, such as pots and pans, or pitchers, were also made of precious metals. For this reason, the temple and its service quarters were called Coricancha, which means the place of gold.[67]

THE TEMPLE'S GOLDEN ALTAR PIECE

The Holy of Holies in the temple in Cuzco housed two treasures, a golden bench or altar and a gold panel or altarpiece. The bench was melted into Spanish bullion. Perhaps the most interesting feature from the Holy of Holies is the great altarpiece that was referred to as "Viracocha's Standard." Fortunately, the Inca Pachakuti Yamqui (Juan Pachacuti) made a crude drawing of the altarpiece and marked on it what he believed the symbols on the altar meant. According to Inca oral tradition "Viracocha's Standard" was created by none other than Manco Capac (Nephi), and thus would have been an item found in the original temple of Manco Capac (Nephi).

According to Sullivan, the symbols on the altarpiece represented important religious concepts. Indeed, they prove that in Manco Capac's

Replica of golden altar of Manco Capac in the Coricancha.

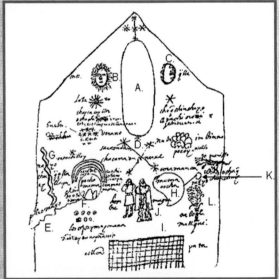

Rough drawing of the altar at the Temple of Viracocha

time the primary god of the Peruvians was Viracocha and not the sun. Sullivan explains that at the very top of the standard is a "male" form of a cross that is represented by the three "equal" stars, (a possible reference to the godhead). Below the cross is a large circle that represents Viracocha, the "sun of the sun" that meant the one who created the sun and its orbits[68]—in other words the first world-age, the Creation. To one side of the oval is the icon of the sun, the male icon, while on the other side is the moon, the female realm.[69] LDS temple seating places men on one side and women on the other. Below the oval symbol of Viracocha is the Inca "female" cross. William Sullivan believes that the male and female crosses represented the "world parents"[70] and Viracocha was their son. He writes: "Here, then, arrayed about the central symbol of Wiraqocha—an oval on the stave—are the world parents. . . . Here also the ultimate, cosmic origin of Wiraqocha's [Christ] androgyny is fully expressed. As the creator of the starry and ecliptic realms, Wiraqocha [Christ] was also their [world parents'—celestial parents'] offspring."[71]

In addition, there is a cluster of twelve or thirteen stars on the altar that could be a reference to the Twelve Tribes of Israel or Viracocha and the Twelve Apostles. Of course, no one today actually knows for certain what Manco Capac meant by the drawings engraved on the golden altarpiece, but one does not need to stretch his imagination far to see that the symbols include the fundamental elements from Lehi's dream. Latin characters have been added to Pachacuti's drawing to identify the author's suggestions of how the symbols could possibly have represented the elements of Lehi's dream.

A. Pachacuti noted that the large golden disk represents Viracocha, whom the Incas called the "Eternal Light." The Lord told Nephi that He was his "light in the wilderness" (1 Nephi 17:13). The display at the Coricancha provides this description: "Wira-qochan (Viracocha) 'Teacher of the world'. The author of the drawing comments that this element was a golden plate, round or oval, that symbolized the creator of the world, Wiraqocha, who was the supreme deity of the Incas according to the Pachacuti Yamqui's chronicle. The plate was made by the order of the first Inca ruler, Manko Qapaq (Manco Capac)."

B. The Sun (Celestial Kingdom or fruit of the Tree of Life)

C. The Moon (Terrestrial Kingdom)

D. Stars (Telestial Kingdom or Southern Cross). Similar symbols of the sun, moon, and stars are found on some Latter-day Saint temples.

E. A twisting river flowing through a canyon. According to the display at the Coricancha, this symbol represented "Pilcomayo (Pillku-mayu), in Quechua—'river of many colors,' probably an extinct name of some specific river of importance (R. Lehmann-Nitsche)." In his dream, Lehi sees his family following the course of a river. The members of Lehi's family were descendents or remnants of the house of Joseph. The "remnant" is a symbol of Joseph's coat of many colors (Alma 46:23).

F. Tall mountains from which the river

flows—exactly the conditions that exist in wadi Tayyib al-Ism, my candidate for the Valley of Lemuel, where Lehi had his dream of the Tree of Life. Undoubtedly, the Valley of Lemuel formed the imagery of Lehi's dream.[72] However, the display in the Coricancha provides another interpretation. It claims that the round sphere represents the "earth." This could be seen as the world, Idumea, or the pride of those in the tall and spacious building of Lehi's dream. The guide at the Coricancha made an interesting observation. He noted that if the ancient Incas knew the world was round, they must have had contact with the ancient Egyptians, who realized that the world was a sphere (1 Nephi 1:2).

G. The Coricancha display suggests that it represents the deity of thunderstorms and lightning, the master of rain. The river in Lehi's dream is characterized as being both of pure waters and of filthy waters. In other words, the river had pure waters until a rain storm transformed it into a muddy torrent.

H. A lake or gulf where those who let go of the iron rod before reaching the tree perished in its depths. The display at the Coricancha notes: "It can be interpreted as the Pacific Ocean or the Titicaca Lake."

I. This figure is believed to have represented a collcampata, meaning terrace of granaries. If this represented a terraced (multileveled) man-made structure, it might also have represented a large and spacious building where people mocked those trying to reach the tree of life; letting go of the rod,

they wandered into the gulf (see H above). Between the river and the terraced structure are seven round objects. The Coricancha display suggests that these are "eyes." The eyes could represent people looking from the river to the man-made structure. The Book of Mormon states that when the people saw the tall and spacious building, "they did cast their eyes about as if they were ashamed" (1 Nephi 8:25–27).

J. Lehi and Sariah looking toward the tree of life. Pachacuti labeled the left figure *hombre* meaning "man," and the right figure *mujer* and *mama* ("woman" and "mother").

K. According to the display at the Coricancha, the small circle and line that goes to the cocha (gulf) represent: "Pucyo (*pukyu*), in Quechua—'water spring.' " In Lehi's dream a straight and narrow path, as well as an iron rod, led to the fountain of living waters" (1 Nephi 11:25, 12:16)

L. The Tree of Life is clearly marked by Pachacuti as "*arbol*," which is Spanish for "tree." The tree appears to be a stylized palm. The Coricancha display reads: "Manko Qapaq [Manco Capac or Nephi] established a cult to his parents [Lehi and Sariah at the tree] symbolized by two trees in Paqariq Tanpu [perhaps the Valley of Lemuel], the mythical place of origin of the Incas." Above the figure of a tree is a grouping that looks like a pile of stones. The Coricancha display suggests that this represents "Pocóy (*poqoy mita*) in Quechua—"the season when the crops ripen." The fruit of the Tree of Life was of perfect ripeness, being most

precious and desirable above all other fruit (1 Nephi 15:36).

DID THE TEMPLE PLATES CONTAIN AN HISTORICAL RECORD?

The Inca temple was lined with golden plates, all of which were melted down by the Spaniards. The existence of golden plates raises an interesting question. Were there inscriptions on the thin golden plates that lined the walls of the temple? Since the plates were destroyed, we will never know if reformed Egyptian characters appeared on some of the plates. However, there was a sacred history recorded on boards adorned in gold and that were kept in the Holy of Holies in the temple in Cuzco. We cannot be certain what these gold-adorned boards were, since they were also destroyed. Sarmiento recorded this interesting facet of the Inca temple:

Besides this they had, and still have, special historians in these nations, an hereditary office descending from father to son. . . . He [Inca Yapanqui] had them [historians] in Cuzco for a long time, examining them concerning their antiquities, origin, and the most notable events in their history. These were painted on great boards, and deposited in the temple of the Sun, in a great hall. There such boards, adorned with gold, were kept as in our libraries, and learned persons were appointed, who were well versed in the art of understanding and declaring their contents. No one was allowed to enter where these boards were kept, except the Inca and the historians, without a special order of the Inca."[73]

In Lehi's era, hieroglyphic characters adorned the walls of Egyptian temples. To this day, calligraphy is a highly praised art form in the Middle East. Large stylized verses of sacred Arabic writing and poetry are commonly found on walls of public buildings, mosques, and private homes in the Middle East. Only authorized Inca-temple priestly historians were allowed to read the boards in the Holy of Holies. The Inca temple boards bring to mind Mosiah's need to teach his son the Egyptian language so they could read the sacred Nephite plates (Mosiah 1:2), something that would have been impossible for the common Nephite to do since they spoke only the language of the people.

At first glance, one might not see the significance of having found an historical record written on wooden boards. However to Latter-day Saints this could be a major clue in locating the Book of Mormon lands. The reason for this lies in the Latter-day Saint interpretation of a prophecy made by Ezekiel:

> The word of the Lord came unto me, saying Moreover, thou son of man, take thee one stick, and write upon it, For Judah, and for the children of Israel his companions: then take another stick, and write upon it, For Joseph, the stick of Ephraim, and for all the house of Israel his companions: and join them one to another into one stick; and they shall become one in thine hand. (Ezekiel 37:15–17).

Latter-day Saints believe that these verses foretell the coming forth of the Book of Mormon, which is the record or stick of Joseph. We believe that in the last days, the Book of Mormon, with the Bible, will together testify of the Savior.

What most students of the Book of Mormon or Bible do not realize is what Ezekiel meant by the word "stick." Elder Boyd K. Packer stated: "The sticks, of course, are records or books. In ancient Israel records were written upon tablets of wood or scrolls rolled upon sticks."[74] Monte S. Nyman, of Brigham Young University notes:

> However, writing on wooden tablets has more recently been discovered. Wooden tablets were discovered and reported to the academic world in 1948. The tablets were discovered in ancient southern Babylonia, the area where Ezekiel was in captivity. *The New English Bible*, a translation sponsored by the Protestant churches and Bible societies in the British Isles, translates Ezekiel 37:15–20 as follows: "These were the words of the Lord to me: Man, take one leaf of a wood tablet and write on it, 'Judah and his associates of Israel.' Then take another leaf and write on it, 'Joseph, the leaf of Ephraim and all his associates of Israel.' Now bring the two together to form a tablet; then they will be a folding tablet in your hand."[75]

If the wooden boards in the Cuzco temple contained the record of the large or small plates of Nephi, then there was a literal "stick of Joseph" found among the pre-Columbian Peruvians.

THE PRIESTHOOD AND TEMPLE KEYS

Cobo wrote, "People came there [the temple] from everywhere with their most precious things to make their vows and sacrifices."[76] That is to say, the Incas gathered to the temple in Cuzco from throughout the Andes. The Prophet Joseph Smith taught that the people of God should gather because:

> The main object was to build unto the Lord a house whereby He could reveal unto His people the ordinances of His and the glories of His kingdom, and teach the people the way of salvation; for there are certain ordinances and principles that, when they are taught and practiced, must be done in a place or house built for that purpose.
>
> It was the design of the councils of heaven before the world was, that the principles and laws of the priesthood should be predicated upon the gathering of the people in every age of the world. Jesus did everything to gather the people, and they would not be gathered, and he

therefore poured out curses upon them. Ordinances instituted in the heavens before the foundation of the world, in the priesthood, for the salvation of men, are not to be altered or changed. All must be saved on the same principles.[77]

We learn from Joseph Smith that the temple ordinances require the lawful authority (keys) and principles of the priesthood, and that if ordinances of salvation are to be valid, the laws and principles cannot be altered by man. In this regard, by the time the Spanish arrived in Cuzco, the temples' practices had been handed down for many generations by an untold number of priests. Thus, the oral traditions would naturally have become distorted. One faded Inca myth provides a possible explanation of how Lehi received the authority to build a temple (requiring the Melchizedek Priesthood) and make sacrifices upon an altar (a duty of the Aaronic Priesthood) (1 Nephi 2:7).

Recalling the story of how Viracocha visited Manco Capac's father, Sullivan writes: "According to a myth recorded by Pachakuti Yamqui, the god Wiraqocha [Viracocha/Christ], just before leaving the 'earth,' via the river Chacamarca, met with the father [Lehi] of the yet-unborn Manco Capac [Nephi] and left for the child his 'staff.'"[78]

A Peruvian paradigm for the Book of Mormon would suggest that Jesus Christ (Viracocha) gave Lehi (Manco Capac's father) his "staff" or priesthood even before Nephi's birth. The Inca's "staff" was the tupayauri. It was a wooden pole with a copper knife affixed to the top and had purple and black ribbons flowing from it.[79] Sullivan notes that the tupayauri staff was "the symbol of Imperial authority among the historical Inca."[80]

Webster's Dictionary provides these definitions for a staff as "a supporting rod . . . a rod carried as a symbol of office or authority."[81] From the scriptures we learn that a staff or rod had priesthood association; for example, the iron rod is the word of God—implying the authority to speak in behalf of the Almighty (1 Nephi 11:25, 15:23–24); the Lord straitened Israel in the wilderness with his rod (1 Nephi 17:41); the Lord will give Moses power in a rod (2 Nephi 3:17); the rod shall come forth out of the stem of Jesse (Joseph Smith in the last days, 2 Nephi 21:1). Finally, the LDS Bible Dictionary states: "Moses' and Aaron's rods represented authority."[82]

Although we have no record that Lehi carried a staff or rod, the Book of Mormon hints that Lehi received the priesthood authorities before the birth of his son, Nephi (Manco Capac). In the first chapter of the Book of Mormon, Nephi tells us that his father, Lehi, received several profound revelations, including, as with Moses, a pillar of fire that spoke unto him (1 Nephi 1:6). Lehi also had a dream in which priesthood officers appeared to him: "God sitting upon his throne [the Father], . . . One descending out of the midst of heaven [the Son, and finally the Holy Ghost]. . . . He [Lehi] was filled with the Spirit of the Lord" (vv. 8–9, 12). "And he also saw twelve others following him . . . they came and stood before my father [Lehi] [perhaps ordaining him with the priesthood and temple keys], and gave him a book, and bade him that he should read" (vv. 10–11).

It seems likely that the book that was given to Lehi contained instructions for the temple and thus indicated to him that the priests in Jerusalem were not following correct priesthood practices. When Lehi read the book, he realized that and said, "Wo, wo unto Jerusalem, for I have seen thine abominations! Yea, and many things did my father read concerning Jerusalem—that it should be destroyed" (1 Nephi 1:13). It is interesting to note that Nephi appears to be telling us that the revelations Lehi had in verses 6–15 were received by Lehi before his "account of my [Nephi's] proceeding *in my days*" (1 Nephi 1:17; emphasis added). In other words, the first fifteen verses of the Book of First Nephi, where Lehi possibly received the priesthood keys, took place before Nephi was born and are, therefore, consistent with the legend of the Incas.

The fact that "the twelve" appeared to Lehi indicates that the quorum members have the stewardship for administering the keys for temple work and the work for the dead for the house of Israel. In Old Testament times, "twelve dead sticks," one for each tribe, were kept in the tabernacle in Israel.[83]

THE LAYOUT OF MANCO CAPAC'S CITY

The division of the Incas geography did not end with their cardinal quartering of the kingdom. Like the Utah towns chartered by Brigham Young, the villages in Peru were laid out according to a cardinal matrix. "Cobo states that the Cuzco region was further partitioned by forty-two abstract lines, or ceques that radiated out, like spokes of a wheel, from the Coricancha [central temple]. The course of these lines was defined by the location of hundreds of sacred objects, or huacas, situated in or around the city of Cuzco."[84] Sullivan explains:

> Between 1976 and 1980, Urton conducted ethnoastronomical fieldwork in a single community, Misminay, in the Department of Cuzco. Among his findings was the fact that the village itself was divided into four quarters by two intersecting footpaths. The footpaths ran intercardinally, that is, one ran northeast-southwest, while the other ran southeast-northwest. These paths crossed in the middle of the village. Noting reports of similar quadri-partitions of villages in contemporary Ecuador and the Ayacucho region of Peru, as well as evidence of similar arrangements by the Inca, Urton concluded that, ideally, *the footpaths were thought to run to the four rising and setting points of the solstice suns on the horizon.*[85]

The question needs to be answered, "Why were the footpaths of ancient Peru aligned in a southeasterly and northwesterly direction and not true north and south?" Sullivan provides an interesting answer, "The mythical 'trajectory' of the god Wiraqocha [Viracocha/Jesus Christ], also stressed one of these intercardinal axes. Wiraqocha first appears at Titicaca (southeast), thence to travel the Andes in a northwesterly direction, finally leaving this world at Manta in Ecuador."[86] In other words, the villages of the Andes were marked off in quarters, with a northeast-southwest dividing footpath being established in remembrance of the mission of Viracocha (Christ) and the path that he walked from his temple in Cuzco to what is today Ecuador.

By the time the Incas finished dividing Peru, they had turned the Andes into a giant solar calendar. Sullivan describes how they did it:

> From the gold-encrusted epicenter of the Inca Empire, the Temple of the Sun in Cuzco, there emanated a system of between forty and forty-two imaginary lines in all directions to the horizon. These lines, called seques, meaning "rays," functioned, among other uses, as a calendar. Each seque, conceptualized as running over hill and dale in an unswervingly straight line to the horizon, passed through or near a number of shrines along the way. Those shrines—called wakas [huacas or temples], either natural or man-made, but each connected to Inca lore and religion numbered on average between seven and

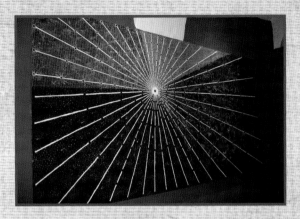

Seques and four quarters dividing the Inca kingdom surrounding the Cuzco central temple, Archeaological Museum Cuzco. .

nine per seque, and there were a total of 328 in all. Zuidema and Urton have pointed out that, according to the Spanish Chronicles, each waka of the seque system was allotted its own day for special propitiation, accounting for 328 days out of the 365 in the year. What about the "missing" thirty-seven days? Zuidema and Urton argue persuasively that these are accounted for by the thirty-seven days of invisibility of the Pleiades (owing to their proximity to the sun) at the latitude of Cuzco.[87]

During my mission I served for six months in Cuzco. While knocking on doors at night in dimly lit neighborhoods, I noticed how the stars would shine all the way down to the horizon. At nearly 11,000 feet above sea level, the night sky is haze-free, and the thin atmosphere allows the stars to be seen until they pass beneath the curvature of the earth. It is easy to see why the Peruvians followed the movements of the planets and stars. They were experts in tracking and mapping the Milky Way. Sullivan explains: "In the same way that men today in rural New England lean on the sides of pickup trucks, feet in slushy snow, and trade opinions on whether the time has come to tap the maples, contemporary Quechua peasants confer about the clarity of the Pleiades and the proper time to plant."[88] Mosley explains:

> The Coricancha [temple/Golden Enclosure] was the sighting center for a remarkable system of radial organization. A sundial is perhaps the nearest analogy, but the grand temple was more akin to the hub of a cosmic dial for tracking multitudes of celestial phenomena and correlating them with terrestrial phenomena. Radiating out of the Coricancha [Nephi's temple or Golden Enclosure], at sighting lines, called ceques, stretched to the horizon or beyond. Also these rays, or adjacent to them some 328 huacas, pillars, and survey points were arranged in a hierarchical manner. Astronomer Tony Aveni of Colgate University notes that the 328 stations represent the days in 12 sidereal lunar months. Given the importance to irrigation, it is not coincidental that one-third of the ceque (seque) points comprised the major springs and water sources of the region.[89]

Bruce W. Warren suggests that the sidereal Mayan lunar calendar that was carved on stones might constitute evidence of the Jaredites having been in Mesoamerica.[90] Current archaeological evidence shows however that the Mayan culture came thousands of years after the Jaredites came to the Americas. Besides, as Warren states, "Those who have some acquaintance with Mesoamerican calendars know that the most widely used calendar was one that is composed of 365 days, or a solar calendar that began with the summer solstice."[91] The Peruvians also used a sidereal calendar to mark the months, one not cut in stone; rather the Incas made the entire city of Cuzco and its surrounding lands a giant solar calendar.

The Nephites used a lunar calendar to mark their months, with the Nephite word for "month" meaning moon (Omni 1:21). The Incas also had lunar months and in both the Quechua and Aymara languages the word for "month" and "moon" are likewise the same word (killa in Quechua and pacsi in Aymara).[92]

New Cuzco

The history of the Book of Mormon is one of repetitive cycles of righteous revivals eventually turning into a loss of faithfulness and destruction. The city of Cuzco had a cyclical past. Sullivan writes that the "Inca civilization was wed to an ancient sorrow, witnessed through its myths to very great cycles of creation and loss. Along with so many other tribes, the Incas had suffered the legacy of warfare and the memory of better days."[93] Indeed Cuzco seems to have been destroyed and rebuilt several times. During my time there, I observed that on a single masonry wall there might be three or four different styles of stonework. Cieza de León wrote of the masonry of the Incas: "In all Spain I have seen nothing that can compare with these walls and the laying of their stones."[94] The interesting aspect of the stonework in Cuzco is that the lower stones of the walls (those laid during the earlier period of construction) exhibited the finer workmanship.

Today it is difficult to assign specific dates to the Inca stone walls that form the foundations of the buildings in Cuzco. Jean-Pierre Protzen wrote in 2000: "Very few individual buildings are unequivocally attributed to a specific Inca ruler, and sites known to have been established by a given ruler are likely to have been modified over the years. Too few sites have been investigated with a view to their construction history to be certain of which features are associated with which construction phase."[95]

What is known is that the Incas whom the Spanish discovered had recently rebuilt most of Cuzco, including its great temple. The Incas were attempting to recreate the golden age of their hero Manco Capac (Nephi). Sullivan continues:

> The Inca Empire was an attempt to set things right, to return to the Andean peoples their birthright of unity in diversity. If it took a certain arrogance to declare themselves the executors of the divine will, the Incas nonetheless attempted to materialize a vision that was self-consciously tempered with historical maturity. . . . Manco Capac, along with his brothers and sisters, "walled up" their dangerous brother Ayar Cachi [Laman]. . . . The Inca Emperors had no purpose greater than the revivification of the legacy of Tiahuanaco [Nephi's camp on the Island in Lake Titicaca].[96]

In other words, the later Incas did not build Cuzco, they only rebuilt the city using some of the existing foundations, and did so trying to emulate the glory of their capital's ancient days. The driving force behind the resurrection of Cuzco was Inca Pachacuti, the king known as the "Builder."

Who exactly were Pachacuti and the other thirteenth-century-AD Incas? Are they candidates for the descendants of the Nephites or the

Lamanites? The Spanish reported that the Inca nobility were fair-skinned. This would hint that they could have been surviving Nephites. Several verses in the Book of Mormon suggest that some Nephites did survive the final war with the Lamanites (Mormon 8:24, Moroni 1:2). Another possibility is that the Incas were remnants of the Privileged Incas, the Tambo Indians who befriended the Nephites, and whose rulers would have been part of the Nephite nobility and become fairer-skinned over time by intermarrying with the Nephites. Finally, the Inca nobility could have been Lamanites who were attempting to adopt parts of the Nephi culture while retaining elements of their own. Possible evidence of this final scenario is found in the physical layout of Cuzco. When the Incas rebuilt Cuzco, they borrowed strong elements of Tiahuanaco architecture.[97] Since Tiahuanaco was on the east end of Lake Titicaca, it was most likely a Lamanite city. The jury is still out, but the fair-skinned Inca nobility of fifteenth-century-AD Peru spoke Quechua. Their tribal language strongly implies that they were descendents of surviving Nephites, or more likely, the Privileged Inca class.

TEMPLE OF VIRACOCHA

The Spanish discovered a second important temple in Cuzco called the Quishuarcancha. Like the Golden Enclosure, it was destroyed by the Spanish. Within the temple was an interesting figure of the Creator of the World, Viracocha (Christ). Cobo writes of this statue: "It was made of gold, the size of a ten-year-old boy, the shape of a shining man standing upright with his right arm raised, his hand almost closed, and his thumb and first finger held up, like a person who is giving a command."[98] Although the description of the statue is brief, the

description of the statue's body positions hint of Solomonic associations.

THE TOWER NEAR THE TEMPLE

Between 160–150 BC the Book of Mormon's wicked King Noah "built a tower [in the city of Nephi] near the temple; yea, a very high tower, even so high that he could stand upon the top thereof and overlook the land of Shilom, and also the land Shelon, which was possessed by the Lamanites; and he could even look over all the land round about" (Mosiah 11:12).

We learn from this verse that the Lamanites lived within site of Cuzco, and from the tower near the temple, the king observed the movements of his enemies. When the cruel elder brother of Manco Capac, Ayar Cachi [Laman], finally freed himself from the cave, he took up residence at Guanacauri, a hill that can be seen "on the horizon of Cuzco."[99] Mosley tells us that "Nearby [the Cuzco temple] towered the tallest of all edifices, a grand spire of exquisite masonry that cast no noontime shadow at zenith. The coming of zenith was precisely foretold from a tower window by observing sunrise over the marked point of the distant horizon."[100]

WALLS, RESORT, AND TOWER ON A HILL NORTH OF THE CITY

"He [King Noah] caused many buildings to be built in the land of Shilom, and he caused a great tower to be built on the hill north of the land of Shilom, which had been a resort for the children of Nephi at the time they fled out of the land" (Mosiah 11:13).

Kocherhans presents an interesting argument for where this second tower of King Noah was located. From verses 12 and 13 of Mosiah 11, Kocherhans lists several features of the city of Nephi.

1. It is apparent from these scriptures that the temple constructed under the direction of Nephi, around 550 BC, was still in existence four hundred years later and still a landmark in the city of Nephi.

2. The city of Nephi appears to be surrounded by sufficient level ground that, from the temple location, an area called Shemlon occupied by Lamanites, could be seen and distinguished from the city of Nephi.

3. To the north of the city of Nephi was a Nephite community called Shilom. It could be seen from the tower by the temple

and distinguished from Shemlon and the north borders of the city of Nephi.

4. On the hill on the north of Shilom was a place of last resort★ or small fort built for the protection of the people. It seems reasonable that the distance to the hill from the borders of the city of Nephi would not have been excessive, in order for the people to reach it in time of attack [★*Resort*: ultimate means of relief, Noah Webster's Dictionary 1828][101]

Kocherhans refines our understanding of what a Nephite "resort" was by citing Alma 48:8, "he had been strengthening the armies of the Nephites, and erecting small forts, or places of resort; throwing up banks of earth around about to enclose his armies, and also building walls of stone." Kocherhans concludes:

After years of research and studying ruins of the western hemisphere, I have found this picture in the book *The Last of the Incas*, by Edward Hyams and George Ordish. On page 153, it shows that a place called Sacsahuaman by the Inca, was an ancient fortress, built on a hill to the north of the city of today's Cuzco, Peru.

Then in Ancient America by Jonathan Norton Leonard, on page 133, I found an aerial picture of the same fortress, with this caption under the picture: "Massive Triple Walls guard Cuzco's Sacsahuaman citadel, whose ruined foundations are visible at top right. Circular walls marked the site of a tower."

[In] the *National Geographic*, December 1973 edition, I found still further

The massive Fortress of Sacsahuaman, Cuzco reminds us of the strength of its builders.

collaboration with this great picture and commentary: "Navel of the world" they called it Cuzco, capital of the Inca Empire. From sketchy Spanish Accounts, artist Donald A. Mackay has "reconstructed the city on its still-surviving foundations. . ." Notice the tower on the north of the city.

Massive stone at Sacsahuaman

On page 776 of the same *National Geographic* issue is a caption that reads: "Rocks of ages underpin much of modern Cuzco, sprawling in the valley beyond the massive hilltop fortress of Sacsahuaman. Pachacuti in the 1400s began rebuilding the city, oldest continually inhabited metropolis in the Americas."

That information also agrees with the Book of Mormon, for we know from the scriptures that the city of Nephi was the main location of both the Nephites and then Lamanites from the time it was established by Nephi and the followers of Jesus Christ throughout Book of Mormon history.

And here in the city of Cuzco is an ancient block wall, again built with the same precision as the rock work on the fortress. This could have been part of the base of the high tower that King

Noah built, or perhaps of the temple that Nephi built.

It was very exciting to finally find a place that physically matches the Book of Mormon scriptures!!

In all my years of research, I have not been able to find any other location in the western hemisphere that matches so precisely the description in the scriptures of the land and city of Nephi, as does this Cuzco, Peru area.[102]

Although I agree with Kocherhans' conclusion, that Cuzco is the best candidate for the city of Nephi in all the Western Hemisphere, it must be remembered that the Inca king Pachacuti rebuilt the city and fortress of Sacsahuaman in the fifteenth century. However, Pachacuti was attempting to rebuild Cuzco in the image of its past glory so one would assume that to some degree he used the original foundations and what was remembered of the city's past layout as a model for its later reconstruction. In this regard, the strategic location of Sacsahuaman suggests that it is highly probable that in ancient times a fort existed at Sacsahuaman. It would also seem logical to assume that like the later Incas, the builders of the ancient fort would have wisely utilized a lookout tower to determine the movements in the surrounding valleys.

By any measure Sacsahuaman was a magnificent "resort." Bauer describes the importance of the fort and notes that archaeologists have now dated the site to an era close to that of King Noah. He writes, "The most important site outside the city but within the Cuzco Basin is the massive site of Sacsayhuaman [Sacsahuaman]. It is located on a steep hill that overlooks the city and provides an impressive view of the valley to

Sun calendar at Sacsahuaman, center was the base of a tall tower.

the southeast. Surface collections at Sacsayhuaman indicate that the site dates back to at least
the Qotakalli Period [AD 200–600]."[103] Michael
Mosley notes:

> The head of the cat was formed by
> the largest and highest edifices, called
> Sacsahuaman. Perched atop a high hill,
> one side of the complex ran along a cliff
> with a commanding view of the city. The
> opposite side of the hill was relatively low
> and encased by three successively higher
> zigzag terraces. Each wall employed the
> finest and most impressive of Inca polygo-
> nal masonry, including individual stone
> blocks weighing from 90 to more than
> 100 metric tons. In plan Sacsahuaman is
> suggestive of an elongated animal head
> topped with the great terraces. A mar-
> velous complex of fine ashlar buildings
> crown a flattened hill, including tall
> towers, and circular and rectangular
> structures. Excavations have revealed
> a complex system of finely cut stone
> channels and drains suggesting ritual
> manipulations of water. Cieza de León
> says that Pachacuti intended Sacsahua-
> man to be a temple that would surpass
> all other edifices in splendor. Garcilaso
> de la Vega relates that only royalty could
> enter the sacrosanct complex because
> it was a house of the sun, of arms and
> war, and a temple of prayer and sacri-
> fice. Construction supposedly employed
> 30,000 workers who labored for several
> generations.[104]

Hiram Bingham, the American explorer who
discovered Machu Picchu, called Sacsahuaman
the "most unbelievable achievement of ancient
man in the Americas."[105] McIntyre writes of

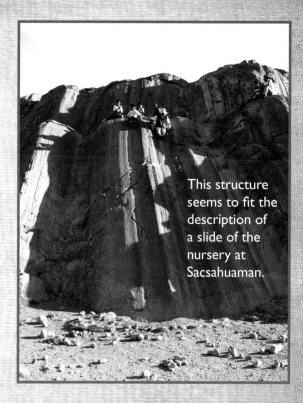

This structure seems to fit the description of a slide of the nursery at Sacsahuaman.

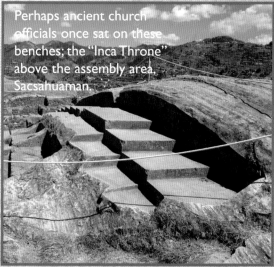

Perhaps ancient church officials once sat on these benches; the "Inca Throne" above the assembly area, Sacsahuaman.

Sacsayhuaman: "Later observers doubted that Indians could haul such huge stones up here and shape them so precisely. They thought it was the devil's doing. Others insisted the Incas knew how to soften stones and mold them like clay. The latest fad attributes construction to extraterrestrial beings."[106]

Today, nothing remains of the buildings at Sacsayhuaman. Following a bitter battle between the Spaniards and an Indian uprising, the Spaniards used the buildings of the fortress as a source of building stones. Within a year of the battle, most of the buildings and towers had vanished.[107]

Besides being a fortress, Sacsayhuanman was an important religious center in pre-Columbian Peru. Bauer notes: "The most notable feature of this area [middle site of Sacsayhuaman] is the famous carved stone, referred to as 'the throne of the Incas.' This carving was a shrine of the Cuzco ceque system and may have held an important role in the Inca rituals that took place in the complex."[108] "The throne of the Incas" was carved from a single massive stone. The throne rests in front of a large open area where thousands of people could gather. The throne consists of one large central seat and twelve smaller seats on its side. Just to the east of the throne is a building that is separated into twelve niches.

Just behind the sacred gathering area next to the Inca throne, is what could be called an ancient playground for children. Long slides were formed in the great rock.

WIMPILLAY—POSSIBLE SITE FOR THE ORIGINAL CITY OF NEPHI

Cuzco is the oldest continuously inhabited city in the Americas. It has been rebuilt several times, subjected to repairs from major

Ruins of town of Wimpillay near Cuzco: our candidate for Nephi's first settlement.

earthquakes, and is today a bustling city. It is impossible to know what ancient remains lie beneath the foundations of the city's occupied buildings and streets. Inca oral traditions place Manco Capac's first settlement at the temple site in Cuzco. However, recent discoveries of the ruins of Wimpillay near the Cuzco airport hint that it could have been the city of Nephi. Initial excavations at Wimpillay point to many features that one would expect to find in the ruins of the early Nephite capital: a sacred temple, a high quality pottery of an elite society, a sacred area on a hill directly above the city—possibly the site of an ancient altar—and a tower. Bauer concludes:

> I currently interpret the site of Wimpillay to be the center of a valley-wide chiefdom during the Late Formative Phase. Closely associated with this center was a ritual precinct, Muyu Orco, which continued to hold special significance in the valley until the arrival of the Spaniards.[109]

Through time, a select few sites grew to occupy disproportionately important roles within the regional settlement patterns. In the Cuzco Basin, it appears that the site of Wimpillay emerged as the center of a small chiefdom-level society during the Late Formative Phase (500 BC–AD 200). The site is the largest Late Formative Phase occupation known in the valley and contains the finest Formative ceramics. Adjacent to Wimpillay is the distinctly round hill of Muyu Orco, the top of which contains a ceremonial sunken court dating to the Late Formative. The emergent leaders of Wimpillay may have controlled the other settlements within a few hours' walk, and toward the end of the period, perhaps the entire valley came to be united under a single elite clan located in this village.[110]

Dating Wimpillay to the Late Formative Phase (500 BC to AD 200) is important. Not only does it place the Cuzco valley settlements within the Book of Mormon time frame, it also places the legendary Manco Capac [Nephi] within the same period. We can assume this because the Spanish found the *huaca* and possibly the mummy of Manco Capac, not in Cuzco, but at Wimpillay.[111]

Wherever Nephi was buried, we owe so much to him. He gave us the precious first chapters of the Book of Mormon. Perhaps, the greatest gift he gave to humanity was his example of how one person, despite obstacles that would have crushed the spirit of most men, can live a pure Christian life. To this day, the descendents of the Incas teach their children:

> *Manco Inca [Nephi], the first inhabitant of these lands, when he died, was taken to heaven to the house and place of this god called Pirua, and that there he was ensconced and feasted by that same god.*[112]

The Snake motif on walls in Cuzco strongly resembles the Snake Motif in the ruins of the People of Lehi Temple.

The author at Ula, Saudi Arabia

Lake Titicaca at Sunset,
12,500 feet above sea level.

LAKE TITICACA BASIN, THE LAND OF ZARAHEMLA

VII

*Neither durst they march down against the city
of Zarahemla; neither durst they cross
the head of Sidon, . . .*

ALMA 56:25

Identifying the Andean city of Cuzco as a candidate for the city of Nephi was facilitated in part by analyzing the striking parallels between the first king of the Nephites, Nephi, and his counterpart, the first king of the Incas, Manco Capac. The first Nephite migration to the land of Zarahemla was achieved by another Moses-like leader, Mosiah. It would seem pertinent then to start our search for the land of Zarahemla by first asking, "Is there found among the oral traditions of the Inca kings a ruler who can be matched with a significant degree of certainty to King Mosiah in the Book of Mormon?"

The Inca ruling class consisted of kings and priestly record-keepers. The early Book of Mormon kings appear to have been the direct descendents of Nephi, while a parallel set of prophet-scribes maintained the sacred plates. When Nephi anointed his successor, he did so "according to the reigns of the kings" (Jacob 1:9), that is, his eldest son succeeded him. Initially, Nephi served as both king and the first

record keeper. Eventually he ordained his much younger brother Jacob to be the record keeper for the next generation (2 Nephi 6:2, Jacob 1:1–2, 17–18). Jacob would have been approximately the same age as Nephi's oldest son, the second Nephite king. During the time the Nephites ruled the city of Nephi, Jacob was succeeded as the record-keeper by Enos, Jarom, Omni, Amaron, Abinadom, and Amaleki. Including Nephi and Jacob there were eight Nephite record-keepers in the city of Nephi.

It was during the life of the eighth Nephite record keeper, Amaleki, that Mosiah and his followers fled the city and resettled among the Mulekites in the land of Zarahemla. If there were an equal number of generations of kings in the city of Nephi before the fall of the city to the Lamanites, then Mosiah would have been the eighth Nephite king. Apparently, he was born a sovereign, for when he arrived in Zarahemla he was selected to become the king of the land (Omni 1:12). It would follow then, that if Mosiah had ruled in the city of Nephi before he led the exodus to Zarahemla, then it is likely that the eighth Nephite king, Mosiah, fled the city of Nephi (Cuzco) after having been warned by God.

How does this compare with the oral traditions of the Inca kings? As discussed earlier, current archaeologists believe that the genealogy of the Inca kings of Cuzco should be divided into two separate civilizations that were divided by a great time span. The first eight Inca kings ruled Cuzco in antiquity, while the remainder ruled just prior to the arrival of the Spanish.[1] According to the oral traditions of the Incas, the eighth Inca king, Viracocha Inca, fled the city before the Chanca Indians (Laman, called Cachi).[2] They also said of the eighth Inca king, "This one was named Viracocha Inca because he was very friendly with his people and affable, governing very calmly, always giving gifts and doing favors. For this reason, the people loved him greatly."[3]

As for the possibility that Inca Viracocha was a pure blooded Nephite, Cástulo Martínez provides some interesting evidence:

Effectively, a few years after the Spanish conquest, Juan Polo de Ondegardo discovered the mummified bodies of three Incan sovereigns and two queens in a house in Cuzco . The mummies had been carefully hidden there before the arrival of Pizarro and his conquistadors. The chronicler verified that one of the mummies had such blond hair that it appeared to be almost white. It was the mummy of the eighth Incan Chief who had taken the name of the god Viracocha, and who most likely married his sister, a woman named *Mama Runta*, or Mother Egg (Juan Polo de Ondegardo y Zárate, *Tratado y Averiguación Sobre los Errores y*

Supersticiones de los Indios [1559]). Garcilaso de la Vega explains that the reason of that term [egg] was because "she was of a much whiter color than all the other Indians" (Garcilaso de la Vega , *Comentarios Reales de los Incas,* Libro Quinto, cap. 1, sección 28 [1609]). In addition, the Peruvian Felipe Guaman Poma de Ayala, corroborates that the emperor Viracocha was actually "a white-skinned, lightly bearded gentleman." The beard, in addition to the color of the skin, is an important element, because those features distinguished them from the Amerindians who were generally beardless (Felipe Guaman Poma de Ayala, *Nueva corónica y buen gobierno* [1615]).[4]

It should be noted that Viracocha Inca also took upon himself the name of the god Viracocha ("Christian"). The Inca storytellers say that one day the king announced to this people "that Viracocha Pacha-yachachic [God] had spoken to him and that god had talked to him that night. Then all of his people stood up and called him Viracocha Inca, which means king and god, and from then on he was called by this name."[5] In the tradition of the Biblical prophets, for example Abram, Jacob, Saul, the eighth Inca king was given a "new name" after hearing the voice of God.

In my opinion, Viracocha Inca is a likely candidate for the Book of Mormon king, Mosiah. Like the eighth Inca king, Mosiah received a revelation from God (Omni 1:12,13), fled the capital city with his people (Omni 1:12), was a king (Omni 1:12), and took upon himself the name of his god (believers in Zarahemla were called Christians, Alma 46:14–15). He must also have been beloved of his people, for Mosiah taught

the people, united them, and was appointed king by both the minority Nephites and the majority Mulekites (Omni 1:18–19).

PUKARA, AN EMPIRE PARALLEL TO ZARAHEMLA

In chapter 4, we briefly examined four reasons why Pukara is a likely candidate for Zarahemla. First, it was populated by the Quechua-speaking people who were disliked throughout history by the Aymara who lived on the opposite end of Lake Titicaca. This fits the Book of Mormon scenario of the warring Nephites and Lamanites who were separated by a strip of wilderness that stretches between two seas. Second, the city of Pukara came into prominence at roughly 200 BC, the period when king Mosiah arrived at Zarahemla. Third, Pukara is 120 miles south of Cuzco, which is how Zarahemla was geographically situated in reference to the city of Nephi ("down" in Quechua means "south"; see Omni 1:13, Mormon 1:6). Fourth, the original land of Zarahemla (Pukara) was bordered by the sea on the west (Pacific) and the sea on the east (Titicaca).

Kolata states of Pukara:

However we interpret the nature of Pukara influence outside of its Altiplano core territory, it is evident that this dynamic Altiplano city was the most powerful and well-integrated political force of its time in the southern Andes. For the first time, with Pukara we see evidence of a corporate art style in the service of elites that had extensive impact throughout the Titicaca basin and the adjoining coastal regions of southern Peru and northern Chile.[6]

A small portion of the Andes mountains north of Pukara. Can you find the secret hiding places of the Gadianton robbers?

PUKARA AND THE MULEKITES

As Mosiah's migration continued south, they eventually discovered a large community of people called the Mulekites, in a land called Zarahemla. The Mulekites left Jerusalem approximately the same time as Lehi. Thus, for Pukara to have been Zarahemla, the Mulekites would have needed to have settled in the promised land on the Altiplano northwest of Lake Titicaca, the area where Pukara was located. Pukara is located approximately 150 miles inland from the Pacific. The Book of Mormon tells us that once the Mulekites crossed the waters and landed, they went "into the land" (Omni 1:16), thus they did

not remain along the Pacific shoreline, but settled inland. After their initial migration, the Mulekites remained at the same place (Omni 1:16).

Since we know from the Inca traditions that the lands around today's Lima, Peru were known by the Indians as the land of the people of Desolation, then Pukara would have been located in the right direction from the Book of Mormon land of Desolation (Helaman 3:3–5). That is, when the Mulekites arrived they found the land northward covered with the bones of dead Jaredites (Omni 1:22); thus the Jaredite bones (in the land of Desolation) were in the "land northward" of Zarahemla where the statement was

originally recorded. Being located southeast of Lima, Pukara matches the general location of Zarahemla.

The existence of the Mulekites raises an interesting question in reference to any candidate for the land of Zarahemla. *How could the Nephites have lived for nearly four hundred years in relative proximity to the Mulekites without having discovered them?* In a Pukara model for Zarahemla the answer is straightforward. There are two possible explanations for this lack of interaction between the Nephites at the city of Nephi (Cuzco) and the Mulekites at Zarahemla (Pukara).

First, there were Lamanites to the immediate south of the city of Nephi. Thus, there was an enemy barrier between the Nephites and Mulekites. This appears to have been the case between Cuzco and Pukara, where Aymara-speaking people lived between the Quechua-speaking people of Cuzco and Pukara.

Second, the Book of Mormon indicates that there was a narrow passage between the land northward and the land southward (Mormon 2:29). The narrow "passage" was a unique feature, and should not be confused with the "narrow strip of wilderness" or "the narrow neck of land" that are cited elsewhere in the Book of Mormon. Furthermore, it appears that the "narrow passage" was a route through a mountain range. Zarahemla was located in the land southward, but north of the city, in the direction of the city of Nephi, where were located the mountains called Manti, whose watershed formed the headwaters of the Sidon River (Alma 22:29). The Manti mountain range, unlike the Andes, ran east to west (Alma 22:27). Thus, the Book of Mormon hints that between the two ancient civilizations was a major geographic barrier, and if the Lamanites controlled the only "narrow passage" through the mountains, it would explain why there was no interaction between the Nephites and Mulekies and why their culture and languages took separate courses for nearly four centuries.

Numerous historical cases show how mountains have isolated two groups of people. Having lived in Switzerland, I was amazed to learn that the people living in the mountainous cantons had their own unique language dialect, which differed significantly from the dialect of the people living in the next valley. The towering Alps virtually isolate the two alpine communities who live within only a few miles of each other.

Although Cuzco and Pukara are only 120 miles apart, the two ancient city-states were separated by a range of glaciered mountains that tower over 20,000 feet. The only passage through the Vilcanota Mountains is the La Raya pass at an altitude of 14,172 feet. Furthermore, the Vilcanota Mountain range runs east to west between the two great Andes cordilleras, thus forming a massive barrier between the Nephites and the Mulekites.

A mountainouss terrain between the two cities of Nephi and the land of Zarahemla would also explain why parties that left Zarahemla got lost in their attempts to find the city of their first inheritance (Omni 1:28–30).

Locating the city of Zarahemla at Pukara would also satisfy another Book of Mormon clue as to the city's location. If the Lamanite (Aymara-speaking) tribes lived in the valleys between Cuzco and the La Raya pass, and also in the lands south of the Mulekites (southeast of Lake Titicaca), then it meant that Lamanites surrounded Zarahemla (compare Alma 22:29).

WHY DID MOSIAH'S PEOPLE LEAVE THE LAND OF NEPHI?

The city of Nephi was a land choice above all other lands, so why would Mosiah and the faithful leave their beautiful city? The answer is found in the decaying morality of the Nephites. There seems to have been a steady falling away from the gospel from the time of Jarom to the time of Amaleki, roughly 317–130 BC. By the time the Lord warns Mosiah to leave the city of Nephi, the prophet-king took with him only "as many as would hearken unto the voice of the Lord" (Omni 1:12), and apparently it took "many preachings and prophesyings" (Omni 1:13) by Mosiah to convince even those people to believe him to the point that they would leave the city of Nephi. This would suggest that most of the Nephites did not leave the land of Nephi.

What was the fate of the Nephites who ignored the Lord's warning and remained in the city of Nephi? Arthur Kocherhans believes that this might have been the first, but not the final destruction of the Nephite nation, and the fulfillment of a prophecy made by Jacob. He writes:

"And now it came to pass that the people of Nephi, under the reign of the second king, began to grow hard in their hearts, and indulged themselves in wicked practices (Jacob 1:15);

"Yea, and they also began to search much gold and silver, and began to be lifted up somewhat in pride" (Jacob 1:16).

Then, Jacob speaks emphatically about the future of the Lehi colony; read the scriptures carefully:

"Wherefore, this people shall keep my commandments, saith the Lord of Host, or cursed be the land for their sakes" (Jacob 2:29).

These scriptures are in harmony with Nephi's prophecy in 2 Nephi 5:25, that the Lamanites shall scourge the Nephites even unto destruction. Jacob also prophesied indicating very clearly the cause leading to the Nephites destruction:

"And the time speedily cometh, that except ye [the Nephites] repent, they [the Lamanites] shall possess the land of your inheritance [the land of Nephi], and the Lord God will lead away the righteous out from among you" (Jacob 3:4).

History shows that the Nephites did not repent and the Lamanites did take possession of their land, and so Mosiah, and those who would follow him, had to leave their homeland, the land of Nephi, and migrate to a new land.[7]

Kocherhans' scenario clearly fits the prophecies of Jacob and could explain why the righteous Nephites abandoned the city of Nephi. However, we do not know what event finally brought down the city. It could have been a prolonged *El Niño* drought (cursed land, Jacob 2:29) or an invasion by a Lamanite army. Kocherhans is more conclusive:

It is important to note that even though the 2nd or small plates of Nephi were supposed to contain the prophecies and ministry, the writers of the last 155 years have only mentioned the wickedness and wars of the Nephites. Abinadom clearly states: "And I know of no revelation save that which has been written, neither prophecy (Omni 1:11).

From the scriptures, we can easily identify the reason why the Nephite civilization was nearly destroyed in about 205 BC. They had become a wicked people, and as for Mosiah leaving the land of Nephi, it sounds to me like the age-old pattern of the righteous having to flee the wickedness. Remember, we just read Omni, verse 7, "Wherefore, the Lord did visit them in great judgement; nevertheless, he did spare the righteous that they should not perish, but did deliver them out of the hands of their enemies.[8]

During the centuries the Mulekites had lived in Zarahemla prior to Mosiah's arrival, the Mulekites had become exceedingly numerous. However, they had no written records with them. For this reason, being isolated, their language became so corrupt that no one in Mosiah's party could understand them. Even more discomforting is that they no longer believed in the existence of their Creator. Since the people of Zarahemla (Mulekites) agreed to unite with the minority Nephites, and since Mosiah was appointed the king of Zarahemla, it seems likely that Mosiah must have left the land of Nephi with a significant number of people. In other words, it was a sizable exodus of the righteous (Omni 1:17–19). This conjecture appears to be confirmed when the combined forces in Zarahemla were able, under King Benjamin (Mosiah's son), to drive the Lamanites out of the land of Zarahemla (Omni 1:24).

Perhaps in an attempt to reclaim their cities in the land of Zarahemla, the Lamanites "came down [south] out of the land of Nephi [which they now controlled], to battle against his people, "But behold, king Benjamin gathered together his armies, . . . until they had slain many thousands

Pukara River.

of the Lamanites" (Words of Mormon 1:13–14).

Amaleki provided us a further clue as to the location of Zarahemla. He recorded that a large number of Nephites, became "desirous to possess the land of their inheritance" and "went up [north] into the wilderness" (Omni 1:27, 28). Again, in Semitic languages and in Quechua, the word *up* implies "north," the direction one would travel from Pukara to Cuzco.

ARCHAEOLOGICAL EVIDENCE FOR ZARAHEMLA AT PUKARA

Archaeologists place Pukara squarely in the historical period of Zarahemla. Elizabeth Klarich

of University of California at Santa Barbara cites:

The Late (or Upper) Formative (500 BC–AD 400) is characterized by the development of the first markedly ranked societies in the region centered at the sites of Pukara in the northwestern basin and Tiwanaku in the southern basin (Stanish et al. 1997; Stanish 2003:137). Stanish defines these polities as complex chiefdoms and, in spite of their scale and influence, argues that many areas of the basin were not under the control of either polity.[9]

Not only did the Pukara civilization start to rise at the time of the arrival of the Mulekites (roughly 500 BC) and fall at the time of the demise of the Nephites (AD 400), but also no evidence can be found that the city was occupied during the subsequent Middle Horizon period;[10] thus, hinting that a genocide had occurred at Pukara. Referring to that time period, Klarich notes: "By AD 400, the Pukara polity had collapsed while Tiwanaku [Lamanites at the south end of the lake] continued to grow and reorganized into an urban center, one that developed into the first archaic state of the Titicaca region."[11] In other words, in an Altiplano paradigm for Zarahemla, the Nephite society disappeared on the northwest end of Lake Titicaca, while their enemies, the Lamanites, continued prospering at Tiwanaku.

In further detail, archaeologists divide the Pukara civilization into three sub-periods, which coincide remarkably well with the three distinct Zarahemla periods mentioned in the Book of Mormon: the Mulekite Period (roughly 550–200 BC), the Nephites (200 BC to AD 30), and the Post-Christ visitation-reconstruction period (AD 30–400). Mujica (1988)[12] divided the Pukara civilization between the Initial Pukara (500–200 BCE), Middle Pukara (200 BC–AD 100), and the Late Pukara (AD 100–300). Steadman (1995)[13] establishes the Pukara periods as: the Initial Pukara and the Classic Pukara 1 (400–100 BC), the Classic Pukara Period (100 BC–AD 100), and the Late Pukara (AD 100–350).

GEOGRAPHIC AND DEMOGRAPHIC CONTEXT

The land of Zarahemla was a hegemony that included many other cities and villages. Alma established at least seven churches in the land

(Mosiah 25:23). Although the capital was the city of Zarahemla, we know that there must have been many small urban centers within a one-day walking distance of Zarahemla. We can infer this because King Mosiah made a proclamation that "this people, or the people of Zarahemla, and the people of Mosiah who dwell in the land. . . thereby . . . may be gathered together; for on the morrow I shall proclaim" (Mosiah 1:10). The Titicaca Basin in the Late Formative Period consisted of the primary regional centers, the capital cities of Tiwanaku and Pukara, which attracted

large populations.[14] Klarich writes, "The Pukara polity is characterized by a three-tiered site hierarchy with the primate non-urban center of Pukara, smaller secondary centers, and villages and hamlets."[15]

The land of Zarahemla had a river that flowed north to south through it and which appears to have defined the land's western border. The river's name was Sidon, and it flowed beside the city of Zarahemla. The Pukara River winds its way through the entire length of the northern Lake Titicaca basin, from the La Raya passage in

At a convert baptism in what I believe is the River Sidon. Rodriques and Delgado families, Pukara River 1970, photograph by the author.

the north (the border between the northeast and southeast Inca quarters) south to Lake Titicaca (sea east). The river's headwaters, course, and drainage into the giant lake suit well the features attributed to the river Sidon, which extended to the "northern parts of the land bordering the wilderness, at the head of the river Sidon" (Alma 22:29).

The land of Melek was on the west side of the river Sidon (Alma 8:3), suggesting that the western border of the land of Zarahemla was the river Sidon. In an Altiplano scenario, Lake Titicaca would have dominated the land's southern borders, and Zarahemla's eastern border would have ended at the Amazon basin where most of the basin's western flanks are covered with a sheet of water six months of the year.[16] In this regard, it should be remembered that the Incas considered the Amazon basin the North Sea. The river, lake, and Amazon flood basin meet the criteria that the Land of Zarahemla was nearly surrounded by water (Alma 22:32).

The Book of Mormon tells us that an extensive range of mountains and wilderness was adjacent to Zarahemla. The terrain allowed the Gadianton robbers to raid the Nephites and then return to their secret places in the mountains where the Nephites could not find them (Helaman 11:25–31, 3 Nephi 1:27). To the immediate east and north of Pukara is one of the greatest mountain wildernesses on earth, the Andes Mountains that separate Cuzco from the Altiplano.

A CIVILIZATION WITH A SOPHISTICATED CULTURE

Distinct from ancient civilizations in Central and North America, the Pukara society, like the Nephite community, had a pastoral component to

The Uros Indians of Lake Titicaca live on floating islands.

its economy (Mosiah 2:3). Kolata defines Pukara as having been an "agro-pastoral society."[17] The Pukara society also possessed a technical and artistic tradition indicative of what one might expect of the Nephites. Kolata explains:

> The cultural and technological sophistication of Pukara was expressed most clearly through its impressive architectural achievements and through its remarkable stone-carving tradition that far surpasses that of Chiripa [Lamanites, early Tiwanaku] in terms of technical skill and sophistication in design. Pukara stone carvers created both full round and flat relief sculptures. The carvers used champlevée and incision techniques to fashion the relief carvings on rectangular stone slabs, or stelae. The flat relief sculptures trend to portray a variety of animals, such as fish, felines, lizards, and serpents, with incised surface detail representing cosmological or mythical symbols. One stela with a notched upper end portrays a magnificent human head wearing an elaborate crown with feather and feline appendages. The sculptures carved in full round are relatively realistic portraits of humans, most often depicted holding or wearing trophy heads.[18]

THE JAREDITES OF ZARAHEMLA

Mosiah learned that a descendent of the Jaredites, Coriantumr, had lived with the people of Zarahemla. (Omni 1:21). This would suggest, that part of the Jaredites lived and fought their last battles in the land of Zarahemla. Three archaeological clues indicate that the Jaredites spent some time at Lake Titicaca.

First, the Nephites found at Zarahemla large stones that had been engraved on by the Jaredites (Omni 1:20). Not only are large monoliths found at Pukara, but large statues are also found at Tiwanaku on the Lamanite site of Lake Titicaca. Dating stone carvings is difficult; however, they are believed to be associated with the early Pukara and Tiwanaku periods when it was possible that the last of the Jaredites were still alive. Urton reports that "Inca informants in the early years following the Spanish invasion told their conquerors that the statues at Tiahuanaco represented an earlier race of giants whose origins were in an era before the appearance of the Inca kings."[19]

Second, as noted in chapter 2, the Uros Indians of Lake Titicaca still build reed boats that compare to those the Jaredites would have seen and possibly built in Mesopatamia (Ether 2:16).

Third, the people of Norte Chico, who qualify as candidates for the Jaredites, used a U-shaped architecture when building their temples."[20] The first settlements in the Lake Titicaca Basin used this same U-shape design for their sacred temples (from circa 900 BC).[21]

CLIMATIC CONDITIONS OF ZARAHEMLA

Zarahemla had a climate very different from the one Nephi described when his family initially pitched their tents along the coast and successfully grew seeds from Jerusalem. A close examination of the eleventh chapter of Helaman indicates three factors about the climate at Zarahemla: One, it was favorable for growing grain. Two, it was an arid environment where grain grew only when rains fell. Three, there was a distinctive "season of grain," thus Zarahemla had a clearly defined rainy season. (Helaman 11:5–6, 13, 17). These three conditions match the climatic pattern of the Altiplano where Pukara is located.

Palaeo-climatologists from the United States and Chile have concluded:

> Along its central portion (15°–22° south), the widening of the Andes produces distinctive meteorological conditions that we refer to as the climate of the Altiplano. Interest in the climate of the Altiplano has grown in recent decades because its variability has a strong impact on the availability of water resources over this semi-arid region and the adjacent lowlands. . .[22]

> The annual rainfall over the Altiplano is largely concentrated in the austral summer months, especially along its southwestern part where more than 70% of the precipitation occurs from December to February.[23]

Accordingly, Danish and Bolivian scientists note about the Altiplano: "The onset and the duration of the rainy season, [indicates] that climate-wise crop production is only possible during 5 months. . . ."[24]

Unfortunately, the arrival of the rainy season in the Andes marks the commencment of the season of sicknesses and death. The Book of Mormon reports that at Zarahemla some "died with fevers, which at some seasons of the year were very frequent"; however, there were "excellent qualities of the many plants and roots which God had prepared to remove the cause of diseases" (Alma 46:40). The Canadian Foreign Affairs Ministry warns travelers to Peru that with the rainy season "water-borne diseases may also become a threat."[25] Indeed water-related infectious diseases are still the leading cause of death of children on the Altiplano,[26] and when the rains wash human and animal waste into the streams and rivers, the water becomes dangerous for human consumption.[27] The New York Times quotes one Peruvian doctor: "Drinking water is drawn from local creeks of uncertain purity . . . we go from 80 cases a month to almost 250 in the rainy season."[28] Although many other illnesses are associated with Andean water, the Center for Disease Control and Prevention calls special attention to Yellow Fever, Malaria, Hepatitis A, and Hepatitis B.[29] Fortunately, God has blessed Peru with some of the most effective natural medicines known, including Coca leaves, Maca, Cats Claw, Anchiote, Quinina, Camu-Camu, and many others.[30]

CLIMATIC VARIATIONS ASSOCIATED WITH ZARAHEMLA

As in the Bible, the history of the Book of Mormon tells of the Lord using climatic changes to influence the faithfulness of His people. When the Jaredites persecuted the prophets

> . . . there began a great dearth upon the land, and the inhabitants began to be destroyed exceedingly fast because of the dearth, for there was no rain upon the face of the earth. And there came forth poisonous serpents, also upon the face of the land, and did poison many people. And it came to pass that their flocks began to flee before the poisonous serpents, toward the land southward, which was called by the Nephites Zarahemla. And it came to pass that there were many of them which did perish by the way; nevertheless, there were some which fled

into the land southward. And it came to pass that the people did follow the course of the beasts, and did devour the carcasses of them which fell by the way, until they had devoured them all. Now when the people saw that they must perish they began to repent of their iniquities and cry unto the Lord. (Ether 9:30–34)

What do we learn from this passage that can help us locate Zarahemla?

1. The climate became much drier where the Jaredites were living (in the land northward).

2. Poisonous snakes left their previous domain and entered the Jaredite lands.

3. The Jaredites had flocks of domesticated animals that fled from the snakes.

4. The people wandered southward, following the "beasts."

5. The Jaredites started living in a land the Nephites would one day call Zarahemla.

We already know that in all of the Americas only the ruins of Norte Chico in Peru have been dated to the period of the early Jaredites, and only the Peruvians domesticated flocks. In this regard, the climatic history of Peru becomes quite informative. Bauer writes:

> By around 3000 to 2000 BC, the climate in the Andean highlands was becoming not unlike that of the modern day [desert coastline/rains in highlands]. In Peru, the coasts became much drier and the highlands started

getting more regular rainfall. It may also be during this interval that El Niño events began (Sandweiss et al. 1996). This had major implications for people and may even be the time when agriculture began to be firmly established in the Andes. This would be consistent with the pollen data examined from both Lake Marcacocha (Chepstow-Lusty et al. 1998) and Lake Paca, as well as macro-fossil evidence also from the Junin area, which indicates cultivation beginning around this time (Pearsall 1980, 1983; Hansen et al. 1994).[31]

A likely scenario is that during the famine, the starving Jaredites left the shoreline where the drought had destroyed their crops and the snakes had scattered their sheep (alpacas). To forestall starvation they followed the wild camelids and deer, which live in the high Andes. As the drought worsened, the wild animals would have wandered higher into the Andes in search of fodder. It would also seem likely that the beasts followed the rains southward. Once in the land

southward (the southern quarter, which included the Lake Titicaca Basin) the Jaredites finally humbled themselves and the rains returned. Whether the Jaredite migration to Zarahemla occurred during the climate change between 3000–2000 BC or during a subsequent drought cycle, we can only speculate. What is known is that Peru is famous for its droughts and that super droughts occurred in Peru around 1500 BC, 900 BC, and 700 BC.[32]

The snakes mentioned in Ether could have been any number of poisonous snakes found in Peru, including vipers and coral snakes. Perhaps the most likely candidate would have been the Ecuadorian coral snake (*micrurus bocourti*) which lives in the moist lands of Ecuador. If the coastline of northern Peru had been moist like today's Ecuadorian shores on Peru's immediate north, then as the climate changed and the mangrove forests disappeared, the snakes could have left the dried marshes and invaded the irrigated pastoral lands of the Jaredites.

Of course, the drought that brought the Jaredites to Zarahemla was not the only climate change that affected the land of Zarahemla. In approximately 18 BC, and in response to Nephi's prayers, the Lord causes:

> [A] work of destruction. . . [that] became sore by famine. And the work of destruction did also continue in the seventy and fifth year [circa 17 BC]. For the earth was smitten that it was dry, and did not yield forth grain in the season of grain; and the whole earth was smitten, even among the Lamanites as well as among the Nephites, so that they were smitten that they did perish by the thousands in the more wicked parts of the land (Helaman 11:5–6).

The Lord lifted the drought circa 16 BC. Scientists have found evidence that a major climatic shift occurred in the Andes starting at the same period. Bauer notes that three distinct periods of climatic changes, the "third phase developing between 10 BC and AD 100. These phases may reflect general drought conditions for the region during these periods."[33]

LA NIÑA—THE EAST WIND

Placing the Nephites high in the Peruvian Andes provides a possible insight into another climatic phenomenon mentioned in the Book of Mormon. Speaking for the Lord, the prophet Abinadi called the Nephites to repent, "lest I will smite this my people with sore afflictions, yea with famine and with pestilence; and I will cause that they shall howl all the day long" (Mosiah 12:4).

This prophecy is a probable implication that the Lord will bring the dreaded El Niño drought to the Andes. The El Niño occurs when the waters of Pacific Ocean off the coast of Peru warm. The warmer waters cause the east winds that cross Peru to subside. As a result, unusually large amounts of rain fall along the coast; however, the moist air from the Amazon can no longer cross over the eastern Andes, and the inhabited highland valleys experience drought conditions. Abinadi further warned the Nephites that if the drought did not cause them to repent, the Lord would also "send forth hail among them, and it shall smite them" (Mosiah 12:6). Having spent over a year as a missionary in that region at altitudes between 10,000 and 12,500 ft. above sea level, I was smitten by hail on a regular basis. Indeed one evening in Juliaca, Peru, Glenn Kimball and I walked through four inches of hailstones.

Hail following a drought suggests that if the people did not repent, the Lord would cause an even greater curse to come upon the people. That is, large amounts of moisture would fall on the scorched earth. If so, the result would be devastating. Abinadi continued: "They shall also be smitten with the east wind; and insects shall pester their land, and also devour their grain" (Mosiah 12:6). Abinadi explained that unlike the slow death from famine, "the east wind . . . bringeth immediate destruction" (Mosiah 7:31).

What many people do not realize is that the El Niño that brings sever drought to the Andes highlands has a wicked sister called La Niña, which causes the exact opposite effect. Occasionally a dry El Niño weather oscillation in the Andes is followed by a very moist La Niña weather pattern.[34] According to the U.S. National Oceanic and Atmospheric Administration (NOAA): "During La Niña, the easterly trade winds strengthen and cold upwellings along the equator and the West coast of South America intensify. Sea-surface temperatures along the equator can fall as much as 7 degrees F below normal."[35] As a result, the strong east wind brings abnormal levels of moisture across the Andes from the Amazon, causing heavy rainfall, hail, and flooding. The heavy and sustained downpours preceded by a long drought that causes the lands to be parched and barren is a formula for "immediate destruction" (Mosiah 7:31).

A La Niña devastated the southern Andes in 2001. A long-lasting rainfall caused widespread flooding and erosion. The storm is known as the great Atacama flood of 2001. The International Red Cross reported that in Bolivia alone the flood affected 238,700 people. The greatest impact was caused by overflowing rivers.[36] With ancient Cuzco (city of Nephi) and Pukara

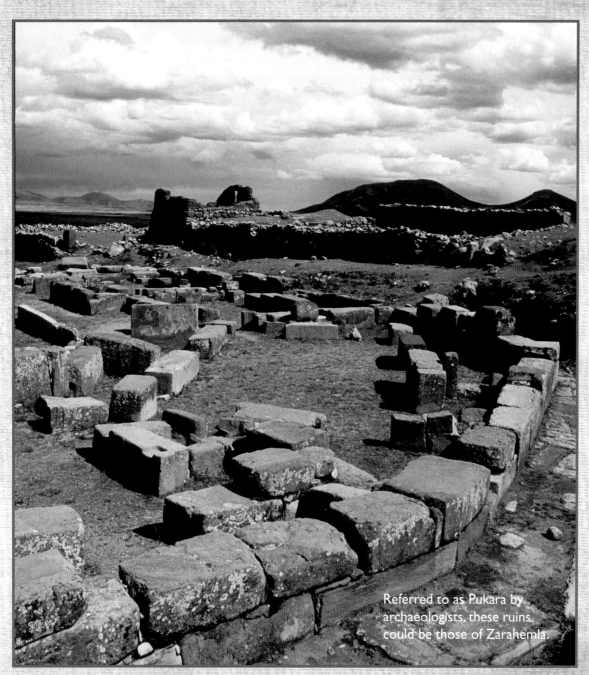

Referred to as Pukara by archaeologists, these ruins could be those of Zarahemla.

(Zarahemla) having been built beside rivers, the fear of an increase in the east wind must have been very real to the cities' inhabitants.

However, according to Abinadi the east wind brought with it more than just immediate destruction from hail and flooding on the Nephites' crops. Abinadi's prophecy reads, "Smitten with the east wind and insects shall pester their land and also devour their grain." In other words, the coming of the east wind could easily be directly associated with pests devouring their crops. While locust swarms are relatively rare in Peru, they do occur after heavy rains.[37] With the La Niña rains, above normal levels of grass appear, which allow the locust swarms to form.

PUKARA, THE CITY OF ZARAHEMLA

Approximately fifty miles northwest of Lake Titicaca and resting below an impressive pinkish sandstone outcrop known as the Peñon are the ruins of the ancient city of Pukara. First viewed by a westerner in 1540 or 1550, Pedro de Cieza de León reported: "What I saw at Pucará were great buildings in ruin and decay and many statues of stone in the shape of human figures and other noteworthy things."[38] A similar account was made in 1681 by Antonio Vásques de Espinosa who described the city's remains as "their marvelous works—there were great proud buildings with many stone statues in the likeness of men and other creatures, very neatly worked."[39] The website of the New York Metropolitan Museum of Art states, "ca. 200 BC Pukara is the largest settlement in the Altiplano north of Lake Titicaca, covering approximately 900 acres. U-shaped courts flanked by fine masonry structures are part of the complex. Three-dimensional stone sculptures depict blocky humans with accentuated ribs and prominent square eyes. Ceramics are slip painted in red, black, white, and yellow, with incisions outlining motifs of frontal humans, spotted cats, llamas and geometric patterns."[40]

Although today little remains of the ancient Pukara, its original size of 900 acres is over four times the size of Old Jerusalem (220 acres). Furthermore, it was a monument city of civic buildings and a temple complex; however, it does not appear to have had a large population. As stated above, Zarahemla was a hub with many surrounding villages. Indeed, the people of Zarahemla "were scattered about upon the face of the land" (Helaman 10:12), and had to be gathered together during time of war for mutual protection (3 Nephi 3:13).

The Nephites migrated to Zarahemla some time around 205 BC.[41] Kolata writes, "In the period between 200 BC and AD 200, Pukara grew to truly urban proportions (Mulica 1978) and took on a distinctly cosmopolitan character, with elegant public buildings and finely constructed private houses. . . . There is little doubt that Pukara was, at one time, one of the most important cities of the southern Andes—a major religious and secular power."[42] Klarich confirms, "The dates have been published in a variety of contexts as the temporal limits of the Classic Pukara (200 BC–AD 200) culture for their association with highly decorative, polychrome, incised ceramics."[43] Bauer notes: "During the Qotakalli Period [Cuzco chronology AD 200–600], the site of Pucara (Pukara), approximately 200 kilometers [120 miles] southeast of Cuzco in the Peruvian Altiplano near Lake Titicaca, reaches its largest area of influence. It is widely believed that Pucara

was the center of one of the earliest and largest complex societies in the south-central Andes."[44]

Given the current body of archaeological data, Pukara stands out as a likely candidate for the city of Zarahemla and the center of the Church of Jesus Christ in the Andes during the Zarahemla period (Alma 6:1,7). In March 1970, I was in the small city of Juliaca on the northern side of the Lake Titicaca Basin. My assigned mission area included the ruins of Pukara, just thirty miles northwest of Juliaca. At that time, the Peruvian Altiplano cities of Juliaca and Puno were still part of the Bolivian Mission. That month Elder Steve Farnsworth, the Mission's Public Relations Representative, received a surprising response to a letter he had sent (with a copy of a mission paper called "Mormon") to President Joseph Fielding Smith. At the time,

President Smith was serving as the President of The Church of Jesus Christ of Latter-day Saints. Mission President Keith Roberts had the letter included in the mission's monthly newsletter. He introduced President Smith's correspondence in these words: "The following letter from President Joseph Fielding Smith was received by Elder Steve Farnsworth in March 1970. It was written March 18, 1970. I think that it is an important statement for this Mission and should be part of your permanent record. Read it often and it will give you a boost in your work."

Dear Brother Farnsworth,

Thank you for your kind letter of March 11, 1970, which just arrived from Bolivia together with a copy of the paper called "Mormon."

Remains of the central courtyard of the Pukara Temple

I am very pleased to know that you are having wonderful success in your field of labor. No doubt a paper in Spanish in that country dealing with the doctrines of the Church would be a great help to you. There is no reason that I know that you should not have remarkable success in that field which at one time was the central country occupied by the people in the Book of Mormon times as we learn from the Book of Mormon. It is my judgement that the missionaries would have remarkable success in this section of the country.

It is indeed a pleasure for me to get a communication from that Land which at one time was headquarters of the Church in Book of Mormon history.

May the Lord continue to bless you and your companions and open the doors before you that you may teach the people. I humbly pray.

Sincerely your brother,
Joseph Fielding Smith
President

JFS.re

Other than Pukara, there was no other antiquity site within the March 1970 Bolivia Mission boundaries that could qualify as a serious candidate for Zarahemla. At the time I first read President Smith's letter, I found it interesting that the prophet referred to the "Land" of the mission instead of simply stating that "Bolivia" had once been the headquarters of the Church. A likely explanation is that the headquarters of the ancient church had been in the "Land" of the Bolivian Mission, but not in Bolivia itself. In March 1970, there were only two cities that

Terraced walls of the Pukara Temple.

were part of the mission "Land," but were not in Bolivia. They were the cities of Puno on the shore of Lake Titicaca and Juliaca. Juliaca, just 30 miles from the ruins of Pukara, is today a Latter-day Saint oasis on the Altiplano, a modern Zarahemla. When Elders Glenn Kimball, Timothy Evans, and I served in Juliaca in 1970, the town had an LDS branch that consisted of about only thirty members, ten of which we had baptized. Today the city of only two hundred thousand people has two LDS stakes and a district.

THE TEMPLE OF ZARAHEMLA

The city of Zarahemla was of great importance to the people of the Book of Mormon. During part of its occupation, the city served as the Nephite capital and the center of the church

(Alma 6:7). It also contained the Church's central temple (Mosiah 1:18). In comparison, Pukara's public buildings were dominated by a massive temple that was erected on man-made terraces. The Pukara ceremonial structure, called the Qalasaya, was built with dressed-stone blocks. Its three large inner courts were flanked by smaller rooms. Klarich provides this description of the massive structure:

The Qalasaya complex consists of a series of stone-lined terraces and platforms rising steeply 32 m (105 feet) over the central pampa. The complex is in the form of a truncated step-pyramid with both straight and curved walls, a series of variously sized platforms, and a variety of interesting architectural features, many of which are only partially exposed.

On the uppermost platform is a series of three sunken courts running north-south that vary slightly in form, orientation, and scale. The Copesco excavations fully exposed the terrace walls and platforms that measure 315m (1033 feet) north-south and 300m (984 feet) east-west and reconstructed the main central staircase (Wheeler and Mujica 1981).[45]

The entrance is off-center on the eastern side of the structure and each of the walls has a central stone-lined burial chamber (Mohr-Chávez 1988).[46]

Having three large rooms adjacent to smaller chambers and a single doorway on the east, the Pukara temple complex hints of having associations to true temple services. Likewise, it appears from the artifacts that have been found at the temple that the people of Pukara worshiped a god with a human body.[47] Stone statues portray their god with human-head images with rayed appendages (artistic convention used in Old World art to symbolize divinity). Other Pukara artifacts include remains of sacrificed burnt offerings on ceremonial burners, and stone images of the Yaya-Uma (Adam and Eve) religion.[48]

THE PUKARA TEMPLE'S PUBLIC MEETING GROUNDS

The Pukara temple complex was unusual in that it featured a large open space where great numbers of people congregated on the western side of the temple. Anthropologist Klarich found this area significant and describes the large open field in these words: "The central pampa (large grass-covered plain) abuts the easternmost, lowest level of the imposing Qalasaya complex and

From the temple looking upon the open-public area of Pukara. Did the Nephites listen to King Benjamin from this field?

expands to cover an area at least 300 m x 300 m (approximately 1 million square feet). The multiple tiers of the stone-lined terraces of the Qalasaya [Temple] rise dramatically above the expanse of this area."[49] Standing on the east side of the temple that was adjacent to the central pampa, the great temple walls would also have provided an acoustical sounding board for a speaker.

The temple's public grounds (central pampa) bring to mind the temple at Zarahemla where "a great number even so many that they did not number them [gathered at the temple]; for they had multiplied exceedingly and waxed great in the land" (Mosiah 2:2) Undoubtedly, the large public area at the Pukara temple could have accommodated the tents the Nephites pitched next to the Zarahemla temple with their doors opening toward the temple so they could hear

the words of King Benjamin (Mosiah 2:6–7).

The public area at the Pukara temple had other features that are of interest in our attempt to identify Zarahemla. These are man-made mounds that were built on the perimeters of the temple's public grounds. There were seven mounds in all.[50] In the Book of Mosiah we learn that there were so many people gathered at the temple to hear King Benjamin that not all could hear his voice, so he had a tower constructed. However, even with the aid of a tower his words could not be heard by all the people, so he had his words read throughout the great congregation (Mosiah 2:8). Obviously, in that day a large number of copies could not have been transcribed in one day. However, a few copies of his speech could have been made and then read at various locations in the congregation. From atop the seven mounds that are located at the perimeter of the public grounds, readers could have spread the king's message to a large multitude.

ZARAHEMLA IN THE IMAGE OF THE BENEVOLENT KING BENJAMIN

Some readers of the Book of Mormon might question if the beloved King Benjamin was "too good" a person to have been a real historical king? So "inclusive" was he as a ruler, that he took laborious steps to make sure that "all" the people could participate in the meeting to which he called them at the Zarahemla temple. Throughout antiquity, it is hard to find kings who expressed real concern for their people and who cared in the least about the opinions of their subjects. Yet there is archaeological evidence that "inclusive" kings actually ruled Pukara during its early period. Anthropologist Klarich studied the leadership strategies of the Pukara rulers. She explains:

> The study of alternative leadership strategies has become a major avenue for tracing the development of institutional inequality in complex societies across the globe. In the Lake Titicaca Basin in Peru and Bolivia, the Later Formative period (500 BC–AD 400) is characterized by the development of two regional population centers, Pukara in the northwest [Nephites] and Tiwanaku in the southeast [Lamanites]. The site of Pukara, the subject of the present study, is typically identified with the features of the Qalasaya complex [the Pukara temple compound], a series of massive terraced platforms with sunken, stone-lined structures, and the presence of sophisticated polychrome pottery and carved monoliths. . . .

The Qalasaya complex and several artificial mounds can be used to trace a shift from inclusive [King Benjamin leadership style] to exclusive leadership strategies at Pukara. The central pampa was originally used as a public space dedicated to the preparation and consumption of suprahousehold-level means and was an integral element of inclusive leadership strategies during the site's early development. Over time, as the monumental architecture of the Qalasaya was reconstructed and ritual activities became more restricted, the central pampa was "cut off" and relegated to the periphery of the ceremonial district.[51]

In other words, the earliest rulers in Pukara, which would be comparable in our scenario to Zarahemla's first Nephite kings—Mosiah and Benjamin—had "inclusive" leadership styles. That is, they treated their people as equals and brought them into the decision-making processes, by talking directly to the people and consulting with them. Since inclusive leaders were rare in antiquity, the architecture of Pukara provides additional evidence that it is a candidate for Zarahemla. By any measure of ancient politics, King Benjamin was unique among ancient leaders. He was so "inclusive" that it appears his temple architecture was designed to allow all his people to hear his words and consult with him. King Benjamin said:

> I have not commanded you to come up hither that ye should fear me, or that ye should think that I of myself am more than a mortal man (Mosiah 2:10).

> But *I am like as yourselves*, subject to all manner of infirmities in body and mind; yet I have been *chosen by this people*, and consecrated by my father that I should be a ruler and a king over this people; and have been kept and preserved by his matchless power, to serve you with all the might, mind and strength which the Lord hath granted unto me (Mosiah 2:11; emphasis added).

> I say unto you that as I have been suffered to spend my days in your service, even up to this time, and have not sought gold nor silver nor any manner of riches of you (Mosiah 2:12).

And it came to pass that when king Benjamin had thus spoken, he sent among them, *desiring to know of his people* if they believed the words which he had spoken unto them. And they all cried with one voice, saying: Yea, we believe the words which thou hast spoken unto us (emphasis added, Mosiah 5:1, 2).

King Benjamin's father, Mosiah, appears to have held similar "all inclusive" meetings. He "assembled together [all the Nephites], and also all the people of Zarahemla, and they were gathered together in two bodies. And it came to pass that Mosiah did read, and caused to be read, the records of Zeniff to his people" (Mosiah 25:4–5).

The archaeological theories of the public grounds next to the Pukara temple certainly bring to mind the events cited in the Book of Mormon, where the kings spoke from the temple walls toward an open field where their people camped in tents and listened to the words of their righteous king. Once the address was completed, the king would then walk into the congregation and receive their council. Klarich proposes:

> The central pampa was an area of interaction in the central ceremonial district and is used to infer both the

motivations of early leaders and the role of the local population in the negotiation of social power.[52]

While superficially the area is unimpressive relative to the architectural grandeur of the surrounding mounds and terraces of the Qalasaya complex, the pampa was a dynamic, bustling area within the central district. Originally used as a public space such as a plaza, the pampa was a vital element of the central ceremonial district during the site's early development.[53]

Based on the public setting of these activities and a lack of highly specialized serving vessels in most areas, the material remains of these events are most consistent with the expectations developed for patron-role or entrepreneurial feasts (Dietler 1966), both elements of inclusionary leadership strategies.[54]

. . . Patron-role feasts and entrepreneurial feasts are inclusionary events in which "hosts attempt to promote solidarity and equality by widely casting invitations to community members and supporters (LeCount 2001:935).[55]

ZARAHEMLA, THE FORTRESS CITY

When the Nephites were threatened, they withdrew from their outer cities and villages and fled to the city of Zarahemla (3 Nephi 3:22,23). The prophet-general Mormon tells us that when he was eleven years old, his father carried him "into the land southward, even to the land of Zarahemla" (Mormon 1:6). Two verses later, he provides the probable reason why they gathered to Zarahemla, "in

Modern city of Pucara with full length of west side protected by the Pukara River.

this year there began to be a war between the Nephites . . . and the Lamanites" (Mormon 1:8). From the limited description we have of Zarahemla, the city must have enjoyed important natural defenses.

Some of Zarahemla's natural defenses are described in the Book of Alma when the Amlicites attacked Zarahemla. To the east of the city was the hill Amnihu. Between the hill and the city ran the river Sidon, which "ran by the land of Zarahemla" (Alma 2:15). Since the river ran north-south, and the hill Amnihu was on the east side, it would appear that the hill Manti, which was near Zarahemla (Alma 1:15), must have been on the city's west side. Since the city was protected by the river Sidon, the hills on both flanks, and of course the man-made fortifications

of the Nephites, we see why it was written of the Lamanites that "neither durst they march down against the city of Zarahemla" (Alma 56:25). As a matter of curiosity, in Bedouin Arabic, which evolved in part from Egyptian, the words *Zara hamla* mean "the flower to leave alone."

No one knows the ancient name of the ruins the archaeologists now call Pukara. However, the geographic setting of Pukara would fit well into what we know of Zarahemla. Nestled in a valley, there is a large hill to the city's east.

The entire east approach to the city was blocked by the Pukara River, and to its immediate west, and rising directly above the temple were the sheer cliffs of hill Llallahhua (a hill whose Quechua name encompasses the Arabic name of god, Allah).

Great stone cliff on east side of temple.
The location fits that of Mount Manti.

Did Samuel stand on these temple walls? Matthew Potter stands on lowest of several layers of Pukara temple walls.

Proposed Crossing Of River By Alma's Army during Amlicite War

CROSSING POINT
River on East
• Tall mountains on West
Balsa Pata (Marshes)
Lagoons
Tall mountains protect west flank
Defensive Mounds

Scale 1: 100,000   3.1 Miles
0   5 km   N

There was a very practical place for the Nephite Army to cross. Once they were on the west side of the river, with fortifications, supplies and reinforcements, it would have been impossible for the Lamanites to try to attack them against the manmade and natural fortifications of Zarahemla. Realizing their vulnerable state the Lamanites and Amlicites armies fled to the northwest.

that of Ammon's small party to find the city of Nephi, to free their Nephite brothers and sisters, and to return with them successfully to Zarahemla. Alma and his converts made a similar exodus to Zarahemla. These expeditions and other movements will be discussed in further detail in the Appendix.

The author, who has traveled extensively in the area, believes that all the movements mentioned in the Book of Mormon are in complete har-mony with the geography of Peru.

SAMUEL'S WALLS

One of the most inspiring events in the Book of Mormon is the visit of the prophet Samuel to Zarahemla. The brave Lamanite climbed the

With such natural barriers to invasion, it is easy to see why in the Quechua language the name "Pukara" means "the stronghold or fortress."[56] The ancient city was a natural place of refuge from enemy attack.

From the Zarahemla period we learn of sev-eral expeditions by the Nephites; for example,

walls of Zarahemla and boldly called the wicked Nephites to repentance (Helaman 13). The unre-pentant Nephites threw stones and shot arrows at him, yet they could not hit the prophet. The events of Samuel's visit fit well into the layout of the city of Pukara, with walls near the temple terraced to a height of one hundred feet. Furthermore, the walls extend to the mountains on the west side of the temple. The setting would have provided considerable space between the prophet and his attackers in the public area below, allowing him enough time to declare his prophecies before they could reach him. Once having finished speaking, Samuel could escape without having to pass through the city; that is, he could proceed west by climbing over the hills on the backside of the temple complex. Klarich notes that "the earliest direct evidence of stone-lined terrace construction is at Pukara, but in this context such construction was used in building retaining walls for the massive platforms of the Qalasaya [temple] complex."[57] Archaeologist Mary Kidder provided this impression of Pukara: "The most apparent feature is a series of terraces, built with rough stone retaining walls, just southeast of the modern town and almost under the cliff of a great rock."[58]

THE REBUILDING OF ZARAHEMLA

As a whole, the people of Zarahemla did not take to heart Samuel's warning, causing the wicked city of Zarahemla to be burned at Christ's death (3 Nephi 8:8, 24). Subsequently, the righteous Nephite nation that followed rebuilt the great city (4 Nephi 1:8). Though only a very small percentage of Pukara has been excavated, there are early indications of the city having burned. Klarich notes of the limited excavations at Pukara:

> Block 3: The fill range from 5–20 cm. thick and contained burned and unburned refuse Late Formative period [BC 500–AD 400] oriented at all angles. The soil was moist and loose with a high density of fired clay (10–20%).[59]

> Underlying deposits included different color clays, a limited number of artifacts, and a substantial concentration of burned wooden beam fragments.[60]

Furthermore, as the Book of Mormon states of Zarahemla, archaeologists have determined that the temple of Pukara was reconstructed sometime between 200 BC and AD 100.[61]

THE END OF ZARAHEMLA

Like Pukara, the Nephite civilization ended circa 400 BC, and with it Zarahemla ceased to exist. If the Nephites and Lamanites co-existed on the Altiplano, it was never a peaceful affair. Archaeological evidences suggest that the Pukara and Tiwanaku civilizations seldom mixed. Ciezo de León was informed by the Indians that:

> Many of these Colla Indians tell that before the rule of the Incas there were two great lords in their province, one called Zapana [Zarahemla] and the other Cari, and that they won many purcarás, which are their fortresses. And that one of them entered the lake of Titicaca, and found on the largest island of that body of water bearded white men with whom he fought until he had killed all of them.[62]

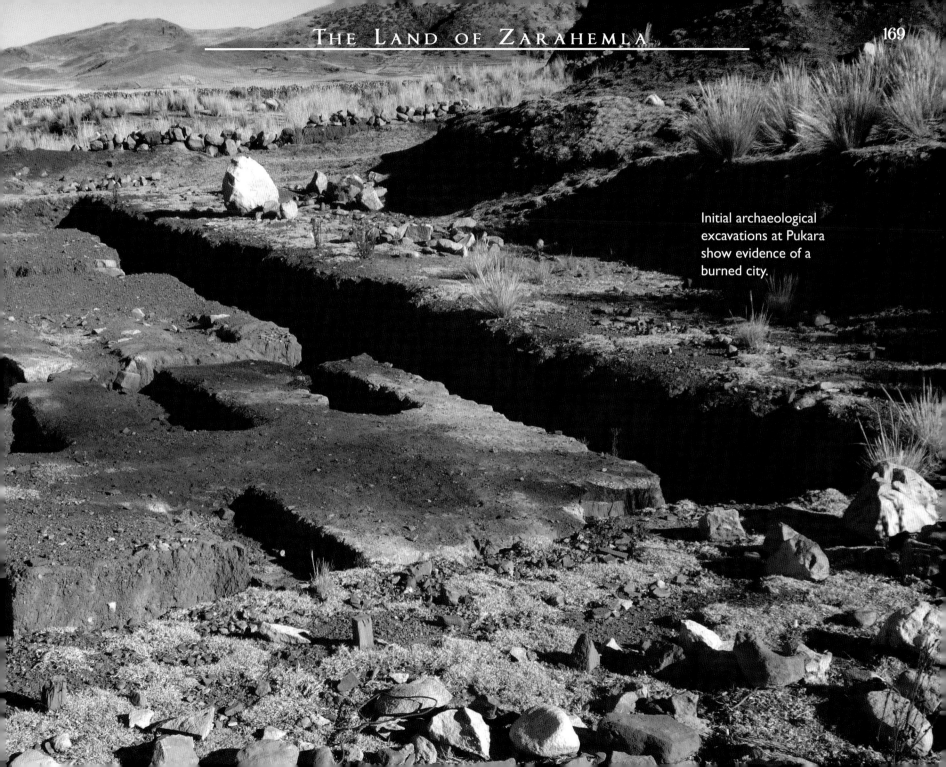

Initial archaeological excavations at Pukara show evidence of a burned city.

A statue of Christ overlooks
Cuzco, Peru from Sacsahuaman.

CHRIST'S MISSION IN THE ANDES

VIII

And when he had said these words, he wept,
and the multitude bare record of it,
and he took their little children, one by one,
and blessed them,

and prayed unto the Father for them.
And when he had done this he wept again.

3 NEPHI 17:21, 22

In the century preceding the birth of Christ, Nephi's promised land was a very dangerous place. The Nephite society suffered from the cancers of idolatry and faithlessness. Wars between the Nephites and Lamanites were growing in frequency and intensity. The Lamanites were gaining strength in the land southward. At one point, the seemingly invincible fortress of Zarahemla fell twice to the Lamanites (Helaman 1:18–27, 4:5). By the time of the coming of Christ, so precarious and wicked were the circumstances in Zarahemla that the Church leaders appear to have moved out of the city and established their headquarters in the city of Bountiful (3 Nephi 11:1, 18).

BOUNTIFUL—WHERE CHRIST APPEARED TO THE NEPHITES

In earlier times, under the righteous kings Mosiah and Benjamin, Zarahemla had prospered. Besides having been a prophet and benevolent ruler, King Benjamin had a gifted military mind. He led campaigns that drove the Lamanites out of the land of Zarahemla (northern Titicaca Basin, Omni 1:24), and established peace in his kingdom for the remainder of his days (Mosiah 1:1).

By the first century BC, another powerful nation was growing on the southern end of Lake Titicaca, the empire of Tiwanaku.[1] As this Aymara-speaking (Lamanite) city grew in power, it became a major threat to Pukara (Zarahemla) on the northern side of the lake. In our Book of Mormon model, it meant that Zarahemla was now facing its traditional Lamanite enemy in the land of Nephi on its northern border (Cuzco, Alma 22:28), as well as a growing threat much closer to home on the south side of the sea on the east (Tiwanaku, Alma 22:33). The Nephites had temporarily blocked in the Lamanites against the eastern shores of the sea in the east (Lake Titicaca, Alma 22:29), yet even to the west of Zarahemla nomadic Lamanite tribes were wandering the wilderness areas of the land of Bountiful (Alma 22:28).

171

In need of safer habitats, the Nephites of Zarahemla had only two choices: 1) to colonize the land of Bountiful to their west (Alma 22:33), or to resettle the shoreline valleys north of Desolation (Alma 22:30), where the Jaredites had once lived. Thus, by 72 BC many Nephites were migrating north and taking possession of "all the land northward, yea, even all the land which was northward of the land Bountiful, according to their pleasure" (Alma 50:11). In a Peruvian context, the route from Bountiful to the Land Northward would have taken the Nephites along the shoreline highway of the Incas, past the narrow neck of land, and on to the shoreline valleys north of the Land of Desolation.

In what was undoubtedly another desperate attempt to find a safer place to live, in 55 BC, Hagoth launched the first of his ships near the borders of the "land Bountiful, by the land Desolation (Alma 62:5), by the narrow neck of land" (Alma 62:5).

The relocation of the Church's headquarters from Zarahemla possibly happened in 35 BC, when the Lamanites "did come down against the Nephites to battle, and they did commence the work of death; yea, insomuch that in the fifty and eighth year of the reign of the judges they succeeded in obtaining possession of the land of Zarahemla; yea, and also all the lands, even unto the land which was near the land Bountiful" (Helaman 4:5).

The archaeological record confirms that during this period there was an extension of Pukara influence from what we believe was Zarahemla to the Nasca Empire, which seems to be a likely candidate for Bountiful. Archaeologists have concluded that the most important civilization to arise west of Pukara in the first century BC

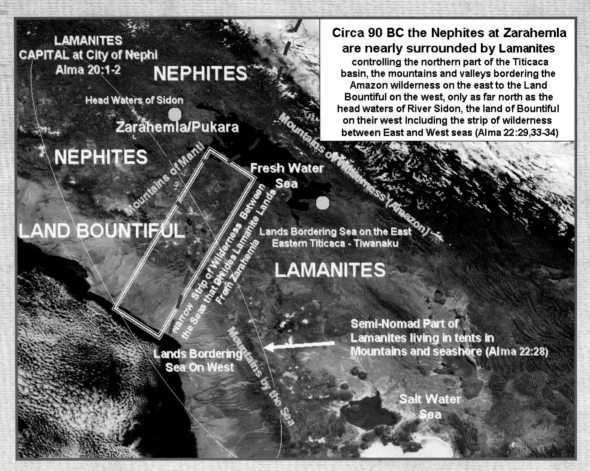

was the Nasca Empire. The Nasca are famous for their huge *lines* (geoglyphs) of animal figures that were created in the desert, but can only be visually appreciated from high in the air. An example of their artistry is the large figure known as the *Tree of Life*.[2]

Anthropologists Helaine Silverman of the University of Illinois and Donald Proulx of the University of Massachusetts define the time period for the rise of the Nasca Empire as an important political and religious center.

It is highly unlikely that Nasca 1 can be earlier than the final century of the first millennium BC. Nasca 1 also can be cross-dated to the Pucara [Zarahemla, 13,000 feet above sea level in the Andeans] style of the Lake Titicaca Basin on the basis of Pucara's use of incised lines to separate areas of slip-painted color. Radiocarbon dates from strata of pure Pucara refuse dated to approximately 150 BC to 100 AD. These dates also support

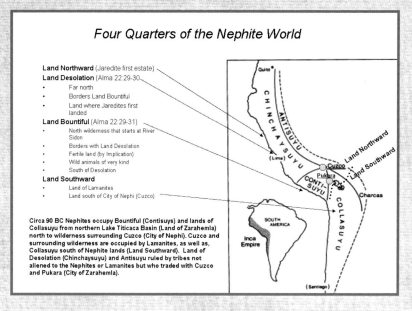

Four Quarters of the Nephite World

Land Northward (Jaredite first estate)
Land Desolation (Alma 22:29-30)
- Far north
- Borders Land Bountiful
- Land where Jaredites first landed

Land Bountiful (Alma 22:29-31)
- North wilderness that starts at River Sidon
- Borders with Land Desolation
- Fertile land (by Implication)
- Wild animals of very kind
- South of Desolation

Land Southward
- Land of Lamanites
- Land south of City of Nephi (Cuzco)

Circa 90 BC Nephites occupy Bountiful (Contisuys) and lands of Collasuyu from northern Lake Titicaca Basin (Land of Zarahemla) north to wilderness surrounding Cuzco (City of Nephi). Cuzco and surrounding wilderness are occupied by Lamanites, as well as, Collasuyu south of Nephite lands (Land Southward). Land of Desolation (Chinchaysuyu) and Antisuyu ruled by tribes not aliened to the Nephites or Lamanites but who traded with Cuzco and Pukara (City of Zarahemla).

the suggestion that Nasca 1 dates to this period of time.[3]

We start from the premise that Nasca was an Andean [Pukara] society. Using the common analytical method of ethnographic analogy, we argue that it is plausible to suggest that ethnographically and ethnohistorically known principles of Andean sociopolitical organization may have operated in Nasca times.[4]

The first mention in the Book of Mormon of a land called Bountiful is found in the twenty-second chapter of the Book of Alma. The footnote to this chapter dates it to 90–77 BC. However, this reference to Bountiful is to a place that already existed. Thus, it is likely that Bountiful was first colonized by the Nephites some time during the late second century BC. Not only is Nasca Period 1 considered to have been an offshoot of the Pukara culture, it also seems

to have the familiar ruling duality that was employed at Zarahemla. That is, there were both secular rulers and a religious hierarchy.[5]

Several specific clues point to the Nasca city of Cahuachi as being a candidate for the Nephites' city of Bountiful. For example, elaborate Nasca pottery depicts war scenes that are consistent with what is known about the battles recorded in the Book of Mormon. The Nephite General Moroni, "prepared his people with breastplates and with arm-shields, yea, and also shields to defend their heads, and also they were dressed with thick clothing" (Alma 43:19). Since a pre-Columbian iron ore mine had never been discovered in the New World, the Book of Mormon's assertion that the Nephites wore armor seemed suspect. Furthermore, "ore" deposits are referred to five times in the Book of Mormon. It was not until 2008 that archaeologists discovered the only known pre-Columbian iron ore mine in the Americas. The mine dates back at least 2,000 years and was discovered at Nasca, Peru.[6]

While the Nephites were dressed well for battle, the unfortunate Lamanite soldiers fought "naked, save it were a skin which was girded about their loins" (Alma 43:20). Painted on Nasca pottery are battle scenes depicting soldiers of varied dress, "from naked to wearing just a loincloth," to one that "depicts a fully clothed Nasca warrior

Nasca lines (the spider) point to the holy city of Cahuachi, perhaps identifying underground water sources.

"Tree of Life"? Geoglyph at Nasca, Peru.

fighting and grabbing the wild hair of a naked savage whose depiction is sp 'other' that he must not be Nasca."[7] As we might expect, the Nasca pottery depicts the naked or loinclothed warriors as having dark skin, while the fully clothed warriors had a fairer skin color.[8]

The eloquent artistry of the Nasca civilization also brings to mind images of the rich Nephite society (Alma 4:6; 45:24; Helaman: 3:36; 4:12; 6:17). The Nasca Lines are some of the true mysteries and wonders of the ancient world. The potters, weavers, embroiderers, and architects of Nasca were highly skilled. For example, Nasca potters used up to eleven slip pigments on a single vessel, which typically were highly polished.[9] Nasca's sophisticated society has been classified as one of the Mastercraftman Cultures of the ancient world.[10]

We also know that the Nephites of the Bountiful period wore costly apparel (Alma 1:6, 32; 4:6; 5:53; 31:28). As mentioned earlier, the Nasca men wore mantles, tunics, turbans, turban

Fair-skinned Nasca man with facial hair. Note the light- and dark-skinned faces on the robe's trim.

Ceramic showing fully armored light-skinned warrior fighting darker-skinned naked warrior.

bands, and head cloths.[11] The women:

adorned their hair with feathers or gold plumes. The main item of clothing worn by females is an ankle-length mantle, which is most often shown wrapped around the body, sometimes fastened with a pin. When drawn on a ceramic vessel, these mantles served as the background for mythical creatures that are drawn on top of them. Beneath the mantles women seem to have worn a long tunic, probably consisting of two rectangles of cloth sewn together to form

Were trees from this Nasca valley sent by ship to the people in the land northward?

coastal fluvial valleys to have become deforested. Whatever the cause for lack of trees, the northern colonists needed to build their houses using cement (Helaman 3:7). Victor Von Hagen writes, the "largest man-made pyramid in all the Americas [near Lima in the Land Northward], was constructed of millions of sun-baked bricks cemented over and frescoed with paintings."[15] However, to the south, the river valleys of the Nasca abounded with trees that could have been placed aboard Inca ships and transported to the Land Northward.

In antiquity the building, launching, and loading of large ships required a natural harbor. The land of Bountiful geographically matches well the Contisuyu, the southwest quarter of the Inca Empire. Contisuyu had at least one, and perhaps more Pacific ports. Roughly, eighty miles south of the Nasca capital was the harbor known as Puerto Inca (Port of the Inca). The protected cove was the closest point on the Pacific to Cuzco and is the place from which fresh fish was delivered to the nobles in Cuzco. The late Inca Empire built a permanent settlement at the harbor, and reason suggests that such an attractive port would have been used in earlier periods.

The Nasca ruins have surrendered the kinds of artifacts that would be expected of any serious candidate as a Nephite archaeological site, including gold-plate technology. Nasca excavations have uncovered gold sheets that were hammered into an "almost uniform thinness."[16]

Finally, we know that General Moroni had strong walls of earth and timber constructed to encircle the entire city of Bountiful (Alma 53:4). Although the ruins of Cahuachi have just started to be excavated, it is already apparent that the

a tubular garment. The major difference between male and female tunics is the length, with some of the later female examples extending to the ankles. Head-cloths were sometimes used.[12]

Since the indigenous natives of Peru had no facial hair, an intriguing piece of Nasca pottery depicts a man who might have been a direct descendent of the Nephites. Painted on the pot is a well-dressed fair-skinned Nasca male depicted with a long moustache and goatee.[13]

Excavated tombs have revealed that the "Nasca craftsmen made gold forehead ornaments, gold mouth masks and other gold items of personal adornment such as head plumes, bracelets, earrings, pendants, clothing plaques, pectorals, and remarkable spear throwers."[14]

The Book of Mormon tells us that Bountiful had timbers that they shipped to the Nephites who had colonized the land northward (Helaman 3:10). The numerous inhabitants who had previously lived in the north, the Jaredites, had deforested the land (Helaman 3:6). I flew from Lima (land of Desolation) north along Peru's barren shoreline and found that it would have been easy for the fragile ecosystems of the

Remains of central Nasca Temple at Cahuachi. Was this where Christ appeared to the Nephites?

Several layers of ten-foot-tall walls that protected the central temple.

city was encircled by several layers of tall earthen walls (see figures on the next page).

CAHUACHI, THE TEMPLE OF BOUNTIFUL

The temple of Bountiful is extremely important to students of the Book of Mormon. After the destruction that occurred at the death of Christ, the surviving Nephites in the area gathered at their temple. The prophet Nephi and the others who would become apostles were all at the temple at Bountiful, and it was, understandably, the place where Jesus Christ appeared to the Nephites (3 Nephi 11:1).

If the Nasca civilization was the land of Bountiful, then we can be fairly certain that the city of Cahuachi with its massive temple was the

city of Bountiful and the very place where Christ first appeared in the Americas. Cahuachi was the capital city in the Nasca lands, which included all the valleys and cities in the Río Grande de Nasca River drainage.[17] Silverman and Proulx give this description: "Cahuachi is located on the south bank of the Nasca River, in a narrow section of the valley at approximately 365 m (1200 feet) above sea level, at a point where subterranean water emerges to the surface. Cahuachi extends in length for some 2 km (1.2 miles) and covers approximately 150 ha (hectares, 370 acres). The site is elaborated over a series of brown, barren, hill-covered river terraces just above the valley floor and beneath the Pampa de Atarco."[18]

The Metropolitan Museum of Art in New York writes of the Cahuachi temple complex: "On the south bank of the Nasca River, is the

dominant ceremonial site in southern Peru. Sprawling over forty low-lying hills capped with adobe structures, it is a pilgrimage center that brought hundreds of worshippers to the region."[19] Silverman and Proulx write:

Silverman's determination that Cahuachi was not an urban site is supported by Giuseppe Orefici's seventeen years of excavation at the site, which further demonstrates its hyperceremonial nature. For example, Orefici has discovered a "Step-fret Temple" (so-called because of a mud frieze decorating its north face). Dated to Nasca 1 [150 BC-100 AD], this is the earliest ceremonial structure thus far identified at Cahuachi; surely there are other Nasca 1 ceremonial constructions waiting to be unearthed. The Step-fret Temple shows that Cahuachi was a sacred site from its earliest Nasca occupation. . . .

On the floor of one of the agglutinate rooms on the north-east side of Strong's Great Temple (Unit 2), Orefici discovered a cache of hundreds of broken panpipes. These rooms may have stored the ritual paraphernalia used in ceremonies as well as been facilities for the curation of damaged and obsolete symbolically charged objects. Strong [1957:31] already had recovered ritual paraphernalia from the Great Temple, including fine pottery, colored feathers, and llama remains suggestive of sacrifice and feasting.[20]

Nevertheless, we need to determine if the religion practiced at the great Cahuachi temple was one that had associations to the Law of Moses and included practices one would expect of the Nephite faith. However, it is one thing to excavate an ancient temple or collect ritual attire and paraphernalia, but another matter altogether to try to decipher the actual beliefs of a people who vanished nearly two thousand years ago. From what archaeologists have discovered at Cahuachi, we can glean the following insights into the beliefs of the Cahuachi people.

First, during early Nasca Periods 1, 2 (150 BC–AD 100) the Nasca faithful performed pilgrimages to the temple. Cahuachi was the principal pilgrimage site where people came to offer sacrifices. Rostworowski argues that at Cahuachi "at a certain time of the year a great number of people—common as well as elite—met there to perform a great taqui and dance according to their ancient rites. . . . After the celebrations everyone returned [home]."[21] We know that the righteous Nephites used the temple at the city of Bountiful as their place of gathering (3 Nephi 11:1). We can also assume that the Nephites would have practiced annual temple pilgrimages. When the temple existed in Jerusalem, the Israelites practiced three "pilgrimage festivals" (chagim): Passover, Pentecost, and Tabernacles (*Pseach, Shavouot, and Sukkot*).

Second, the Nasca people offered animal sacrifices. Orefici excavated the burial site of more than sixty sacrificed llamas in an area immediately south-east of one of the small mounds near the temple, and he has recovered the remains of one hundred fifty-four adult and sixty-five young camelids in construction fill in ceremonial mounds at Cahuachi.[22]

Third, like the Nephites (Alma 1:2–3, 16), the Nasca appear to have had a lay priesthood. Silverman and Proulx note: "We do not see evidence of Nasca religion having been a state cult in which the religious officiators were supported by the labor of others."[23]

Fourth, the Nasca temple rites were probably memorized and passed on from one generation to the next, and with the ordinances performed according to a strict tradition. Victor Turner of Cornell University writes that the Nasca temple

priests would have possessed "a body of codified and standardized ritual knowledge [learnt] from older priests and later transmit[ted] to successors."[24] Since Nephi modeled his temple after the one in Jerusalem, it would follow that the Nephites observed the same ceremonial rites. As noted, the Nasca offered animal sacrifices. Among the famous Nasca geoglyphs (lines) is a giant figure labeled "Round Eyed Human Effigy."[25] The geoglyph covers an entire hillside and depicts a human holding his left arm to the square, while the right arm is indistinguishable.

Fifth, music was a primary means for expressing the Nasca faith. Orefici writes "For the Nasca people, music was one of the indispensable means of expressing the collective religious spirit, constituting a true and proper choral language with which it was possible to communicate with the divine."[26] Figurines of individuals playing panpipes, trumpets, and drums have been discovered in Nasca ruins.[27] Instruments used on the temple grounds in Jerusalem, though not in the ceremony itself, included silver trumpets, flutes, harps, lutes, and brass cymbals.[28]

Sixth, a central theme in the Nasca faith was asking God for agricultural fertility. Silverman and Proulx note, "In the situational context of rites, . . . it is significant that the painted harvest festival textiles depict scores of farmers who are finely dressed in human garb and carry plants."[29] Praying and sacrificing for a good harvest is well inside the context of the Nephite faith. The Book of Mormon's Amulek instructed the Nephites to pray "unto him when ye are in your fields, yea, over all your flocks, . . . Cry unto him over the crops of your fields, that ye may prosper in them. Cry over the flocks of your fields, that they may increase." (Alma 34:21, 24–25). Of course, praying and sacrificing for successful harvests and

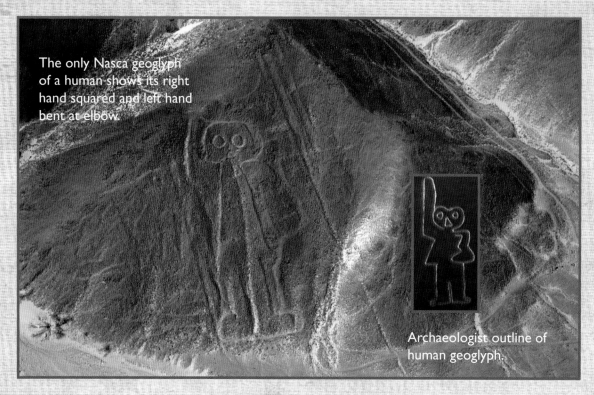

The only Nasca geoglyph of a human shows its right hand squared and left hand bent at elbow.

Archaeologist outline of human geoglyph.

for strength against one's enemies are common elements of most faiths. Still, this practice of the people at Cahuachi between 150 BC and AD 100 provides additional evidences that the early Nasca period religion was harmonious with that of the Nephites.

Seventh, and most important, we know that the Nasca people believed in Viracocha [Christ], the bearded white God of Peru. Urton of Harvard University recorded ethnographic testimony from people living at Cerro Blanco in the Nasca valleys. He writes:

In ancient times, before there were aqueducts [filtration galleries] in the valley, a great drought occurred and the people had no water for years. The people began crying out to their god, Viracocha or Con. They cried and screamed the word nanay [Quechua for "pain"]. . . . The people went en-mass to the foot of Cerro Blanco, which was their principal templo or adoratorio; this was the place where they spoke to the gods. At that moment, Viracocha/Con descended from the sky to the summit of the mountain and heard the weeping of his people. He was so moved by their cries that he began weeping and tears flowed from his eyes.[30]

We learn from the above Nasca oral tradition that 1) their god was Viracocha, the bearded white god of the Andes; 2) the Nasca people believed that they had a personal relationship with Vira-cocha, even to the point that he could intervene on their behalf and end a drought; 3) that Vira-cocha answered prayers; 4) that special prayers were offered at the temple; and 5) that even in the heavens their god had the form of a man who could "hear," have compassion, and "weep" tears of concern and love. Although our knowledge is still quite limited, I am amazed at the similarities that seem to exist between the Nasca people and the account of the Nephites of Bountiful who, according to the Book of Mormon:

saw that they were about to perish by famine, and they began to remember the Lord their God; and they began to remember the words of Nephi.

And the people began to plead with their chief judges and their leaders, that they would say unto Nephi; Behold, we know that thou art a man of God, and therefore cry unto the Lord our God that he turn away from us this famine, lest all the words which thou hast spoken concerning our destruction be fulfilled.

. . . the Lord did turn away his anger from the people, and caused that rain should fall upon the earth, insomuch that it did bring forth her fruit in the season of her fruit. And it came to pass that it did bring forth her grain in the season of her grain.

And behold, the people did rejoice and glorify God (Helaman 11:7, 8, 17, 18).

THE SIGNS OF CHRIST'S COMING TO THE AMERICAS

The events surrounding the coming of Jesus Christ to the promised land included miraculous geological events. It should be remembered that the account of the calamities that we read about in the Book of Mormon was not recorded on the day that the events occurred, but is a summarization made nearly four hundred years later by Mormon.

Two similar events suggest that earthquakes and volcanic eruptions were messianic signs for the Nephites and Lamanites. The first of these two catastrophic events took place during Nephi's and Lehi's missions. While they were held in prison circa 30 BC, the earth shook and a cloud of darkness formed. The earth shook again and the prison walls trembled. The Lamanites could not flee because of the cloud of darkness. The people repented, and the cloud dispersed, but then the prophets were encircled by a mysterious fire that did not harm them (Helaman 5:23, 27, 28, 31, 33, 34, 42–44).

In 1980, I lived in the state of Washington and witnessed the eruptions of Mount St. Helens. The first signs of the volcano's awakening were earthquakes. When the volcano finally exploded, a sizeable earthquake occurred, the north side of the mountain collapsed, and a monstrous cloud of pyroclastic debris killed every living thing within twelve miles of its northern slope. The superheated lava, ash, and gases that formed the pyroclastic blast ignited fires wherever it touched. The energy from the eruption created a thunder and lightning storm that encircled the mountain. Following the initial eruption, what was left of Mount St. Helens shot a massive ash plume miles into the air. Although I was living one hundred miles to the north of the volcano, on several occasions my city was engulfed in a thick cloud of volcanic ash. The ash cloud was so thick that it darkened the sky to the point where one could not see the sun. The ash fell like heavy powdered snow, covering everything with several inches of dust-like ash.

The second volcanic eruption-like event in the Book of Mormon took place at the time of the Lord's death. Mormon recorded that major catastrophes took place throughout all the land, a prime indicator that multiple volcanic eruptions occurred. He wrote that an earthquake did "shake the whole earth" (3 Nephi 8:6), a great storm with thunder and lightnings arose (3 Nephi 8:5–6), the city of Zarahamla caught fire and burned (3 Nephi 8:8), the earth (lava or lahar) was carried up upon the city of Moronihah, and there became a *great mountain* (over the four hundred years to Mormon's time a volcanic cone must have formed where the city had been once been; emphasis added, 3 Nephi 3:8). The quaking of the earth lasted for about three hours (3 Nephi 8:19), which seems more indicative of a volcanic eruption than an autonomous earthquake. After the quaking, an odd darkness came "upon the face of the land" (3 Nephi 8:19). The darkness appears to have had a physical cause, perhaps volcanic ash. The darkness came "upon the face" or surface of the land. Mormon described it as "mists of darkness." Again this seems indicative of thick clouds of volcanic ash, but could also have included smoke from the fires that were ignited by lava, or pyroclastic clouds. So heavy was the darkness (ash fall?) that neither candles, torches, nor wood could be lit, nor could the sun, moon, or stars be seen (3 Nephi 21–22). We also know that some cities sank into the depths of the sea (3 Nephi 9:14), indicating that the accompanying earthquakes must have shifted ground levels along seismic plates.

The oral traditions of the Incas include stories strikingly similar to the record found in the Book of Mormon. Calderwood notes:

Betanzos began his manuscript by referring to ancient legends of a time when the land and the provinces of Peru were dark and neither firelight nor daylight existed, and Peru was inhabited by people whose name had long been forgotten. The fact that Betanzos started his account with this legend is indicative of the importance the natives placed on the event of total darkness when there was neither sun light nor apparently fire of any kind. . . . Betanzos emphasized that there was no light from any source. Betanzos then relates that during this time of total darkness, the people were visited by a lord whose name was Contiti Viracocha [Ticci Viracocha], who went to the area known as Tiahuanaco.[31]

In Poma de Ayala's description of these calamites, Calderwood sees a close parallel to the events in the Book of Mormon that took place at the death of Christ:

God punished them by sending down fire from heaven to burn them, mountains fell upon them and covered them over, some villages were covered with water, other villages were swallowed up by the earth, all as a punishment sent by God. . . . during the time of the Incas, mountains fell down, rocky cliffs and crags were brought down, volcanoes erupted and rained fire from hell upon them, sand flattened a city and the surrounding areas, earthquakes killed many, tidal waves hit the coastal region killing many. God also sent plagues and pestilence, hail storms, and heavy snows killed many people and animals.[32]

The early Spaniards in Peru actually experienced events similar to what we read about in the Book of Mormon. One colonist wrote: "A number of calamities affected our country. . . for instance, fire rained down upon the town of Cacha in the Collao. The volcano of Putina erupted and caused a rain of dust. Also the city of Arequipa and the surrounding district were leveled to the ground."[33] As the Spanish conquistadors attacked Quito, they experienced the eruption of one of the great Andean volcanoes. Cieza de León wrote: "The fire that it had within destroyed many Indian houses, killed many men and women and it threw into the air so many ashes as dense as smoke that one could not see while these ashes floated, and the amount that I said was all over. So much fell that those who did not know how believed that from the heavens it was raining ashes, which fell more than twenty days."[34]

From the brief description we have of the calamities in the Book of Mormon, it appears that the city of Bountiful experienced earthquakes, lighting, thunder, and a thick darkness. Further east, in the land of Zarahemla, the city of Moroni sank into the east sea, and the city of Zarahemla burned. At an almost equal distance, between Cahuachi (city of Bountiful) and Pukara (city of Zarahemla), stands a great volcano. It is called El Misti. Like the mermaids of the Lorelei, the mountain is both incredibly beautiful and notoriously dangerous. For certain, El Misti should be admired from a distance. The volcano is located just east of Peru's second largest city, Arequipa, and stands as a constant reminder of the city's eventual doom.

Is the beautiful El Misti volcano guilty as charged of having taken part in the Book of Mormon calamities of the first centuries BC and first century AD? Seismologists can show that over the last 14,000 years, El Misti has erupted twenty times. The volcano's average interval between eruptions is once every 700 years. However, according to the Smithsonian Museum, El Misti was very active around the time of the Lord's mission on earth. At that time, two of El Misti's eruptions came close together. Though it is not possible to precisely date volcanic eruptions, scientists believe that one of El Misti's eruptions occurred around 80 BC (plus or minus 75 years). Another eruption occurred AD 90 (plus or minus 300 Years).[35] Today El Misti's massive symmetrical cone has a mile-wide cap (summit). Scientists also believe that a "pyroclastic flow traveled 12 km (7 miles) south (from El Misti) about 2000 years ago."[36] El Misti's Meridian-of-time lava flow leads me to wonder if the city of Moronihah, which was covered by earth, might be found encrusted by or beneath the massive mountain.

It is unlikely that even El Misti alone could have caused all the destruction that was recorded in the Book of Mormon. The Andes Mountains are part of the Pacific Ring of Fire, and its volcanoes are the tallest mountains in the entire ring. Indeed, the Andes could be defined as a garden of volcanoes. The calamities that took place at the time of Christ's death were felt on both sides on the earth, thus the powerful force that triggered the events would have been strong enough to have caused eruptions all along the Ring of Fire. There are several other major volcanoes in central and southern Peru that could have been El Misti's accomplices. For example, the Smithsonian cites one violent volcano just a few miles from El Misti:

This majestic beauty has a
violent past. Mt. Misti Volcano,
Arequipa, Peru.

Huaynaputina (whose name means "new volcano") is a relatively inconspicuous volcano that was the source of the largest historical eruption of South America in 1600 AD. The volcano has no prominent topographic expression and lies within a 2.5-km-wide (1.85 miles) depression formed by edifice collapse. . . . This powerful fissure-fed eruption may have produced 20 cu km (7.7 sq. miles) of dacitic tephra, including pyroclastic flows and surges that traveled 13 km (8 miles) to the east and SE. Lahar reached the Pacific Ocean, 120 km (73 miles) away. The eruption caused substantial damage to the major cities of Arequipa and Moguengua, and regional economies took 150 years to fully recover.[37]

As the birth of Christ approached, Zarahemla became an extremely wicked city. Its inhabitants rejected the words of Nephi to the point where the prophet could not stay among them. Gadianton robbers ruled the judgment seats, and the city was void of justice. Zarahemla's righteous were punished while the wicked openly committed adultery, thievery, and murder. Nephi labeled her as a city of "great iniquity" (Helaman 7:3–6). Their abominations were so grievous that the Lord personally made certain that the city of Zarahemla and its inhabitants were cleansed by fire (3 Nephi 9:3).

It appears as though Zarahemla became Lake Titicaca's sister city to the brothel-infested Roman city of Pompeii. Duke University professor Paul Baker states, "Lake Titicaca is also well situated to receive volcanic ash from the adjacent active arc—there are several active volcanic centers within 200 km (75 miles) from the lake (including the well known Sabancaya and

Huaynaputina). The lake will provide an import record of volcanism and volcanic ashes."[38]

NASA's website "Visible Earth" recently featured another volcano that could have contributed to the destruction that cleared Peru of the wicked at the time of Christ's death. The website includes a picture of a volcano and its ash plume. The subtitle of the picture reads: "Ash and volcanic gas rose from the Ubinas Volcano in southern Peru in late April and early May 2006, prompting evacuations. . . . after a series of explosions sent ash, gas, and lava fragments more than three kilometers (nearly two miles) into the air, said the U.S. Geological Survey in its weekly Volcanic Activity Report. The fumes caused respiratory problems, and livestock fell ill or died after eating ash-coated grass. . . . Ubinas sits in southern Peru, due west of Lake Titicaca."[39]

As for evil doers in the city of Moroni, they experienced a different fate—they sank with their city into the depths of the sea of the east (Alma 50:13, 3 Nephi 8:9, 9:4). According to our model for the Book of Mormon in Peru, this would imply that at least one ancient city should be found under the blue waters of Lake Titicaca. Along with the city of Moroni, the cities of Onihah, Mocum, and Jerusalem were also submerged (3 Nephi 9:7). In 2002 "Peruvian divers found pre-Inca stairways, ramps and walls beneath the waters of Lake Titicaca, . . . The remains were found at a depth of 6.5 to 26 feet on the eastern side of the lake. . . . They are built with interlocking stones. . . . oceanic engineer and expedition member Gustavo Villavicencio told reporters. . . . 'There are studies that show that the lake used to be . . . around 66 to 98 feet lower, and that was where ancient Peruvians built.' "[40]

Just off the northeast shore of the Isle of the Sun, are the remains of an even more impressive sunken city. The city was discovered by the French oceanographer Jacques Cousteau. Named the city of Mancapampa, the ruins were discovered 20 meters (65 feet) below the surface of Lake Titicaca. Situated between three small islands, Cousteau's divers recovered pottery and gold artifacts, some of which are on display in the Museo de Oro (Museum of Gold) on the Isle of the Sun. In 2000, Italian divers discovered a wall that ran for 2,600 feet, a long road and a 660-ft by 160-ft temple 100 feet under Lake Titicaca (initial dating estimated to AD 500–1000).[41] My Aymara Indian guide on the Isle of the Sun told me that his people believe many other sunken cities and temples lie beneath the waters of Lake Titicaca.

Finally, we know that the Incas were perhaps the ancient world's greatest highway builders, and that at the death of Jesus Christ, the Nephite highways were broken up and the level roads were spoiled (3 Nephi 8:13). Undoubtedly, even the most skeptical observer has to agree that Peru possessed all the geological attributes required for a region to have experienced the calamities mentioned in the Book of Mormon.

CHRIST APPEARS TO THE NEPHITES AND LAMANITES

The comparisons between the Inca oral traditions of the physical visitation of their god Viracocha to Peru and the account of the visitation of Jesus Christ in the Book of Mormon are truly amazing. H. Osborne writes of the appearance of Viracocha to the ancient Incas: "There suddenly appeared, coming from the south, a white man of large stature and authoritative demeanor. This man had such great power that he changed the hills into valleys and from valleys made great hills, causing streams to flow from the living stone" (compare 3 Nephi 9:8).[42]

Cabello Valboa attributes this event to the events that occurred when Christ was crucified. He wrote:

> There is a story, passed down by tradition from fathers to sons, that one day, all of a sudden, the earth shook, and the sun (outside of its normal trajectory) was darkened and the rocks were broken up by smashing some against the others, and many graves of men dead since many years earlier were seen open. Many of the animals were greatly disturbed. By conjecture and numerous indications, this appears to have taken place on the holy day of the crucifixion and death of our Redeemer Christ because it was also said that within a few years there were seen in some areas of Peru certain men of venerable presence and appearance with long beards who dealt justly with everyone.[43]

Calderwood cites Father Francisco de Avila's description (1598) of this ancient event:

> In ancient times the sun died.
> Because of his [sun's] death it was
>   night for five days.
> Rocks banged against each other.
> Mortars and grinding stones began
>   to eat people.
> Buck llamas started to drive men.[44]

Calderwood continues "Father Francisco de Avila inserted his opinion of the event when he exclaimed that 'Here's what we Christians think about it. We think these stories tell of the

darkness following the death of our Lord Jesus Christ. Maybe that is what it was.' "[45]

Quoting the chronicler Cieza de León, Hammond Innes relates:

> Before the Incas came to reign in these kingdoms or were known there, these Indians tell a thing that far exceeds all else they say.
>
> They state that a long time went by in which they "did not see the sun; . . ." It finally emerged out of Lake Titicaca and shortly afterwards "out of the regions of the south there came and appeared among them a white man, large of stature, whose air and person aroused great respect and veneration."
>
> Because he could work miracles, "making plains of the hills and of the plains mountains, and bringing forth springs in the living rock," they called him "the Maker of all things, their Beginning, Father of the Sun. . ." They say that in many places he instructed people how they should live and spoke

to them lovingly and meekly, exhorting them to be good and not do one another harm or injury, but rather to love one another, and use charity to all.[46]

Osborne continues that Viracocha was "a bearded man of tall stature clothed in a white robe which came down to his feet and which he wore belted at the waist."[47] "He walked with a staff and addressed the natives with love, calling them his sons and daughters. As he traversed all the land he worked miracles. He healed the sick by touch. He spoke every tongue even better than the natives. They called him Thunupa or Tarpaca, Viracocha-rapacha or Pacaccan."[48]

To someone who has not read the Book

of Mormon account, it must seem odd that the Peruvian god seems to have had the dress, manners, and appearance of a holy man from Palestine during the era of Christ's earthly mission. Urton notes: "The native chronicler Pachacuti Yamqui strongly averred that the creator, known to him by the names Thunupa, Tarapaca and Thunupa Viracocha, was the apostle St. Thomas, whereas the native chronicler Guaman Poma identified Viracocha as St. Bartholomew."[49] It is easy to see why Viracocha stood out from the native Peruvians; he was a "white man of large stature, whose air and person aroused great respect and veneration,"[50] and had blue eyes.[51]

THE DEAD RISE FROM THEIR GRAVES IN PERU

Matthew recorded that at the time of Christ's death "the graves were opened; and many bodies of the saints which slept rose" (Matthew 27:52). Calderwood points out:

Miguel Cabello Valboa's account, as noted earlier, includes this strange phrase about the time of upheaval: "y muchos sepulcros de hombres muertos de mucho tiempo atras se vieron abiertos." (Author's translation: "*and many graves of men, dead since many years earlier, were seen open*.") If the phrase only referred to cemeteries that had been destroyed by an earthquake or a flood, which happens periodically in the Andes, the memory of the event would not have been passed forward for centuries.

In the Book of Mormon, Samuel the Lamanite prophesied that the graves would be opened and yield up their dead at the time of the resurrection of Jesus

Christ. Subsequently, when Jesus Christ examined the Nephite records during his brief visit to the New World, he observed that the Nephites had not recorded the fulfillment of this prophesy and questioned Nephi whether any resurrected saints had appeared and administered unto the surviving Nephites and Lamanites. When Nephi affirmed that the event had occurred as prophesied, Jesus commanded that it should be recorded (See 3 Nephi 23:11,13).[52]

THE LORD HEALS THE HEART OF THE ANDES—ISLAND OF THE SUN

The marvelous mission of Jesus Christ to the Nephites at the temple in Bountiful is recorded in the Third Book of Nephi, chapters 11 to 26. Few passages of scripture can compare in glory to these sixteen chapters, for they reveal much about the personality of our Savior. These sacred pages are an eyewitness account of our great God who healed the sick, taught the eternal truth of salvation and exaltation, blessed the children, prayed to the Father for humanity, and wept tears of love. While at Bountiful the Lord called twelve disciples, organized his church, and structured the daily affairs of the Nephite society so that the people had all things in common (3 Nephi 26:17–21). Fortunately the visitation to the Nephites was recorded on the golden plates and has been passed down to us as the heart of the Book of Mormon. As precious as these chapters are, they are not a full account of the Lord's mission in the Americas.

Charles Mann reminds us, "By the time of Christ's birth, two of these early polities had become dominant: Pukara on the northern, Peruvian edge of the lake and Tiwanaku on the opposite, Bolivian side."[53] There were two great civilizations in the Book of Mormon, the Nephites and the Lamanites, both sharing in some degree the blood of the house of Israel. We know that the Lamanites were also taught the gospel and became Christians at the time Jesus visited the Americas. Thus, either the Lord himself visited the Lamanites or He commanded his disciples to minister to them. After reading the oral traditions of the Incas, it is my opinion that both Jesus Christ and his disciples visited the Lamanites in their two strongholds. Their first stronghold was their traditional capital at the city of Nephi (Cuzco); and the second, the newly risen empire in the land southward (Tiwanaku on the south side of Lake Titicaca).

After the Lord told the Nephites about the Lost Tribes of Israel (3 Nephi 15:15) and that they, the Nephites, were also his "sheep" (3 Nephi 15:24), He continued by stating:

I have *other sheep*, which are not of this land, neither of the land of Jerusalem, neither in any parts of that land round about whither I have been to minister. For they of whom I speak are they who have not as yet heard my voice; neither have I at any time manifested myself unto them.

But I have received a commandment of the Father that I shall go unto them, and that they shall hear my voice, and shall be numbered among my sheep, that there may be one fold and one shepherd; therefore I go to show myself unto them (emphasis added, 3 Nephi 16:1–4).

It is widely held that these verses refer to the Lost Tribes of Israel. However, this seems unlikely. Just ten verses before, the Lord has already told the Nephites about the Lost Tribes (3 Nephi 15:15), and now He is telling them that he has even "other" sheep (3 Nephi 16:1). I believe that the other sheep were the Lamanites in the Americas, and that He still had to visit them and make them part of his fold. In this regard, we know that at the time of Christ the animosity between the Nephites and Lamanites was temporarily healed. They became one fold with one shepherd for at least the next two hundred years (4 Nephi 1:15, 18).

The conversion of the Lamanite nation is not recorded in the Book of Mormon. The golden plates contain only the record of the Nephite people (Jacob 1:2). Therefore, the Book of Mormon would not mention the details of the Lord's visit to non-Nephites. The pacification of the hearts of the Lamanites did not happen by osmosis. Someone had to convert them and teach them the gospel. However, it appears that the Lamanites had no written language, and thus, any knowledge of Christ visiting them would have been passed down to their descendants through their oral traditions.

Even so, the Nephite record might allude to the Lord's visit to the Lamanites. While the Lord was at Bountiful he commanded his twelve disciples, as he did in the Old World, to take "journeys" where they could preach the gospel and baptize in the name of Christ. While abroad from the land of Bountiful, the disciples gathered to pray. While in supplication, Jesus Christ appeared to them (3 Nephi 27:1)—presumably in a place outside of the land of Bountiful. Since the Lord had organized his church among the Nephites and baptized them, it would seem likely that the disciples were not teaching the Nephites whom the Lord had already converted, but were serving among their Lamanite brothers. This would

Possible Course of Christ's Mission in the Americas

Manta

Cuzco/City of Nephi

Cacha

Isle of the Sun

Bountiful
Nasca Temple

imply that the Lord reappeared in the Americas, this time in the land of the Lamanites.

The question remains. In the surviving oral history of the Andean people is there a memory of a visit by Christ? The answer is clearly "yes." There still exists in the Andes the prevailing belief among the Inca and Aymara people that their ancestors were visited by a bearded white god who appeared at Lake Titicaca and from there walked north through the Andes ministering and teaching the people. Urton writes:

> For instance, the space traversed by characters in the myth begins at the lake and proceeds north-westward to the coast of Ecuador. The more detailed narration of encounters between the creator and people— those occurring in Cacha and Urcos—centre on the Vilcanota, or Urubamba river valley, which courses north-westward near Cusco and within the Cusco valley itself. Thus the myths of the origins of the world told by informants in the Inca capital project a vital connection between Lake Titicaca, the site of one of the principal highland civilizations of pre-Inca times (Tiahuanaco) [Lamanites on southeast end of Titicaca], and Cusco [City of Nephi], the successor capital.[54]

> . . . Cieza (de León) says that the creator, who had the appearance of a tall white man, traveled along the highland route healing the sick and restoring sight to the blind by his words alone.[55]

According to the various accounts, Viracocha appeared on the Island of the Sun in Lake Titicaca. At the time of Christ, the Island of the Sun would have been within the Lamanite lands, though it was the same place where Manco Capac

(Nephi) had temporarily lived with his family. After teaching the people and performing miracles, Viracocha left Lake Titicaca and proceeded north. Alden Mason tells us that Viracocha, with the aid of two assistants, covered the three main corridors of the Andes.

> Viracocha himself, with his two assistants, journeyed north. . . He traveled up the cordillera, one assistant went along the coast, and the other up the edge of the eastern forest. . . The Creator proceeded to Urcos, near Cuzco, where he commanded future populations

to emerge from a mountain. He visited Cuzco, and then continued north to Ecuador. There, in the province of Manta [perhaps another "Manti" far to the north], he took leave of his people and, walking on waves, disappeared across the ocean.[56]

From this account, we learn that Viracocha taught the people that he would command "future" populations to emerge from a mountain. When warning the people in Palestine about the Last Days, Jesus Christ referred them to the revelations of Daniel (see Matthew 24:15). Viracocha's description of a future people being command by the Lord to "emerge from a mountain" is strikingly close to Daniel's prophecy of a people of the Church in the last days coming forth as a stone being cut from a mountain (Daniel 2:44–45).

When the Lord served among the Jews, He did not minister alone. Beside him were the apostles, whom he eventually sent forth two-by-two to share the good news to the world. According to Peruvian oral traditions, their white god "sent out disciples to various districts which Viracocha had indicated for them."[57] According to another account, Viracocha assigned himself and his assistants to specific mission areas. Sarmiento recorded:

> He [Viracocha] ordered his two servants to charge [write] their memories with the names of all tribes that he had depicted, and of the valleys and provinces where they were to come forth, which were those of the whole land. He ordered that each one should go by a different road, naming the tribes, and ordering them all to go forth and people the country. His servants,

obeying the command of Viracocha, set out on their journey and work. One went by the mountain range or chain which they call the heights over the plains on the South Sea (Lake Poopó in the Altiplano in Bolivia). The other went by the heights which overlook the wonderful mountain ranges which we call the Andes, situated to the east of the said sea. By these roads they went, saying with a loud voice "Oh you tribes and nations, hear and obey the order of Ticci Viracocha Pachayachachi, which commands you to go forth, and multiply and settle the land" [compare Genesis 1:28]. Viracocha himself did the same along the road between those taken by his two servants, naming all the tribes and places by which he passed. At the sound of his voice every place obeyed, and the people came forth, some from lakes, others from fountains, valleys, caves, trees, rocks and hills, spreading over the land and multiplying to form the nations which are to-day in Peru."[58]

We cannot be certain what was meant by the people being commanded to go forth, be named, multiply, and settling the land; however, I like to conjecture that the people came forth to be baptized, and took upon them the name of Christ (as *Viracochas*). Another possible meaning for the new names is that the tribes were being organized into the ancient Church's equivalent of wards and stakes. The command to multiply and settle the land could have meant that the faithful were asked to have families and repopulate Peru (since all the wicked had been killed), and to resettle the areas that had become desolate.

This last command of Viracocha to settle the land brings to mind images of Brigham Young calling the Mormon pioneers to spread out and settle the fertile valleys of Utah, Idaho, Wyoming, Arizona, Colorado, New Mexico, California, Nevada, and even Alberta in Canada. In the literal sense, the Mormons used their skills in irrigation to make the arid North American West blossom like a rose. So effective were the Saints' irrigation skills that at times the LDS Church was invited to send pioneers to colonize barren lands which earlier settlers were unable to farm. For example, Buffalo Bill Cody and the Governor of Wyoming asked the Church to build the Sidon Canal to the Lovell Valley. The amazing canal is still in use.

Francisco de Avila wrote of the legend of Viracocha, "He caused terraces and fields to be formed on the steep sides of ravines, and sustaining walls to rise up and support them. He also made irrigation channels to flow. . . and he went in various directions, arranging many things."[59] The engineering feats of the ancient Peruvians are renown, none more so than their vast network of terraced farms and long irrigation systems. Cieza de León believed that the Incas were unsurpassed in their ability to construct irrigation canals over difficult terrain.[60]

During Viracocha's journey north from Lake Titicaca to Cuzco a significant event took place. At Rachi, seventy-three miles south of Cuzco, Viracocha approached the lands of the Cacha tribe. Again, if we switch the last "a" in Cacha to an "i," we derive Cachi, the name of the violent eldest brother of the original four Inca brothers. Cachi is our counterpart to Laman. Thus, the people of Cacha (Canas or Lamans) were possibly Lamanites. Betanzos recorded the following tradition:

Remains of Temple dedicated
to the White Bearded God,
Viracocha at Rachi, Peru.

When he [Viracocha] came to a province which they call Cacha, which belongs to the Canas Indians and is eighteen leagues from the city of Cuzco, Viracocha called out these Canas Indians. They came out armed, however, and did not know Viracocha when they saw him [Lamanites did not recognize Christ]. They all came at him with their arms to kill him. When he saw them coming, he understood what they were coming for and instantly caused fire to fall from heaven, burning a range of mountains near the Indians. When the Indians saw the fire, they feared they would be burned. Throwing their arms to the ground, they went straight to Viracocha and all threw themselves on the ground before him. When he saw them thus, he took a staff in his hands and went where the fire was. He gave it two or three blows with his staff, which put it completely out, whereupon he told the Indians that he was their maker. The Canas Indians built a sumptuous guaca, which means a shrine or idol, at the place where he stood when he called the fire from heaven and from which he went to put it out.[61]

Sarmiento recorded the same story, but noted that those who tried to kill Viracocha, when they saw the fire, "were terrified at the fearful fire. They came down from the hill, and sought pardon from Viracocha for their sins. Viracocha was moved by compassion."[62] Urton summarizes several accounts in his description:

> However, when Viracocha approached a village called Cacha, in the district of Canas (south-east of Cusco), the people came out of the town in a threatening manner, saying they were going to stone him. Betanzos says the people rushed at Viracocha with weapons.
>
> Viracocha dropped to his knees and raised his hands toward the sky, as if seeking aid. The sky immediately filled with fire, and the terrified people of Cacha [Lamanites] approached Viracocha, asking him to forgive and save them. The fire was then extinguished, but not before it had burned the rocks around there so that large blocks were consumed and became as light as cork [indicative of lava rock]. Betanzos says that he himself traveled to Cacha to investigate this mythic incident and clearly saw the scorched earth [possibly barren lava flows] resulting from this cataclysmic event.[63]

What I find interesting is that once the Indians realized that the white Viracocha was not a Nephite enemy, but their god, they "approached Viracocha, asking him to forgive their sins and save them." I ask, Who can forgive sins and save one's soul but Jesus Christ? To honor the site of this great miracle the Inca erected at Rachi a massive temple to Viracocha. The temple measured 100 m (328 ft) long by 20 m (66 ft) wide by 15 m high (48 ft).

After what appears to have been an encounter with Lamanite tribesmen at Cacha (possibly Shemlon in the Book of Mormon), Viracocha traveled to Tambo of Urcos, eighteen miles from the city of Cuzco. Tambo was the place where Manco Capac (Nephi) won the allegiance of the Tambo Tribes who helped him acquire and rule Cuzco. At Tambo, Viracocha climbed a mountain and sat down on its peak. It was here that he called the ancestors to come forth from the grave. I like to think that at Tambo, Viracocha called forth the great Nephite ancestors who had lived in the land of Nephi, that is, Jacob, Enos, and Abinadi. Such an event was foretold in the Book of Mormon (Helaman 14:25). To commemorate the great event, Urton writes of this sacred place:

> In homage to the time when the creator sat atop this mountain, the people of Urcos built a bench of gold there and placed a statue of Viracocha upon it. Molina tells us that the image of Viracocha at Urcos was called Atun-Viracocha ("great creator") and that the statue was in the form of a man with a white robe hanging down to his feet.[64]

When the Spanish arrived they melted down the statue of Viracocha and the bench. The bench alone had enough gold in it to make 16,000 to 18,000 pesos (large coins) of fine gold.[65]

In the Old World, Jesus Christ ended his journeys at the great temple in Jerusalem. Viracocha was destined for Cuzco, the place where I believe the Nephites built the first temple in the promised land. When Viracocha reached the city, he brought forth from the grave another ancestor. Urton tells us that Viracocha called up out of the earth (resurrected) the great Lord for whom the land was originally named.[66] From a Book of Mormon paradigm of Peru, this would mean that when Jesus Christ reached the city of Nephi, he called forth from the grave, the newly resurrected body of the great Nephi, the first king for whom the land was named.

As Viracocha left Cuzco, he promised the leaders that they also "should emerge from the earth after he left."[67] In other words, from that time on, at the command of Viracocha (Christ) all men shall come forth from the grave.

Betanzos summarizes the final phase of Viracocha's mission, "He went on, continuing his work, until he reached the province of Puerto Viejo. There he met the others whom he had sent out, as has been said. He went out across the sea with them; they say that he and his companions walked on water as if on land."[68] Thus, Viracocha ended his mission in Peru with a parallel miracle to one Jesus Christ performed on the Sea of Galilee. He walked on water, and did so with his disciples, and as he left, he promised his people that one day he would return.[69]

THE NAMES OF VIRACOCHA

If Viracocha was the Christ, why did the Peruvians call him Viracocha and not Jesus Christ? There are at least four reasons why the Incas would not have called their white god "Jesus." First, the resurrected Christ was a God, whose Hebrew names *YHWA* or *El* would have been sacred and not appropriate for common usage. Second, as we shall discuss later, Viracocha is only a "descriptive"

name for the Inca god, probably not his actual name. In the Bible we find that in reverence for the Lord's actual name, *YHWA* or *EL*, the believers substituted a number of "descriptive" names, like the First Born, the Holy One of Israel, and so on. Third, the secret language used by the Incas, which we are presuming to be Reformed Egyptian was lost. Since Nephi used the Lord's name (Jesus Christ) while writing on the plates, we can assume that within the Egyptian-speaking Nephite inner circle they knew Him as Jesus the Christ. Fourth, in the Quechua and Aymara languages of the commoners, it is unlikely that the Lord's name could have been rendered by the native translation of "Jesus Christ." While referring to Hugh Nibley's research, Dana Pike explains:

It is worth noting that in the Book of Mormon there appear names that are technically theophoric, but which do not employ the root of either *YHWH* or *EL*. In the biblical text such theophoric names are traditionally efforts to venerate pagan deities. In the Book of Mormon, however, they appear referential to Jehovah but also serve as evidence of a strong Egyptian influence. One prime example of this is the name Ammon, which means "the one who is not known, the secret one whom we can't name, whose name is not know to us." Ammon, Amon or Amun was the great and universal god of the Egyptian empire. It was also the most common name among the Nephites. Anciently the name was frequently used in the building of other Egyptian names, Omni being a good example of this, as it means "he who belongs to Amon."[70]

In Quechua, the language of the Inca populace,

the name of the Peruvian gods would have been transliterated, not translated, from the Nephite private language of Egyptian. Elder Bruce R. McConkie wrote: "Since God revealed himself to Adam by certain names, we might suppose that those names, or variants of them, would be preserved among succeeding generations, even though people coming later developed false religions. It is also, not uncommon for important names to be carried from one language to another by transliteration rather than translation."[71]

Valuable information can be acquired about the divine calling and character of Jesus Christ by knowing the descriptive names his Old World disciples gave him (Creator, the Good Shepherd, the Only One of Israel, the Master, The Living Water, the Tree of Life, the Mediator, the Word, and so). In the same manner, vital information about Viracocha's calling and character can be learned by knowing the substitute names he was given.

VIRACOCHA—THE CREATOR

To the Peruvians, Viracocha was the source of all reality, and was often called the Creator or Creator God. Sullivan writes "Cuni Raya Vira Cocha is said to have existed from very ancient times. Before he was, there was nothing at all in the world. It was he who first gave shape and force to the mountains, the forest, the rivers, and all sorts of animals, and to the fields for humankind's subsistence as well."[72] The Nephites knew Jesus Christ was their creator (2 Nephi 9:5, Mosiah 3:8, 5:15).

VIRACOCHA—THE RELATIONSHIP BETWEEN TWO ABSTRACT REALTIES

According to Sullivan, the Spanish conquistadors were puzzled by the name Viracocha

(Wiraqocha). They thought it sounded like words which combined meant "foam or fat of the sea." When the Spanish presented their meaning to the Indians, the native Peruvians laughed. Sullivan suggests that the name of the Andean white god had a completely different meaning. He relates:

> I was therefore amazed to find the word *wira*, written in the Spanish convention of the day as *uira*, in Bertonio's Aymara dictionary. . . .
>
> . . . *wira* was an abstract term standing for the concept of obliquity. It is probably best translated as "tilted plane." In the language of Wiraqocha's homeland, his name meant "tilted plane of the (celestial) sea. . ."
>
> Therefore the meaning, in Aymara, of the name of the Aymara god Wiraqocha denotes the *relationship of two abstract planes*.[73]

Given Sullivan's meaning of Viracocha's name, we can now speculate on what is meant by the god who is "the relationship of two abstract planes." Could these planes or realities represent the spiritual and the physical, the Celestial and the Terrestrial, and the plane between the two realities being the veil or the body of Christ (Hebrews 10:18–20)? The Apostle John wrote: "No man cometh unto the Father, but by me" (John 14:6), and "No man hath ascended up to heaven, but he that came down from heaven, even the Son of man" (John 3:13). Paul taught that Christ was the one and only mediator between God and men (1 Timothy 2:5). In the Americas the Nephites believed that their god was "the great mediator" (2 Nephi 2:28). The Jaredites before them believed that their god could appear to them in two spheres, the spirit and the flesh (Ether 3:16).

VIRACOCHA—THE STAFF GOD

Since great antiquity, Viracocha was known as the "staff god" whose personage was that of a male human. Sullivan notes "Tunapa Wiraqocha is always described as carrying a staff."[74] This title might provide direct evidence that Viracocha is the Messiah. Ada Habershon writes:

> In Numbers xvii we have a beautiful type of the resurrection of the Lord Jesus Christ, in the budding of Aaron's rod. The twelve rods were laid up before the Lord. All were equally dead, and there was no sign of life in them; but when the morning came a wondrous miracle had taken place—one rod, that on which was inscribed the name of Aaron, had become full of life: buds and blossoms and fruit had all appeared. No eye saw the change take place; when Moses came in the morning there was abundant evidence of life, reminding us of that morning when the women came to the sepulcher at the rising of the sun, and found that He whom they sought was not dead but was risen.[75]

VIRACOCHA—BEARER OF THE MILLSTONE

Sullivan mused:

> the empty interpretation of the name of the god Wiraqocha as meaning "foam of the sea" had been established in print as early as 1551, and nothing written since has replaced this reading as standard. This same ground had been gone over numerous times already. The idea, then, of searching the dictionaries appeared at the outset merely an exercise in futility.

Conditioned as I was by the literature, I assumed that finding a meaning for the name Wiraqocha was hopeless.

What tipped the balance in favor of going forward—however tentatively—was the thought that I could at least look up one or two of Wiraqocha's other titles, just to be sure there was nothing there. I began with the name "Tunapa," found throughout the Chronicles as a title of Wiraqocha, but used especially often (more than twenty times) by Pachakuti Yamqui, the indigenous nobleman from the Lake Titicaca [Zarahemla] region. Quechua [Nephite language] and Aymara [Lamanite language] abound in compound words. I knew that in both languages the verb apay means "to carry." Then I looked up tuna. It means "millstone." Tunapa Wiraqocha was the "bearer of the mill."[76]

In other words, one of Viracocha's titles was "the bearer of the millstone." We know that Jesus Christ alone took upon himself the punishment for our sins. He suffered the crushing forces of humanity's aggregate transgressions. If it were not for the Savior, the millstones that we have chained to ourselves by transgressing God's laws would be our eternal burdens. (see Matthew 18:6, D&C 121:17–22). Through the Atonement the Lord will carry that burden for us.

VIRACOCHA—THE GRINDSTONE (GRAIN PRESS)

Viracocha was also known as the grindstone: Sullivan reports that "Con is an ancient epithet for the god Wiraqocha, "*Con* Ticce Wiraqocha." According to Quechua lexicons both early and recent, the word *con* refers literally to thunder

Nasca pottery depicting people with fair skin and people with a darker skin,
Jose Antonini Museum, Nasca, Peru.

and, by metonymy, to the sound made by spherical grindstones—rolling thunder. The closest cognates of con are the Quechua and Aymara words for "grindstone," spelled *qhona* and *ccuna*.[77]

In Palestine, where olive trees grow, Christ's suffering in the olive garden of Gethsemane has been likened unto the olive-press. In the garden Jesus took upon himself the sins of every person who has lived or ever will live in the universe. The burden Jesus suffered is incomprehensible to man, though the image of an olive being crushed into virgin oil can help one understand in a small measure the nature of what the Lord endured for us. Only the great pressure of the press can draw out the healing olive oil. From the greatest pressure ever endured by a man, drops of innocent blood flowed from every pore of the Savior's body, He open the doors of eternal life for those who repent and follow him.

When Christ visited the Nephites and Lamanites in the New World, there were no olive trees. Thus an oil press could not be used as a metaphor for the Lord's suffering. However, the Incas had invented an ingenious grain press or rocker made of two grindstones. The pressure between the stones crushed their grain into fine flour. The ancient Andean grindstone was a two-piece press or mortar-type mill.[78]

VIRACOCHA—THE BEGINNING

The Apostle John taught that "*in the beginning was the Word*" (John 1:1), meaning Jesus Christ. Viracocha was called *Ticci* Viracocha.' *Ticci* is Quechua for "source," "beginning," "foundation," "prime cause," "originator of time."[79]

VIRACOCHA—THE MASTER

The Apostle Matthew wrote, "*One is your Master, even Christ*" (Matthew 23:8). The first definition of "master" in Webster's Dictionary is "a male teacher."[80] Sullivan writes, "Among Wiraqocha's manifold titles is pachayachachi, literally 'world teacher, and there is concordance among the sources that his mode of teaching was one of love and kindness, delivered with great solicitude."[81]

VIRACOCHA— FOUNTAIN OF THE SUN

In Psalms, we read of Christ, "By the word of the Lord were the heavens made" (Psalms 33:6). Another title of Viracocha is found in a series of hymns recorded by Pachakuti Yampui: vilca ulcaapu, which means "lord fountainhead of the sun." In other words, Viracocha gave birth to the sun and the other heavenly bodies.[82] Sullivan found the relationship between the "fountain" and the "creator of the heavenly bodies" to be significant. He writes:

Finally, the great importance attached to this image by the Incas is most clearly manifest in the magnificent Inca shrine on the Island of the Sun in Lake Titicaca. On the eastside of the island, the Incas fashioned a long stairway leading from the water's edge upward to a fountain gushing forth from the very cliffside where Wiraqocha [Viracocha/Jesus Christ] was said to have created the sun, the moon, and the stars. The water from this fountain, which is faced in flawless Inca masonry, pours into a large, equally perfect stone basin, thence to flow back into the lake via two channels flanking the stairway.[83]

The imagery used by the Incas for Viracocha is not foreign to Christians. The straight and narrow path leads to the head of the fountain (1 Nephi 8:20). Lehi's iron rod leads to the fountain of living waters (1 Nephi 11:25). Moroni wrote that men should come to the "fountain of all righteousness" (Ether 8:26, 12:28). Lehi beheld one descending from heaven whose luster is above the sun at noonday (1 Nephi 1:9). While a sign of the birth

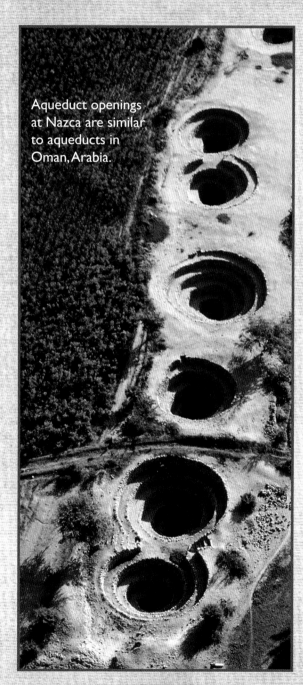

Aqueduct openings at Nazca are similar to aqueducts in Oman, Arabia.

of Christ was no darkness at the setting of the sun (Helaman 14:4), at his death, the sun was not seen.

VIRACOCHA—THE GOD OF FIRE

When the Savior visited the Nephites, fire came from the heavens and surrounded the people (3 Nephi 17:24). On arriving in Bountiful, the Lord told the people that he personally burned the city of Zarahemla and its inhabitants. There was also the time when Viracocha was attacked by the Cacha tribe, and he brought down fire from the heavens. Little wonder then, that one of the names the Peruvians had for their white god was "fire."[84]

VIRACOCHA—THE TREE OF LIFE

Perhaps the most important descriptive name for Jesus Christ in the Book of Mormon is the Tree of Life. Sullivan writes:

> Tunapa Wiraqocha is always described as carrying a staff. Further, Ludovico Bertonio, the author of the 1611 Aymara dictionary cited throughout this study, sometimes wrote Wiraqocha's title as "Tunuupa." Here lies a clue to the origin of the word tunas, rocker mill, an invention that appears on the archaeological horizon about 200 BC, when the Aymara-speaking civilization [Lamanites] around Lake Titicaca—the seat of Wiraqocha—began its florescence. The word tunu is found both in Aymara and Quechua. Bertonio lists: Tunu. The top of a large tree. Holguín records the Quechua meaning: Tunu.

The central support pillar of a round house.

These linguistic indicators pointed me directly back to the cosmological drawing of Pachakuti Yamqui [drawing of the golden altar in Temple in Cuzco] where the tuna, the "pillar/tree/mill" carried by Tunapa Wiraqocha, reappears as the central organizing principle of the diagram.[85]

As described in chapter 6, it is possible that all the essential symbols of Lehi's dream of the Tree of Life were found on the altarpiece in Inca temple at Cuzco. The Inca's called the altarpiece, Viracocha's shield.

THE INCA HYMN TO VIRACOCHA

Osborne tells us that the Incas had a beautiful song they sang about Viracocha's visit to their homeland. He writes:

> And they heard it from their fathers, who in turn had it from the old songs which were handed down from very ancient times. . . . They say that this man traveled along the highland route to the north, working marvels as he went and that they never saw him again. They say that in many places he gave men instructions how they should live speaking to them with great love and kindness and admonished them to be good and to do no damage or injury one to another, but to love one another and show charity to all. In most places they named him Ticci Viracocha.[86]

CONCLUSION

I remember seeing with my own eye old Indians who, upon seeing Cuzco, stared
at the city and gave a great cry, which then turned to tears of sadness,
as they contemplated the present and recalled the past. . .

PEDRO DE CIEZA DE LEÓN, 1553

As manifested by the oral traditions of the North and South American native tribes, ample evidence exists that Jesus Christ visited the Nephites and the Lamanites. The Peruvian legends tell of the bearded white god traversing through the towns and villages of the Andes and finally leaving his people from the shores of today's Ecuador. During his earthly mission, the Lord was called exclusively to the house of Israel. Thus, it is doubtful that he actually visited other peoples in the Americas. What we do know is that Jesus Christ showed himself unto the lost tribes of Israel (3 Nephi 17:4).

Since Christ told those He visited in the Americas about his people in Jerusalem, we could speculate that He would also have told the Lost Tribes about his "sheep" both in Jerusalem and in the Americas. For this reason, the oral traditions of the Karen people of Burma (today's Myanmar) are of interest to students of the Book of Mormon. Tudor Parfitt is a Reader in Modern Jewish Studies at the School of Oriental and African Studies and the Director of the school's Center for Jewish Studies. In his book, The Lost Tribes of Israel, the History of a Myth, Parfitt relates the following:

> Western missionaries active in the country had formed the view that the Karen ethnic group was itself of Jewish extraction. This view is still held by some people, and, as will be shown, has a bearing on the claims to Jewishness of many thousands of people on the Burmese-Indian border, some of whom have already immigrated to Israel.[1]

> Quite clearly there were striking and seductive similarities between their legends and those of the Jewish scriptures: an example was the Karen story of creation, which "was almost parallel to the Mosaic account in Genesis."[2]

> Francis Mason of the American Baptist Foreign Mission Society arrived in Burma in 1814 and in time became convinced that the Karen were part of

the Lost Tribes of Israel. He had certainly reached this conclusion by 1833: on 6 December of that year he announced from his headquarters in the "head waters of the Tenesserim" to Mr. Maingy the British Civil Commissioner, who had requested a report of the Karen, "the discovery of a fragment of the descendants of the Hebrews." "I sit down in the midst of the Karen jungle," he wrote, "to redeem my pledge and give you some account of the traditions existing among the Tayoy Karens." In a passionate letter Mason listed the traits that proved their distinguished lineage: the nature of their god Pu or Yuway, their belief in angels and Satan, the fall of man, the dispersion of Babel, the future destruction of the world, their love of God, their tradition of being a wandering people, their freedom from idolatry and so on. "There can scarcely be a rational doubt that the Yuwah of the Karens is the Jehovah of the Hebrews . . . from the foregoing I am constrained to believe the Karens to be descendents of the Hebrews. Look at them, sir; is not the Jew written in their countenance?"[3]

Above all, it is the cult of the high god Yuwah or Ywa, reminiscent of the Hebrew YHWH, which excited the Christians and later Jews and inspired them with the certainty that here must be some long-lost relic of the ancient religion of the Hebrews. . . . According to Father Plaisant, the early Baptist missionaries had got it about right: Yuwah created the earth, he made man and all living creatures, he was omniscient, omnipotent, perfect and

eternal. According to the priest, in the days after the creation, Yuwah set aside the 'book of gold' for the Karen, who failed to come and get it. It was therefore entrusted to his younger "white brother." Therefore. . . the latter obligingly built a boat for Ywa and transported him across the ocean, whence Ywa ascended to heaven. In their sacred songs, the Karen look forward to the return of the White Brother and their book, as well as to the advent of Ywa.[4]

If the Karen are from the Lost Tribes of Israel, then it seems likely that someone must have told them that Nephi acquired the plates from the unfaithful Laban, that the Lord commanded him

to build a ship, that the Lord guided Nephi to a New World, that Christ ascended into heaven, that their white brother would come back (perhaps Latter-day Saint missionaries), and that the gold book would be returned. Who gave the Karen this information if it were not the Lord? However, the Lord promised another tribe of Israel that the gold record would return for them. They were Lamanites.[5]

WHAT HAPPENED TO THE LAMANITES AND THEIR NEPHITE BROTHERS?

As discussed before, the Incas believed in a cyclical concept called pachacuti or world ages.

According to Urton, the Incas believed there were five pachacutis that roughly endured a thousand years. Pachacutis were "episodes of the destruction of the inhabitants of the world and their replacement by a new race."[6] The Book of Mormon records four such repopulations of the promised land: the great flood, the destruction of the Jaredites, the cleansing of the wicked at the coming of Christ, and the annihilation of the Nephites.

Zarahemla was rebuilt at what we have assumed to be Pukara (4 Nephi 1:8). However, the Nephites turned wicked, and by AD 322[7] they were at war with the Lamanites (Mormon 1:10, 13). The battles started at the borders (mountains) of Zarahemla and the river Sidon (Mormon 1:10). By AD 400 only Moroni remained of the Nephite elite. Klarich writes that "by AD 400, the Pukara polity had collapsed"[8] and there was no evidence that the city was occupied thereafter.[9]

The other great city of the Nephites, Bountiful, had a similar fate. The city of Cahuachi and its great temple were already abandoned by Nasca 3 [AD 200–400],[10] nor was it used any longer as a burial site or great civic-ceremonial place or place of pilgrimage.[11] The abandonment of Cahuachi suggests that its elite class of rulers and priests had vanished.

With the abandonment of Cahuachi, the culture of the Nasca took a marked change. Silverman and Proulx noted a significant decline in the religious practices of the Nasca.[12] Richard P. Roark identified a "major iconographic change (in Nasca ceramics) from religious themes to militaristic ones."[13] The Nasca 3 Period covers the period of Nephite decline, and the time in which the Nephites became increasingly wicked. The moral degeneration of the Nasca people can be seen by the motifs depicted on their ceramics.

Though the theory has been challenged, John H. Rowe believes that the most notable feature of Nasca 3 sites became "fortifications walls." Such walls would be expected if the Lamanites were threatening the very existence of the Nephites. Furthermore Rowe "believed that the rapid rise and fall of their (enemy) Acarí sites [Cachi/Laman] were causally attributable to the decline of Cahuachi and the collapse of a short-lived Nasca 3 state."[14]

THE WAR THAT ENDED THE NEPHITE CIVILIZATION

The series of battles that ended with the death of all the Nephite elite started in the mountains of Zarahemla, which I believe was the Lake Titicaca Basin. A likely scenario is that the Lamanites from the south side of the lake (Tiwanaku) attacked the Nephites on the north end of the lake. According to Kolata the people of Tiwanaku engaged in a war for dominance over Pukara, and it was a war they won:

That the entire Lake Titicaca basin population did not voluntarily embrace Tiwanaku state religion with messianic fervor is made apparent in the archaeological record. We now know that a major stone stela from the site of Arapa near Puno on the northern shores of the lake was broken at its base in antiquity, transported over 150 kilometers (92 miles) by raft, and incorporated into one of the palace complexes at Tiwanaku (Chávez, 1975). This stela was associated stylistically with the early, north Titicaca basin urbanized culture of Pukara. The implication of this violent political and ideological act is clear: in the process of subjugating the northern Titicaca basin, a ruler of Tiwanaku ritually debased and appropriated a sacred emblem of the concentrated spiritual power, or huaca of the Pukara nation, and in so doing, demonstrated both the religious and secular superiority of the Tiwanaku state.[15]

The take over of what were once Nephite lands by the Lamanites is evidenced by the corpus of art in the Pukara colonies of northern Chile. Circa AD 400–600 the style of art changed from Pukara to Tiwanaku.[16] Clearly, something had happened to Pukara (Zarahemla). Its influence was gone, and Tiwanaku (the Lamanites) stood in its place.

HILL CUMORAH, THE NEPHITES' LAST STAND

Driven from Zarahemla by the Lamanites, the Nephites needed a place of refuge. In roughly AD 350, Mormon entered a "treaty with the Lamanites and the robbers of Gadianton, in which we did get the lands of our inheritance divided. And the Lamanites did give unto us the land northward [north of la Raya Pass], yea, even to the narrow passage which led into the land southward [narrow neck of land/Lurin Valley]. And we did give unto the Lamanites all the land southward (Mormon 2:28–29)."

Having been driven from the lands of Zarahemla and Bountiful and knowing that the Lamanites were about to break the truce Mormon wrote: "I did cause my people that they should gather themselves together at the land Desolation, to a city which was in the borders [mountains], by the narrow [mountain] pass which led into the land southward" (Mormon 3:5). Once again, the narrow neck of land became the Nephites' strategic line of defense between the Nephites and their enemies (Mormon 3:6). Despite the Nephites' efforts, the Lamanites broke through the Nephite defenses and entered the land of Desolation. Initially, the Nephites were successful in Desolation, but the greater forces of the Lamanites turned the tide through a series of bloody battles (Mormon 3:7–5:6). Eventually, only those Nephites who could outrun the Lamanites survived (Mormon 5:7).

Mormon faced a dire situation. He reasoned that the most favorable battleground for the Nephites to stand a chance of prevailing against the overwhelming force of the Lamanites was a narrow mountain battlefield. For this purpose, Mormon wrote an epistle to the king of Lamanites to do battle in the land of Cumorah. The Lamanites agreed to the site, so the Nephites marched southward and pitched their tents around about the hill Cumorah. As the battle commenced, Mormon and the surviving remnant of his army found themselves fighting to the death; although some Nephites survived by deserting to the Lamanite side (Moroni 8:24) or by denying the Christ (Moroni 1:2). Of the Nephite elite only Moroni remained to lead a lonely life, which included a long journey northward to what is today the state of New York.

The question begs to be answered, "Where was the Peruvian hill Cumorah?" We can start by listing what we know about Cumorah.

Was this the site of the Nephites' last stand? La Raya Pass, Peruvian Andes

- Cumorah was both a "land" and a "hill," thus it was not in the lands northward, southward, Desolation, Bountiful, Nephi, or Zarahemla.

- To reach the land Cumorah, the Jaredites had to travel southward from Desolation (Ether 15:10).

- The hill appears to have been in "Lamanite" controlled territory, for Mormon had to petition the Lamanite king to be able to gather his army there for the final battle.

- Since twenty-four Nephite survivors of the battle of Cumorah fled into the land southward, it means that the hill Cumorah was on the north border of the land southward. The land southward was east of the land Bountiful. (Mormon 8:2).

- It was a land with many waters, rivers, and fountains (Mormon 6:2–4).

- It was a place that had a name familiar to both the Nephites and the Lamanite generals (it was no common hill, but a specific place known to both groups).

- The terrain could help an inferior number of soldiers hold back a much larger force (Mormon 6:4).

- Tens of thousands of warriors fought on top of hill Cumorah, thus it must have been a large area or mountain (Mormon 6:8–15).

So where is the Hill Cumorah? I do not know. However, I believe a case can be made for the battle of Hill Cumorah having been fought at the La Raya pass. The high pass is narrow and provides an area where large armies could convene on both sides, yet allow a small force to use the natural bottleneck to fight a superior army on only one front. The La Raya pass would have given Mormon a similar advantage as that enjoyed by King Leonidas of Sparta at the Battle of Thermophyla. The gutsy king led three hundred Spartans and seven hundred Theban volunteers and slaves in a three-day last stand against a Persian army of several hundred thousand soldiers.

The Nephites' last stand was fought on "top" of the hill Cumorah. This means that Cumorah was not a small hill, but a sizable battleground. La Raya pass reaches its summit at 4,321 m above sea level (14,172 feet). The summit of the pass or "top" is surrounded by the glaciered peaks of the Vilcanota mountains on both sides. The Incas believed that Mount Vilcanota (at 20,644 feet) was the highest mountain on earth, and the sacred fountainhead of the sun.[17] Thus there is little doubt that the ancients knew of the mountain and could use it as a meeting place for staging a war.

Cumorah had lakes, rivers, and fountains. Lakes dot the Vilcanota mountains, including a small lake at the base of Mount Vilcanota. The two most important rivers of the Inca originate on the opposite sides of the La Raya pass, the sacred Vilcamayu River (a.k.a. the Urubamba) and the Pukara river. Mount Vilcanota was perhaps the most important fountain in all southern Peru. The mountain provides the headwaters of the Vilcamayu River that was held sacred by the Incas and was well known to the ancients. The

Urubamba River

waters flowed north from the pass reminding the Incas of the journey of their god Viracocha.[18]

The thermal fountains at the La Raya pass were famous. The Spanish priest Acosta wrote: "This spring, when it rises at the cliff at (mount) Vilcanota of which I have spoken, is like lye-water, ashen colored, and everywhere steaming with smoke like something burning, and so it runs for a long stretch until the multitude of other waters which enter into it put out the fire and smoke which it has at its sources."[19]

Finally, the traditional borderline between the Inca northeast and southeast quarters passed through the La Raya pass. Being in the mountain wilderness between the Land of Nephi and the Land of Zarahemla it would have been under Lamanite control. The twenty-four Nephite soldiers who survived the last battle could have fled

down the passage into the land southward where they were eventually hunted down and killed.

Evaluating the clues, my tentative candidate for the battlegrounds of Cumorah is La Raya pass; the land of Cumorah is the Vilcanota mountain range; and hill Cumorah is the great Vilcanota—the noblest of all mountains in the eyes of the Incas.

Calderwood summarizes an oral tradition recorded by Montesinos that parallels remarkably well with the final days of the Nephite civilization. It encompasses a great battle in mountain passes, and the end of the Inca nobility.

There were also many people who were announcing or prophesying about the destruction and expulsion of the inhabitants from Cuzco.

Huaman Tacco Amauta's successor, King Titu Yupanqui Pachacuti, was filled with melancholy and occupied his time making sacrifices and praying to the gods [perhaps Mormon during the period when he refused to lead the Nephi army]. When Titu Yupanqui Pachacuti finally came out of his dark mood, it was just in time to fortify his armies for an attack by a large army coming from the Colloa area of Bolivia around Lake Titicaca. The king's spies also discovered another army of fierce warriors was coming from the eastern slopes of the Andes. Montesinos noted that among the two enemy armies some warriors had dark skins which implied that the Cuzco inhabitants had light skins. These two huge armies began to overrun lands and cities. The rulers of the lands in the paths of these two armies could not defend their territory alone. Consequently, Titu Yupanquie Pachacuti decided to gather all of his forces to form a large enough army to resist the advancing forces.

He also divided his army into several combat forces, sending one against the Collao army and another to fight the army from the Andes in the dangerous mountain passes and at the key river and bridge sites. Titu Yupanqui Pachacuti also took the bulk of his army into the high mountains where he constructed fortifications including numerous platforms, deep pits, and trenches. He also built a series of walls, which were constructed in such a manner that each wall, only had one entrance. When one was breeched by the invaders, they would then face another wall higher up which

also had only one entrance. These walls continued in this fashion to the top of the mountain where Titu Yupanqui Pachacuti had his tent and headquarters.

When the invaders arrived at the fortified area, Titu Yupanqui Pachacuti gave them battle and was killed along with thousands of warriors and captains on both sides. . . .

Montesinos added that with this great battle, the Peruvian monarchy was destroyed. The descendants of the former Cuzco natives did not return to the Cuzco area for more than four hundred years. Montesinos claims that the Inca Indians lost their ability to read and write during this exile period.[20]

HOW DID THE PLATES REACH NEW YORK STATE?

Jerry Ainsworth, has spent much of his life searching for the original hill Cumorah. Like many other Book of Mormon scholars, he believes that there are at least two hills "Cumorah"—the one where the Nephites made their last stand, and the hill in New England in which Moroni hid the plates of the Book of Mormon. Ainsworth writes, "I discovered just a few years ago that Joseph Smith may not have been the first to call the hill in New York 'Cumorah.' That tradition probably started with early church leaders and caught on. . . . Cumorah near Palmyra is just a plain little hill with grass and trees on it, only a bit more prominent than others in the immediate vicinity, not likely to be a place where the leaders of two great nations had gathered all their people together."[21]

For the purpose of this discussion, let us assume that the original hill Cumorah rises above

the La Raya pass in Peru, and that the mountain has a cave that still holds the large depository of plates which Heber C. Kimball reported ten men could not carry.[22] That said, the question begs to be answered: How did Moroni transport the plates of the Book of Mormon and the Urim and Thummim from Peru to what is today New York? The load must have been heavy, but as it turned out, not so bulky and unwieldy that Joseph Smith could not carry these precious items from a hill near Manchester to his home in Palmyra.

We might consider two possible ways the gold plates could have reached New York, where in 1827 the angel Moroni presented the sacred library to the Prophet Joseph Smith (JSH 1:51,59). One way could be that the Lord simply relocated the sacred records from South America to a site near the home of Joseph Smith, just as He had placed the Liahona outside Lehi's tent.

A second consideration is that Moroni himself could have transferred the plates to New York, a task that would not have been as difficult as it might at first appear to be.

If we consider the time-frame of Book of Mormon events, we realize that from the time Moroni finished his initial work with the plates and the time they were buried in the hill, he would have had ample time to achieve the feat. Furthermore, when we consider that the Lamanites sought the life of the young Nephite military leader (Moroni 1:1–3), it seems reasonable to believe that Moroni used his time to get as far away from the Lamanites and the site of the final battleground as possible. Moroni wrote that "I wander whithersoever I can for the safety of mine own life" (Moroni 1:3). The battle at the Hill Cumorah took place in AD 385 (Mormon 6:5). It was not until AD 421 that Moroni finally sealed up the plates in the earth

(Moroni 10:1, 2). In other words, Moroni wandered for roughly thirty-six years before hiding the plates in a stone box. If he had wandered only five miles per day, over the course of thirty-six years Moroni could conceivably have walked a distance of nearly 70,000 miles. It seems only reasonable that by the time Moroni deposited the plates, he had migrated far from the battleground at the original Hill Cumorah.

We can speculate as to how Moroni actually transported the heavy plates to New York. Two likely routes would merit consideration, each journey being significantly less challenging than Nephi's saga in helping to bring the brass plates and his extended family from Jerusalem to the promised land. The first route would have included a long water passage. Moroni's wanderings could conceivably have occurred in three stages. First, he would have to have taken the plates from the Andean highlands down to the Amazon basin. The Incas knew that the waters of the Urubamba River flowed north from the La Raya pass down to the Amazon basin and eventually reaching the northern sea (Atlantic Ocean). The Urubamba River drops precipitously down the backside of the mountains. White-water rapids would have made even a canoe trip an unlikely proposition. Inca traders used caravans of surefooted llamas to transport trade goods from the highlands to the Amazon jungle. Moroni was probably a large man, similar to his father (Mormon 2:1). Undoubtedly, he could have wrapped the plates and Urim & Thummim in strong Inca cloth and carried the plates on his back down the Andes. However, a more likely scenario is that he would have packed such weighty metal items on the backs of llamas for the trip down the bank of the Urubamba River to the Amazon basin.

At the eastern base of the Andes, the Urubamba River becomes navigable, and shortly thereafter joins the mighty Amazon River. Here Moroni would have found a valuable resource to aid him in his mission—Amazon hardwoods, including the long, straight Peruvian mahogany (*Switenia macrophylla*) from which timbers could be cut to build a strong ship. Mahogany trees grow in abundance along the lower Urubamba River.[23] Using mahogany wood and Peruvian shipwrights, the explorer Gene Savoy actually constructed a replica of an ancient ship and sailed it from Peru to Hawaii in 1997.[24]

As discussed earlier, the Peruvians had a long seafaring history, and Moroni would have had plenty of time to construct a sturdy oceangoing boat to transport his precious cargo down the Amazon River, up the Atlantic coast, and further up the Hudson River.

From the Hudson River to Manchester, New York, Moroni could have carried the sacred articles or pulled them using a wooden sled. The ancient Egyptians used wooden sleds to haul the two-and-a-half-ton stone blocks used to construct the Great Pyramids the three miles from the quarry on the Giza Plateau to the building site.[25] Of course, the effort would have been far easier if he were to have pulled a sled during the time of winter snows.

A second feasible route from Peru to New York would have taken Moroni and his small llama caravan north along the Inca highway to what is today Columbia. Once on the shores of the Gulf of Mexico, he could have constructed a canoe and crossed the gulf to North America in a vessel similar to the canoes the Indians of the Caribbean constructed to trade with the mainland. Archaeologists have discovered that the Saladoid culture of Venezuela used ocean-going canoes to trade with Puerto Rico as far back as 500 BC. Some of the artifacts found in Puerto Rico could have come from as far away as Chile.[26]

Irrespective of the method that was used to get the golden plates and the Urim and Thummim into the hands of Joseph Smith, the fact is that he did receive those precious items and translated those plates into what we have today as the Book of Mormon. Since additional discoveries, such as those described in this book, are coming forth all the time, perhaps we will not have to wait a lifetime to have answers to some of the questions that currently occupy our minds. Until then, let us have patience and appreciate the new findings that are coming to light.

THE GREAT LAMANITE EMPIRE AT LAKE TITICACA

If Cuzco was the city of Nephi, then the Lamanites or Nephites who lived in the city did not fair well there after the Lamanite victory destroyed the Nephite society. Within two hundred years of the fall of the Nephites, the Cuzco Valley was invaded from the north by the Wari tribe who held the valley for four centuries. In contrast, the Lamanites at the south end of the Lake Titicaca basin were busy building one of the great civilizations of the first millennium AD

According to Charles Mann, with the fall of Pukara (Nephites), Tiwanaku, (the new Lamanite capital), became a "predatory state."

It was not the centrally administered military power that the term conjures. Instead, it was an archipelago of cities

Statue of the weeping
God, Temple of the Sun,
Tiwanaku, Bolivia

An image of Viracocha
adorns the Gate of the
Sun at Tiwanaku, Bolivia.

that acknowledged Tiwanaku's religious preeminence. "State religion and imperial ideology, . . . awed by its magnificence, fearful of the supernatural powers controlled by its priesthood, local rulers subordinated themselves." Central to this strategy of intimidation was Tiwanaku city. A past wonder of the world.[27]

Mann continues: "Flush with wealth, Tiwanaku city swelled into a marvel of terraced pyramids and grand monuments. Stone breakwaters extended far out into Lake Titicaca, thronged with long-prowed boats made of reeds. With its running water, closed sewers, and gaudily painted walls, Tiwanaku was among the world's most impressive cities."[28]

University of Chicago archaeologist Alan L. Kolata, estimates that by AD 1000 Tiwanaku had an estimated population of 115,000 people, with another 250,000 people living in the surrounding area. Paris would not reach such a number for another 500 years.[29]

Mann summarizes: "The two states, Wari and Tiwanaku, were probably the greatest of Inka's [late Inca empire AD 1200–1532] forerunners, and certainly the predecessors from whom they took the most. In their separate ways, both were children of Norte Chico [Jaredites]. They worshipped figures in Staff God poses."[30] In other words, the Lamanites never fully forgot their god, Viracocha. Indeed, the most famous of all the images of Viracocha is found on the Gateway of the Sun at Tiwanaku, Mann describes as, "the so-called Gateway of the Sun, cut from a single block of stone. Covered with a fastidiously elaborate frieze, the twelve-foot gateway focuses the visitor's eyes on the image of a single deity whose figure projects from the lintel: the Staff God."[31]

THE LAMANITE MISSIONARIES TO NORTH AMERICA

As Mann indicated, Tiwanaku grew more through the influence of its religion than through military dominance. The priests of Tiwanaku grew wealthy from the spread of their religion, and they had an amazing skill—their ability to construct reed boats that could travel long distances across open seas.

It is my conjecture that Lamanite missionaries—with a determination similar to that of Paul in his efforts to convert Rome—boarded ships to spread the knowledge of a white god who could save humankind. M. Wells Jakeman and other LDS scholars have likened the traditions of Mexico to the Book of Mormon account of the Nephites. Quoting Jakeman: "Later they united with another people called the Tulteca [Toltecs] ("people of the place of abundance or bountiful"), said to have been of the same ancestry— the first of several successive groups of this name, indicated to have been a highly civilized people and the followers of the famed "Fair God Quetzalcoatl."[32]

If Jakeman is correct, then the first civilization in Mesoamerica to worship the "Fair God" were the Toltecs who ruled central Mexico during AD 1000–AD 1200. It is important to remember that anthropologists believe that the earliest time in which Quetzalcoatl became the dominant Mesoamerican god was during the tenth century AD, and it was not until the Xochicaoco's political class started claiming the divine right to rule in the name of the white god Quetzalcoatl that the deity took the main stage in Mesoamerican

mythology. Soon thereafter, the Toltec nobility began using the name Quetzalcoatl in reference to their right to rule.[33]

Of course, the religion of the tenth-century Lamanite missionaries would have been very different from the true faith. Although the Lamanites believed in a white god, they killed any Nephite who would not deny the Christ (Moroni 1:2). Furthermore, one can only wonder how the pagans in Mesoamerica would have adapted a new deity imported by South Americans. Just as the fallen religions of the Old World Christians held to stories of a flood, an Exodus, and a Savior, by the time of Joseph Smith the common concept of God among the Christian faith had changed from a Heavenly Father, in whose image man was created, to a formless spirit that filled the universe.

The Peruvian image of Viracocha was always that of a god with normal features that included a fair skin, a beard, and blue eyes. The image of Viracocha at Lake Titicaca, though abstract, is clearly that of a god in the form of a man. In contrast, the fair god of Central America is depicted as a beast-fable god. Quetzalcoatl's icons are of humans that have taken on animal characteristics (see at left one icon of Quetzalcoatl) or are entirely the image of a beast, that is, a plumed serpent.

In my opinion, such beast-fable images are clearly warning signs that the white-god traditions in Mesoamerica were distorted, and were probably the images of a faith that had a limited understanding of the true gospel. One possible explanation for such a perverted representation of Jesus Christ in Mesoamerica is that when the Mayans adopted the tradition of a white god, instead of accepting the tradition in its proper

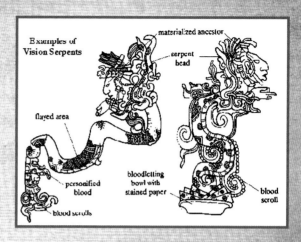

Is this something you would worship? Classical images of the Mesoamerican serpent god Quetzalcoatl.

form, they superimposed the white god of Peru over their existing pagan deity. In other words, it is possible that the post–Book of Mormon Mayans, Toltecs, and Aztecs blended the imported Peruvian white god of the Lamanites into a hybrid god with attributes of their serpent god Quetzalcoatl, a mythological snake god that dates to the early Olmecs (see drawing above).

In like fashion, the belief in a white god could have been spread by South American and Mesoamerican missionaries further north into what is today Mexico, the United States, and Canada. Taking this theory one step further, the Lamanite missionaries from Peru would have passed on the blood of the house of Israel, though in only trace amounts, among all the Native American people. It is also likely that the capable ancient Inca mariners spread Nephite and Lamanite bloodlines throughout the Americas and deep into the Pacific Islands. Michael De Groote notes:

According to [Scott] Woodward, even if you assume we knew what DNA to look for, finding DNA evidence of Book of Mormon people may be very difficult. When a small group of people intermarry into a large population, the DNA markers that might identify their descendents could entirely disappear even though their genealogical descendents could number in the millions.

This means it is possible that almost every American Indian alive today could be genealogically related to Lehi's family but still have retained no identifiable DNA marker to prove it. In other words, you could be related genealogically to and perhaps even feel a spiritual kinship with an ancestor but not have any vestige of his DNA.[34]

NEO-NEPHITE REMNANT RETAKE THE LANDS OF INHERITANCE

The Wari in Cuzco and the Tiwanaku in the Lake Titicaca basin kept themselves separated. Even though they shared borders, no Tiwanaku artifacts have been found in Cuzco and vice versa. They intermingled, but did not mix, a social phenomenon called "interdigitization."[35]

By the end of the first millennium AD the Wari influence declined in Cuzco, and the valley entered a four-century period called the Killke or Late Intermediate Period. As the Wari pulled out, the Cuzco area that we have supposed to be the land of Nephi was ruled by local tribes, which were native to the valley. This unstable localized period ended in the early fifteenth century when Pachacuti Inca Yupanque led his people in a military victory over their revival tribe the Chanka.[36] The battle marked the birth of the late Inca

Empire. As Nigel Davies summarizes, "When he [Pachacuti] became ruler, the Incas formed only a modest village community, at his death they were the mightiest empire in South America."[37] By the time the Spanish arrived a little more than a century later, it is estimated that the Incas ruled eight million people.[38]

The ancient roots of these neo-Incas, who rebuilt the city of Cuzco and its temple and repaired the ancient roads and irrigation systems, is not certain. The Inca kings claimed that they were descendents of Manco Capac (Nephi), and the original four Viracocha brothers who brought prosperity to Peru. The native Peruvian Poma de Ayala wrote that he believed that some of the Indians were descendents of Jews, for they had blond hair, blue eyes, and beards and looked like Jews.[39] This would imply that they were remnants of actual Nephites. This is possible, since the Nephites who denied Christ were not killed by the Lamanites (Moroni 1:2), and the Lord promised that at least some of the Nephites—the direct descendents of Joseph (son of Lehi)—would not be utterly destroyed (2 Nephi 3:3) because they would hearken to the words of the Book of Mormon (2 Nephi 3:22–23; see also 2 Nephi 9:53).

The neo-Incas believed in the god Viracocha, made sacrifices to him, had a secret language that they spoke only among themselves, used Quechua as the common tongue, and had a rich oral tradition that has amazing parallels to the Nephites in the Book of Mormon record. Another, and perhaps more feasible, explanation is that neo-Incas were mostly the remnants of the Tambo tribes who helped Nephi colonize Cuzco. Again, the Tambo tribes were among the "Inca Privileged class," who helped rule the empire under the Inca

Viracocha at Tiwanaku holding two things. Could they be sticks or books?

royals, and probably intermarried within the royal Nephite elite. They would have been, in a very limited sense, the remnants of the Nephites.

Whoever the neo-Inca were, they were determined to recover their heritage and the land of their origin, the Lake Titicaca Basin (Zarahemla). As the fifteenth century opened, the Inca army poured into the Lake Titicaca Basin and conquered the city of Tiwanaku. Kulmar notes: "Once in power, they [the Incas] started rebuilding Cuzco [1000–1200 AD]. They called their new empire Tahuantinsuyu [1200–1533 AD] and patterned it after what they remembered of their original religion, culture, and history. They tried to build at Cuzco the civilization the White God Viracocha had taught them when he came to them on the Altiplano."[40]

However, Tahuantinsuyu was not the kingdom of Nephi. The Incas practiced a corrupted form of the gospel of Viracocha. On the Altiplano, the god Viracocha was called the sky god. The neo-Incas, like Solomon in the Bible, mistakenly required all the tribes they conquered to bring their idol gods to the temple at Cuzco.[41] Viracocha was no longer the only god of the Incas; he now ruled over a host of pagan deities. To appease the powerful tribes to the north, the Inca elite transformed their Viracocha deity into the *Inti*, the Sun god, one of the local tribe's heathen gods.[42] They started calling themselves the *Incas*, or children of the Sun. They rebuilt the temple of Ayar Manco, but now called it the Temple of the Sun. The Incas had always practiced the offering of crops and spotless male animals, but on their return to power in Cuzco the neo-Inca sacrificed virgins and young boys.

Little wonder that Pachacuti Inca Yupanque, the first neo-Inca king, knew that the days of his

empire were numbered. Idolatry has always led to only one end—destruction. The practice brought war and destruction to the Nephites (Alma 50:21), and the idolatry of the Jaredites brought a "curse upon the land, and they should be destroyed if they did not repent" (Ether 7:23) —in the end they didn't. (Pachacuti) Inca Yupanque had built the temple to the sun god, had created over 200 idols, and was the first Inca ruler to declare himself the "son of the Sun." He replaced the white god Viracocha who had been the chief god of the Incas with a sphere of burning gas. He "called himself *Capac Capa apo yndi chori*, which means king and unique lord son of the Sun."[43]

Having betrayed the white god, Inca Yupanque's guilt must have awoken his conscience. Betanzos relates a prophecy made by Inca Yupanque:

He [Inca Yupanque] let them know . . . after the days of his grandson Huayna Capac there would be pachacuti, which means "change of the world." Those lords ask him if that change of the world would be from floods, fire, or pestilence. He told them it would not be for any of those reasons but, rather, because white, bearded, and very tall men would come. They would go to war with these men and in the end these men would subjugate them. There would be no more Inca lords like them. What he was telling them was to enjoy the good life as long as they could because few lords would survive after the days of his grandson Huayna Capac.[44]

THE FIFTH INCA PACHACUTI— WORLD AGE OF DESTRUCTION AND REPOPULATION

Before the white god Viracocha left Peru, he gave his people one last sermon. The Catholic Sarmiento recorded: "Intending to leave the land of Peru, he [Viracocha/Christ] made a speech to those he had created, apprising them of the things that would happen. He told them that people would come [the gentiles/Spanish], who would say that they were Viracocha their creator, and that they were not to believe them; but that in the time to come he would send his messengers [LDS missionaries] who would protect and teach them."[45]

Sarmiento summarized what he thought of the legend of Viracocha and his mission in the Andes: "This absurd fable of their creation is held by these barbarians and they affirm and believe it as if they had really seen it to happen and come to pass."[46] As the world now realizes, the barbarians were not the Peruvians, but the Spanish conquistadors who murdered, raped, and robbed the innocent Incas who had gracefully welcomed the Spaniards to their homeland. Betanzos reported the first message the Inca king received of Pizarro's arrival. As we can see, it is a direct fulfillment of the Viracocha's prophecy. "The Inca asked them [the Inca messengers], 'What do these men [Spaniards] call themselves?' They [the messengers to the Inca] only knew that they called them viracocha cuna, which means 'gods.' "[47]

Before reaching Peru, Pizarro spent four years exploring the mangrove forests and rivers of the Pacific shoreline of what is today Columbia and Ecuador. He and his men fought extreme starvation, deadly malaria, and Indians who rained arrows on them. Almagro, Pizarro's partner, said that Pizarro suffered "hunger and hardships never heard or seen by men before."[48] Having lost most of his men, and accumulating massive debts trying to explore the southern land from Panama, Pizarro finally reached a northernmost city controlled by the Incas. Pizarro was on his last leg. Had the Incas wanted to crush him it would have been an easy chore. Cieza de León recorded the first encounter the Spanish had with a member of the Inca ruling tribe from Cuzco. The Indian was the residing deputy who ruled the local people. Cieza de León recorded the welcome the ruler and the city gave the first Europeans to reach Peru.

They were quite astonished, believing that such people were sent by God's hand and that it would be proper to give them a warm reception. Then ten or twelve balsas were prepared—replete with food and fruit, many jugs of water and chicha, and fish and a lamb that the virgins of the temple gave to take to them. The Indians went to the ship with all this without any guile or malice, but rather with joy and pleasure to see such people. . . . Among them was an orejón, one of those with the deputy who resided there, who said to the captain that they could safely come on land without being harmed and provision themselves with water and whatever they needed.[49]

The Spaniards were possibly more stunned at what they saw in Peru than the Indians were at seeing the Spanish ships, horses, swords, and guns. Cieza de León continued:

Alonso de Molina saw many buildings and notable things in Tumbez. Both he and the Black [a black African member of Pizarro's conquistadors] were well served with food. The latter walked here and there wherever they wanted to see him, as something so new and by them never seen before. Alonso de Molina saw the fortress of Tumbez, irrigation channels, many planted fields, and fruits and some sheep. Many Indian women— very beautiful and well attired, dressed according to their fashion—came to talk to him. . . . When he arrived at the ship, he [Molina] was so overwhelmed by what he had seen that he did not relate anything. He said that the houses were of stone, and that before he spoke to the lord, he passed through three gates where they had gatekeepers who guarded them, and that they served him in cups of silver and gold.[50]

On hearing Molina's report, Pizarro had difficulty believing him. He decided to send Pedro de Candia ashore to verify what had been reported. Candia reported an Inca fortress that had six or seven walls, and many riches inside. He saw many silversmiths and a temple with walls with gold and silver sheets. When he returned to the ship he was sent with balsas boats with "plenty of maize, fish, and fruit to go along. And to the captain he sent with Candia a beautiful ram and quite a fat lamb."[51]

In the meantime, the lord of Tumbez sent runners to the Inca (emperor) Huayna Capac to announce the arrival of the Spaniards. However, what appears to have been the smallpox virus was spreading throughout South America faster than the Spanish. Before word reached the king, Huayna Capac had already died.[52] His son, the crown prince died a few days later, which suddenly left the throne in dispute. A bloody civil war broke out and never again would an Inca king rule Peru. Indeed, with the death of Huayna Capac, just days before the arrival of Pizarro, his grandfather's deathbed prophecy was fulfilled that stated: "After the days of his grandson Huayna Capac there would be pachacuti, which means 'change of the world' and there would be no more Incas [kings] like before."

In the meantime the Spaniards sailed south to survey the wealth and extent of the Inca Empire. It was becoming obvious to them that Peru was fabulously wealthy. Cieza de León wrote, "Undoubtedly (Peru) was the best and the richest in the world."[53] At their next stop, near present-day Trujillo, one sailor was so impressed by the Inca society, that he asked for and was granted permission to leave the ship and live with the Indians. It was reported that the "Indians came out joyously to receive them, bring them the food from their land to eat; they provided them with water and firewood, and they gave them five sheep. A sailor named Bocanegra, seeing such fine land, left the ship with the Indians . . . . He wanted to remain among such good people as were those Indians."[54] Despite the warm and gentle nature of the Indians living under the Inca domain, the greedy Spanish were busy assessing how many soldiers and horses they would need to return and subjugate the Peruvians.[55]

Pizarro eventually disembarked in Peru with a tiny army and quickly disclosed his true nature. Cieza de León relates:

> The considerable reputation of the Spaniards had already spread among the Indians—very different from what they had originally thought and believed: that they were holy people, not disposed to kill or steal or do harm, but were friendly and peaceful toward them. Whereas now, according to those from that time who are still around, they say they [the Spaniards] were cruel people without justice or truth because they went from land to land like thieves, pillaging and killing those who had not offended them, and that they brought large horses who ran like the wind and swords that cut anything within reach, and they said the same about lances.[56]

One of the two sons of Huayna Capac who fought for the throne of the dead Inca was Atahualpa. If Atahualpa's great-grandfather Inca Yupanque had not blasphemed the Lord enough by calling himself "the son of the Sun," what Atahualpa did certainly confirmed that the Inca royalty no longer respected the power of their white Viracocha.

Just a few days before Atahualpa learned of the arrival of Pizarro, he sent some lords to make a sacrifice at a large *guaca* (temple or shrine)[57] to the white god Viracocha. At the time, he was marching toward Cuzco to battle his half-brother for the vacant throne. On route to Cuzco, Atahualpa had severely punished those who had sided with his enemy. Betanzos relates that at the temple to the white god an "old man who was there. . . . He said the Inca, son of the Sun (Atahualpa), should not kill so many people because Viracocha, who had created the people, was angry about it. He wanted him to know that from it no good would come to Atahualpa."[58]

The Inca was so furious that he "climbed to the *guaca* where the idol [statue of the white god] was. Atahualpa gave the idol such a blow in the neck with a battle-ax he carried that he cut off the head. They then brought there the old man. . . Atahualpa also beheaded him with his battle-ax."[59] In a craze of anger, Atahualpa stopped his

army's march to Cuzco, and commanded his men to completely destroy the temple of Viracocha.

While camped at the *guaca*, waiting for his men to finish destroying the temple of Viracocha, the first words came to the Inca that white men had arrived.[60] It was the first warning Atahualpa would hear that the *fifth pachacuti* had arrived. It was the "last days" for the Inca Empire. Tens of thousands of warriors had already died in the civil war. Atahualpa's advance army of one hundred and forty thousand men were already at Cuzco and were engaged in bloody battles with his half-brother Huascar's army of one hundred thirty thousand warriors.[61] After the initial engagement, estimates of death on both sides ranged from forty to sixty thousand men.[62] Tens of thousands more would die before Atahualpa's army captured Huascar.

At the same time, even greater killers were depopulating Peru. Diamond writes:

> Atahualpa's presence at Cajamarca thus highlights one of the key factors in world history: diseases transmitted to people lacking immunity by invading peoples with considerable immunity. Smallpox, measles, influenza, typhus, bubonic plague, and other infectious diseases endemic in Europe played a decisive role in European conquest, by decimating many people on other continents. . . . Throughout the Americas, diseases introduced with Europeans spread from tribe to tribe far in advance of the Europeans themselves, killing an estimated 95 percent of the pre-Columbia Native American populations.[63]

By the time Pizarro's tiny force reached Atahualpa at the city of Cajamarca, Atahualpa's

advance army had taken Cuzco and had captured his half-brother. Yet Atahualpa with his combined army of over two hundred thousand men would never claim the throne in Cuzco. As his men tore asunder the temple of Viracocha, Atahualpa's fate was sealed. Within days he would lose his kingdom of eight million people and his life to an army of only 169 Spaniards (Cieza de León claims there were only 160 Spaniards and lists them by name).[64]

Betanzos interviewed an eyewitness account of when Atahualpa heard of the Spaniards' arrival. "Moreover, I must tell you that while I was with the Inca at the guaca (huaca) in Guamachuco from whence I left, two Tallanes came to him from Tangarala and they carried news that Viracocha had emerged from the sea and many other *viracochas* [white people] came with him. It is believed that they are the ancient *viracochas* [Nephites] that created the people."[65]

It is easy to understand why the Spaniards believed that the turmoil that engulfed the Inca Empire was by providence. Cieza de León concluded, "Hence, you see the great calamity of that time in Peru and how apparent it is that God permitted the entry of the Spaniards at the time of such upheaval never before seen by those born there. The hatred these Indians had for each other was already great; no friendship or any *fief* were maintained, nor did they honor religion."[66]

Atahualpa seems to have made two profound mistakes. First, he destroyed the statue and temple of Viracocha and killed the old priest. Second, he did not remember the prophecy that the departing Viracocha gave that murderous people would come claiming they were Viracochas (gods). If he had, Atahualpa would have summoned all his forces to Cajamarca in an attempt to destroy the Spaniards. As a result, he quickly witnessed for himself that the Spanish were not gods that came to bless the Incas; they were *runa quicacha*—destroyers of people. By the time Atahualpa's second messenger, named Ciquinchara, arrived, it was already too late. The messenger reported:

Let me tell you, unique lord [Atahualpa], that I have accompanied them all the way to Caxas. While I was with them I tried to learn what kind of people they are in order to determine if it were the Contiti Viracocha [Jesus Christ] and the viracochas [Nephites] who came in ancient times and created the world and the people in it.

Since I had wanted to find out about this, I saw and understood that they are men like us because they eat and drink, dress and mend their clothes, and have relations with women. They perform no miracles nor do they raise or level mountains nor create people nor produce rivers and springs in areas that need water [create irrigation systems]. When they travel through arid regions, they carry water with them in jars and gourds.

The Viracocha that created the world in ancient times made all this that I stated. These people don't do anything like that. Rather, I have seen that they covet all they see and if it be to their liking they take it whether it be young women, gold or silver tumblers, or fine clothes.

In the same manner, they have Indians bound with quilla guascas, which means "iron ropes," who bear their burdens and petacas that contain their clothing. These Indians are treated badly. Wherever the Spaniards go, they appropriate everything, leaving nothing. They take it so easily you would think it were theirs.

They are very few. I have counted between one hundred and seventy and one hundred and eighty. Their number does not surpass two hundred. To me they seem to be quitas pumarangra, which means "leaderless people" wandering about and thieving.

The Inca was stunned by what he heard. Since he had taken them for gods and wanted to serve and worship them, he was saddened at having learned this news and he said to Ciquinchara: "Tell me, then, why do you all call them Viracocha?" And Ciquinchara said: "I don't call them viracocha but, rather, supai cuna, which means 'devils.' "[67]

Even after Ciquinchara's report of the evil intentions of the Spaniards, Atahualpa was reluctant to fight the white ones, fearing they might be gods. The morning he was to march to Cajamarca to meet Pizarro, the Inca drank himself into a drunken state of mind that cost him his empire and his life.[68] Diamond describes what happened in the city square where Pizarro finally met Atahualpa riding his litter and accompanied by 40,000 men:

Governor Pizarro now sent Friar Vincente de Valverde to go speak to Atahualpa, and to require Atahualpa in the name of God and of the King of Spain that Atahualpa subject himself to the law of our Lord Jesus Christ and to the service of His Majesty the King of Spain. Advancing with a cross in one hand and the Bible in the other hand, and going among the Indian troops up to the place where Atahualpa was, the Friar thus

addressed him: "I am a Priest of God, and I teach Christians the things of God, and in like manner I come to teach you. What I teach is that which God says to us in this Book. Therefore, on the part of God and of the Christians, I beseech you to be their friend, for such is God's will, and it will be for your good."

Atahualpa asked for the Book, that he might look at it, and the Friar gave it to him closed. Atahualpa did not know how to open the Book, and the Friar was extending his arm to do so, when Atahualpa, in great anger, gave him a blow on the arm, not wishing that it should be opened. Then he opened it himself, and, without any astonishment at the letters and paper he threw it away from him five or six paces, his face a deep crimson.

The Friar returned to Pizarro, shouting, "Come out! Come out, Christians! Come at these enemy dogs who reject the things of God. That tyrant has thrown my book of holy law to the ground! Did you not see what happened? Why remain polite and servile toward this over-proud dog when the plains are full of Indians? March out against him, for I absolve you!"

The governor then gave the signal to Candia, who began to fire off the guns. At the same time the trumpets were sounded, and the armored Spanish troops, both cavalry and infantry, sallied forth out of their hiding places straight into the mass of unarmed Indians crowding the square, giving the Spanish battle cry, "Santiago!" We had placed rattles on the horses to terrify the Indians. The booming of the guns, the blowing of the trumpets, and the rattles on the horses threw the Indians into panicked confusion. The Spaniards fell upon them and began to cut them to pieces. The Indians were so filled with fear that they climbed on top of one another, formed mounds, and suffocated each other. Since they were unarmed, they were attacked without danger to any Christians. The cavalry rode them down, killing and wounding, and following in pursuit.[69]

In the confusion that followed, Atahualpa was taken captive by the Spaniards. As Diamond concludes, "If night had not come on, few out of the more than 40,000 Indian troops would have been left alive. Six or seven thousand Indians lay dead, and many more had their arms cut off and other wounds[70] (compare 1 Nephi 15:17; 2 Nephi 10:18, 26:15–19).

Just as king Noah sealed his own fate by condemning the prophet Abinadi to burn, Atahualpa seems to have condemned himself when he cut off the head of the statue of Viracocha and then beheaded the old temple priest and ordering that his body be burned. After filling a large room almost to the ceiling with gold, a ransom Atahualpa paid for his release, Pizarro broke his promise to the Inca and had Atahualpa garroted and his body burned.[71]

Cieza de León called the betrayal and murder of Atahualpa by the Spaniards "the most ignoble act the Spaniards have ever done in all this empire of the Indies, and as such it is condemned and viewed as a great sin."[72] Apparently God did not pardon the Spaniards who executed Atahualpa. According to Cieza de León, "those who are blamed for his death died disastrous deaths:

Pizarro was stabbed; Almagro was garroted; Friar Vicente was killed by the Indians in Puná; Riquelme died suddenly; and Pedro Sancho, the notary, was put to a cruel death in Chile by a garrote and a rope."[73]

The Spanish conquistadors not only murdered, plundered, and raped their way through Peru, by killing the empire's elite class, they left, and as Cieza de León puts it "all of Peru was in disarray."[74] Cieza de León notes, "He [Pizarro] had stayed in Cajamarca more than seven months, and that beautiful and plentiful province was in such a state that [the Spaniards] were saddened to see how they were leaving it, remembering how flawless they had found it."[75]

Centuries after the conquistadors killed tens of thousands of Peruvians, the native Peruvians continued dying from the European diseases. Henry Dobyns has studied early death records in Peru, and calculates that nine out of every ten natives were killed by typhus, influenza, smallpox, diphtheria, and measles. He writes: "They died by scores and hundreds. . . . Villages were depopulated. Corpses were scattered over the fields or piled up in the houses or huts. . . . The fields were uncultivated; the herds were untended [and] the price of food rose to such an extent that many persons found it beyond their reach. They escaped the foul disease, but only to be wasted by famine."[76]

The Inca Empire was gone forever, but not the legacy of their ancient forefathers. As for the shameful deeds of the Spaniards, Cieza de León penned, "Through our sins, wars have never been lacking in this kingdom, and the natives have been so molested and abused that most of the people are gone from it, which is a great shame because it happened in such a short time."[77]

In an attempt to rest his soul in peace, Don Mancio Serra de Leguisamo, the last known survivor of the original conquerors of Peru wrote in the preamble of his will:

> We found these kingdoms in such good order, and the said Incas governed them in such wise that throughout them there was not a thief, nor a vicious man, nor an adulteress, nor a bad woman admitted among them, nor were there immoral people. The men had honest and useful occupations. The lands, forest, mines, pastures, houses and all kinds of products were regulated and distributed in such sort that each one knew his property without any other person seizing it or occupying it, nor were there law suits respecting it. . . .

> The motive which obliges me to make this statement is the discharge of my conscience, as I find myself guilty. For we have destroyed by our evil example, the people who had such a government as was enjoyed by these natives. They were so free from the committal of crimes or excesses, as well as women, that the Indian who had 100,000 pesos worth of gold or silver in his house, left it open merely placing a small stick against the door, as a sign that its master was out. With that, according to their custom, no one could enter or take anything that was there. When they saw that we put locks and keys on our doors, they supposed that it was from fear of them, that they might not kill us, but not because they believed that anyone would steal the property of another. So that when they found that we had thieves among us, and men who sought

to make their daughters commit sin, they despised us.[78]

Cieza de León recorded a very interesting note, that after the Indians of Peru realized how poorly they were faring in combat against the Spanish; they sat aside their alliance to their sun god and tried to return to their white god Viracocha.

> Although the Indians knew how badly they fared in combat, they encouraged themselves, believing that it would please God [Viracocha] to defend them without allowing the immense harm that

was coming their way. They made great sacrifices. They have the Sun as their sovereign god, but during greatest adversity, they ask favor of the great god of the heavens, maker of everything created, whom—as I have said many times—they call Ticci Viracocha.[79]

REMNANTS OF THE CHILDREN OF LEHI

Many conquistadors believed that the inhabitants of the New World were descendants of the lost tribes of Israel. One of the more controversial, but interesting accounts was recorded by

Menasseh Ben Israel, a Jewish Rabbi who was born in Lisbon in 1605. In his book *Voices from the Dust*, Calderwood provides this summary of Ben Israel's account.

Ben Israel wrote that he personally believed that the Indians were Israelites. The nucleus for Ben Israel's ideas came from an Israelite visitor to the New World, Aharon Levi, who spent some time in Columbia in the 1600's, and subsequently returned to Holland on 18 December 1644 to report that he had discovered a colony of white Indians hidden in the jungle who revealed to him their Israelite background. Aharon Levi claimed to be a *marrano* Jew [a Jew who changed his name and adopted Catholicism to avoid the Inquisition] and a member of the Tribe of Levi. He also used the Spanish name of Antonio Montesinos in his attempt to pass himself off as Catholic and avoid the Inquisition.

Levi reported to Ben Israel and a group of Portuguese Jews that some two and a half years earlier, he left the West Indies to travel to Quito, Ecuador. He obtained a pack of mules and hired several Indians under the leadership of Francisco, a local Indian chief, to help him make the trip. Levi stated that some time after this trip, he was in the city of Cartagena, Colombia, where he was placed under arrest by the Inquisition. While in jail, entrusting himself to God, he offered the following prayer "Blessed be the name of the Lord, that did not make me idolatrous, barbarian, black, or Indian." Levi claimed that upon saying "Indian," it suddenly came

to him that these Indians were Hebrews. The thought so startled him that he decided that he must be losing his mind. Every day during the following week he offered the same prayer and every day he received the same strong impression that the Indians were Hebrews.

As soon as he obtained his freedom, he sought out Francisco with whom he had established a good relationship in order to find out whether there might be any truth to the idea that the Indians were Hebrews. During the ensuing conversation, Levi revealed to Francisco that he, Aharon Levi, was an Israelite from the Tribe of Levi and that his God was Adonay.

Francisco told Levi that if he would obey Francisco in everything, he would take him to a place where Levi could find out the answers to his questions concerning Israelites in the Americas. The following day, Francisco arrived at Levi's hut and instructed him to leave his sword and cape behind and take only some food and a walking stick. The two men walked for eight days into the interior of Colombia until they finally came to a wide river. Taking a large handkerchief from around his waist, Francisco signaled to the other side of the river. Shortly thereafter three men and one woman crossed the river by canoe. The four strangers left the canoe and approached Levi and Francisco. When the men approached Francisco, he immediately bowed down in a sign of great respect. With a demonstration of considerable kindness, the men lifted Francisco up, spoke briefly with him and

then approached Levi. Using Francisco as an interpreter, they began to speak to Levi.

The men began their discourse by citing a scripture which Levi recognized was from the Book of Deuteronomy 6:4 which states, "Hear, O Israel: The Lord our God is one Lord." The men, still using Francisco as an interpreter, made the following additional declarations:

"First: Our Father is Abraham, Isaac, Jacob, Israel, and holding up three fingers mentioned these four. Then adding Ruben, they held up four fingers.

Second: Those who want to live with us, we will give them lands.

Third: Joseph lives in the middle of the ocean (holding up two fingers together and then opening them) in two parts.

Fourth: In the near future, we will come out to look around and to walk around. (Upon saying that they made signs with their eyes and stomped with their feet.)

Fifth: Some day we will all speak, and we shall come out as if the earth gave us birth.

Sixth: A messenger will go forth.

Seventh: Francisco will later tell you a little more. (They held up their fingers showing a little.)

Eighth: Give us a place where we can prepare ourselves, and do not delay. They moved their hands from one place to another.

Ninth: Twelve men will be sent who can write. (Each man made a sign that the twelve men would have beards.)"[80]

Calderwood further cites an account by Cabello Valboa which suggests that the Spanish saw a form of the Hebrew Passover being practiced in the Americas. Valboa wrote:

Some new islands were discovered and, upon arriving at one of them, we encountered where the natives had built a solemn temple and they gathered every day at the temple to celebrate their holidays, and in the first quarter of the new moon, they looked for a male lamb without spot or blemish and they sacrificed it. They then sprinkled the blood of this lamb around the frames of their doors.[81]

From this account, Cabello Valboa was convinced that these were descendants of the Jews.[82]

THE MARVELOUS WORK AND WONDER CONTINUES

Viracocha's prophecy that evil and deceitful men would come to Peru and claim that they were Viracochas also contained a prophecy of hope: "that in the time to come he would send his messengers who would protect and teach them."[83] In a small way, I believe that by serving a mission in Bolivia and Peru, I participated in the fulfillment of God's words that the gospel would be delivered by Gentiles to the remnant of the Lamanites and Nephites (2 Nephi 30:3).

I thank the LDS Church for the opportunity I had to serve a mission to both the Quechua and Aymara Indians. What a great opportunity it was to testify of the Book of Mormon in the lands where I believe Jesus Christ ministered to the Nephites and the Lamanites. To this day, one vivid image from my mission stands out above the others.

When I arrived in South America, I saw its native people still crushed to their knees by poverty and ignorance. The Quechua and Aymara people have suffered the hopelessness brought on by corrupt governments, false religious doctrines, and by having had their culture systemically erased.

The image I remember so well took place in Cuzco. The Peru Mission was sponsoring a Book of Mormon exhibition. The expo was well attended. I was working the sidewalk like a carnival barker, inviting people to take ten minutes and walk through the exhibits. Among the hundreds of people who entered the exhibition was a large middle-aged Quechua Indian. His large stature, wide shoulders, and barrel chest reminded me of a mature Nephi. But this was no Nephite king. His clothes were worn. His Indian hat and rough hands suggested he was a farmer from the countryside. As is the norm with the Indians, the man's eyes were lowered in respect to my American nationality. As disturbing as such sociological conditions are, I had become accustomed to, but not accepting of, the depleted self-esteem that plagues my Indian brothers and sisters.

After ten minutes, the large Indian exited the exhibition. He had heard a message about the Book of Mormon and had seen the pictures of Nephi, Alma, Moroni, and Jesus Christ in the Americas. Gripped tightly in his right hand was a copy of the Book of Mormon that he had purchased. His head was now held high; a gentle smile highlighted his face, and his countenance seemed to communicate, "I cannot wait to share the true history of our people with my children." His strong hand held the book as if it were made of pure gold.

WHERE HAS THIS BOOK TAKEN US?

Like voices from the dust, scientific findings are now pointing to the Book of Mormon as the ancient history of the people who lived in the Andes. The data is new, yet compelling. The substantial body of Peruvian archaeological, agricultural, metallurgic, economic, geographic, and mythological records is in harmony with the history contained on the pages of the Book of Mormon. On the other hand, the actual civilizations described in the sacred book have little in common with what is known about the ancient civilizations north of Panama.

Peru provides the student a rational approach for studying the landscape and people of the Book of Mormon. From the shoreline of the Pacific to the snowcapped Andes, there is a clear archaeological template for commencing an in-depth study of the historical sites and artifacts of the ancient Nephite and Lamanite nations. Within the borders of ancient Peru, which include modern Ecuador, Bolivia, Chile, and the Peru of today, we find an area that provides the next generation of Book of Mormon explorers with an unsurpassed combination of beauty, mystique, and seemingly endless opportunities to discover still new unheard voices from the dust.

Will the next generation of explorers unlock the alphabet of the *quipo* strings? Will they find the sunken city of Moroni beneath the majestic blue waters of Lake Titicaca? Will some bright LDS grade-school student in South America track the battlegrounds of the Nephites until he or she finds the hill Cumorah and touches its hidden treasure of sacred plates? Might a crew of young Polynesians build a replica of Hagoth's ship and retrace their ancestors' fearless voyages from South America to the isles of the sea? Who will be intelligent enough to decipher the timeline of oral traditions of the bearded white god throughout North and South America—and in

David Richardson giving food to poor Peruvian children.

so doing, discover the footsteps and DNA markers of ancient Nephite and Lamanite missionaries? Will yet another young scholar, recover the lost language of the Inca nobility and confirm that "Manco" was indeed the commoners' name for the great man we know as Nephi? Most important, are you the one who will compile an irrefutable body of evidence that the bearded white God Viracocha, who shed tears of love for his people, was Jesus Christ, the Savior of the World?

I believe these and many more questions will be answered by scholars of the Book of Mormon within the coming decades, and it is my testimony that we are at the dawn of the age of which Joseph Smith spoke:

> When Lehi went down by the Red Sea to the great Southern Ocean, and crossed over to this land, and landed a little south of the Isthmus of Darien [Panama,[84] see explanation in end note], and improved the country according to the word of the Lord, as a branch of the house of Israel, and then read such a goodly traditionary account as the one below, we can not but think the Lord has a hand in bringing to pass his strange act, and proving the Book of Mormon true in the eyes of all the people. The extract below, comes as near the real fact, as the four Evangelists do the crucifixion of Jesus. Surely "facts are stubborn things." It will be as it ever has been, the world will prove Joseph Smith a true prophet by circumstantial evidence, in experiments.[85]

THE LORD'S PROMISE TO THE LAMANITES

Viracocha promised to send not only teachers to the people of the Andes, but also protectors. The missionaries are the teachers who bring the gospel to the Lamanites. Who are the protectors of our Lamanite brothers? I believe that the responsibility to protect the Native Americans rests squarely upon the shoulders and in the hearts of every person who believes in the Book of Mormon and wants to fulfill his obligations in carrying out its covenants.

HOW CAN WE HELP?

As followers of the Book of Mormon, it is imperative that we reach out to assist the fallen Lamanite nations, be they in Peru, Brazil, Mexico, Utah, or among any other Native American people. The Book of Mormon promises:

> And after our seed is scattered the Lord God will proceed to do a marvelous work among the Gentiles, which shall be of great worth unto our seed; wherefore, it is likened unto their being nourished by the Gentiles and being carried in their arms and upon their shoulders. (1 Nephi 22:8)

In November 1983, over a decade after our missions, Tim Evans, David Richardson, and I returned to Peru. Tim was my companion in Juliaca near Pukara (Zarahemla). David was my companion in Cuzco (the city of Nephi). We did not return as tourists, or even as former missionaries coming to check on the welfare on our converts. We were there to obtain legal status in Peru for the Andean Children's Foundation, a

non-profit organization that Tim established for helping the needy children in Peru and Bolivia. We filed the necessary legal documents in Lima then visited orphanages and Catholic relief organizations to see how we could help.

Since that trip, I have spent all but five of the ensuing twenty-four years working overseas, where I have been researching the Book of Mormon. David, seen on the previous page giving bread to the small children, has worked non-stop for the *World Farmers Cooperative Foundation,* establishing farming cooperatives for poor farmers in Third World nations and most recently establishing micro-loan programs for the world's poorest. Tim Evans, on the other hand, has lengthened his stride even further in fulfilling the sacred promise the Lord made to the Lamanites.

Tim, a dentist by profession, realized that the number-one killer in the world of children is water-born diseases. Knowing this, Tim focused his efforts on developing a concept for a low-cost and easy-to-maintain water pump. He received a grant for turning the concept into a reality. Using his own farm as a proving ground, Tim perfected an easy-to-maintain pump that costs only forty

Timothy Evans inspecting a new well in Bolivia

dollars. The organization he founded is now called Ascend Alliance, which promotes humanitarian travel tours for installing fresh-water projects, building schools, educating women, and for dental and medical volunteerism. Since its start as the Andean Children's Foundation in 1983, the Ascend Alliance has installed over 1,500 wells on the Altiplano of Bolivia and Peru.

I am proud of my missionary companion, for Tim, his wife Melissa, and their supporters are responsible for having saved tens of thousands of lives. The volunteers and supporters of Ascend Alliance now organize and fund projects throughout the world. The Alliance allows everyone to finance or personally work on projects that make a real difference. I strongly encourage anyone

One of 1,500 Ascend Alliance wells with pumps on the Altiplano.

interested in helping to redeem our needy brothers and sisters, regardless of their race or religion, to visit www.ascendalliance.com.

Of course, Tim, Dave, and I are not alone. Returned missionaries are heeding the call of the Book of Mormon to return and lift up the people they once taught. Similar projects have been led by returned missionaries in locations from Mongolia to Ethiopia and from Guatemala to Tonga. The Lord's promise to the poor is not something we can conveniently ignore or justify away. For those who believe in the Book of Mormon, we all know that. It is our calling. For you who are now doing your part in this marvelous work and wonder, or who will pledge to do so, I conclude, *Que te vaya con Dios. May you journey with God.*

Royalties from this book are donated to Ascend Alliance.

A great mountain barrier
and wilderness lie between
Pukara and Cuzco.

APPENDIX I
POSSIBLE SECOND AND THIRD NEPHITE EXODUSES TO ZARAHEMLA

King Mosiah (son of King Benjamin) sent sixteen strong men to inquire concerning the people who had returned to the city of Lehi-Nephi (city of Nephi renamed after Lamanites control possession of it). These men were led by Ammon. After a long search, they found their brethren who had been held captive by the Lamanites.

I have proposed that the city of Zarahemla was the ruins of the city now call Pukara on the Altiplano of Peru just 80 km from the shores of Lake Titicaca.

The Land of Zarahemla was the northern end (Peruvian side) of the Altiplano (the plain on the north side Lake Titicaca). As one follows the Pukara River (river Sidon) to its headwaters, it leaves the plain and enters into a mountainous wilderness (Manti borders and southern wilderness).

The border between the land of Zarahemla and the land of Nephi was the La Raya pass through the mountains at 14,172 feet above sea level. Once through the pass, one could follow the sacred Inca river Urubamba through a series of valleys until it reaches the Cuzco Valley. These valleys, south of the City of Nephi, were occupied by the Lamanites. Thus the sixteen Nephite men could not have used the La Raya pass to find the City of Nephi which was located at the northern end of the Cuzco Valley.

Art Kocherhans takes to guns in 1980s for protection against Leftist Rebels while searching for the Sidon River (Montrego River)

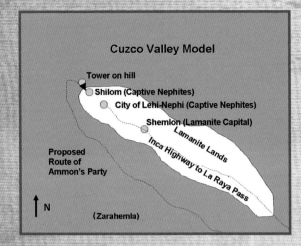

Cuzco Valley Model

Tower on hill
Shilom (Captive Nephites)
City of Lehi-Nephi (Captive Nephites)
Shemlon (Lamanite Capital)
Lamanite Lands
Inca Highway to La Raya Pass

Proposed
Route of
Ammon's Party

N

(Zarahemla)

Indian women leading llama and alpacas up trail from Cuzco past the fortress of Sacsahuaman.

The City of Lehi-Nephi (or Nephi) was the city of Cuzco, Peru.

The Book of Mormon city of Shilom: appears to have been a village north of Cuzco, just below the famous ruins of Sacsahuaman. Arthur Kocherhans was the first to suggest the tower north of Shilom as having been the great ancient tower that stood atop the hill north of Cuzco where the fortress of Sacsahuaman still stands.[1]

From the tower next to the temple in the city of Lehi-Nephi, one could see the Lamanite town of Shemlon which was within eyesight of Lehi-Nephi and on its south. In the opposite direction one could see from the tower the Nephite city of Shilom to the north (Mosiah 11:12). We can infer that Shilom was to the north, because King Noah had constructed many buildings at Shilom, and on a hill north of the town he had another tower built (Mosiah 11:13). Since there was a hill north of Shilom, it again seems likely that Shilom must have been north of the city of Lehi-Nephi and south of the tower on the hill (otherwise, if Shilom was south of the city and a hill was north

of it, then how could it have been seen from the first tower next to the temple? There would have been a hill between the two towers.

WHAT THE BOOK OF MORMON STATES

Ammon's party left Zarahemla (Pukara) and went in the "up" direction (Mosiah 7:2), which in Semitic, and Quechua (Peru's languages), means "north" in search of the City of Lehi-Nephi. Cuzco (city of Lehi-Nephi) is north of

the ruins of Pukara (Zarahemla). As they traveled north they entered a wilderness where they wandered for forty days (Mosiah 7:4), implying that they were in a wilderness and became seriously lost. After forty days in the wilderness they finally reached the "hill" which is north of the land of Shilom, where they pitched their tents.

To reach Cuzco (the City of Nephi) from Pukara (Zarahemla), one would have to travel north into a wilderness of high desert mountains. The towering mountains ascend well over 20,000 feet and present a substantial barrier between

Beautiful streams like these running off the Andes provide irrigation for the valleys below.

Pukara and Cuzco. They could not have used the La Raya pass because the Lamanites lived in the lands south of the city of Nephi-Lehi—that which appears to have been the inhabitable fertile valleys that run along the Urubamba River south of Cuzco all the way to the La Raya pass.

Unable to take the La Raya pass, Ammon's party would have had to forge a trail around the Andes, thus wandering in a high desert wilderness for several weeks. They not only had to avoid the glaciers, they also had to avoid villages of the Lamanites. The foothills and mountain ranges north of Pukara (Zarahemla) appear to be the mountains referred to in the Book of Mormon as the mountains of Manti and the south wilderness which was beyond the mountains ("borders" means "mountains" in Semitic languages; see Alma 16:6–7). The headwaters of the Pukara river (river Sidon) flows from these mountains south past Pukara (Zarahemla) into Lake Titicaca (sea of the east).

Once Ammon's party found their way around the mountains, the logical way to reach the Nephites north of the Lamanites was to avoid Shemlon and the other Lamanite cities (in the Cuzco valley). In other words, they could not have traveled in a direct course up the Cuzco Valley for it was inhabited by the Lamanites, so they needed to circumvent the valley of Cuzco and then join it at its northern end, where the hill with the tower stands at the northern end of the Cuzco valley. Thus they detoured around the mountains eventually coming to the Cuzco valley (land of Nephi) from the North. This explains why they first traveled "up" (north) from Zarahemla, and then the short distance back "down" (south) from the hill into the town of Shilom. This last-minute change of direction

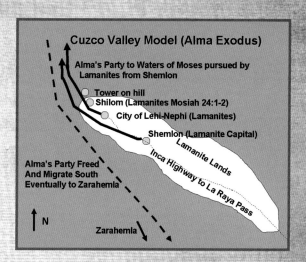

Cuzco Valley Model (Alma Exodus)

Alma's Party to Waters of Moses pursued by Lamanites from Shemlon

Tower on hill
Shilom (Lamanites Mosiah 24:1-2)
City of Lehi-Nephi (Lamanites)
Shemlon (Lamanite Capital)
Lamanite Lands
Inca Highway to La Raya Pass

Alma's Party Freed And Migrate South Eventually to Zarahemla

N

Zarahemla

is confirmed a short period later when Ammon leads the Nephites at the city of Lehi-Nephi to Zarahemla.

Their exodus to Zarahemla appears to have been along the same route that Ammon used to reach the city of Lehi-Nephi. They leave at night while the Lamanites are in a deep sleep from the wine the Nephites gave them. The Nephites took their flocks and went through the back side of the city (the side not facing the Lamanites guards on the south; Mosiah 22:6), and "traveled around Shilom (in north direction) and then "bent their course towards the land of Zarahemla" (turned south once outside the Cuzco Valley; Mosiah 22:11).

From their camp, three men on the hill north of Shilom— Amaleki, Helem, and Hem—went down (Mosiah 7:6) into Shilom, a Nephite town, where they were discovered by king Limhi's guards (Mosiah 7:5–9). The Book of Mormon accounts fit exactly the geography of what existed at the northern end of the Cuzco valley. It would have been true in antiquity that north of Cuzco (the city of Lehi-Nephi) a hill with a tower was located north of the city. To travel from the hill into the valley to Cuzco, where a tower stood next to the temple, one would have passed through a town just below the hill. A *National Geographic* illustration of ancient Cuzco clearly shows an ancient setting that fits perfectly the City of Lehi-Nephi. It depicts the trail that leads from the hill (with a tower) down into the valley of Cuzco, past an ancient village (Shilom) that once stood below Sacsahuaman, and then leads to Cuzco (city of Nephi).[2]

ALMA'S JOURNEY TO THE WATERS OF MORMON AND TO ZARAHEMLA

One more exodus was made from the city of Nephi (Lehi-Nephi) to Zarahemla. It was the journey of Alma's converts who fled for their lives from the city to a wilderness camp at the waters of Mormon. For a season the waters of Mormon appear to have been an effective hideaway, "being in the borders [mountains] of the land having been infested, by times or at seasons, by wild beasts. Now, there was in Mormon a fountain of pure water, and Alma resorted thither, there being near the water a thicket of small trees, where he did hide himself in the daytime from the searches of the king" (Mosiah 18:4–5). The small trees did not stand alone, but were part of a forest (Mosiah 18:30). (Machu Picchu is covered with forest).

Several locations within fifty miles of Cuzco could have been the waters of Mormon. I like to think that with their thick tropical forests, the spectacular mountains around Machu Picchu would be an ideal hideaway from King Noah's search parties. Near Machu Picchu and beside the Vilcanota River are the hot-water springs (fountains) of Aguas Calientes.

Eventually Alma's people fled from the waters of Mormon for eight days through a wilderness area to the City of Helam. (Mosiah 23:3)—"very beautiful and pleasant land, and a land of pure water" (Mosiah 23:4), called the land of Helam, or city of Helam. (Mosiah 23:20). Helam appears to have been in the mountains. However, at Helam, Alma's people are discovered by the Lamanite army (Mosiah 23:25–26). Alma has the people of Helam deliver themselves into bondage to the Lamanites (23:29). Helam must be far into the wilderness hinterlands, for the Lamanite army was lost and could not find their way back to the land of Nephi. Alma shows them the way (Mosiah 23:35, 37). Alma leads his people to freedom by traveling all day then pitching tents in valley they called Alma (Mosiah 24:20); however, Alma was warned to leave the valley immediately. for the Lamanites were pursuing them (Mosiah 24:23). Alma's party traveled twelve days in the wilderness and came to Zarahemla (Mosiah 24:25).

THE BATTLE WITH THE AMLICITES

The Amlicites attacked the Nephites on the hill of Amnihu, which was east of the river Sidon, the river that ran by Zarahemla (Alma 2:15). The Nephites overpowered the Amlicites on Amnihu and pursued them up river to the valley of Gideon (Alma 2:20), which was to the east of Zarahemla and the river Sidon (Alma 5:7).

At Gideon the Nephites pitched their tents and sent scouts to spy on the Amlicite camp which was in the land of Minon (above, meaning north of the land of Zarahemla), and on the trail to the land of Nephi (Alma 2:22–24, which was to the north, as is Cuzco). At the land Minon, the Amlicites joined a large Lamanite army that was attacking the Nephites from the north (land of Nephi or Cuzco) (Alma 2:24). The Nephite scouts saw the Nephite civilians fleeing to the south, undoubtedly toward their fortress city of Zarahemla (Alma 2:24).

Hearing that the Lamanites were attacking the land, Alma had his army break camp and march southward to defend the city of Zarahemla (Alma 2:26). As the Nephite army crossed the river Sidon near Zarahemla, they were attacked by the Lamanites and the remainder of the Amlicites

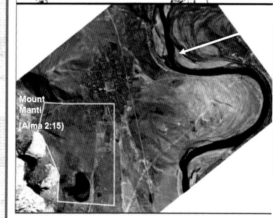

Amlicite Battle for Zarahemla

Mount Manti
(Alma 2:15)

Nephite army tries to cross river Sidon to west side fortifications at Zarahemla, however they must first drive the Lamanites and Amlicites back. The Nephites then successfully cross the river to their fortifications. Lamanites and Amlicites flee to north and west. Bodies of the enemy dead are thrown into the River and their bones end up in the sea (Lake Titicaca).

(Alma 2:27). Alma and his men fought with such strength that the Lamanites "fled back from before Alma [at the river] and the Nephites "slew and drove them [Lamanites] back [away from the river]" (Alma 2:32–33). The Nephites killed so many Lamanites at the place where they crossed the river,

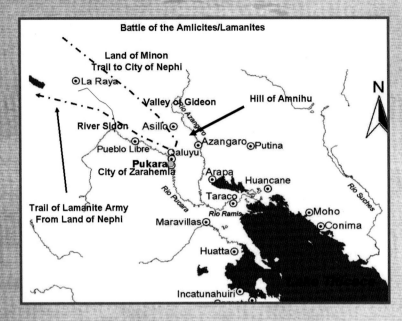

Battle of the Amlicites/Lamanites

that they were forced to throw the bodies of the dead Lamanites into the river to make room to recross the river (Alma 2:34). The Lamanite bodies floated down the river into the East Sea (Lake Titicaca).

Alma returned to the western (or Zarahemla) side of the river to fight the Lamanites from fortified positions (Alma 2:34). Seeing that the Nephites had crossed the river to Zarahemla, the Lamanites and Amlicites realized the battle was lost and fled west and north, beyond the borders (mountains) of the land (Alma 2:35–36). Alma, probably with reinforcements, and seeing the enemy forces had divided to the west and north, ordered his army to pursue the enemy (Alma 2:35–36). Alma's army periodically attacked their fleeing enemy, even unto the wilderness of Hermounts; where there were wild and ravenous beasts (Alma 2:37). Many died from their

wounds and were devoured by those "beasts and also the vultures of the air" (Alma 2:38). The mountains to the north and west of Lake Titicaca Basin, especially the Colca Canyon, has the largest population of the great vultures of the Andes, the condors—the largest of all flying birds.

THE BATTLE IN THE SOUTHERN WILDERNESS

The Lamanites attacked and destroyed the wicked people of Ammonihah (Alma 16: 3). We are not told where Ammonihah was, except we know it was not in the land of Zarahemla (Alma 15:18), and that it was a three day journey north of the mountainous wilderness of Melek (Alma 8:3). Melek seems to have been quite a distance to the west of Zarahemla and the river Sidon (Alma 8:3). The western orientation of the land of Melek seems to be confirmed since Alma went "over" to Melek from Zarahemla, not up (north) or down (south) to the reach the land (Alma 8:3). Therefore, we can assume that the city of Ammonihah was somewhere outside the Titicaca Basin.

After attacking the city of Noah and taking its inhabitants captive, Zoram, the Nephite commander, lost track of the Lamanites. Subsequently he asked Alma to inquire of the Lord where he could find the victorious Lamanite army. Alma prayed unto the Lord, and then told Zoram that the Lamanite army, apparently thinking they could attack Zarahemla, had crossed the river Sidon and entered the wilderness of Manti (16:6). Since the hill Manti was near the city of Zarahemla, we will place the wilderness of Manti on the west or opposite side of the mountain in back of Pukara (Zarahemla). The southern branch of the Pukara river (Sidon) runs north from the city then breaks off to the west and then south behind what we assume is the hill Manti. Zoram left Zarahemla, crossed over the river Sidon, then defeated the Lamanite army beyond the land of Manti, in the southern wilderness (Alma 16:8).

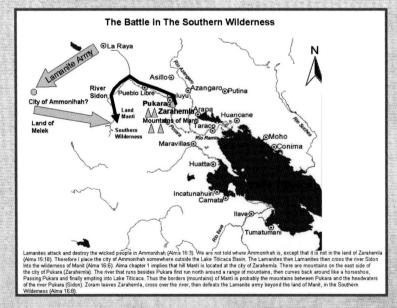

The Battle in The Southern Wilderness

Lamanites attack and destroy the wicked people in Ammonihah (Alma 16:3). We are not told where Ammonihah is, except that it is not in the land of Zarahemla (Alma 15:18). Therefore I place the city of Ammonihah somewhere outside the Lake Titicaca Basin. The Lamanites then cross the river Sidon into the wilderness of Manti (Alma 16:6). Alma chapter 1 implies that hill Manti is located at the city of Zarahemla. There are mountains on the east side of the city of Pukara (Zarahemla). The river that runs beside Pukara first run north around a range of mountains, then curves back around like a horseshoe, Passing Pukara and finally empting into Lake Titicaca. Thus the borders (mountains) of Manti is probably the mountains between Pukara and the headwaters of the river Pukara (Sidon). Zoram leaves Zarahemla, cross over the river, then defeats the Lamanite army beyond the land of Manti, in the Southern Wilderness (Alma 16:8).

APPENDIX III
On DNA Research and the Book of Mormon

Simon Southerton, a senior research scientist with the Commonwealth Scientific and Industrial Research Organization (CSIRO) in Canberra, Australia summarizes the gap he perceives existed between science and the Book of Mormon account:

> Ten centuries ago a handful of Norse sailors slipped into Newfoundland, established small colonies, traded with local natives, then sailed back into the fog of history. In spite of the small scale of their settlements and the brevity of their stay, unequivocal evidence of their presence has been found, including metalwork, buildings, and Norse inscriptions. Just six centuries earlier, the Book of Mormon tells us, a climatic battle between fair-skinned Nephites and dark-skinned Lamanites ended a millennial dominion by a literate, Christian Bronze Age civilization with a population numbering in the millions. Decades of serious honest scholarship have failed to uncover credible evidence that these Book of Mormon civilizations ever existed. No Semitic languages, no Israelites speaking these languages, no wheeled chariots or horses to pull them, no swords or steel to make them. They remain a great civilization vanished without a trace, the people along with their genes.[3]

Critics like Southerton have difficulty with the Book of Mormon because they simply do not understand the geographic and demographic context of the book. Indeed the same can be said for South American archaeology as a whole. It is just now becoming understood. Mann notes:

> Peru, anthropologist Henry F. Dobyns [working in Peru in the 1960s] learned, was one of the world's cultural wellsprings, a place as important to the human saga as the Fertile Crescent. Yet the area's significance had been scarcely appreciated outside the Andes, partly because the Spaniards so thoroughly ravaged Inka culture, and partly because the Inka themselves, wanting to puff up their own importance, had actively concealed the glories of the cultures before them. Incredibly, the first full history of the fall of the Inka empire did not appear until more than three hundred years after the events it chronicled: William H. Prescott's *History of the Conquest of Peru*, published in 1847.[4]

Indeed, when I left in 1969 to serve for two years in the Andes South Mission, there was still no serious successor to Prescott's history of Peru.

Undoubtedly the Nephites' and Lamanites' bloodlines represented only a very thin ruling class veneer that ruled over a large populace of aboriginals. The same is probably true for the Polynesians. Hagoth and other Peruvian traders would have made a very small dent in the aborigines' bloodlines. In each case any Hebrew DNA was but a mere drop of Israelite blood in an ocean of indigenous DNA. Given the scenario presented in this book, the only possible way of finding remnants of Middle Eastern DNA in Peru is to extract it from an ancient mummy of the long extinct Nephite ruling class, a pure "Lehite," that is, Nephi or Mormon. Since the Spanish burned the mummies believed to be those of the original eight Inca kings found at Will-pillay, the probability of finding Middle Eastern DNA in the present-day Peruvian Amerindian is highly unlikely. Perhaps odd variants will hint of possible links to the Middle East, but compelling DNA evidence may never be found among living Amerindians.

It seems the Lamanites intermarried freely with the indigenous tribes while the Nephites, at least for a period, practiced polygamy and took concubines of native women and are known to have married Lamanites.[5] A parallel genetic history can be found in the lineage of the Yemen Jews, a much larger community of people who left Jerusalem and settled among a non-Jewish people. Geneticists Steven Jones describes their history:

> Between 1948 and 1951 a whole community of devout Jews was airlifted from Yemen to Israel in Operation Magic Carpet. It was one of the first and most dramatic statements of the Law of Return. The Yemenites saw themselves as a prototype of the Diaspora, driven from their native land and keeping separate from the Islamic people around them. Their dialect and religious customs are subtly different from those of other Jews. They are, in some ways, a living fossil of ancient Judaic practice. While other Jews have changed, those in Yemen have stayed the same, holding steadfastly to their beliefs.

> They trace their origin to the days of King Solomon, a thousand years before Christ, to a small group of Jews who arrived at the southern end of the Arabian Peninsula—in fact to the city of Sana'a, much later claimed as a homeland by the Lemba [an African tribe that claims Israeli lineage]. Jews certainly did migrate there more than two thousand years ago. Soon, though, there were some remarkable developments. From the fourth century onwards, the paganism of the locals began to give way to a religion in which one God was elevated above others. By AD 500 most of the state was Jewish. However, this brief flowering of Judaism in a foreign land did not last. In one of the forgotten religious conflicts of history, Yemen was defeated, in AD 525 by Christian invaders from Ethiopia.

> Some Jews remained. Who they were, history does not say. Perhaps they were—as modern Yemenite Jews believe—the original group who had moved to Yemen centuries before. Perhaps, though, they retained no direct connection with those migrants from Israel. There was, no doubt, plenty of mixing with locals when the state had taken up Judaism. What is more, some of those who retained a Jewish identity when Yemen fell to militant Christianity may themselves have been converts, with no biological descent from Israel at all.

> The genes tell a more equivocal story. The Yemenites are, in fact, biologically distinct from other Jews. None of the cystic-fibrosis mutations found among Yemenites is present in other members of their faith; and none of the screening tests for the disease effective in nine-tenths of world Jewry can be used in those of Yemenite origin. What is more, some genes for blood groups and enzymes common in Yemenites are not found in other Jewish groups, but are frequent in Arabs. Some genes link them to Ethiopians; and some are found only among the Yemenites themselves. Their biological heritage reflects, not unbroken descent from the people of Israel at the time of Solomon, but intermixture, due partly to intermarriage and partly to conversion at the moment when their state briefly took up the Jewish faith. Many of those returned on eagles' wings to what they saw as their ancient home were in fact being exiled from the land of their ancestors. This discovery caused a certain embarrassment to those who made it and has still not been widely advertised in the Yemenite community.[6]

Answering Simon Southerton's question of where the genes of the Book of Mormon people are is easy. The DNA is where it has always been. The genes of the majority of the people of the Book of Mormon lands were the genes of the people who lived in South America before Lehi's family arrived. In other words, the history of the Book of Mormon lands covers a large indigenous populace that was colonized by tiny groups of Jaredites, Lehites, and Mulekites.

LIST OF MAPS

PHOTOGRAPHY CREDITS

ENDNOTES

INTRODUCTION

1. Michael de Groote, "Hebrew DNA found in South America?" *Deseret News* (Salt Lake City), 12 May 2008, http://www.deseretnews.com/article/1,5143,700225191,00.html.

2. Kenneth W. Godfrey, "What is the Significance of Zelph in the Study of Book of Mormon Geography?" (Provo, UT: Maxwell Institute, 1999), 70–79, http://farms.byu.edu/display-print.php?table=jbms&id=202, March 29, 2008, 4.

3. B. H. Roberts, *New Witness for God*, vol. 3., 501.

4. *Encyclopedia of Mormonism*, vol. 1, "Book of Mormon Geography."

5. Roberts, *New Witness for God*, 501.

6. Andrew Jenson, *Church Chronology*, November 2, 1851 (Saturday).

7. Orson Pratt, *Journal of Discourses*, February 11, 1872, vol. 14, 325.

8. John L. Sorenson and Matthew Roper, "Before DNA" *Journal of Book of Mormon Studies* 12, no. 1 (2003): 6–23.

9. John E. Clark, "Archaeology, Relics, and Book of Mormon Belief," *Journal of Book of Mormon Studies* 14 (2005): 38–39.

10. No author stated, "The 'Origins' of Cahokia Mounds," 6/25/2008, 1, http://www.cahokiamounds.com/mystery_01.html.

11. Alma 49:4 mentions building defensive ridges (or walls) of earth, but structures like those built by the "mound builders" are not described in the Book of Mormon.

12. No author stated, "Paleoamerican Origins," *Smithsonian Encyclopedia*, Smithsonian Institute: http://www.si.edu/Encyclopedia_SI/nmnh/origin.htm.

13. Hugh Nibley, *The Prophetic Book of Mormon* (Provo, UT: F.A.R.M.S.), 221–22.

14. Charles C. Mann, *1491: New Revelations of the Americas Before Columbus* (New York: Vintage Books, 2006), 30.

15. Brian S. Bauer, *Ancient Cuzco: Heartland of the Inca* (Austin: University of Texas Press, 2004), 1.

16. Mann, *1491: New Revelations of the Americas,* 315.

17. Ibid., 123.

18. Gavin Menzies, *1421: The Year China Discovered the World* (New York: Bantom Books, 2003), 237–75.

19. Author unknown, "Cosmology of Tawantinsuys," http://interpres/cz/worag/cosmol/tawan.htm, 2.

20. David G. Calderwood, *Voices from the Dust* (Austin: Historical Publications, Inc, 2005), 46.

21. Gary Urton, *The Legendary Past: Inca Myths* (Austin: University of Texas Press, 1999), 44–46.

22. Calderwood, *Voices from the Dust*, 29.

23. Ibid.

24. Mann, *1491: New Revelations of the Americas*, 315.

25. Urton, *The Legendary Past*, 28.

26. Calderwood, *Voices from the Dust*, 40.

27. Irving A. Leonard, *Books of the Brave* (originally published by Harvard University Press, 1949). Republished in 1992 with an introduction by Rolena Adorno by the University of California Press, xxv, as quoted by Calderwood, *Voices from the Dust*, 40.

CHAPTER 1

1. John L. Sorenson and Matthew Roper, "Before DNA" *Journal of Book of Mormon Studies* 12 (2003), 6–23.

2. Joseph Fielding Smith, Jr., *Doctrines of Salvation* (Salt Lake City: Bookcraft, 1954), 3:232–233; see also *Church News*, 10 September 1938.

3. John Sorenson, "A Reconsideration of Early Metal in Mesoamerica," *Katunob 9* (March 1976):1–18. Cited by Jeff Lindsay at http://www.jefflindsay.com/LDSFAQ/FQ_metals.shtml#ores

4. John Sorenson, *An Ancient American Setting for the Book of Mormon*, 279–80. Cited by Jeff Lindsay at http://www.jefflindsay.com/LDSFAQ/FQ_metals.shtml#ores

5. "Copper, Bronze, and Brass," Journal of Book of Mormon Studies 9 (2000), 1.

6. Juan de Betanzos, *Narrative of the Incas*, translated and edited by Roland Hamilton and Dana Buchanan from the Palma de Mallorca manuscript, (Austin: University of Texas Press, 1996), 90.

7. Pedro de Cieza de León, *The Discovery and Conquest of Peru: Chronnciles of the New World Encounter*, edited and translated by Alexander Parma Cook and Noble David Cook, (London: Duke University, 1998), 360.

8. Bernabe Cobo, *History of the Inca Empire*, translated by Roland Hamilton, (Austin: University of Texas, 1996), 231–32.

9. John Sorenson, *An Ancient American Setting for the Book of Mormon*, 278–80: The earliest piece so far probably dates back to around the first century BC. It is a bit of copper sheathing found on top of an altar at Cuicuilco in the Valley of Mexico [Bryon Cummings, "Cuicuilco and the Archaic of Mexico," University of Arizona, Bulletin IV, no. 8 *Social Science Bulletin*, 4 (Tucson, 1933), 38–39; Robert F. Heizer and James A. Bennyhoff, "Archaeological Investigation of Cuicuilco, Valley of Mexico, 1957," *Science* 127, no. 3292 (1958): 232–33]. Metal work in the Americas was first developed in Peru and then much later transferred north to Mesoamerica. Celia Heil, "The Significance of Metallurgy in the Purhepecha Religion," in *Across Before Columbus?* Ed. by Donald Y. Gilmore and Linda S. Mc Elroy, New England Antiquities Research Association (NEARA), Laconia, NH, 1998, 43–51, "South American metallurgical technology . . . seems to have moved northward with the coastal maritime trade, and this knowledge is apparently included the skills of smelting, hot and cold hammering, and casting by both lost wax and open molds. The Chavin of Peru appear to have been the innovators in metallurgy, probably before 500 BC, followed by artisans of Colombia and Ecuador. It could have been even earlier, however, as some samples have been dated to about 1500 BC in the high Andes, where hammering was the method, and there was particular interest in color." Also Richard L. Burger and Robert B. Gordon, "Early Central Andean Metalworking from Mina Perdida, Peru," *Science*. Vol. 282, no. 5391 (6 Nov. 1998), states "Copper and gold artifacts in context" online abstract of the Science article, 1108–1111. The date dated to approximately 3120 to 3020 carbon-14 years before the present (approximately 1410–1090 calendar years BC) "recovered in excavation at Mina Perdida, Lurin Valley Peru, show that artisans hammered native metals into thin foils, in some cases with intermediate anneals. They gilded copper artifacts by attaching gold foil. The artifacts show that fundamental elements of the Andeans' metallurgical tradition were developed before the Chavin horizon, and that on the Peruvian coast the working of native copper preceded the production of smelted copper objects."

10. Mann, *1491: New Revelations of the Americas*, 91–92.

11. George Potter, documentary film, *The Jaredites* (Bear River City, UT: Nephi Project, 2003).

12. William R. Phillips, "Metals of the Book of Mormon (Provo, UT: FARMS, 2000), 36–43. http://home.exetel.com.au/wvduivenvoorde/WAMM-Report130.pdf

13. "Excavations and Restoration of the Complex of Khor Rori, Interim Report (October 2000–April 2001)," (Pisa: University of Pisa, 2001), 12–15, 45.

14. "Copper, Bronze, and Brass," Journal of Book of Mormon Studies 9 (2000), p.na. see http://farms.byu.edu/display-print.php?table=jbms&id=226

15. Ali Shahri, Khor Rori historian, conversation with author, 23 September 2006.

16. On exhibit at the Museum of the Frankincense Land, Salalah, Oman (November 30, 2008).

17. Urton, *The Legendary Past,* 53.

18. No author stated, "Archaeologist 'Strike Gold' with Finds of Ancient Nasca Iron Ore Mine," *Science Daily,* http://www.science-daily.com/releases/2008/01/080129125405.htm, 3 February 2008.

19. Gavin Menzies, *1421: The Year China Discovered the World,* (New York: Bantam Books, 2003), 145.

20. Rod Ewins, "Barkcloth and the Origins of Paper," paper presented at the First National Paper Conference in Hobar Australia, May 1981, 4, published in the Conference Papers, distribution to conferees only by Papermakers of Australia; http://www.justpacific.com/pacific/papers/barkcloth~paper.html.

21. Mike Xu, "Transpacific Contacts?" Dr. Xu of Texas Christian University, provides a comparison of Olmec motif characters to Chinese Shang writing (6 February 2007), see presentation at http://www.chinese.tcu.edu/www_chinese3_tcu_edc.htm.

22. Adrian Gilbert, *The End of Time: The Mayan Prophecies Revisited,* (Edinburgh: Mainstream Publishing, 2007), 40–41.

23. John Sorenson, "Was There Hebrew Language In Ancient America? An interview with Brian Stubbs," *Journal of Book of Mormon Studies* 9 (2000): 54–63; refer to Arnold Leesburg, *Comparative Philology: A Comparison between Semitic and American Languages* (Leyden: Brill, 1908).

24. "A Survey of Some Vowel Systems," http://www.compulink.co.uk/~morven/lang/vowels.html

25. Edward P. Stabler, "The Finite Connectivity of Linguistic Structure," (Los Angeles: UCLA), www.linguistics.ucla.edu/people/stabler/eps-conn.pdf, January 2007), 5,

26. Mary LeCron Foster of the University of California, Berkeley, in "Old World Language in the Americas: 1," an unpublished paper read at the annual meeting of the Association of American Geographers, San Diego, 20 April 1992; and also in her "Old World Language in the Americas: 2," an unpublished paper given at the annual meeting of the Language Origins Society, Cambridge University, September 1992; copies are in the possession of John Sorenson and Matthew Roper, cited by Sorenson and Roper in "Before DNA."

27. Cobo, *History of the Inca Empire,* 266.

28. Ibid., 107.

29. Loren McIntyre, "Lost Empire of the Incas," *National Geographic,* 144, no. 6 (December 1973): 764.

30. Mann, *1491: New Revelations of the Americas,* 397.

31. Juha J. Hiltunen, *Ancient Kings of Peru: The Reliability of the Chronicle of Fernando de Montesinos* (Helsinki: Suomen Historiallinen Sevra, 1999), 354.

32. Mann, *1491: New Revelations of the Americas,* 303.

33. John Noble Wilford, "String and Knot, Theory of Inca Writing," *New York Times,* 12 August 2003. Article reports on news conference with Dr. Gary Urton's research on Quipus. His research is funded by the National Science Foundation, the Dumbarton Oaks Foundation, Harvard's Faculty of Arts and Sciences, and the John D. and Catherine T. MacArthur Foundation, which in 2001 awarded Urton a MacArthur Fellowship. Nicholas Wade, " Untying the Knots of the Inca" (*New York Times,* 19 August 2005).

34. Galen Brokaw, quoted by Mann, *1491: New Revelations of the Americas,* 395.

35. Mann, *1491: New Revelations of the Americas,* 397.

36. Urton, *The Legendary Past,* 25.

37. Cobo, *History of the Inca Empire,* 254.

38. Ibid., 254–55.

39. Gareth Cook, "Untangling the Mystery of the Inca," *Wired,* January 2007, 145–46.

40. Wilford, "String and Knot."

41. Cook, "Untangling the Mystery of the Inca," 147.

42. Wilford, "String and Knot."

43. Cook, "Untangling the Mystery of the Inca," 146.

44. Catherine Julien, quote by Mann, *1491: New Revelations of the Americas,* 398.

45. Gilbert, *The End of Time,* 26.

46. Ibid., 32.

47. Ibid., 33.

48. Calderwood, *Voices from the Dust,* 328.

49. Pedro de Gamboa Sarmiento, *History of the Incas* written circa AD 1570, translated by Clements Markham, (Cambridge: The Haklugy Society 1907) 28–58. Available at http:www.sacred-text.com/nam/inca/inca01.htm. 1.

50. Alonzo L. Gaskill, *The Lost Language of Symbolism: An Essential Guide for Recognizing and Interpreting Symbols of the Gospel* (Salt Lake City: Deseret Book, 2003), 161.

51. Sullivan, *The Secret of the Incas,* 233.

52. Ibid., 234.

53. Calderwood, *Voices from the Dust*, 330.

54. Diego Durán, *The History of the Indies of New Spain*, (originally written in 1581 but not found until 1850 and partially published in 1867), translated, annotated, and with an introduction by Doris Heyden (University of Oklahoma Press, 1994), 57.

55. John E. Clark, "Geography," *To All The World: The Book of Mormon Articles* from the *Encyclopedia of Mormonism*, 97–101, (Provo, UT: Maxwell Institute, 2008), http://maxwellinstitute.byu.edu/publications/bookschapter.php?book, 2–3.

56. Charles Stanish and Amanda B. Cohen, "Introduction to 'Advances in Titicaca Basin Archaeology-1,' (Los Angeles: UCLA, 2007), 4, http://www.ioa.ucla.edu/stanish/publications/1_advances-fm_copy.pdf.

57. Michael Coe, "Mormons and Archaeology: An Outside View," *Dialogue: A Journal of Mormon Thought*, 8, no. 2 (Summer 1973), 42.

58. Mann, *1491: New Revelations of the Americas*, 197.

59. Calderwood, *Voices from the Dust*, 410.

60. Clark, "Geography," 2.

61. Alan L. Kolata, *The Tiwanaku: Portrait of an Andean Civilization* (Cambridge, MA: Blackwell Publishing, 1993), 40–41.

62. Kolata, *The Tiwanaku*, 43.

63. Ibid., 47–48.

64. Mann, *1491: New Revelations of the Americas*, 73–74.

CHAPTER 2

1. Mann, *1491: New Revelations of the Americas*, 203.

2. Laurent Beisie, "Civilization Lost?" *The Christian Science Monitor*, 3 January 2002, http://www.csmonitor.com/2002/0103/p11s1-woam.html, 2.

3. Mann, *1491: New Revelations of the Americas*, 205.

4. "Special Project Caral-Supe," 21 January 2008, http://www.caralperu.gob.pe/civilization_andes_ing.htm.

5. Ruth Shady Solis, *The Caral-Supe Peru, The Caral-Supe Civilization, 5000 Years of Cultural Identity in Peru*, (Lima: Projecto Especial Arqueológico Caral-Supe, I.N.C., 2005), 7.

6. Bruce R. McConkie, *Mormon Doctrine*, "Mahonri Moriancumer," 463.

7. Sorenson, "A Reconsideration of Early Metal in Mesoamerica," *Katunob* 9 (March 1976): 1–18. Cited by Jeff Lindsay at http://www.jefflindsay.com/LDSFAQ/FQ_metals.shtml#ores

8. Ibid.

9. 1 Kings 6:1 states that the exodus from Egypt occurred 480 years before the fourth year of Solomon's reign over Israel. Exodus 12:40 says that the children of Israel dwelt in Egypt for 430 years. At the time they entered Egypt, Jacob was 130 years old (Genesis 47:9). Isaac was 60 years old when Jacob was born (Genesis 25:26). Abram/Abraham was 100 years old when Isaac was born (Genesis 21:5). Genesis 11:10–26 gives us the genealogy of Abram back to Noah's son Shem, who is said to have begat Arphaxad two years after the Flood. The remaining ancestors of Abram and the ages when they begat their sons are all provided for us. From Shem to Abram, the total is 292 years. So, the computation of the date of the Flood would start in the fourth year of Solomon's reign (967 BCE). Add up the years in the unbroken chain of events back to Shem's begetting of Arphaxad (adding two more to get us back to the end of the Flood) and we get 1,494 years; see Mark Bakke, http://members.aol.com/JAlw/flood_myth.html.

10. Mann, *1491: New Revelations of the Americas*, 20.

11. "Olmecs," http://wsu.edu/~dee/CIVAMRCA/OLMECS.HTM

12. John E. Clark, "Debating the Foundation of Mormonism and Archaeology," speech given at the 2005 Conference of the Foundation for Apologetic Information and Research. Text available at http:www.fairlds.org/FAIR_Conference/2005_Debating_the_Foundations_of_Mormonism.html, (1 March 2008).

13. No author stated, "Archaeologists Shed New Light On America's Earliest Known Civilization," *Science Daily*, 4 January 2005, http://www.sciencedaily.com/releases/2005/01/050104112957.htm

14. Mann, *1491: New Revelations of the Americas*, 109.

15. Betanzos, *Narrative of the Incas*, 77.

16. Pedro de Cieza de León, *Incas of Pedro de Cieza de León*, (Norman, OK: University of Oklahoma Press, 1959 [1553])109, 113.

17. Ibid., 311.

18. Noah Webster, *American Dictionary of the English Language*, original edition 1828, (Chesapeake, Virginia, American Christian Education, 2006). See "Cattle."

19. William J. Hamblin, "Basic Methodological Problems with the Anti-Mormon Approach to the Geography and Archaeology of the Book of Mormon," *Journal of Book of Mormon*

Studies vol. 2 (Spring–Fall 1993): 194. (This article cites John L. Sorenson, *Geography of Book of Mormon Events*, 360).

20. "Arch," *Meridian Webster's Ninth New Collegiate Dictionary*, (Springfield, MA: Merriam-Webster, Inc, 1990), 100.

21. William Sullivan, *The Secret of the Incas, Myth, Astronomy, and the War Against Time* (New York: Three Rivers Press: 1996), 240.

22. http://252/chapmanresearch/elephant.html

23. Robin Lloyd, "Big Pig-Like Beast Discovered," *Live Science* (LiveScience.com, 2 November 2007) http.//news.yahoo.com/s/livescience/20071102/sc_livescience/bigpiglikebeastdiscovered, 3 November 2007.

24. Urton, *The Legendary Past*, 37.

25. Ibid., 34–35.

26. Martín de Murúa, *Historia General del Perú de los Orígenes al timo Inca*, originally written in 1611, (Información y Revista, S. A., Hermanos García Noblejas, 41 – 28037 Madrid. Historia, 1986), 49–50.

27. "The Book of Ether," *Evening and Morning Star* (Aug. 1832), 22.

28. Cobo, *History of the Inca Empire*, 94–95.

29. Ibid., 95.

30. Urton, *The Legendary Past*, 36.

31. Ibid.

32. Molina, Fr., "Relacion de las fabulas y ritos de los Yngas,' in H. Osborne, *South American Mythology*, 61

33. Pedro de Gamboa Sarmiento, *History of the Incas*, written circa AD 1570, translated by Clements Markham, (Cambridge: Haklugy Society, 1907) 28–58. Available at http:www.sacred-text.com/nam/inca/inca01.htm. 32.

34. John L. Sorenson, "Ancient Voyages Across the Ocean to America: From 'Impossible' to 'Certain,' " (Provo, UT: Maxwell Institute, 2005), 4–5.

35. Hiltunen, *Ancient Kings of Peru*, 354.

36. Janne M. Sjodahl, quoted on on-line at http://search.ldslibrary.com/article/view/976113, 8 January 2008.

37. Calderwood, *Voices from the Dust*, 287.

38. James Adair, *Adair's History of the American Indians*. 2d ed., edited by Samuel Cole Williams, (New York: Promontory Press, 1986), 229.

39. Cobo, *History of the Inca Empire*, 65–66.

40. "Insights: An Ancient Window," *The Newsletter of the Foundation for Ancient Research and Mormon Studies*, 1990, no. 3, (1990): 3. "Savoy's discoveries seem to open new areas of potential research, according to Dr. Ray Matheny, his host in Provo. While much remains to be done to verify his findings and determine their significance, he deserves credit for efforts in a geographic area that others shun because of the physical difficulty of doing research there."

41. Rev. Charles Forster, B.D., *The Historical Geography of Arabia* (London: Darf Publishers Limited, 1984), 77–133.

42. Ibid., 115.

43. Ibid., 12,

44. Some early Bible translations call Jerah "Jared" (see Smith and Sjodahl's commentary on the Book of Ether). Also, *Jared* in 1 Chronicles 1:2 is *Jered* according to Smith's Bible Dictionary (London, 1863, 1:964).

45. Genesis 10:9: Ophir's uncle is Peleg who lived when earth was divided. Ophir's brother is Jerah (Jared) 10:26, Jerah, Ophir, and other brothers move to Mesha at Sephar with a mountain on the east; 10:30—many scholars believe Sephar is Zopher or Dhofar in Oman, which harbor was called Mosha (Mesha) by the Greeks. The tallest mountain in all southern Oman is Mt. Samban on the east end of Dhofar. During their lifetimes, God confounds their languages, and the people are scattered (11:9).

46. McConkie, *Mormon Doctrine*, 463.

47. George Potter and Richard Wellington, *Lehi in the Wilderness: 81 New Documented Evidences that the Book of Mormon Is a True History* (Springville, UT: Cedar Fort Inc., 2002).

48. Ali Ahmed Ali Ash-Shahri, *Dhofar: Its Ancient Inscriptions and Writings and the Language of AAD* (Dhofar: Omani Ministry of Culture, no date), 30–35.

49. Bertram Thomas, *The Arabs* (London: Thornton Butterworth, 1937), 262. Nigel Groom also notes the similarity between the names of *Zufar* (*Dhofar*) and *Ophir*: *Zufar* is sometimes proposed as a likely word etymologically close to *Ophir*, while the nineteenth-century traveler Vod Wrede observed that the Mahra of south Arabia, who lived adjacent to Zufar and whose language has very ancient origins, used the word *ofir* to mean "red" and called themselves the tribe of "Ofir," meaning the "red country." (Nigel Groom, *Frankincense and Myrrh: A Study of the Arabian Incense Trade* [London: Longman, 1981], 49–50.) The Book of Mormon Commentary draws a correlation between Ophir and Bountiful: One of the sons of Joktan was so named. Very early some place, famous for its gold, also became known as Ophir. The name signifies, it is said, "red," or, as a name of a certain place, a "fruitful place," the same as "Bountiful," a prominent name in the story of the Book of Mormon.

50. George Potter, documentary film, *The Jaredites* (Bear River City, Utah: Nephi Project, 2004).

51. Mann, *1491: New Revelations of the Americas,* 209–212.

52. Calderwood, *Voices from the Dust,* 56.

53. Mann, *1491: New Revelations of the Americas,* 199–200.

54. Ibid., 201

55. Ibid., 19.

56. Ibid., 205.

57. Ibid., 206.

58. Randolph E. Schmid, "Andean find pushes earliest date of metalworking back 1,000 years," *The Associate Press,* 5 November 1998 (Washington), 1, 2, http://www.latinamericanstudies.org/inca/metal.htm.

59. The bronze plate discovered at Khor Rori is on display at the Frankincense Museum in Salalah, Oman. Observed by the author September 2006.

60. Calderwood, *Voices from the Dust,* 382–83.

61. Mann, *1491: New Revelations of the Americas,* 19.

62. Ibid., 206.

63. Kolata, *The Tiwanaku,* 41.

64. Mann, *1491: New Revelations of the Americas,* 207.

65. Noah Webster, *American Dictionary of the English Language,* original edition 1828; see "silk".

66. Mann, *1491: New Revelations of the Americas,* 207.

67. Calderwood, *Voices from the Dust,* 392.

68. Mann, *1491: New Revelations of the Americas,* 208–209.

69. Beisie, "Civilization Lost?" 2.

70. Mann, *1491: New Revelations of the Americas,* 186.

71. Ibid., 18.

72. Urton, *The Legendary Past,* 59.

73. Mann, *1491: New Revelations of the Americas,* 92.

74. John Hemming, *The Conquest of the Incas* (New York: Harcourt, Inc., 1970), 25.

75. P. J. Capelotti, "Easter Island and the Ra and *Viracocha* Expeditions," http://www.personal.psu.edu/faculty/p/j/pjc12/Easter%20Island%20and%20the%20Ra, (6/13/2007), 14.

76. Alan L. Kolata, *Valley of the Spirits: A Journey into the Lost Realm of the Aymara* (New York: John Wiley & Sons, 1996), 82.

77. Kolata, *The Tiwanaku,* 47.

78. McIntyre, "Lost Empire of the Incas," 739.

79. Kolata, *The Tiwanaku,* 19.

80. Mann, *1491: New Revelations of the Americas,* 249.

81. Julian H. Steward and Louis C. Faron, *Native Peoples of South America* (New York: McGraw-Hill, 1959), 46

82. Cieza de León, *Discovery and Conquest of Peru,* 59

83. Ibid., 112 (footnote 2) and 115.

84. Betanzos, *Narrative of the Incas,* 141.

85. Ibid., 148.

86. Ibid., 317.

87. Ibid., 235.

88. Ibid., 249.

89. Richard W. Bulliet, "Why They Lost the Wheel," *Saudi Aramco World,* May/June 1973, 24, No. 3 (Drahran, Saudi Arabia: 1973): 22–25.

90. For example see, Ron Shinnick, "Llama Driving, A Historical Perspective of Driving in the Southeastern U.S.," http://www.ssla.org/carting_driving.htm, 21 March 2007.

91. Bulliet, "Why They Lost the Wheel," 22–25.

92. Sarmiento, *History of the Incas,* 135–36.

93. Urton, *The Legendary Past,* 15.

94. Ibid.

95. Sullivan, *The Secret of the Incas,* 226.

96. Diego González Holguín, *Volcabulario de la lengua general de todo el Perú llamada lengua Quichua o del Inca* (Lima: Instituto de Historia, Universidad Nacional Mayor de San Cristobal de Humanaga, 1952), 54.

97. Joseph Fielding Smith, *Doctrines of Salvation,* vol. 3, 323.

98. "The Book of Ether," *Evening and Morning Star* (Aug. 1832), 22.

CHAPTER 3

1. Mann, *1491: New Revelations of the Americas,* 71.

2. Urton, *The Legendary Past,* 59; see also Thor Heyerdahl, 253.

3. Sarmiento, *History of the Incas,* 44.

4. Kolata, *The Tiwanaku,* 79–81.

5. The Metropolitan Museum of Art (New York), "Timeline of Art History, Central and Southern Andes, 1000 BC–AD 1," http://www.metmuseum.org/toah/ht/04/sac/ht04/sac.htm. Accessed February 12, 2007, 2.

6. Conversation with F. Al-Zamil, February 17, 2007.

7. http://www.netspace.org/~ewinard/cave-

church/meaning/htm.

8. Arthur Cotterell, *The Illustrated Encyclopaedia of Myths and Legends* (London: Guild Publishing, 1989, 174; and Osborne, *South American Mythology*), 68–88.

9. Kolata, *Valley of the Spirits*, 69.

10. See George Potter and Richard Wellington, *Lehi in the Wilderness*, 18.

11. Urton, *The Legendary Past*, 15.

12. Betanzos, *Narrative of the Incas*, 72.

13. Ibid., 269.

14. Cobo, *History of the Inca Empire*, 8.

15. Thor Heyerdahl, *Aku-Aku: The Secret of Easter Island* (London: George Allen & Unwin, 1988), 253.

16. John A. Tvedtnes, "A Brief History of the Limited Geographic View of the Book of Mormon," *Meridian Magazine*, 31 October 2007, 5.

17. Calderwood, *Voices from the Dust*, 315–32.

18. Ibid., 320 (quoting Pizarro, Spanish edition, 241).

19. Ibid., 322.

20. Guthrie, James L. "Human Lymphocyte Antigens: Apparent Afro-Asiatic, Southern Asian, and European HLAs in Indigenous American Populations," *Pre-Columbiana*, vol. 2 and 3 (Dec. 2000/June 2001): 90–163. Available online at NEARA.org. See Summary # 5, 6, 10, 12.

21. Cieza de León, *Incas of Pedro de Cieza de León*, 64.

22. Urton, *The Legendary Past*, 32.

23. Ibid., 32–33.

24. Arthur J. Kocherhans, *Lehi's Isle of Promise* (Fullerton, CA: Et Cetera, 1989), 117.

25. Kocherhans, *Lehi's Isle of Promise*, 109–110.

26. Mann, *1491: New Revelations of the Americas*, 86.

27. Helaine Silverman and Donald A. Proulx, *The Nasca: The Peoples of America* series (Oxford: Blackwell Publishing, 2002), 40.

28. Cieza de León, *Discovery and Conquest of Peru*, 112.

29. Cobo, *History of the Inca Empire*, 236.

30. No author, "Nevados de Chilán Biological Corridor" *The Nature Conservancy*, 27 June 2007, http://nature.org/wherewework/southamerica/chile/work/art5115.html. "The huemel, an Andean deer that is Chile's national symbol, counts on the Nevados de Chilián for food and shelter. The endangered animal might look like a deer, but it behaves more like a mountain goat."

31. Kocherhans, *Lehi's Isle of Promise*, 112, 114.

32. Ibid., 114; see also "Chile, major mining and manufacturing centers," *Rand McNalley for World Book*.

33. Urton, *The Legendary Past*, 54.

34. Sullivan, *Secret of the Incas*, 25.

35. Betanzos, *Narrative of the Incas*, 29.

36. Sullivan, *Secret of the Incas*, 24.

37. H. Osborne, *South American Mythology* (London: Paul Hamlyn, 1968), 74.

38. bid., 74.

39. Ibid., 74.

40. Sarmiento, *History of the Incas*, 31.

41. Calderwood, *Voices from the Dust*, 190.

42. Ibid., 203, 246–247, 248–250.

43. Sullivan, *Secret of the Incas*, 26

44. Cited by Sullivan, *Secret of the Incas*, 27.

45. Sullivan, *Secret of the Incas*, 27.

46. Ibid., 28.

47. Ibid., 29.

48. Urton, *The Legendary Past*, 41.

49. Ibid., 41, 42.

50. Felipe Guaman Poma de Ayala, *Nueva Corónica y Buen Gobierno*, 41. Original manuscript finished in 1615, but not discovered until 1908 by Richard Pietschmann and published in 1936. Transcript, Prologue, Notes y Chronology by Franklin Pease. (This edition was printed in Venezuela by Biblioteca Ayacucho Caracas, Venezuela, 1978.)

51. Cieza de León, *Discovery and Conquest of Peru*, 416.

52. Ibid., 436.

53. Sullivan, *Secret of the Incas*, 47.

54. Betanzos, *Narrative of the Incas*, 161.

55. Ibid., 168.

56. Sarmiento, *History of the Incas*, 168.

57. Cieza de León, *Discovery and Conquest of Peru*, 260.

58. Cieza de León, *Discovery and Conquest of Peru*, 274.

59. Sullivan, *Secret of the Incas*, 307, 308.

60. Elizabeth Ana Klarich, *From the Monumental to the Mundane: Defining Early Leadership Strategies at Late Formative Pukara, Peru*, Dissertation (Santa Barbara: University of California San Barbara), 19.

61. Bauer, *Ancient Cuzco*, 51.

62. Betanzos, *Narrative of the Incas*, 94.

63. Ibid., 94–95.

64. Calderwood, *Voices from the Dust*, 172–174.

65. Ibid., 179.

66. Sullivan, *Secret of the Incas*, 56–57.

67. Ibid., 57.

68. Calderwood, *Voices from the Dust*, 180–181.

69. Betanzos, *Narrative of the Incas*, 105.

70. Ibid., 105.

71. The Metropolitan Museum of Art (New York), "Timeline of Art History, Central and Southern Andes, 1000 BC—AD 1, http://www.metmuseum.org/toah/ht/04/sac/ht04/sac.htm. (February 12, 2007), 1.

72. Sullivan, *Secret of the Incas*, 157.

73. Ibid., 174.

74. Ibid., 219.

75. Ibid., 219.

76. Betanzos, *Narrative of the Incas*, 129.

77. Ibid., 103.

78. Ibid., 109.

79. Ibid., 111.

80. Sullivan, *Secret of the Incas*, 125.

81. Sarmiento, *History of the Incas*, 27

82. Mann, *1491: New Revelations of the Americas*, 81.

83. Betanzos, *Narrative of the Incas*, 99.

84. The Church of Jesus Christ of Latter-day Saints, "All Is Safely Gathered In, Family Home Storage" 2007.

85. Polo De Ondegardo, "Report by Polo De Ondegardo, Manuscript in the National Library at Madrid," 4 to, on parchment, B. 135, See http://www.sacred-texts.com/nam/inca/rly/rly4.htm), 8/30/2006, 3.

86. Bauer, *Ancient Cuzco*, 98.

87. Cobo, *History of the Inca Empire*, 218–219.

88. Ibid., 221.

89. Calderwood, *Voices from the Dust*, 259.

90. Sullivan, *Secret of the Incas*, 103.

91. Ibid., 221.

92. Calderwood, *Voices from the Dust*, 241.

93. Silverman and Proulx, *The Nasca*, 73.

94. Alan Sawyer, quoted by Silverman and Proulx, *The Nasca*, 62.

95. Silverman and Proulx, *The Nasca*, 63.

96. Hemming, *Conquest of the Incas*, 60, 61.

97. McIntyre, "Lost Empire of the Incas," 780.

98. Kolata, *The Tiwanaku*, 167.

99. Betanzos, *Narrative of the Incas*, 168, 179.

100. Ibid., 174.

101. Cobo, *History of the Inca Empire*, 109.

102. Betanzos, *Narrative of the Incas*, 178.

103. Mann, *1491: New Revelations of the Americas*, 93.

104. Sullivan, *Secret of the Incas*, 48.

105. Richard Harris, "Oldest Solar Observatory in Americas Found in Peru," National Public Radio, April 28, 2007, (http://www.npr.org/templates/story/story.php?storyId=7658847,) 1

106. McIntyre, "Lost Empire of the Incas," 766.

107. Kolata, *The Tiwanaku*, 7.

108. Sullivan, *Secret of the Incas*, 212.

109. Klarich, *From the Monumental to the Mundane*, 80; author cites Couture, 2002; Janusek, 2003; Goldstein, 1993, 2003.

110. Klarich, *From the Monumental to the Mundane*, 46.

111. Mann, *1491: New Revelations of the Americas*, 24.

112. Sullivan, *Secret of the Incas*, 212.

113. Kolata, *The Tiwanaku*, 8.

114. T. Bouyee-Cassagne, "Urco and Uma: Aymara concepts of space," in J. Murra, N. Wachtel and J. Revel (eds.), *Anthropological History of Andean Polities* (Cambridge: Cambridge University Press, 1986), 209.

115. Kolata, *The Tiwanaku*, 34.

CHAPTER 4

1. Sullivan, *Secret of the Incas*, 48.

2. Polo De Ondegardo, "Report by Polo De Ondegardo, Manuscript in the National Library at Madrid," 4 to, on parchment, B. 135) see http://www.sacred-texts.com/nam/inca/rly/rly4.htm), 8/30/2006, 3.

3. De Ondegardo, "Report," 5–6.

4. Cobo, *History of the Inca Empire*, 214.

5. Ibid., 213.

6. Kolata, *Valley of the Spirits*, 61.

7. Mann, *1491: New Revelations of the Americas*, 3.

8. Ibid., 4.

9. Ibid., 5.

10. Ibid., 13.

11. Betanzos, *Narrative of the Incas*, 309.

12. De Ondegardo, "Report," 1.

13. Calderwood, *Voices from the Dust*, 298.

14. Hugh Nibley, *Old Testament and Related Studies*, Eds. John W. Welch, Gary P. Gillum, and Don E. Norton, *The Collected Works of Hugh Nibley*, vol. 1 (Salt Lake City: Deseret Book, 1986), 135.

15. Potter and Wellington, *Lehi in the Wilderness*, 3.

16. Conversation between Hugh Nibley and author at Brigham Young University, August 13, 2001.

17. Arthur J. Kocherhans, *Nephi to Zarahemla* (Orem, Utah: Granite Publishing, 2002), 48–49.

18. Janne M. Sjodahl, *An Introduction to the Study of the Book of Mormon*, 118–119.

19. Ibid.

20. Urton, *The Legendary Past*, 36–37.

21. Hemming, *Conquest of the Incas*, 16.

22. Bauer, *Ancient Cuzco*, 73.

23. Osborne, *South American Mythology*, 87.

24. Urton, *The Legendary Past*, 15.

25. Mann, *1491: New Revelations of the Americas*, 71.

26. Cieza de León, *Discovery and Conquest of Peru*, 264.

27. Menzies, *1421: The Year China Discovered the World*, 546.

28. Kocherhans, *Nephi to Zarahemla*, 24.

29. Cobo, *History of the Inca Empire*, 223.

30. Hammond Innes, *The Conquistadors* (New York: Alfred A. Khopf, 1969), 259.

31. McIntyre, "Lost Empire of the Incas," 780–81.

32. Ibid., 782.

33. Calderwood, *Voices from the Dust*, 427.

34. Cook, "Untangling the Mystery of the Inca," 144.

35. Cobo, *History of the Inca Empire*, 229.

36. Ibid., 230.

37. Calderwood, *Voices from the Dust*, 288.

38. Bauer, *Ancient Cuzco*, 154.

39. Urton, *The Legendary Past*, 39–40.

40. Ibid., 39.

41. Sullivan, *Secret of the Incas*, 37, 51.

42. Ibid., 226.

43. Ibid., 223.

44. No author stated, "Travel across the 'Narrow Neck of Land,' (Provo, Utah: Maxwell Institute, BYU, 2000) 10 June 2008, 1, http://maxwellinstitute.byu.edu/display-print.php?table=insights&id=132.

45. General Authorities of the LDS Church have told the Hawaiians that they are descendents of Hagoth. The narrow neck of land was where Hagoth built his ships, and seafaring culture was south of the Hawaiian Islands (Hagoth sailed north). Hagoth's sailing from Peru was possibly replicated by the Inca Tupa Inca Yupanqui, who sailed to the islands he called *Hahua Chumpi* and *Nina Chumpi*. Calderwood cites: "Manuel Ballasteros Gambrios. . .wrote that in Quechua *Chumpi* means a belt or ring and *Nina* means fire. Ballasteros suggests that Tupa Inca Yupanqui may have discovered some islands surrounded by fire or where there was an active volcano. This similarity in the sounds between Hahua or Hawa and Hawaii cannot be overlooked nor considered mere coincidence" (Calderwood, *Voices from the Dust*, 372). Furthermore the narrow neck of land was a place where a person could cross it in one and a half days. These two characteristics would seem to eliminate both the Isthmus of Tehuantepec or Panama as the place where he built his ship. Neither are located in a southerly direction from Hawaii or the Polynesian Islands. The Isthmus of Tehuantepec with a width of 137 miles could not have been traveled in one and a half days. It is tempting to look at a map of the Western Hemisphere and conclude that the narrow strip of land mentioned in the Book of Mormon is the Isthmus of Panama, which is only thirty at its narrowest width. A boots-on-the-ground look will provide another perspective. Panama is nearly impossible to cross. So impassible is the Isthmus of Panama that the 29,800 mile–long Pan-American Highway from Circle Alaska to Puerto Montt has never been completed. There remains the fifty-four-mile gap in the highway due to the Darién Jungle along the Panama-Columbia border. To this day, the Darién remains an untamed rainforest full of quicksand, swamps, and insects. Another evidence that the Panama Isthmus was impassible in one day is the fact that it remains isolated while lying between large civilizations to its north and south. On the one hand, the lack of DNA diversity among the Ngöbé native Indians of Panama indicates that they had little contact with outside groups, and their DNA shows that the Ngöbé did not intermarry with other people for thousands of years. On the other hand, there is possible evidence that Hagoth and his people sailed from South America. Genetic research by Dr. Rebecca Cann of the University of Hawaii indicates that there exist DNA links between four tribes in South America and the Polynesians in Samoa (see "New Light," Maxwell Institute, (Provo, Utah: 2000), http://farms.byu.edu/display.php?id=217&table-jbms). To date, no DNA links have been found between Polynesian nations and the indigenous people in Mesoamerica.

46. *Merriam Webster's*, 694.

47. Noah Webster, *American Dictionary of the English Language*, original edition 1828, (Chesapeake, Virginia, American Christian Education, 2006). See "line," 11.

48. F. Richard Hauck, *Deciphering the Geography of the Book of Mormon* (Salt Lake City: Deseret Book, 1988), 12.

49. Webster, *American Dictionary of the English Language*; see "pass."

50. *Merriam Webster's*, 908.

51. Webster, *American Dictionary of the English Language*; see "point."

52. Hauck, *Deciphering the Geography*, 12–13.

53. Sullivan, *Secret of the Incas*, 223.

54. Cieza de León, *Discovery and Conquest of Peru*, 181–183, see footnotes 3 and 4 on page 183.

55. Cobo, *History of the Inca Empire*, 225.

56. Hemming, *Conquest of the Incas*, 31.

57. UNESCO, World Heritage, "Archaeological Complex of," http://whc.unesco.org/en/tentativelist/512/ (accessed 5 July 2007).

58. Karen E. Stothert, "The Villa Salvador Site and the Beginning of the Early Intermediate Period in the Lurin Valley, Peru," *Journal of Field Archaeology* 7, no. 3 (Autumn, 1980): 279.

59. Clark, "Geography," 2.

CHAPTER 5

1. "Lehi . . . landed on the continent of South America in Chili [Chile] thirty degrees south latitude." This is a statement attributed to Joseph Smith, Jr. by Apostle Franklin D. Richards and Apostle James A. Little, and accepted by Orson Pratt, and printed in the footnotes of the 1879 edition of the Book of Mormon (see *Encyclopedia of Mormonism*, vol. 1, "Book of Mormon Geography").

2. See http://www3.nationalgeographic.com/genographic/altas.html.

3. No author stated, "Thousands of Humans Inhabited New World's Doorstep for 20,000 years," *Science Daily*, 13 February 2008, http://www.sciencedaily.com/release/2008/02/080213090524.htm (type Mulligan into Search box), (credit: Kitchen, A, Miyamoto MM, Mulligan, CJ, *A Three-Stage Colonization Model for the People of the Americas*).

4. Carrie A. Moore, "Intro Change in Book of Mormon spurs discussion," *Deseret Morning News*, 9 November 2007, http://deseretnews.com/dn/view/1%2C1249%2C695226049%2C00.html.

5. Michael F. Whiting, "DNA and the Book of Mormon: A Phylogenetic Perspective," *Journal of Book of Mormon Studies* 12, Issue 1, (2003), 24–25.

6. Hugh Nibley, *Collected Works of Hugh Nibley*, vol. 8, 223–224.

7. Heyerdahl, *Aku-Aku*, 253.

8. Betanzos, *Narrative of the Incas*, 13.

9. Ibid., 14.

10. Ibid., 17.

11. Ibid., 13–14.

12. Sarmiento, *History of the Incas*, 45.

13. Potter and Wellington, *Lehi in the Wilderness*, 142.

14. Betanzos, *Narrative of the Incas*, 226.

15. Ibid., 311.

16. Ibid., 237.

17. Cieza de León, *Discovery and Conquest of Peru*, 108.

18. Jared Diamond, *Guns, Germs, and Steel: The Fates of Human Societies* (New York: W. W. Norton & Company, 1997), 73.

19. Ibid., 76.

20. Sarmiento, *History of the Incas*, 44.

21. Ibid., 45.

22. Ibid., 44.

23. Cobo, *History of the Inca Empire*, 108.

24. Sjodahl, *Introduction to the Study*, 303.

25. Betanzos, *Narrative of the Incas*, 72.

26. Brigham Young, *Journal of Discourses*, vol. 11, 10 February 1867, 326–27.

27. Hugh Nibley, *Collected Works of Hugh Nibley*, vol. 6, 72–73.

28. Noah Webster, *American Dictionary of the English Language*; see "unite."

29. Bauer, *Ancient Cuzco*, 29.

30. Cobo, *History of the Inca Empire*, 237.

31. Bauer, *Ancient Cuzco*, 89.

32. LDS Bible Dictionary (Salt Lake City: The Church of Jesus Christ of Latter-day Saints, 1979), 699.

33. Urton, *The Legendary Past*, 41.

34. Bauer, *Ancient Cuzco*, 15, 17.

35. Ibid., 17.

36. Pedro Pizarro, *Relacíon del Descubrimiento y Conquita de Los Reinos del Perú*. Original manuscript presented in Arequipa, Peru on 28 March 1572. First printed in the late 1870's (current edition with notes and preliminary considerations by Guillermo Lohmann Villena and Pierre Duviols by Pontifica Universidad Catolica del Peru, 1896) 241, quoted by Calderwood, *Voices from the Dust*, 320).

37. Betanzos, *Narrative of the Incas*, 272.

38. Calderwood, *Voices from the Dust*, 321.

39. Carolyn Dean, *Inka Bodies and the Body of Christ: Corpus Christi in Colonial Cuzco* (Durham, NC: Duke University Press, 1999), 192, 258 n. 14.

40. Kocherhans, *Nephi in Zarahemla*, 80.

41. Kocherhans, *Lehi's Isle of Promise*, 117.

42. "Lehi. . . landed on the continent of South

America in Chili [Chile] thirty degrees south latitude," This is a statement attributed to Joseph Smith, Jr. by Apostle Franklin D. Richards and Apostle James A. Little, and accepted by Orson Pratt and printed in the footnotes of the 1879 edition of the Book of Mormon; see *Encyclopedia of Mormonism*, vol. 1, "Book of Mormon Geography."

43. Héctor Hugo Varela, José Alberto Cocilovo, Calogero M. Santoro and Francisco Roth-hammer, "Microevolution of Human Archaic Groups of Arica, Northern Chile, and Its Genetic Contribution to Populations from the Formative Period," *Revista Chilena De Historica Natural*, v. 79 n. 2, (Santiago: 2006), 185–193. http://www.scielo.cl/scielo.php?pid=S0716-078X2006000200005&Script=sci_arttext (accessed October 17, 2006).

44. Varela, et al, "Microevolution," 9.

45. Cieza de Léon, quoted by Silverman and Proulx, *The Nasca*, 41.

46. Sullivan, *Secret of the Incas*, 116.

47. Merriam Webster's, 1020, see "rod."

48. Bauer, *Ancient Cuzco*, 157.

49. Cobo, *History of the Inca Empire*, 105.

50. Ibid., 108.

51. Ibid., 109.

52. Ibid., 110

53. Urton, *The Legendary Past*, 52.

54. Sarmiento, *History of the Incas*, 47.

55. Ibid., 61.

56. Bauer, *Ancient Cuzco*, 172.

57. Ibid., 41–43, 186.

58. Steve Jones, *In the Blood, God, Genes, and Destiny* (London: Harper Collins Publishers, 1996), 80–82.

59. Sullivan, *Secret of the Incas*, 136.

60. Mann, *1491: New Revelations of the Americas*, 397.

61. Juha Hiltunen, "Separating Invention from Possible Inherited Traditions in the Chronicle of Montesinos," *Traditional High Cultures*, 7 January 2008. http://www.traditionalhigh-cultures.com/HiltunenPaper.htm .

62. Bill Cooper, "The Kings of the Ancient Britons: Chronology," *The Early History of Man*—Part 3, *Bible Believers*, 1 January 2008, http://www.biblebelievers.org.au/nation08.htm.

63. Hugh Nibley, *Collected Works of Hugh Nibley*, vol. 6, 46–47.

64. Bauer, *Ancient Cuzco*, 160.

65. Lynn Hilton and Hope Hilton, *Discovering Lehi: New evidence of Lehi and Nephi in Arabia* (Springville, UT: Cedar Fort Inc., 1996), 91.

66. Hugh Nibley, *Collected Works of Hugh Nibley*, vol. 6., 76.

67. Calderwood, *Voices from the Dust*, 306–307.

68. Urton, *The Legendary Past*, 45.

69. *The Facts on File Encyclopedia of World Mythology and Legend*, (London and Oxford 1988), 657.

70. McIntyre, "Lost Empire of the Incas," 741.

71. Charles Stanish, "An Archaeological Summary of the Island of the Sun and the Moon," published 30 May 2007, http://www.ioa.ucla.edu/staff/stanish/islands/archinfo.html.

72. Aymara Indian guide John to author, 5 June 2008, Isle of the Sun, Lake Titicaca, Bolivia.

73. Charles Stanish and Amanda B. Cohen, "Introduction to Advances," 5.

74. Victor Wolfgang Von Hagen, *The Incas of Pedro de Cieza de Leon*, translated by Harriet de Onis (Norman, OK: University of Okla-

homa Press, 1959), 93.

75. Sarmiento, *History of the Incas*, 47.

76. Ibid., 49.

77. Bauer, *Ancient Cuzco*, 17; see map 2.1 "The Inca heartland and its ethnic groups."

78. Urton, *The Legendary Past*, 47.

79. Ibid., 48.

80. Michael Mosley, *Incas and Their Ancestors* (New York: Thames and Hudson Publishing, 1992), 54–55.

81. Orson Pratt, in the *Journal of Discourses*, vol. 12, December 27, 1868, 342.

82. Betanzos, *Narrative of the Incas*, 277.

83. Sarmiento, *History of the Incas*, 62.

84. Urton, *The Legendary Past*, 48–49.

85. Sarmiento, *History of the Incas*, 48–49.

86. Ibid., 49.

87. Ibid.

88. Gaskill, *Lost Language of Symbolism*, 99.

89. Dean, *Inka Bodies and the Body of Christ*, 100.

90. Sarmiento, *History of the Incas*, 49.

91. Hiltons, *Discovering Lehi* 91.

92. Sullivan, *Secret of the Incas*, 235.

93. Sarmiento, *History of the Incas*, 51

94. Ibid, 48.

95. Betanzos, *Narrative of the Incas*, 14.

96. Ibid., 16–17.

97. Urton, *The Legendary Past*, 48–49.

98. Sarmiento, *History of the Incas*, 46.

99. Cobo, *History of the Inca Empire*, 114.

100. Jones, *In the Blood, God, Genes, and Destiny*, 46.

101. Paul A. Baker, Sherilyn C. Fritz, and Geoffrey O. Seltzer, "Lake Titicaca: An Archive

from South American Paleoclimate", December 2001, http://www.ariweb.org/geotimes/dec01/feature_titicaca.html (accessed February 2007).

CHAPTER 6

1. McIntyre, "Lost Empire of the Incas," 764.
2. Cieza de Léon, *Discovery and Conquest of Peru,* 317–319.
3. Bauer, *Ancient Cuzco,* 106 (quoting Garcilaso de la Vega, 1966: 417–430 [1609: Pt. 1, Bk. 7, Chs. 8–11]).
4. Bauer, *Ancient Cuzco,* 110 (cites Sancho, 1971: 153–154 [1534]).
5. Bauer, *Ancient Cuzco,* 129–130.
6. Ibid., 110.
7. Ibid., 114,
8. Garcilaso de la Vega, *Royal commentaries of the Incas and general history of Peru*, part 1, translated by Harold V. Livermore (Austin: University of Texas, University Press, 1966), 504.
9. Bauer, *Ancient Cuzco,* 7.
10. Betanzos, *Narrative of the Incas*, 13.
11. Bauer, *Ancient Cuzco,* 40.
12. Ibid., 41.
13. Urton, *The Legendary Past,* 52.
14. *LDS Bible Dictionary,* 786–7.
15. Urton, *The Legendary Past,* 50.
16. Bauer, *Ancient Cuzco,* 26.
17. Urton, *The Legendary Past,* 51.
18. Ibid.
19. Ibid., 40.
20. Bauer, *Ancient Cuzco,* 6.
21. Ibid., 41.
22. Ibid., 44.

23. Cobo, *History of the Inca Empire,* 106.
24. Ibid., 245.
25. Sarmiento, *History of the Incas,* 73 (footnote 2).
26. Ibid., 73.
27. Bauer, *Ancient Cuzco,* 155.
28. Ibid., 157.
29. Ibid., 3.
30. Cobo, *History of the Inca Empire,* 110.
31. Bauer, *Ancient Cuzco,* 139.
32. Ibid., 157.
33. Ibid., 157.
34. Sullivan, *Secret of the Incas,* 297.
35. Ibid.
36. Bauer, *Ancient Cuzco,* 149.
37. Joseph Fielding McConkie, *Gospel Symbolism* (Salt Lake City: Bookcraft, 1985) 102–103.
38. Bauer, *Ancient Cuzco,* 143.
39. Bauer, *Ancient Cuzco,* 146.
40. Ibid., 143.
41. Ibid.
42. Ibid., 139.
43. Ibid., 144.
44. Ibid., 144.
45. Ibid., 145.
46. Ibid., 145.
47. Betanzos, *Narrative of the Incas,* 16.
48. Mosley, *Incas and Their Ancestors,* 74–79.
49. Bauer, *Ancient Cuzco,* 148.
50. Ibid.
51. Mosley, *Incas and Their Ancestors* 74–79.
52. Bauer, *Ancient Cuzco,* 157.
53. Gaskill, *Lost Language of Symbolism,* 156.

54. Urton, *The Legendary Past,* 49.
55. Bauer, *Ancient Cuzco,* 148.
56. http://www.yahrzeit.org/text_link/temple_text1/textpage224.htm.
57. Mann, *1491: New Revelations of the Americas,* 79.
58. http://en.allexpert.com/e/s/so/solomon's_temple.htm.
59. Cieza de León, *Discovery and Conquest of Peru,* 321, footnote 2; see also Hemming, *Conquest of the Incas,* 132–34.
60. H. Osborne, *South America Mythology* (London: Paul Hamlyn, 1968), 81.
61. 3 Nephi 9–28.
62. Sullivan, *Secret of the Incas,* 319.
63. *The Jewish Encyclopaedia,* vol. II (New York, Funk, and Wagnell, 1925), 105.
64. Gaskill, *Lost Language of Symbolism,* 92.
65. Hemming, *Conquest of the Incas,* 134.
66. LDS Bible Dictionary, 607.
67. http://inkasperu.com/tours/jpg_files/jpg_photos/titicaca/puno_pucara_pueblo.jpg, 25 November 2007.
68. Sullivan, *Secret of the Incas,* 106–107.
69. Ibid., 103, 106.
70. Ibid., 104.
71. Sullivan, *Secret of the Incas,* 103–105.
72. Potter and Wellington, *Lehi in the Wilderness,* also see George Potter documentary film, *The Tree of Life* (Bear River City, Utah: Bear River Training and Consultancy, 2005).
73. Sarmiento, *History of the Incas,* 41–42.
74. Boyd K. Packer, "Scriptures," *Ensign,* Nov. 1982, 51.
75. Monte S. Nyman, *Abomination of Desolation*

(Springville, UT: Cedar Fort Inc., 2006), 24–25.

76. Cobo, *History of the Inca Empire*, 249.

77. Joseph Smith, *Teachings of the Prophet Joseph Smith*, sel. Joseph Fielding Smith (Salt Lake City: Deseret Book, 1976), 308.

78. Sullivan, *Secret of the Incas*, 116.

79. Ibid., 127.

80. Ibid., 127.

81. *Merriam Webster's*, 1146,

82. LDS Bible Dictionary, 763.

83. Gaskill, *Lost Language of Symbolism*, 281.

84. Bauer, *Ancient Cuzco*, 154.

85. Sullivan, *Secret of the Incas*, 43.

86. Ibid., 44.

87. Ibid., 33.

88. Ibid., 36.

89. Mosley, *Incas and Their Ancestors*, 74–79.

90. Bruce W. Warren, "Mesoamerican Jaredite Calendar Relationship?" *Ancient America Foundation* (AAF) Newsletter, 10 April 2007, 1, http://www.ancientamerica.org.

91. Ibid., 2.

92. Cobo, *History of the Inca Empire*, 252.

93. Sullivan, *Secret of the Incas*, 318.

94. Hemming, *Conquest of the Incas*, 124.

95. Bauer, *Ancient Cuzco*, 93.

96. Sullivan, *Secret of the Incas*, 316.

97. Kolata, *Valley of the Spirits*, 104.

98. Cobo, *History of the Inca Empire*, 135.

99. Sullivan, *Secret of the Incas*, 235.

100. Mosley, *Incas and Their Ancestors*, 74–79.

101. Kocherhans, *Nephi to Zarahemla*, 70–71.

102. Ibid., 73–79.

103. Bauer, *Ancient Cuzco*, 98–99.

104. Mosley, *Incas and Their Ancestors*, 74–79.

105. McIntyre, "Lost Empire of the Incas," 764.

106. Ibid.

107. Betanzos, *Narrative of the Incas*, 157–158.

108. Bauer, *Ancient Cuzco*, 100.

109. Ibid., 44.

110. Ibid., 186.

111. Ibid., 182.

112. Sullivan, *Secret of the Incas*, 115–116.

CHAPTER 7

1. According to the oral traditions recorded by Juan de Betanzos, Viracocha Inca had a son named Inca Yapanki. This younger son, refused to leave Cuzco, and with his three friends defeated the entire army of the Chanca. The story of Inca Yapanki's conquest of the Chanca army with only his own efforts and that of three friends makes him a superhero in Inca traditions. It is said that "he fought the Chanca with such bravery that (according to the legend) the very stones rose up to join the fray" (Mann, *1491: New Revelations of the Americas*, 76) The legendary drama that subsequently took place between him and his father, Viracocha Inca, was so Shakespearian in nature, that many scholars question where it actually took place. Mann writes, "The family story makes such terrific melodrama that it seems reasonable to wonder whether it actually happened. . . . some scholars dismiss the chronicles entirely" (Mann, *1491: New Revelations of the Americas*, 76). The Spanish chronicler, Jesuit Bernabé Cobo dismissed the ties of the later Incas to the Viracocha four brothers as "ludicrous" (Mann, *1491:*

New Revelations of the Americas, 75). In my opinion the storybook rise to power of Inca Yapanki, as the first Inca who declared himself the son of the sun, is an attempt to legitimize his right to rule by creating the story that his father was Viracocha Inca, a person that seems to have lived nearly two thousands years before him. Remember, Inca Yapanki was not the legitimate heir to the throne; he took it from his older brother Inca Urqon. Thus, Inca Yapanki not only made up an heroic story of how he defended the nation, he also created a false genealogy tracking his lineage back to the first colonizers of Cuzco—the famed Manco Capac [Inca] and the other kings for the first eight generations of Cuzco rulers. Cuzco was colonized in 500 BC, not seven generations before Inca Yapanki, who lived during the fifteen century AD. Having the Inca empire's founder legendized by wild tales of his conquest and savvy is reminiscent of the myth that George Washington chopped down his father's cherry tree. Creating a false genealogy that claims he was a descendant of Manco Capac is no more surprising than the European monarchs having creating false genealogies to claim that they were descendants of the house of David (Jones, *In the Blood, God, Genes, and Destiny*, 80–82). In other words, the first eight generations of Cuzco rulers, from the city's founder Manco Capac until Viracocha Inca's abandonment of the city, appears to be the actually story of the first eight rulers of Cuzco, but Inca Yapanki's Herculean account is out of context with time and realism.

2. Betanzos, *Narrative of the Incas*, 22.

3. Ibid.

4. Cástulo Martínez, *El Descubrimiento de América Crónica de Horror y Atropello a los Dere-*

chos Humanos translated by Cástulo Martínez (Las Paz, Bolivia: Librería Editorial Juventud: 2001) provided to author by Cástulo Martínez by email on 3 January 2009.

5. Betanzos, *Narrative of the Incas*, 18.

6. Kolata, *The Tiwanaku*, 77.

7. Arthur J. Kocherhans, *A True and Ancient Record*, (Orem, UT: Granite Publishing, 2002), 104–105.

8. Kocherhans, *Nephi to Zarahemla*, 112.

9. Klarich, *From the Monumental to the Mundane*, 45.

10. Ibid., 67.

11. Ibid., 45.

12. E. Mujica, "Peculiaridades del proceso histórico temprano en la cuenca norte de Titicaca." *Una propuesta inicial. Boletín del laboratoriao de arquelogía* 2:75–122, quoted by Klarich, *From the Monumental to the Mundane*, 69.

13. L. H. Steadman, *Excavations at Camata: an Early Ceramic Chronology for the Western Titicaca Basin, Peru.* Unpublished PhD dissertation, University of California, Berkeley: 1995.

14. Klarich, *From the Monumental to the Mundane*, 45.

15. Klarich, *From the Monumental to the Mundane*, 20; see also C. S. Stanish, *Ancient Titicaca: The Evolution of Complex Society in Southern Peru and Northern Bolivia* (Berkeley: University of California Press, 2003), 111.

16. Mann, *1491: New Revelations of the Americas*, 3.

17. Kolata, *The Tiwanaku*, 70.

18. Ibid., 71–73.

19. Urton, *The Legendary Past*, 21.

20. Mann, *1491: New Revelations of the Americas*, 269.

21. Ibid., 258.

22. Rene Garreaud, Mathiasu Vuille, and Amy C. Clements, "The Climate of the Altiplano: observed current conditons and mechanisms of past changes," *Palaeogeograph, Palaeoclimate, Palaeoecology* 194 (2003): 6.

23. Ibid, 8.

24. M. Garcia, D. Raes, S.-E Jacoben, T. Michel, "Agroclimatic constraints for rain fed agriculture in the Bolivian Altiplano," *Journal of Arid Environments* 71, Issue 1 (October 2007): 109.

25. Canadian Foreign Affairs Ministry, "Peru," Foreign Affairs and Internationl Trade Canada, see Voyage.gc.ca, (accessed 15 May 2008).

26. Dr. Timothy Evans, discussion with author, Oakley, Utah, September 2007.

27. During the author's mission he was warned by the Peruvian Health Ministry and the Peru Mission to not drink tap water during the rainy season.

28. Nathaniel C. Nash, "Youth Trampled in Peru's Gold Rush," quoting Dr. Carlos Manrique, *New York Times,* 17 May 2008, originally printed 26 August 1991; see http://query.nytimes.com/gst/fullpage.html?res=9DOCE4DF1431F935A1575BCOA967958260.

29. Center for Disease Control and Prevention, "Health Information for Travelers to Peru," 17 May 2008, http://wwwn.cdc.gov-health information for Peru.

30. No author stated, "Herbals and Alternative Medicine," *Peru Herbals*, 17 May 2008, http://www.peruherbals.com/3030/medicine.html.

31. Bauer, *Ancient Cuzco,* 25.

32. Ibid., 29.

33. Ibid., 26.

34. Josyane Ronchail & Robert Gallaire, "ENSO and rainfall along the Zongo valley (Bolivia) from the Altiplano to the Amazon basin," Smithsonian/NASA ADS Physics Abstract Service, http://absabs.harvard.edu/abs/2006IJCli.26.1223R, (accessed 3 December 2007), 1.

35. US National Oceanic and Atmospheric Administration, "Answers to La Niña," http://www.elnino.noaa.gov/lanina_new_faq.html, (accessed 3 December 2007), 1.

36. International Red Cross and Red Crescent Societies (IFRC), "Bolivia Floods Appeal No. 05/01 Situation Report No. 3." http://www.reliefweb.int/rw/rwb.nsf/db900sid/OCHA-64BQ3E?OpenDocument, (accessed 3 December 2007), 1.

37. Stephen Cviic, "Peru battles locust plague," BBC NEWS, http://bbc.co.uk/1/hi/world/americas/800771.stm, (accessed 3 December 2007), 1.

38. Cieza de León, *Incas of Pedro de Cieza de León,* 277–278.

39. Ibid., 238.

40. The Metropolitan Museum of Art (New York), "Timeline of Art History, Central and Southern Andes, 1000 BC—AD 1, http://www.metmuseum.org/toah/ht/04/sac/ht04/sac.htm. (accessed February 12, 2007), 2.

41. Kocherhans, *Nephi to Zarahemla*, 112.

42. Kolata, *The Tiwanaku*, 70–71.

43. Klarich, *From the Monumental to the Mundane*, 62.

44. Bauer, *Ancient Cuzco*, 50.

45. Klarich, *From the Monumental to the Mundane*, 57.

46. Ibid., 58.

47. Ibid., 65.

48. Ibid., 19.

49. Ibid., 6.

50. S. J. Chávez, *The Conventionalize Rules in Pucara Pottery Technology and Iconography: Implications of Socio-Political Development in the Northern Titicaca Basin*, Unpublished PhD Dissertation, Michigan State University, 49.

51. Klarich, *From the Monumental to the Mundane*, xii, xiii.

52. Ibid., 11.

53. Ibid., 12.

54. Ibid., 262.

55. Ibid., 75.

56. Klarich, *From the Monumental to the Mundane*, 51, quoting Rowe: J. H. Rowe, "Sitios históricos en la region de Pucara, Puno", Revisita del Instituto Arqueológico 6(10/11): 66–75.

57. Klarich, *From the Monumental to the Mundane*, 40.

58. Mary B. Kidder, *No Limits but the Sky: The Journal of an Archaeologist's Wife in Peru* (Cambridge, MA: Harvard University Press, 1942), 342.

59. Klarich, *From the Monumental to the Mundane*, 165.

60. Klarich, *From the Monumental to the Mundane*, 310.

61. Ibid., 63, 260.

62. Calderwood, *Voices from the Dust*, 327,

CHAPTER 8

1. The Metropolitan Museum of Art (New York), "Timeline of Art History, Central and Southern Andes, 1000 BC—AD 1, http://www.metmuseum.org/toah/ht/04/sac/ht04/sac.htm. (accessed February 12, 2007), 2; also Klarich, *From the Monumental to the Mundane*, 93.

2. The German archaeologist Marie Reiche spent 50 years studying the Nasca lines. She believed the Tree of Life geoglyph was attributed to the Nasca people (see http://www.latinamericanstudies.org/nazca/nazca-lines.htm. However, more recent theories suggest that the Tree of Life might have been made in post-colonial times by Spanish guano diggers to direct their ships.

3. Silverman and Proulx, *The Nasca*, 38.

4. Ibid., 239.

5. Ibid., 266.

6. No author stated, "Archaeologist 'Strike Gold' with Finds of Ancient Nasca Iron Ore Mine," *Science Daily*, http://www.sciencedaily.com/releases/2008/01/080129125405.htm, (accessed 3 February 2008).

7. Silverman and Proulx, *The Nasca*, 231–32.

8. Ibid., 138–139, 216, 232.

9. Ibid., 149.

10. Ibid., 11–12.

11. Ibid., 73.

12. Ibid.

13. Ibid., 74.

14. Ibid., 156.

15. Victor W. Von Hagen, quoted by Kocherhans, *Nephit to Zarahemla*, 123.

16. Silverman and Proulx, *The Nasca*, 160.

17. William Duncan Strong, *Paracas, Nazca and Tiahuanacoid Cultural Relationships in South Coastal Peru*. Memoir no. 13 (Menasha: Society for American Archaeology, 1957), 32.

18. Silverman and Proulx, *The Nasca*, 98.

19. Metropolitan Museum of Art (New York), "Timeline of Art History, Central and Southern Andes, AD 1—AD 500", http://www.metmuseum.org/toah/ht/05/sac/ht05sac.htm, (accesed February 12, 2007), 2.

20. Silverman and Proulx, *The Nasca*, 102.

21. María Rostworowski, "Origen religioso de los dibujos y rayas de Nasca," *Journal de la Société des Américanistes*, 79:193.

22. Silverman and Proulx, *The Nasca*, 102.

23. Ibid., 197.

24. Victor Turner, religious specialist, *Magic, Witchcraft and Religion: An Anthropological Study of the Supernatural*, eds. Arthur C. Lehmann and James E. Myers (Palo Alto: Mayfield Publishing Co., 1985), 82.

25. See figure at http://www.latinamericanstudies.org/nazca/nazca-lines.htm.

26. Giuseppe Orefici, *Nasca: arte e societá del popolo dei geoglifi* (Milan: Jaca Books, 1993), 145.

27. Silverman and Proulx, *The Nasca*, 201.

28. Alfred Edersheim, "Instrumental Music in the Jerusalem Temple, http://www.piney.com/Edershi.html, (accessed 16 September 2007).

29. Silverman and Proulx, *The Nasca*, 205.

30. Urton, "Report of fieldwork in Nazca, Peru," unpublished manuscript in the possession of Helaine Silverman, quoted by Silverman and Proulx, *The Nasca*, 208.

31. Calderwood, *Voices from the Dust*, 126.

32. Calderwood, *Voices from the Dust*, 127, quot-

ing Felipe Guaman Poma de Ayala, *Nueva Corónica y Buen Gobierno*, 65. Original manuscript finished in 1615, but not discovered until 1908 by Richard Pietschmann and published in 1936. Transcription, prologue, notes, and chronology by Franklin Pease. (This edition was printed in Venezuela by Biblioteca Ayacucho Caracas, Venezuela, 1978.)

33. Huaman Poma, *Letter to a King*, quoted by Kocherhans, *Nephi in Zarahemla*, 130.

34. Cieza de León, *Discovery and Conquest of Peru*, 282–83.

35. Smithsonian National Museum of Natural History, Global Volcanism Program, http://volcano.si.edu/world/eruptionlist.cfm, (accessed February 2007).

36. http://users.bendnet.com/bjensen/volcano/southamerica/peru-misti.html.vol

37. Smithsonian, National Museum of Natural History, Global Volcanism Program, "Huaynaputina", February 2007, http://www.volcano.si.edu/world/volcano.cfm?vnum=1504-03=.

38. Paul Baker, "Drilling for Scientific Purposes in the Tropical-Subtropical Andes: Lake Titicaca, Bolivia/Peru," new full-proposal ICDP-12/12/00 (accepted 01/15/2000), http:/www.icdp-online.de/sites/tpl/tpl_proposal_co.htm?label+ICDP-12/00 (accessed February 2007).

39. NASA, "Mount Urinas, Peru," *Visible Earth: A Catalog of NASA Images and Animations of Our Home Planet*, http://visibleearth.nasa,gov.view_rec.php?id=20663 (accessed February 2007).

40. Michele Kurtz, "Scuba Divers find pre-Inca ruins in Lake Titicaca" *Cyber Diver News Network*, 31 October 2002, htt://www.cdnn.

info/industry/021031/i021031.html (accessed February 2007).

41. No author stated, "Ancient temple found under Lake Titicaca," BBC New Online, 23 August 2000, http://news.bbc.co.uk/2/hi/americans/892616,stm.

42. Osborne, *South American Mythology*, 74.

43. Miguel Cabello Valboa, Miscelánea Antártica, *Una Historia del Peru Antiguo*, written in manuscript form in 1586, introduction and notes by Luis E. Vacarcel (first published by the Universidad Nacional Mayor de San Marcos, Facultad de Letras, Instituto de Etnología, Lima, 1951), 237.

44. Calderwood, *Voices from the Dust*, 125, quoting Father Francisco de Avila, *The Huarochiri Manuscript, A Testament of Ancient and Colonial Andean Religion*, translated from Quechua by Frank Salomon and George L. Urioste (Austin: University of Texas Press, 1991).

45. Ibid.

46. Innes, *The Conquistadors*, quoted by Kocherhans, *Nephi to Zarahemla*, 133–34.

47. Osborne, *South America Mythology*, 78.

48. Ibid., 81.

49. Urton, *The Legendary Past*, 37.

50. Hemming, *Conquest of the Incas*, 97.

51. Osborne, *South America Mythology*, 87.

52. Calderwood, *Voices from the Dust*, 134.

53. Mann. *1491: New Revelations of the Americas*, 258.

54. Urton, *The Legendary Past*, 39.

55. Ibid., 38.

56. J. Alden Mason, *The Ancient Civilizations of Peru* (London: Penguin Books, 1991), 135. See also Garcilaso de la Vega, *The Royal Com-

mentaries of the Incas* (New York: Orion Press, 1961), 132–33, 147–48.

57. Osborne, *South America Mythology*, 76.

58. Sarmiento, *History of the Incas*, 34.

59. Francisco De Avila, "A Narrative of the Errors, False Gods, and Other Superstitions and Diabolical Rites in Which the Indians of the Province of Huarochiri lived in Ancient Times," in *Narratives of the Rites and Laws of Yncas*, vol. XLVIII, trans. and ed. Clemens R. Markham (London: Hakluyt Society, 1873), 124.

60. Calderwood, *Voices from the Dust*, 428.

61. Betanzos, *Narrative of the Incas*, 10.

62. Sarmiento, *History of the Incas*, 35.

63. Urton, *The Legendary Past*, 38.

64. Ibid., 38–39.

65. Betanzos, *Narrative of the Incas*, 11.

66. Urton, *The Legendary Past*, 39.

67. Ibid., 39.

68. Betanzos, *Narrative of the Incas*, 11.

69. Sarmiento, *History of the Incas*, 187.

70. Dana M. Pike, "Theophoric Names," in *The Anchor Bible Dictionary*, David Noel Freedman, ed. 6 vols. (New York: Doubleday, 1992), 4:1018; see also Nibley, *Lehi in the Desert, World of the Jaredites, There Were Jaredites*, 25; and Nibley, *Approach to the Book of Mormon*, 286.

71. McConkie, *Mormon Doctrine*, 29–30.

72. Sullivan, *Secret of the Incas*, 232.

73. Ibid., 109.

74. Ibid., 102.

75. Ada Habershon, *Study of the Types* (Grand Rapids, MI: Kregel Publications, 1974), 47.

76. Sullivan, *Secret of the Incas*, 86.

77. Ibid., 89.

78. Ibid., 101.

79. Ibid., 98.

80. Merriam Webster's, 731.

81. Sullivan, *Secret of the Incas*, 98.

82. Ibid., 66.

83. Sullivan, *Secret of the Incas*, 67.

84. Ibid., 100.

85. Ibid., 103.

86. Osborne, *South America Mythology*, 74.

CONCLUSION

1. Tudor Parfitt, *The Lost Tribes of Israel, The History of a Myth* (London: Phoenix, 2004), 123.

2. Ibid, 125.

3. Ibid.

4. Ibid., 127.

5. Preface to the Book of Mormon.

6. Urton, *The Legendary Past*, 41.

7. Book of Mormon, 469, footnote date.

8. Klarich, *From the Monumental to the Mundane*, 45.

9. Ibid., 67.

10. Silverman and Proulx, *The Nasca*, 38.

11. Ibid., 119, 120.

12. Ibid., 250.

13. Ibid., 9.

14. Ibid., 87.

15. Kolata, *The Tiwanaku*, 248–49.

16. Ibid., 76.

17. Sullivan, *Secret of the Incas*, 36.

18. Ibid., 66–67.

19. Ibid., 99.

20. Calderwood, *Voices from the Dust*, 307–309.

21. Jerry L. Ainsworth, http://www.mormon-sites.org/page3.html, (accessed 4 February 2008), 3.

22. *Journal of Discourses,* 28 September, 1856.

23. Stuart White, "Cedar and Mahogany Logging in Easter Peru," *Geographical Review* 68, no. 4 (Oct. 1978): 394.

24. Andean Explorers Foundation & Ocean Sailing Club, http://www.aefosc.org/newsite/index.php?con=expeditions_grandophir_feathered_fs3 (accessed 3 February 2008).

25. "The Great Pyramid at Giza," University of Maryland Physics Research Group http://www.physics.umd.edu/perg/abp/aha/pyramid.htm (accessed 3 February 2008).

26. "Jade Axes Proof of Vast Ancient Caribbean Network, Experts Say," *National Geographic News,* http://news.nationalgeographic.com/news/2006/06/060612-caribbean_2.html (4 February 2008).

27. Mann, *1491: New Revelations of the Americas,* 258.

28. Ibid., 24.

29. Ibid.

30. Ibid., 252.

31. Ibid., 259

32. M. Wells Jakeman, "The Chronicles of Mesoamerica," from *Ancient America Foundation Newsletter,* no. 25/91.32, 10 February 1955. Also found in Ross Christensen, "Progress in Archaeology: an Anthology," 1963. See Newsletters, www.ancientamerica.org.

33. http://en.wikipedia.org/wiki/Quetzalcoatl#References

34. De Groote, "Hebrew DNA found in South America?" 2.

35. Mann. *1491: New Revelations of the Americas,* 262–63.

36. Bauer, *Ancient Cuzco,* 71–72.

37. Ibid., 72.

38. Ibid., 1.

39. Pomo de Ayala, *Nueva Corónica,* 49.

40. Tarmo Kulmar, *Zum Problem des Kulturheros in der Inka-Religion, Mitteilungen feur Antropologie und Religionsgeschichte.* B. (Meunster: Ugarit-Verlag, 1999), 5.

41. De Ondegardo, "Report," 8.

42. Kulmar, *Zum Problem des Kulturheros,* 101–109.

43. Betanzos, *Narrative of the Incas,* 92–93.

44. Ibid., 128.

45. Sarmiento, *History of the Incas,* 36.

46. Ibid., 37.

47. Betanzos, *Narrative of the Incas,* 235.

48. Cieza de León, *Discovery and Conquest of Peru,* 130.

49. Ibid., 107.

50. Ibid., 109.

51. Ibid., 112–13.

52. Ibid., 113.

53. Cieza de León, *Discovery and Conquest of Peru,* 118.

54. Ibid., 117.

55. Ibid., 122.

56. Ibid., 153.

57. Betanzos, *Narrative of the Incas,* 316–317.

58. Ibid., 231–232.

59. Ibid., 232.

60. Ibid., 236.

61. Cieza de León, *Discovery and Conquest of Peru*, 188.

62. Ibid., 189.

63. Diamond, *Guns, Germs, and Steel*, 77–78.

64. Cieza de León, *Discovery and Conquest of Peru*, 241–42.

65. Betanzos, *Narrative of the Incas*, 245.

66. Cieza de León, *Discovery and Conquest of Peru*, 188.

67. Betanzos, *Narrative of the Incas*, 248–49.

68. Ibid. 261–62.

69. Diamond, *Guns, Germs, and Steel*, 71–72.

70. Ibid., 73.

71. Betanzos, *Narrative of the Incas*, 274.

72. Cieza de León, *Discovery and Conquest of Peru*, 252.

73. Ibid., 257.

74. Ibid., 259.

75. Ibid., 263.

76. Mann, *1491: New Revelations of the Americas*, 102.

77. Cieza de León, *Discovery and Conquest of Peru*, 267.

78. Clements Markham, *The Incas of Peru*, Second Edition (London: John Murray, 1970), 300.

79. Cieza de León, *Discovery and Conquest of Peru*, 285.

80. Calderwood, *Voices from the Dust*, 63–65, quoting from *Menasseh Ben Israel, Esto Es Esperanca de Israel, Sobre El Origen de los Americanos*, published in Amsterdam, 1650 by Semuel Ben Israel Soeiro. (Reprinted in Madrid, 1881, Editorial Plata S.A. 1974.)

81. Valboa, *Una Historia*, 195.

82. Calderwood, *Voices from the Dust*, 70.

83. Sarmiento, *History of the Incas*, 36.

84. Some Book of Mormon scholars have conjectured that the Isthmus of Darien was in Central America. Clearly this was not what Joseph Smith thought. Undoubtedly he was referring to Panama, and the fact that Nephi's [ship] landed "somewhat south of Panama." The 1828 Webster's Dictionary states: "Isthmus: A neck or narrow slip of land by which two continents are connected. . . . as the *isthmus* of Darien, which connects North America and South America" Noah Webster, *Noah Webster's First Edition of An American Dictionary of the English Language*, republished in facsimile edition (San Francisco: Foundation for American Christian Education, 2006.) A copy of the Noah Webster's 1829 Dictionary that was in the home of Peter Whitmer is in the possession of the Harold B. Lee Library of Brigham Young University.

85. *Teaching of the Prophet Joseph Smith*, Sect. 5, 1842–43, 267.

APPENDICES

1. Kocherhans, *Nephi to Zarahemla*, 213.

2. Loren McIntyre, "Lost Empire of the Incas," *National Geographic* 144, no. 6 (December 1973): 774.

3. Simon Southerton, *Losing a Lost Tribe* (Salt Lake City: Signature, 2004), 199.

4. Mann, *1491: New Revelations of the Americas*, 71.

5. Calderwood, *Voices from the Dust*, 336–37.

6. Jones, *In the Blood, God, Genes, and Destiny*, 156–57.

SELECTED BIBLIOGRAPHY

Adair, James. *Adair's History of the American Indians.* 2d ed. Edited by Samuel Cole Williams. New York: Promontory Press, 1986.

Alden, Mason, J. *The Ancient Civilizations of Peru.* London: Penguin Books, 1991.

"Archaeologists Shed New Light On America's Earliest Known Civilization." *Science Daily,* 4 January 2005, http://www.sciencedaily.com/releases/2005/01/050104112957.htm

Baker, Paul, Sherilyn C. Fritz, and Geoffrey O. Seltzer. "Lake Titicaca: An Archive from South American Paleoclimate," December 2001, http://www.ariweb.org/geotimes/dec01/feature_titicaca.html (February 2007).

Baker, Paul. "Drilling for Scientific Purposes in the Tropical-Subtropical Andes: Lake Titicaca, Bolivia/Peru," new full-proposal ICDP-12/12/00 (accepted 01/15/2000). http:/www.icdp-online.de/sites/tpl/tpl_proposal_co.htm?label+ICDP-12/00 (accessed February 2007)

Bauer, Brian. *Ancient Cuzco, Heartland of the Inca.* Austin: University of Texas Press, 2004.

Beisie, Laurent, "Civilization lost?" *The Christian Science Monitor,* 3 January 2002, http://www.csmonitor.com/2002/0103/p11s1-woam.html.

Betanzos, Juan de. *Narrative of the Incas.* Translated and edited by Roland Hamilton and Dana Buchanan from the Palma de Mallorca manuscript. Austin: University of Texas Press, 1996.

Bible Dictionary, LDS Version. Salt Lake City: The Church of Jesus Christ of Latter-day Saints, 1979.

Bible, King James Version. Salt Lake City: The Church of Jesus Christ of Latter-day Saints, 1979.

"The Book of Ether." *Evening and Morning Star.* Aug. 1832.

Book of Mormon. Salt Lake City: The Church of Jesus Christ of Latter-day Saints, 1979.

Bouyee-Cassagne, T. "Urco and Uma: Aymara concepts of space." In J. Murra, N. Wachtel and J. Revel, eds. Anthropological History of Andean Polities. Cambridge: Cambridge University Press, 1986.

Bulliet, Richard W. "Why They Lost the Wheel." *Saudi Aramco World.* May/June

1973, vol. 24, no. 3. Drahran, Saudi Arabia, 1973.

Calderwood, David G. *Voices from the Dust.* Austin, TX: Historical Publications, Inc, 2005.

Capelotti, P. J. "Easter Island and the Ra and Viracocha Expeditions." http://www.personal.psu.edu/faculty/p/j/pjc12/Easter%20Island%20and%20the%20Ra. Accessed June 13, 2007.

Chávez, S. J. *The Conventionalize Rules in Pucara Pottery Technology and Iconography: Implications of Socio-Political Development in the Northern Titicaca Basin,* Unpublished Ph.D. Dissertation, Michigan State University, 49.

The Church of Jesus Christ of Latter-day Saints, "All Is Safely Gathered In, Family Home Storage." 2007

Cieza de León, Pedro de. *Incas of Pedro de Cieza de León.* Norman, OK: University of Oklahoma Press, 1959.

———. *The Discovery and Conquest of Peru, Chronnciles of the New World Encounter.* Edited and translated by Alexander Parma Cook and Noble David Cook. London: Duke University, 1998.

Clark, John E. "Archaeology, Relics, and Book of Mormon Belief." *Journal of Book of Mormon Studies* 14, no. 2 (2005).

———. "Geography." *To All The World: The Book of Mormon Articles* from the *Encyclopedia of Mormonism*. Provo, UT: Maxwell Institute, 2008.

Cobo, Bernabe. *History of the Inca Empire*. Translated by Roland Hamilton. Austin: University of Texas, 1996.

Coe, Michael. "Mormons and Archaeology: An Outside View." *Dialogue, A Journal of Mormon Thought* 8, no. 2. Summer 1973.

Cook, Gareth. "Untangling the Mystery of the Inca." *Wired*, January 2007, San Francisco.

Copper, Bill. "The Kings of the Ancient Britons: Chronology." *The Early History of Man—Part 3*. Bible Believers, http://www.biblebelievers.org.au/nation08.htm.

"Copper, Bronze, and Brass," *Journal of Book of Mormon Studies* 9 (2000), 1.

Cotterell, Arthur. *The Illustrated Encyclopaedia of Myths and Legends*. London: Guild Publishing, 1989.

Civic, Stephen. "Peru battles locust plague," BBC NEWS, http://bbc.co.uk/1/hi/world/americas/800771.stm, (accessed 3 December 2007).

De Avila, Francisco. "A Narrative of the Errors, False Gods, and Other Superstitions and Diabolical Rites in Which the Indians of the Province of Huarochiri lived in Ancient Times." *Narratives of the Rites and Laws of Yncas*, vol. XLVIII. Trans. and ed. by Clements R. Markham. London: Hakluyt Society, 1873.

De Groote, Michael. "Hebrew DNA found in South America?" *Deseret News,* 12 May 2008, http://www.deseretnews.com/article/1,5143,700225191,00.html.

De la Vega, Garcilaso. *Royal commentaries of the Incas and general history of Peru*, part 1. Trans. by Harold V. Livermore. Austin: University of Texas, 1966.

De Murúa, Martín. *Historia General del Perú de los Orígenes al timo Inca*. Originally written in 1611. (Published by Información y Revista, S.A., Hermanos García Noblejas, 41 – 28037 Madrid. Historia, 1986.).

De Ondegardo, Polo. "Report by Polo De Ondegardo, Manuscript in the National Library at Madrid," 4, on parchment B. See http://www.sacred-texts.com/nam/inca/rly/rly4.htm), accessed Aug. 30, 2006.

Dean, Carolyn. *Inka Bodies and the Body of Christ, Corpus Christi in Colonial Cuzco*. Durham, NC: Duke University Press, 1999.

Diamond, Jared. *Guns, Germs, and Steel: The Fates of Human Societies*. New York: W.W. Norton & Company, 1997.

Durán, Diego *The History of the Indies of New Spain*, originally written in 1581 but not found until 1850 and partially published in 1867. (Translated, Annotated, and with an Introduction by Doris Heyden. Published by University of Oklahoma Press, 1994).

Edersheim, Alfred. "Instrumental Music in the Jerusalem Temple," http://www.piney.com/Edershi.html, (accessed 16 September 2007).

"Elephant and the Book of Mormon." http://chapmanresearch.org/BOM_Studies.html

Erins, Rod. "Barkcloth and the Origins of Paper." Paper presented at the First National Paper Conference in Hobar Australia, May 1981, 4. Published in the Conference Papers, distribution to conferees only by Papermakers of Australia; http://www.justpacific.com/pacific/papers/barkcloth~paper.html.

"Excavations and Restoration of the Complex of Khor Rori, Interim Report," October 2000–April 2001. Pisa: University of Pisa, 2001.

The Facts on File: Encyclopedia of World Mythology and Legend. London and Oxford, 1988.

Forster, Rev. Charles, B.D. *The Historical Geography of Arabia*. London: Darf Publishers Limited, 1984.

Foster, Mary LeCron. "Old World Language in the Americas: 1." An unpublished paper read at the annual meeting of the Association of American Geographers, San Diego, 20 April 1992; and also in her "Old World Language in the Americas: 2," an unpublished paper given at the annual meeting of the Language Origins Society, Cambridge University, September 1992. Copies are in the possession of John Sorenson and Matthew Roper, cited by Sorenson and Roper in *Before DNA*, *Journal of Book of Mormon Studies* 12, no. 1 (2003): 6–23.

Gaskill, Alonzo L. *The Lost Language of Symbolism: An Essential Guide for Recognizing and Interpreting Symbols of the Gospel*. Salt Lake City: Deseret Book, 2003.

Groom, Nigel. *Frankincense and Myrrh: A Study of the Arabian Incense Trade*. London: Longman, 1981.

Habershon, Ada. *Study of the Types*. Grand Rapids, MI: Kregel Publications, 1974.

Hamblin, William J. "Basic Methodological Problems with the Anti-Mormon Approach to the Geography and Archaeology of the Book of Mormon." *Journal of Book of Mormon Studies* 2 (Spring–Fall 1993).

Harris, Richard. "Oldest Solar Observatory in Americas Found in Peru." National Public Radio, April 28, 2007, http://www.npr.org/templates/story/story.php?storyId=7658847.

Hauck, F. Richard. *Deciphering the Geography of the Book of Mormon*. Salt Lake City: Deseret Book, 1988.

Hemming, John. *The Conquest of the Incas*. New York: Harcourt, Inc., 1970.

Heyerdahl, Thor. *Aku-Aku: The Secret of Easter Island*. London: George Allen & Unwin, 1988.

Hilton, Lynn and Hope Hilton. *Discovering Lehi: New evidence of Lehi and Nephi in Arabia*. Springville, UT: Cedar Fort Inc., 1996.

Hiltunen, Juha J. *Ancient Kings of Peru: The Reliability of the Chronicle of Fernando de Montesinos*. Helsinki: Suomen Historiallinen Sevra, 1999.

———. "Separating Invention from Possible Inherited Traditions in the Chronicle of Montesinos." *Traditional High Cultures*, 7 January 2008, http://www.traditionalhighcultures.com/HiltunenPaper.htm.

Holguín, Diego González. *Volcabulario de la lengua general de todo el Perú llamada lengua Quichua o del Inca*. Lima: Instituto de Historia, Universidad Nacional Mayor de San Cristobal de Humanaga, 1952.

Innes, Hammond. *The Conquistadors*. New York: Alfred A. Knopf, 1969.

International Red Cross and Red Crescent Societies (IFRC). "Bolivia Floods Appeal No. 05/01 Situation Report No. 3." http://www.reliefweb.int/rw/rwb.nsf/db900sid/OCHA-64BQ3E?OpenDocument, (accessed 3 December 2007).

Jakeman, M. Wells. "The Chronicles of Mesoamerica," *Ancient America Foundation Newsletter* 25, 10 February 1955. Also found in "Progress in Archaeology: An Anthology" by Ross Christensen, 1963. See Newsletters, www.ancientamerica.org

"Jaredites in the Bible," http://www.zaksite.co.uk/whyprophets/prophets/ophir.htm.

The Jewish Encyclopaedia, vol. II. New York: Funk & Wagnalls, 1925.

Jones, Steve. *In the Blood, God, Genes, and Destiny*. London: Harper Collins Publishers, 1996.

Kidder, Mary B. *No Limits but the Sky: The Journal of an Archaeologist's Wife in Peru*. Cambridge, MA: Harvard University Press, 1942.

Klarich, Elizabeth Ana. *From the Monumental to the Mundane: Defining Early Leadership Strategies at Late Formative Pukara, Peru, Dissertation*. Santa Barbara: University of California Santa Barbara.

Kocherhans, Arthur J. *Lehi's Isle of Promise*. Fullerton, CA: Et Cetera, 1989.

———. *Nephi to Zarahemla*. Orem, UT: Granite Publishing, 2002.

———. *A True and Ancient Record*. Orem, UT: Granite Publishing, 2002.

Kolata, Alan L. *The Tiwanaku: Portrait of an Andean Civilization*. Cambridge, MA: Blackwell Publishing, 1993.

———. *Valley of the Spirits: A Journey into the Lost Realm of the Aymara*. New York: John Wiley & Sons, 1996.

Kulmar, Tarmo. *Zum Problem des Kulturheros in der Inka-Religion, Mitteilungen feur Antropologie und Religionsgeschichte. B.* Meunster: Ugarit-Verlag, 1999.

Kurtz, Michele. "Scuba Divers find pre-Inca ruins in Lake Titicaca." Cyber Diver News Network. Lima, Peru, 31 October 2002, htt://www.cdnn.info/industry/021031/i021031.html. (February 2007).

Leonard, Irving A. *Books of the Brave* (originally published by Harvard University Press, 1949). Republished in 1992 with an introduction by Rolena Adorno by the University of California Press.

Lloyd, Robin. "Big Pig-Like Beast Discovered." *Live Science*. LiveScience.com, 2 November 2007.

Mann, Charles, *1491: New Revelations of the Americas Before Columbus*. New York: Vintage Books, 2006.

Markham, Sir Clements. *The Incas of Peru*. 2nd Ed. London: John Murray, 1970.

"Insights: An Ancient Window." *The Newsletter of the Foundation for Ancient Research and Mormon Studies*, no. 3, (1990).

McConkie, Bruce R. *Mormon Doctrine*. Salt Lake City: Bookcraft, 1958.

McConkie, Joseph Fielding. *Gospel Symbolism*. Salt Lake City: Bookcraft, 1985.

McIntry, Loren. "Lost Empire of the Incas." *National Geographic* 144, no. 6 (December 1973).

Merriam Webster's Ninth New Collegiate Dictionary, (Springfield, Massachusetts: Merriam-Webster, Inc, 1990).

Metropolitan Museum of Art (New York). "Timeline of Art History, Central and Southern Andes, 1000 BC–AD 1," http://www.metmuseum.org/toah/ht/04/sac/ht04/sac.htm. (February 12, 2007).

———. "Timeline of Art History, Central and Southern Andes, AD 1–AD 500," http://www.metmuseum.org/toah/ht/05/sac/ht05sac.htm, (February 12, 2007).

Molina, Fr. "Relacion de las fabulas y ritos de los Yngas," in H. Osborne, *South American Mythology*.

Moore, Carrie A. "Intro Change in Book of Mormon spurs discussion," *Deseret Morning News*, 9 November 2007, http://deseretnews.com/dn/view/1%2C1249%2C695226049%2C00.html.

Mosley, Micheal. *Incas and Their Ancestors*. New York: Thames and Hudson Publishing, 1992.

NASA. "Mount Urinas, Peru." *Visible Earth: A Catalog of NASA Images and Animations of Our Home Planet.* February 2007, http://visibleearth.nasa.gov.view_rec.php?id=20663.

Nibley, Hugh. *The Prophetic Book of Mormon*. Provo, UT: FARMS, 1989.

———. *Old Testament and Related Studies.* Ed. John W. Welch, Gary P. Gillum, and Don E. Norton. *The Collected Works of Hugh Nibley*, vol. 1. Salt Lake City: Deseret Book, 1986.

———. *Collected Works of Hugh Nibley*, vol. 6. Salt Lake City, Deseret Book.

"Nevados de Chilán Biological Corridor." *The Nature Conservancy*, 27 June 2007, http://nature.org/wherewework/southamerica/chile/work/art5115.html, "

Nyman, Monte S. *Abomination of Desolation*. Springville, UT: Cedar Fort Inc., 2006.

"Olmecs," http://wsu.edu/~dee/CIVAMRCA/OLMECS.HTM

Orefici, Giuseppe. *Nasca: arte e societá del popolo dei geoglifi*. Milan: Jaca Books, 1993.

Osborne, H, *South America Mythology*. London: Paul Hamlyn, 1968.

Packer, Boyd K. "Scriptures," *Ensign*, Nov. 1982.

Parfitt, Tudor: *The Lost Tribes of Israel: The History of a Myth*. London: Phoenix, 2004.

Phillips, William R. "Metals of the Book of Mormon." *Journal of Book of Mormon Studies* 9, no. 2 (2000).

"Pig-like beast discovered in South America" http://www.msnbc.msn.com/id/21600289, 3 November 2007.

Pike, Dana M. "Theophoric Names." In *The Anchor Bible Dictionary*. David Noel Freedman, ed., 6 vols. New York: Doubleday, 1992.

Pizarro, Pedro. *Relacíon del Descubrimiento y Conquita de Los Reinos del Perú*. Original manuscript presented in Arequipa, Peru on 28 March 1572. First printed in the late 1870's. Current edition with notes and preliminary considerations by Guillermo Lohmann Villena and Pierre Duviols by Pontifica Universidad Catolica del Peru, 1896.

Poma de Ayala, Felipe Guaman, *Nueva Corónica y Buen Gobierno*. Original manuscript finished in 1615, but not discovered until 1908 by Richard Pietschmann and published in 1936. Transcript, Prologue, Notes, and Chronology by Franklin Pease. This edition was printed in Venezuela by Biblioteca Ayacucho Caracas, Venezuela, 1978.

Potter, George. *The Jaredites*. Documentary film. Bear River City, UT: Nephi Project, 2003.

Potter, George and Richard Wellington. *Lehi in the Wilderness: 81 New Documented Evidences that the Book of Mormon Is a True History*. Springville, UT: Cedar Fort Inc., 2002.

Potter, George. *The Tree of Life*. Documentary film. Bear River City, UT: Bear River Training and Consultancy, 2005.

Reich, Marie. See http://www.latinamericanstudies.org/nazca/nazca-lines.htm.

Ronchail, Josyane and Robert Gallaire. "ENSO and rainfall along the Zongo valley (Bolivia) from the *Altiplano* to the Amazon basin." Smithsonian/NASA ADS Physics Abstract Service. See http://absabs.harvard.edu/abs/2006IJCli.26.1223R.

Rostworoski, María. "Origen religioso de los dibujos y rayas de Nasca." *Journal de la Société des Américanistes.*

Sarmiento, Pedro de Gamboa. *History of the Incas.* Written circa AD 1570. Translated by Clements Markham. Cambridge: The Haklugy Society 1907.

Schmid, Randolph E. "Andean find pushes earliest date of metalworking back 1,000 years." *The Associate Press,* 5 November 1998 (Washington).

Shinnick, Ron Shinnick. *Llama Driving: A Historical Perspective of Driving in the Southeastern U.S.,* http://www.ssla.org/carting_driving.htm 21 March 2007.

Silverman, Helaine and Donald A. Proulx. *The Nasca: The Peoples of America Series.* Oxford: Blackwell Publishing, 2002.

Sjodahl, Janne M. "Introduction to the Study of the Book of Mormon." http://search.ldslibrary.com/article/view/976113.

Smith, Joseph, Jr. *Teachings of the Prophet Joseph Smith, sel. Joseph Fielding Smith.* Salt Lake City: Deseret Book, 1976.

Smith, Joseph Fielding, Jr. *Doctrines of Salvation.* Salt Lake City: Bookcraft, 1954.

Smithsonian National Museum of Natural History. Global Volcanism Program, http://volcano.si.edu/world/eruptionlist.cfm.

Sorenson, John L. and Matthew Roper. "Before DNA." *Journal of Book of Mormon Studies* 12, no. 1 (2003).

Sorenson, John L. "A Reconsideration of Early Metal in Mesoamerica," *Katunob* 9 (March 1976):1–18. Cited by Jeff Lindsay at http://www.jefflindsay.com/LDSFAQ/FQ_metals.shtml#ores

———.*An Ancient American Setting for the Book of Mormon,* 279–80. Cited by Jeff Lindsay at http://www.jefflindsay.com/LDSFAQ/FQ_metals.shtml#ores

———. *An Ancient American Setting for the Book of Mormon.* Provo, UT: FARMS, 1996.

———. "Was There Hebrew Language In Ancient America? An interview with Brian Stubbs." Provo, UT: FARMS, 2000. Refers to Arnold Leesburg, *Comparative Philology: A Comparison between Semitic and American Languages.* Leyden: Brill, 1908.

"A Survey of Some Vowel Systems." http://www.compulink.co.uk/~morven/lang/vowels.html

Southerton, Simon. *Losing a Lost Tribe.* Salt Lake City: Signature, 2004.

Stabler, Edward P. "The Finite Connectivity of Linguistic Structure." Los Angeles: UCLA, www.linguistics.ucla.edu/people/stabler/eps-conn.pdf.

Stanish, Charles and Amanda B. Cohen, "Introduction to "Advances in Titicaca Basin Archaeology-1." Los Angeles: UCLA, 2007, http://www.ioa.ucla.edu/stanish/publications/1_advances-fm_copy.pdf.

———. "An Archaeological Summary of the Island of the Sun and the Moon." Published 30 May 2007, http://www.ioa.ucla.edu/staff/stanish/islands/archinfo.html.

Steward, Julian H. and Louis C. Faron. *Native Peoples of South America.* New York: McGraw-Hill, 1959.

Stothert, Karen E. "The Villa Salvador Site and the Beginning of the Early Intermediate Period in the Lurin Valley, Peru." *Journal of Field Archaeology* 7, no. 3 (Autumn 1980).

Steadman, L. H., *Excavations at Camata: an Early Ceramic Chronology for the Western Titicaca Basin, Peru.* Unpublished Ph.D. dissertation, University of California, Berkeley: 1995.

Stronge, William Duncan. *Paracas, Nazca and Tiahuanacoid Cultural Relationships in South Coastal Peru.* Memoir no. 13. Menasha: Society for American Archaeology, 1957.

Sullivan, William. *The Secret of the Incas, Myth, Astronomy, and the War Against Time.* New York: Three Rivers Press: 1996.

Thomas, Bertram. *The Arabs.* London: Thornton Butterworth, 1937.

Turner, Victor. *Magic, Witchcraft and Religion: An Anthropological Study of the Supernatural,* ed. Arthur C. Lehmann and James E. Myers. Palo Alto: Mayfield Publishing Co., 1985.

Tvedtnes, John A. "A Brief History of the Limited Geographic View of the Book of Mormon." *Meridian Magazine.* 31 October 2007.

UNESCO, World Heritage. "Archaeological Complex," http://whc.unesco.org/en/tentativelist/512/.

United States National Oceanic and Atmospheric Administration. "Answers to La Niña," http://www.elnino.noaa.gov/lanina_new_faq.html.

Urton, Gary. *The Legendary Past, Inca Myths.* Austin: University of Texas Press, 1999.

Valboa, Miguel Cabello. *Miscelánea Antártica, Una Historia del Peru Antiguo.* Written in manuscript form in 1586. Introduction and notes by Luis E. Vacarcel. First published by the Universidad Nacional Mayor de San Marcos, Facultad de Letras, Instituto de Etnología, Lima, 1951.

Varela, Héctor Hugo, José Alberto Cocilovo, Calogero M. Santoro, and Francisco Rothhammer. "Microevolution of Human Archaic Groups of Arica, Northern Chile, and Its Genetic Contribution to Populations from the Formative Period." *Revista Chilena De Historica Natural,* 79 no. 2 (Santiago: 2006): 185–93.

Von Hagen, Victor Wolfgang. *The Incas of Pedro de Cieza de Leon.* Translated by Harriet de Onis. Norman, OK: University of Oklahoma Press, 1959.

Warren, Bruce W. "Mesoamerican Jaredite Calendar Relationship?" *Ancient America Foundation (AAF) Newsletter,* 10 April 2007, http://www.ancientamerica.org.

Webster, Noah. *American Dictionary of the English Language.* Original edition 1828. Chesapeake, VA: American Christian Education, 2006. See "Line."

Whiting, Michael F. "DNA and the Book of Mormon: A Phylogenetic Perspective." *Journal of Book of Mormon Studies* 12, no. 1 (2003).

Wilfrod, John Noble. "String, and Knot, Theory of Inca Writing." *New York Times,* 12 August 2003.

Xu, Mike, "Transpacific Contacts?" Dr. Xu of Texas Christian University provides a comparison of Olmec motif characters to Chinese Shang writing. See presentation at http://www.chinese.tcu.edu/www_chinese3_tcu_edc.htm.

Young, Brigham. *Journal of Discourses,* vol. 11, 10 February 1867.